A THEATER IN YOUR HEAD

BY KENNETH THORPE ROWE

Write That Play
Romantic Love and Parental Authority in Sidney's Arcadia
University of Michigan Plays, Book I (*editor*)
University of Michigan Plays, Book II (*editor*)
University of Michigan Plays, Book III (*editor*)

A Theater
in Your Head

KENNETH THORPE ROWE

Funk & Wagnalls Company · New York

Preface

Although I have drawn freely upon the literature of drama as the occasions of illustrative reference seemed to demand, for the convenience of my readers in gaining the most effective experience I have concentrated on about twenty plays for recurrent illustrative reference and analysis under different topics through the book. These plays were selected as well known, probably already familiar to many readers, and readily available. The greater number are in widely distributed anthologies and bookstores. Other well-known plays have been selected for a single detailed analysis under one topic.

It is a pleasure to take this opportunity to express my appreciation to the University of Michigan for its contribution of a sabbatical leave of absence, during which part of the book was written; to my students through the years for their many questions and observations; to associates and friends in the theater, professional and amateur; to my wife; and to my publishers.

Acknowledgment is made, in the course of the book, of the courtesy of the publishers who have given permission for quotation from copyrighted material, and of the generosity of the several people who have made available for illustrative use materials from their own work in the theater.

Kenneth Rowe
Ann Arbor, Michigan, 1959

Contents

List of Plates

Note: *All plates will be found between pages 86 and 87.*

Experiencing the Play

1

A Theater in Your Head

Before any work of literature can be honestly evaluated it must be understood. To be understood it must have been experienced. To experience a play by reading is an act of creative imagination. The author has written the play in terms of a collaboration with the theater for its full realization. The text of the play is the author's scenario for the fulfillment of his conception by the complex art of the theater in which scene design, lighting, properties, costume, make-up, acting, and directing all make their contribution to communication of the play to an audience.

One's memories of theater are filled with the work of the playwright's collaborators: Robert Edmund Jones's noble façade of the Mannon mansion which dominated *Mourning Becomes Electra* with O'Neill's intention of continuity with Greek tragedy; Aline Bernstein's mellow room for the New York Civic Repertory Theater production of *The Cherry Orchard* which added meaning to Gayef's apostrophization of the old bookcase; the elongated shadows of the tossing arms of the Negroes singing through the storm scene in *Porgy* under Reuben Mamoulian's staging. Or it may be costume. *Oklahoma!* opens on "a radiant morning." The stage was flooded with clear strong light and the perspective of the set opened the stage into the space of fields and sky, but no element of the original production did more for the lyric mood than the crisp cotton dresses of the chorus of farm girls maintained in newly laundered freshness for each performance. Above all, plays live in one's mind in the actors: Helen Hayes as plain Maggie in *What Every Woman Knows* making Barrie's definition of charm believable and unforgettable; the bravura of Cyrano's famous "No thank you!" speech, with twelve repetitions of the thematic phrase in thirty-eight lines, exalted in a pyrotechnic display of virtuosity by Walter Hampden; the rounded heavy droop of Lee Cobb's back and shoulders which made visual and complete the stage direction for Willy Loman's entrance in *Death of a Salesman,* "carrying two large sample cases. . . . Even as he crosses the stage to the doorway of his house, his exhaustion is apparent." My earliest memory of theater is entirely of actors, directed, of course, but I knew nothing of that, and in costumes and make-up which seemed to me as inseparable from the actors as their skins. My parents took me when I was nine years old to see *Twelfth Night* presented by the Ben Greet Players in the local opera house. Mr. Philip Ben Greet (after 1929 Sir Philip) was one of the pioneers in releasing Shakespeare from the trappings of nineteenth-century staging and the star system. He toured the United Kingdom and America presenting Shakespeare's plays with a few low neutral screens for background and a table, a bench, and a stool on any bare platform available, from opera house to school assembly room or community hall. That production of *Twelfth Night* is as complete in my mind today as any play seen in the past year: Viola with gallant shoulders, Orsino handsome and gentle with close-cropped red hair, Olivia a tall slender lady delicate and gracious, Sir Toby speaking fuzzily through whiskers and ale, lank-haired Sir Andrew and portly Malvolio, and the rest, and the words of Shakespeare.

Whether it is the opening production of a new play with the author corporeally present in conference with production staff and cast, or a revival of a play by Shakespeare or Chekhov, the play is brought effectively into the theater through a meeting of minds between the playwright and his fellow artists. Just as truly, the realization of a play through reading requires a collaboration from the reader. It is not enough to be receptive; a play demands active projection of imagination. That is the challenge and the satisfaction of reading plays. A comparatively small percentage of people are capable of writing a good play (although the number is much larger than is revealed by current cramped production conditions, or than one would suppose from the complaints of producers looking for scripts). Cultivation of the necessary technique and discipline and a wholehearted exercise of imaginative energy should enable most people with sincere interest in drama to have the creative experience available in the reading of plays. Such a person will find himself possessed of a richly furnished theater in his head.

The imaginative responsibility of the reader of a play becomes clear if one considers the proportion in the typical novel given to description of the sights and sounds of the story. Streets, houses, rooms and their furnishings, front yards, back yards, gardens, landscapes are delineated in verbal detail. Changing light is diffused upon the scene by words. By words the characters are drawn to the mind's eye of the reader, and by words the passing expressions, postures, gestures, together with the tone, volume, and inflections, are given life. The action itself is made vivid by verbalization of the accompanying impacts upon the senses. These are the contributions of the theater and of the creative reader to the text of a play, derived in part from a few lines of stage directions, but primarily from within the body of the play where the quality and being of the characters must be discerned in what they do and say and the total existence and meaning of the play must be found.

The play and the novel, each of which is an extended fictional narrative with dramatic structure, are often associated, but the drama as a literary form, whether in verse or prose, is more closely akin to poetry than is the novel. Like poetry, it is a concentrated, economical mode of expression which depends for its effect on suggestion and evocation. It is due to the nature of drama itself that poetic drama historically has been far more characteristic of the theater than prose. In spite of the overbalance of prose in our own time, when we think of the great names of drama, Aeschylus, Sophocles, Euripides, Aristophanes, Marlowe, Shakespeare, Corneille, Racine, Molière, Calderón, Schiller, Goethe, we think of poets. Even Ibsen, a master of prose drama in an age of prose, reached his height, many would say, in *Peer Gynt*. A poetic novel is conceivable only as a tour de force. In spite of Henry James's protest to Hugh Walpole, "How can you say I do anything so foul and abject as to 'state'?" (in reply to a letter anent *The Ambassadors*), the special capacity of the novel is for fullness of effect through direct, explicit, and detailed statement. James's peculiar novelistic art was communication with avoidance of explicit statement by the cumulation of innumerable skirtings of the subject, as though a circle were to become defined by the points of contact of a great many tangents. The novels of Henry James are more poetic than the average novel in the degree of their progression by suggestion and evocation, and more than ordinarily remote from poetry and the drama in their lack of clarity and intensity in brief space, line by line. James had an acute ambition for success in the theater but never succeeded in writing an effective play. Ironically, over three decades after his death, two plays, *The Heiress* and *The Innocents,* adapted from the stories of two of his novels, *Washington Square* and *The Turn of the Screw,* were successfully produced on Broadway. The art of Henry James was that of the novel, the art of Ruth and Augustus Goetz and of William Archibald that of the drama.

The growing popularity of plays for reading, as indicated by increase in publication, suggests that our time is not completely overwhelmed by passive forms of entertainment, a criticism frequently voiced. There is some strong undercurrent of need and impulse for active participation. In the twenties and thirties, when the motion pictures had taken over the opera houses which in every town of a few thousand once accommodated the road-theater, and theater had become almost confined to New York, there was the nation-wide movement of community theaters. People commenced making their own theater and have continued increasingly to do so, especially since World War II. The young men returning from the armed services overseas brought with them a theater interest startling in its extent and earnestness. Schools and departments of drama were flooded, and G.I.'s organized new theater ventures throughout the country. Moreover, they had written plays and were writing plays by the hundreds, men who had never written a play before. The fact of theater interest in any degree as an outcome of war was unexpected and bewildering to many educators and social analysts. War, however, was an intensification of the machine age, regimentation, overwhelming impersonal force, minimization of the individual will, inhuman. The people of the theater in every branch, commercial and noncommercial, did splendid service in taking theater entertainment to the armed forces and in organizing theater activity among the men themselves. In theater in the midst of war men found a vigorous and direct channel for freedom of mind and expression, and an area where the standard of values is concretely human.

In drama there is an immediacy of sense of life in the characters. They are moving and speaking before us, whether on the stage of physically realized production or in the theater in the reader's head. The trend of psychological analysis in the modern novel has gone to an extreme in the search for the full reality until it often has lost the impact of essential reality. In the maze of conscious and unconscious impulse and impression the characters become dreamlike. It is true that this drifting consciousness is recognizable reality to many readers today, gaining a response from their own introspective haze; but that is the curse that has come upon us with a world of data and forces disproportionately complex to the finite mind and will. By sheer reaction and necessity, however, a new dynamism of individual moral responsibility is arising. The advance of machinery and science, having passed from an easy hope of Utopia to a terrifying burden, has become a challenge, a terrifying challenge, perhaps, but fear and courage have always gone hand in hand. Science has moved acceleratively until we are in a world of swift and devastating change, elemental forces of nature no longer striking impersonally out of the dark, but unleashed by man upon himself, precipitating a race between destruction and revitalization of the eternal human capacity for individual moral decision and action.

This is a dynamic age and drama is the most dynamic form of literature, which may be one reason for the growing response to drama as reading as well as to the theater. In a play the mind of the character is stripped down to reveal the essential line of action. From Aristotle's definitions to the present, drama has been recognized as an action, a situation of decision and conflict running its course to a resolution, and the dramatic reality of a character lies in the choice which is made and what he does in pursuance of that choice. Drama and the immediate necessity of our time are meeting upon that ground. Leading playwrights in France, England, and the United States have been making a common assertion. The constructive center of the existentialist philosophy of Jean-Paul Sartre as expressed in his plays is the brushing away of the retreat from

responsibility into the maze of psychological and sociological forces
for a tonic assertion that what a man does gives him identity and
being. Christopher Fry reveals in his plays an acute poetic consciousness of the ghostly or dreamlike diffusion of human personality
which so much contemporary literature, especially of the novel, has
been content to reflect, and cuts through to the core of identity in
action: Moses in *The Firstborn* declares, "I live. I do this thing. I
was born this action," and is akin to Anouilh's Antigone and to
Sartre's Orestes in *The Flies*. The underlying principle of Arthur
Miller's major plays from *All My Sons* through *Death of a Salesman*
to *The Crucible* is the individual responsibility of moral choice. This
dynamic view of life is fundamentally dramatic and finds its natural
form in drama.

Drama has historically attracted and given scope to minds of great
vitality, from Aeschylus and Euripedes, to Shakespeare and Ben
Jonson, to Ibsen and Strindberg. The vitality of drama for our own
time is attested both by the number and quality of plays being written
in the face of adverse theatrical conditions for production, also by
the vigor of attempted escape from those conditions in what we now
call the off-Broadway theater. Inflated production costs, a shortage
of theaters, theater union restrictions, and too great a concentration of
population which generates an oil-boom or gold-rush atmosphere of
gambling for the long-run smash hit all have operated to narrow the
New York commercial theater as an outlet for plays. Yet there is
produced in New York on and off Broadway a notable dramatic
literature. Back of that production is a dramatic literature in manuscript far exceeding the theater resources of any single city. The
pressure of this vitality of dramatic writing is meeting with a general
creative theater impulse and we have the beginning of a broadly
national base for the production of new plays and the interacting
stimulus for an advancing theater and dramatic literature.

At present publication of plays is largely dependent upon previous
production. The publication of more plays directly from manuscript
would greatly enrich our literature and also give added impetus to
the national expansion of our theater. Opportunity to compare a
production with one's own interpretation and mental staging of the
play is one of the higher excitements of theater-going. Wide reading
of a play generates demand for its production. That Shakespeare

is the best box-office author in our theater is not solely because of the quality of his plays but also because they have been read. Similarly, the now customary publication of successful Broadway plays during or immediately following the New York run contributes to building the road audience for those plays. However, even with an expanding theater, opportunity to see plays is narrowly limited compared to the availability to experience of a published play. For the play that is published, produced or not produced, seen or not seen in a theater of brick or stone or wood, there is always the theater in your head.

There are two kinds of experience of a play to the mind's eye and ear. Each is rewarding in itself, each may lead to the other: precedence is determined by the character of the play and the temperament and background of the reader. One may mentally stage the play, experiencing scenery, lighting, and acting, or one may experience the play ideally, the scene which it is the function of scenery and lighting to suggest, the characters which it is the function of acting to create. For even as the text of a play is a scenario for the theater, the theater itself is a window to the imagination of the audience, magic casements opening on the idea, the vision, of the dramatist. Shakespeare, who was producer and probably director as well as author, in the Choruses of *Henry V* spoke for all time when he wrote:

> ....*Can this cockpit hold*
> *The vasty fields of France? Or may we cram*
> *Within this wooden O the very casques*
> *That did affright the air at Agincourt?*

and appealed to the audience to "eke out our performance with your mind." The more than literal representation is as true for a drawing-room comedy as for the heroic play, *Henry V*. Communication of the idea, the feeling, of wit is the essence of staging *The Way of the World* or *The Importance of Being Earnest*. The nature of the process is as varied as is the scope of drama. For *Henry V* Shakespeare's problem was to project the mind of the audience into a physical fact, of battlefields, beyond the compass of stage representation. In staging *King Lear* the problem of the storm scene is to avoid such close suggestion of a storm of mere wind and rain as to fail to suggest warring elements and moral chaos. All the scenes of Hauptmann's *The Weavers* are interiors; yet from within the stage set of one poverty-stricken weaver's hut in Act Two we gain a mental picture of hut after hut stretching away into a kind of limbo of misery, and from the off-stage singing of the "Weaver's Song" in the third, fourth, and fifth acts there is left an indelible image on the mind's eye of masses of weavers marching across the land in the inexorable rhythm and misery-forced momentum of revolt. The projection may devolve entirely upon the actor. When Katharine Cornell in a great scene of an extremely imperfect play, the close of the second act of Maxwell Anderson's *The Wingless Victory,* delivered one of the most highly pitched and sustained passions in modern drama, the walls of the theater fell down, stage and audience disappeared, and one was out alone in space with the anger and pride and agony of Oparre the princess. All the arts of the stage are the medium between the audience and this play beyond the stage. The imagination of the reader may reach the dramatist's full conception through a mental staging of the play, or his imagination may strike out boldly for the ultimate vision and return to build up step by step the sustaining structure of a stage form. His experience will be most complete by an interaction of the two approaches through successive readings and by a correlated cultivation of literary perception and acquaintance with the theater. That, I think, is how the most successful directors work. The reader has unlimited resources at his command for the theater in his head. No actor or actress is otherwise engaged whom he desires for his production. He may select at will among stage designers. The right theater is always at his command. The budget has no ceiling—the only "angel" he needs is his own imagination.

2

The Playwright's Collaborator : The Theater

THE PHYSICAL STRUCTURE AND CONVENTIONS

The first theater was a clear spot of ground encircled by a group of people drawn to see and hear one of their number enact by panto-mime or dance, speaking, chanting, or singing, a story of his own improvisation. Playwright and actor were one; there was no stage, no scenery, no lighting other than from the unregulated sun, fire, or torches. There was drama, simple but absorbing. Already there was the collaboration between playwright and theater; how he told his story was in response to and determined by the conditions of presentation. As the theater became elaborated in different ways in different backgrounds, by musical accompaniment, by a chorus, by addition of actors and of a platform to lift them to view and project their voices, by costume, make-up, masks, by varied fixed and permanent structures for audience and production, the play has taken form in response to awareness in the mind of the playwright of the theater for which he was writing. The collaboration which culminates in the functioning of actors, and in our theater of today, of a director, scenic designer, costume designer, lighting director, and a corps of technicians, possibly a choreographer, composer, and musicians, begins in the study of the playwright. Present as a voice to his imagination is a theater structure with its conventions and facilities which suggests, admonishes, and inspires: this is the effect you want; no, that will not do; ah, here is a marvelous opportunity I offer you—take it!

To read a play not only imaginatively but with an intelligent imagination it is necessary to know something of the theater for which it was written. Mental staging of *King Oedipus* or *Antigone* need not, should not, be an archaistic reconstruction of the theater of Dionysus since the ultimate objective is the play beyond the theater; but to feel the intensification of the drama and the breadth of movement given by the Choral Odes separating the major units of dramatic action, the thin line of poetry on the printed page must swell into the unison song of a Chorus of twelve or fifteen people, delivered not statically but accompanied by expressive dance movements. The Chorus in its highly formalized representation of a group of real people in an involved yet detached relation to the dramatic action, as the Theban Suppliants in *King Oedipus,* Theban Elders in *Antigone,* is the foundation of the proper empathy in the experience of Greek tragedy. Certainly, without going into minutiae of scholarship, to have in mind the occasion and setting of the original performance of the Greek tragedies, a festival of worship and tradition uniting an entire community, the spacious symmetry of the hillside amphitheater seating twenty thousand spectators, the open sky and surrounding temple-crowned hills, is recreative of the spirit in which they were written.

For experiencing a play of Shakespeare the *décor* and structure of the theater as a setting are comparatively unimportant. The Elizabethan theater was a versatile theater which provided for direct interaction between an audience and the heart of a play in independence of surroundings. What is important is the form and conventions of the stage. To read the first act of *Hamlet,* which establishes the isolation and loneliness of Hamlet as the psychological and moral climate for the shattering impact of the meeting with his father's ghost, without knowing that the Elizabethan stage was an open platform on which one scene followed another in immediate succession with no visual break of a curtain or interval for change of act, would be to miss the effect of one of Shakespeare's shrewdest utilizations of the techniques offered by his stage. In Scene One, by lines and situation Shakespeare establishes the mood of cold and darkness on the battlements of Elsinore followed by the awesome appearance of the Ghost. The scene ends on reference to Hamlet. Horatio, Marcellus, and Bernardo make their exeunt. Immediately follows the pageantry of the ceremonial entrance of King and Queen and all the court. The stage is filled with the figures of the actors in brilliant Elizabethan costume, creating the light and warmth of the interior of the castle in bold juxtaposition to the atmosphere of the preceding scene. In the midst of this scene yet isolated from it, linked with the outer darkness by the mourning black of his apparel, alone among the festive costumes, is the figure of Hamlet (Shakespeare's skill is wasted on a *Hamlet* in modern dress).

The Court departs to the marriage festivities; Hamlet is alone on the stage, the first soliloquy; enter Horatio, Bernardo, and Marcellus to recount to Hamlet their meeting with the Ghost. Because the stage has not been emptied this is still nominally Scene Two, but the Elizabethan stage without illusionary scenery or lighting became what the lines made it, and we are back in the mood of the battlements, darkness and the presence of the Ghost, when the scene ends with Hamlet again alone, his mind on foul deeds and the night to come. He exits. Scene Three, enter Laertes and Ophelia, and we are in the home of Polonius, again a sharp juxtaposition of contrast, this time the human warmth of family intimacy, of affectionate concern for one another, against the isolation of Hamlet's loss of his father, detestation and distrust of his uncle, and spiritual separation from his mother. The scene ends with Ophelia's obedience to her father's injunction and awareness for the audience that Hamlet is cut off from Ophelia's love. The preparation is complete for the opening of Scene Four by the entrance of Hamlet, Horatio, and Marcellus at midnight on the battlements and the progression to Hamlet's encounter with the ghost of his father, for which Shakespeare again skillfully utilizes his stage to separate Hamlet from his companions without interrupting the flow of action. It has now become a commonplace of modern production of Shakespeare to find some means of circumventing more or less effectively the structure of our stages to keep the close movement from scene to scene in which he wrote the plays. But if in reading *Hamlet* one allows our modern habitual identification of a scene change with a curtain and an interval to intrude a mental lag in following Shakespeare's carefully built close contrasts and linkages, something will have been lost of the emotional background, of the aloneness in knowledge and responsibility, of Hamlet's cry at the end of Act One: "The time is out of joint;—O, cursed spite! That ever I was born to set it right."

Shakespeare could not raise or lower a curtain on his main stage; he capitalized on the special effects made available by his stage. Similarly, nineteenth- and twentieth-century playwrights do not merely open and close scenes with the curtain but have integrated its mechanics with dramatic effect, as indicated by the frequency of the stage directions "Fast curtain" and "Slow curtain." The modern stage, however, by lighting, mechanics, and the inventiveness and artistry of scenic designers, has become a very flexible instrument inside the original architectural inflexibility of our theaters of proscenium arch and curtain. In consequence, in reading contemporary plays one may find perhaps greater variety of effects written in reliance upon fulfillment in the theater than has belonged to any other drama. For example, the complicated staging by Jo Mielziner of *Death of a Salesman* achieved, with freedom from disruption of curtains and intervals for change of set, articulation and blending of the many scenes, and simultaneous awareness of elements which on first reading of the text can be experienced only successively in time. The flexibility of the great theaters of the past, the Greek and Elizabethan, was inherent in the basic physical structure. That of our theater today depends upon directors, scenic designers, and technicians.

The current movement of central staging gives promise of permanence and growth, particularly in terms of what to my mind is the truer theater form, the three-quarters-round or projecting stage rather than complete arena. This form is, of course, a return to inherent flexibility of structure. A scattering of new plays have already been written directly for central staging and we may in the not far distant future have a whole new body of playwriting of conscious collaboration with its opportunities and techniques.

THE PRODUCER

After a play has been written in awareness of its theater as a physical structure and set of conventions, a second process of collaboration begins in the progress of the play to full life in the theater, this time with persons. First in order, in the present organization of the professional theater in this country, comes a producer. (In England what is termed the director in the United States is known as the producer, in Germany and Russia the *régisseur,* in France the *metteur en scène.* In England what is known as the producer in the United States is the manager, and in France *régisseur* refers to the stage manager. For convenience in this text "director" and "producer" will be used as in the United States.) Producers are not always thought of as a creative part of the theater, and some are not. All that it takes to be a producer, for one play at least, is possession of the necessary right in a script and enough money, his own or from other people; theoretically he might hire a manager to carry on from there. Actually established producers are the line of continuity in our theater, with everything else in the open market, and perform an extremely complex function. The producer finds a script to his liking, the money, the theater, the director, scene designer, actors, and other creative people as required, a stage manager, and all the people necessary to the practical execution of the production. He is responsible for the publicity, sale of tickets, meeting the payroll, maintaining the production through its run, possibly organizing and maintaining road companies, and making all final decisions. Functions are delegated in varying degrees through permanent staff and those engaged for the production, but the total organization centers in the producer's office, which is a very active place. With all this on their hands there are creative producers. A few, like George Abbott, habitually direct their productions; others, like Guthrie McClintic, Eddie Dowling, and Jed Harris, do so sometimes. Theresa Helburn and Lawrence Langner of the Theatre Guild, with a large organization and permanent staff, nevertheless kept so directly in contact with details all through the course of each production and worked in such close cooperation with author, director, designers, and cast, that over the years Theatre Guild productions have come to have an established character. In the twenties, although he was director of his own productions, it was as producer that Arthur Hopkins made his most creative contribution to a change in the professional theater in New York by such moves as giving the young designer Robert Edmond Jones freedom of opportunity for

application of the new stagecraft in his *Richard III* and *Macbeth,*
and by the then daring selection of plays such as *The Hairy Ape* by
the young Eugene O'Neill. In that period of the twenties the Theatre
Guild as a producing organization, then comprising a board of six
members, accomplished more than any single force to change the
scope of Broadway theater. They introduced the new European
dramatists, the new stagecraft, and new American plays as unusual
to Broadway as Elmer Rice's *The Adding Machine,* Dorothy and
DuBose Heyward's *Porgy,* and Eugene O'Neill's *Strange Interlude.*
By number of plays, a basic six a year, and fully professional
level of production made possible by their subscription system of
financing, the Guild bridged the gap between experimental theater
as an amateur enthusiasm and the professional theater. In the thirties
such plays as Maxwell Anderson's *Winterset* and Thornton Wilder's
Our Town were presented by other producers, and in 1959 Norman
Corwin's *The Rivalry* and Archibald MacLeish's *J.B.* were produced respectively by Cheryl Crawford and Joel Schenker, and
Alfred de Liagre, Jr.

Although the circumstances of the professional Broadway theater
emphasize finance, a producer is an organizer of theater and, according to motivation other than or in addition to making money, is in
greater or less degree creative. The professional producers I have
known have enjoyed being responsible for giving life in the theater
to plays. Most of the off-Broadway theaters were organized on some
creative principle and are managed by their organizers, some as
producers only, some as producer-directors. Outside the New York
theater the term *producer* is seldom used, but in community theaters
and in professional, amateur, and university theaters throughout the
country the function of producer is being performed by directors,
boards, administrative heads of community theaters, heads of university departments and schools of drama, and theater committees.
Many of those community and university units are organizers of
theater on a large scale with extensive programs of production, two
or three theaters in continuous operation, and several directors putting on plays simultaneously. Some of the older and larger community institutions, like the Cleveland and the Pasadena Playhouses,
have from the beginning given production of new plays an important
place in their programs; some, like the theater organized by Margo

Jones in Dallas, are basically theaters of new plays, and it is becoming widespread practice to do an occasional new play or regularly one a season. Since the pioneer work of George Pierce Baker at Harvard in 1908, later at Yale, and of Frederick Koch at the University of North Carolina in 1918, with introduction in another ten years of major development of playwriting in association with production at the University of Michigan, University of Iowa, Stanford University, and others, production of new plays, the basic creativity of theater, has become widespread in universities. University theaters have also been especially creative in experimental work in staging and scene design, including so far-reaching an innovation as that of arena theater by Glen Hughes at the University of Seattle. The noncommercial theater in all its forms has been and is becoming increasingly an important area in giving theater life to new plays. It should go a great deal further.

The work of directors, scene designers, and actors, the subjects of following chapters, has more immediate and extensive bearing on experiencing of plays through reading than has that of producers and producing organizations. A basic appreciation, however, of the functioning which creates the situation within which the playwright and all his other personal collaborators of the theater work is desirable, as is an understanding of the creative interplay and overlapping that frequently occurs between the activities of organization and administration and those of direction and design.

3

In the Theater : The Director

Plays have always necessarily been directed in some manner but
the director as a separate profession is a modern development. In
the earlier centuries of great dramatists the dramatists were themselves engaged in bringing on their own plays, although our knowledge of the directorial aspect of production in the Greek theater and
the Elizabethan theater is very incomplete. We know that in the
Greek theater of the fifth century B.C. the training of the chorus
was an important function, and that Aeschylus, Sophocles, Euripedes,
and Aristophanes all trained their own choruses. Aeschylus and
Sophocles also made important contributions to the devices and procedures of staging. In the Elizabethan theater directorial function is
ascribed at least to Ben Jonson and Shakespeare among the dramatists. The informal biographer of the seventeenth century, John
Aubrey, who knew people who knew Ben Jonson, stated he "was
never a good actor, but an excellent instructor." The commonly held
belief that Shakespeare instructed the actors for the Globe Theater
is derived to a considerable degree from the convincing ring of the
voice of a director in Hamlet's famous speech of advice to the
players. In the seventeenth century Molière was not only a principal
playwright and an actor for his company, but as head of the company
assumed all the responsibilities both of the modern producer and
director.

With the eighteenth century and through the nineteenth came a change. The leading actors from Garrick to Irving and Booth became the theater managers and directors of their productions. The star system as the basic attraction in the theater developed; plays were cut, adapted, and staged to enhancement of the star's part; playwriting declined. We speak of the period as an actor's theater. Actually it was a star actor's theater. At the height of the system the princes of the theater might lavish attention on the *décor* of the production, the scenery and costumes, while leaving the acting of the company to the individual actor. The star often prepared his part in isolation, and determined the "business" in which he instructed the stage manager orally or by a prompt-book. The members of the company "got up" their parts and were then rehearsed together by the stage manager for the business. The star met with them for a few rehearsals, sometimes only delivering cues and leaving the remainder of lengthy speeches to be read by a stand-in. In general, the supporting actors were expected to leave sufficient clear space around the star, not to move farther downstage than his position at any time, and to do nothing in the background to distract the audience's attention when he was speaking. The directing even by Edwin Booth of Shakespeare, with his great reverence for "our immortal plays," seems from the records to have been centered around the star part and conceived more in terms of acting of characters than of the play. It is significant that he could speak of Shakespeare's works as "those poems which I reveal to them."

There can be no doubt from contemporary accounts that the eighteenth and nineteenth centuries in Europe, on the Continent and in England, and in the United States produced a remarkable number of actors and actresses with very great power over audiences. Madame Modjeska performed the experiment of inserting into a performance before an American audience a recitation of the Polish alphabet and held the audience spellbound. Mrs. Siddons' biographer Thomas Campbell, while admiring the splendor of the performance, deplored "the perplexity to popular taste" in his surmise that her Margaret of Anjou probably "persuaded half her spectators that Franklin's *Earl of Warwick* was a noble poem . . . a tragedy as good as any of Shakespeare's." * It is probable that less of over-

* *Life of Mrs. Siddons,* Harper and Bros., New York, 1834, pp. 121-122.

whelming emotion is experienced in the theater today, but quite possibly more of meaning.

With the revitalization of drama by the realistic and naturalistic movement in approximately the last third of the nineteenth century, the modern director emerged. The model of closely molded ensemble playing and unification of all the details of production by one mind had already been set by George II, Duke of Saxe-Meiningen, in the theater company he established and maintained from 1874 to 1890. The character of the Meiningen productions influenced the directors to come as an instrument to a new purpose. André Antoine founded the *Théâtre Libre* in Paris in 1887, Stanislavsky the Art and Literature Society in 1888 which was the prelude to the Moscow Art Theatre, and Otto Brahm the *Freie Buehne* in Berlin in 1889 to give opportunity for production and the right kind of production to the revolutionary new plays. These men undertook to free the playwright from the control of the actors; the director was the author's representative; the sole function of the theater was communication of the play. Actually, of course, they were creating a new school of acting oriented to the play rather than the part, or worse, projection of the actor. Both Antoine and Stanislavsky acted in their companies. As the revolution in playwriting of serious concern for truth of life passed on from its initial phase of naturalism into varied forms, symbolism, expressionism, and "selective realism," new directors and theaters appeared, dedicated like the first group to the play, but offering new flexible theater forms and varied styles of production. One of the most influential, Jacques Copeau, announced for the opening of his theater that "The *Théâtre du Vieux Colombier* is open to all efforts, provided that they reach a certain level and of a certain quality," and "we are preparing a place of refuge for future talents." *

From around 1900 on there developed a different type of theater and conception of the director. There is a supreme single art of the theater in which the director is a kind of super-artist. The play is raw material in the hands of the director at the same level as the

---

* Quoted in *Actors on Acting*, ed. Toby Cole and Helen Krich Chinoy, Crown Publishers, New York, 1949, p. 223, from "Un Essai de renovation dramatique," *Etudes d'art dramatique, critiques d'un autre temps*, Editions de la Nouvelle Revue Française, Paris, 1923, pp. 243-246, trans. Joseph M. Bernstein.

voices and bodies of the actors, the form of the stage, the elements of scenic design, lighting, music and dance, all to be molded freely at his will into a theatrical work of art. The high priest of this cult was Gordon Craig, and since he theorized more than he directed he finally went so far as to state, as the ideal for the art of the theater, elimination of the written play—as it limits the freedom of the director—and substitution of super-marionettes for the intractable human actors. Craig wrote a great deal with a peculiarly exciting authoritative eloquence which had spreading power. Practicing directors did not dispense with playwrights and actors, but there was a sequence of authoritarian creators of theatrical theater culminating in the great *régisseurs* such as Meyerhold in Russia and Reinhardt in Germany. One did not speak of a play produced by Meyerhold or Reinhardt but of a Meyerhold or a Reinhardt production of the play. The truly constructive part of Craig's theories came out of his emphasis on the physical aspects, the sense impressions, of theater. He and his immediate predecessor, Adolphe Appia, may be considered together as the founders of the new stagecraft of plastic form and lighting and impression which was applied by men such as Copeau to the service of the play, to the release of its inner spirit to the imagination.

The function of the director in the modern theater was established in repertory companies founded by the directors. These men were producer-directors. The two functions have since largely become separated, although we still have Jean-Louis Barrault with his own company in France in which he is director and chief actor. The early directors came to that function by various routes; some had previously acted, although not formidably, some had written plays, some had been dramatic critics. The significant thing is that once they had created the function of director for themselves, they were primarily directors and secondarily anything else. There were variations from the pattern. Stanislavsky became a great actor in the Moscow Art Theatre and its *régisseur,* with Nemirovitch-Danchenko as his director of plays. Some of the greatest of the dramatists, Strindberg for his last plays and Pirandello, founded intimate or small art theaters in which they staged their own plays. Shaw and Galsworthy directed their own plays without being theater managers. In France, Louis Jouvet was equally actor and director.

The Abbey Theatre of Dublin in its long and honorable history from its opening as the Irish Literary Theatre in 1899 to the present, followed a varied pattern of its own. It was organized by a group of literary people who learned about theater by engaging in it, has been governed by a board, and never had a *régisseur* or single outstanding director, although William Butler Yeats and Lennox Robinson successively as managers each exercised over an extended period a sustaining force and guidance. Both were principal playwrights of the theater, they both directed plays, and Robinson appeared with some frequency as an actor. Actors and playwrights became directors, in some periods there was one director, at other times there were different directors for the plays of a season. Like its great predecessors, the *Théâtre Libre, Freie Buehne,* Moscow Art Theatre, and J. T. Grein's Independent Theatre in London, the Abbey existed to foster new drama. Unlike them it was never unified towards any dramatic theory other than plays by the Irish, of and first of all for Ireland. Even Yeats with his initial devotion to an idea of a theater of noble poetry left theory to follow talent when he brought John Millington Synge, the playwright of the Irish peasantry, into the Abbey Theatre. The Abbey developed competent directors rather than directors of individually brilliant style, and no theater has been more successful in producing playwrights.

Today in England, some of the most distinguished actors, Sir John Gielgud, Sir Cedric Hardwicke, and Sir Laurence Olivier, are also among the most accomplished directors. In the United States a few playwrights, John Van Druten and Elmer Rice, have not only directed their own plays but others with distinction. On the whole, however, directing has become a separate profession in which the director is engaged by the producer to be responsible for the theater form of a play selected by the producer. The development of the modern director, originating to free the playwright from the actors, has now come full circle and today a rising criticism of our theater is that the playwright and his play are too subject to the control and individual styles of directors.

There are inherent reasons for the definition and enlargement of the function of the director in the modern theater. The Greek and Elizabethan stages were more fixed structures than ours (because of what the new stagecraft has accomplished inside our fixed structure), the conventions were more unified and, certainly in the Greek theater, more formalized. Also the Greek theater in its great century and the Elizabethan theater were producing only their own plays. Out of the transitional process of the seventeenth century the eighteenth and nineteenth centuries possessed a new fixed structure but one which opened the way to a steadily increasing emphasis on scenery and stage effects. In these two centuries also developed the revival under new stage conditions of plays from earlier periods. A consequence was the rise of the director, first in the capacity of actor-director. The new drama of realism of the later nineteenth century was a prose drama for scenic illusion of reality in the theater. The old poetic drama for a stage without scenery was more self-creative of its production, demanding primarily good speaking of the lines by the actors. The new realistic drama required a complex process of production; then, as varied styles of playwriting developed under the freedom of form and convention made possible by the new stagecraft, production became more complex and interpretative; and finally, under the magnitude and complication of the process of production in the commercial theater today, specialization has been increased. The playwright writes the play, a producer selects and finances it, a director stages it, and other specialists, as the scenic designer, rise high alongside the director in their functions.

For the reading of plays, whatever improper balance of power or misapplications of power there may be, to understand the place and functioning of directing is of primary importance. This can be accomplished only through study of the activity of directors. How some of the great directors have defined and analyzed their function follows.

André Antoine: "In my opinion, modern directing must perform the same function in the theater as descriptions in a novel. Directing should—as, in fact, is generally the case today—not only fit the action in its proper framework but also determine its true character and create its atmosphere.

"The first time I had to direct a play, I saw clearly that the work was divided into two distinct parts: one was quite tangible, that is, finding the right *décor* for the action and the proper way of grouping the characters; the other was impalpable, that is, the interpretation and flow of the dialogue." *

Otto Brahm: "The most important task in directing actors . . . is the task of being sensitive to the inner spirit of a work and of projecting in its representation the individual tone and mood born by that certain work and none other. He who wishes to bring a dramatic creation to stage-life must be capable of perceiving these basic mood-creating tones and of making them resound in the audience through the medium of his performers." †

Jacques Copeau: "Once the stage is set in accordance with the needs of the action as envisaged in its broad lines, the action itself must be organized, act by act, scene by scene, speech by speech, down to the slightest details. As he devises the action he is going to propose to his actors—their places, their distances from one another, the movements they make, their relations with the stage set, the furniture and the props, the pace of their speeches and their silences, the varying tempo of their entrances and exits—the director bears in mind the truthfulness of the characters, the expression of their emotions, the demands of the script, the logic of events, the positions on stage, the lighting effects, the naturalness of the players and group symmetry. He aims at achieving clear representation, well-defined movement, varied rhythm, and sustained harmony. All his steps are motivated by a unity of style and guided by one over-all idea. But he must be careful not to allow this idea to become too obvious, not to force it to the point of pedantry and abstraction . . . for the triumph of his art is the creation of life." ‡

Louis Jouvet: "In the limbo where the production takes form, in the slow growth during which the features are shaped, where it is foreseen in imagination, where the dramatic leaven is mysteriously at work, the director watches with patience, discretion and tender-

---

* From the translation of "Causerie sur la mise en scène," *La Revue de Paris,* Vol. 10, Apr. 1, 1903, 596-612, in *Directing the Play,* ed. Toby Cole and Helen Krich Chinoy, Bobbs-Merrill, Indianapolis and New York, 1953, pp. 80 and 84.

† Quoted by Herbert Henze in "Otto Brahm and Naturalist Directing," *Theatre Workshop,* April-July, 1937, pp. 14-15.

‡ From the translation of *"La mise en scène,"* *Encyclopédie Française,* Dec., 1935, 1764, 1-5, in *Directing the Play,* Cole and Chinoy, pp. 150-151.

ness over the straggling elements he has assembled to give life to the playwright's work. His job is accomplished through intuition, understanding, foresight, through a special alchemy composed of words, sounds, gestures, colors, lines, movements, rhythms and silences, and including an imponderable which will radiate the proper feeling of laughter or emotion when the work appears before the public.

"The profession of the director suffers from the disease of immodesty, and even the most sincere people do not escape it. Their license to work freely with the plays of other people, to dabble with them and make them over, is an established and accepted convention, and after a few hours of conversation with himself or with a colleague a man must have a steady head and firm foothold to resist the dizziness in which, convinced of what he would like to believe, he approaches the conclusion that Shakespeare or Goethe understood nothing of the theater." *

Harold Clurman: "The director's essential work is to set down the 'notes'—the moment-to-moment inner and outer action which each actor is to play. This is the theater's most intimate and mysterious process. For it is not a matter of *telling* the actor what to do or even of explaining the playwright's and director's intention, but of both firing the actor's imagination and placing it on the right track so that the actor can proceed to the desired destination with an impulse that is as much his own as that of the author's mind or the director's will. Different directors use different methods to bring about that inspired moment when the unity we behold is actually the fruit of a triple generation—the dramatist's text, the director's spirit, the actor's being." †

Imaginative reading of a play should receive some initial stimulus from this directorial bird's-eye view of the scope and complexity of the contribution of the theater to fulfillment of a playscript. These five directors reveal two points of view in common, the authoritativeness of the director for the interpretative unification of all the ele-

* From "The Profession of the Producer, II" (Rosamond Gilder, translator), *Theatre Arts,* June 1937, 57-64; also in *Directing the Play,* Cole and Chinoy, pp. 175-180.
† "The Director's Job," *New Republic,* Aug. 15, 1949, 20-21.

ments of theater in each production, and respect for the script, the function of the director first to penetrate, then to find means to reveal, the content, the truth of the play.

Directors inevitably have their personal bents which color their work. Antoine became a director through interest in the new naturalistic drama. He wrote to the critic Sarcy: "In modern works written in the vein of realism and naturalism, where the theory of environment and the influence of exterior things have become so important, is not the setting the indispensable complement to the work?" *

David Belasco is notorious for devotion in unimaginative and surface terms to completeness and accuracy of detail from life in his stage settings. He had one perception, however, in the pursuit of which he developed the mechanics of one of the theater's most important instruments for more imaginative application by later directors and designers. "Lights," he wrote, "are to drama what music is to the lyrics of a song. No other factor that enters into the production of a play is so effective in conveying its mood and feeling." †

Elia Kazan is notable for his search into the meaning of a play. Once he has committed himself to direct a play it becomes an object of faith on which he fixes with a yogi-like concentration. Nevertheless he is particularly apt to see a play and its characters in social terms where another director, or reader, by a similar process would arrive at a different perception. For example, in his notebook of preparation for directing *A Streetcar Named Desire* appears the following entry: "Blanche is a social type, an emblem of a dying civilization, making its last curlicued and romantic exit. All her behavior patterns are those of the dying civilization she represents. In other words her behavior is *social*. Therefore find social modes! This is the source of the play's stylization and basic color. Likewise Stanley's behavior is *social* too! It is the basic animal cynicism of today. 'Get what's coming to you! Don't waste a day! Eat, drink,

* The entire letter is printed in *Antoine and The Théâtre-Libre,* by Samuel Montefiore Waxman, Harvard University Press, Cambridge, 1926, pp. 132-140.
† *The Theatre Through the Stage Door,* ed. Louis V. DeFoe, Harper and Brothers, New York, 1919, p. 56.

get yours.' This is the basis of his stylization, of the choice of his props." *

Clearly this perception of social placement was a releasing mechanism of insight into the play for Kazan, one of the major progressions toward the unity of his extraordinarily illuminating production. Yet I believe it is possible for a differently motivated reading or production of the play also to be illuminating. No human mind sheds a hard white all-embracing light upon a play or other work of art, but each mind lights it from an angle and with a tone of its own.

Tyrone Guthrie, like most English directors (except George Bernard Shaw as director of his own plays), pays high respect to the contribution of ideas from the actors to the developing direction of a play. Perhaps the level of training of English actors and a general national respect has something to do with this characteristic attitude of the directors. In this country we have no equivalent recognition of public service to the English "Sir" and "Dame" that has been bestowed with some frequency on actors and actresses, and no indication that our government would so bestow it if we had. I recall Dr. Guthrie's remarking in a letter some years ago that he did not prepare a prompt script of elaborate notes and diagrams in advance of rehearsal because he believed as much as possible should be left to the corporate creation which he considered to be the essence of theatrical art; and in a lecture delivered before the Royal Society of Arts in London, March 10, 1952,† he begins disarmingly: "Producing a play clearly requires the co-ordinated efforts of many people, and the producer is no more than the co-ordinator. His work may, and I think should, have creative function, but not always." His next sentence opens the bag for the cat to emerge: "The important thing is gathering together the different pieces and welding many disparate elements into one complete unity, which is never, of course, fully achieved in artistic matters."

Tyrone Guthrie is probably the most individually, some would say individualistically, creative and forceful director in action any-

* *Directing the Play,* Cole and Chenoy, p. 297.
† Transcribed for printing in *Directing the Play,* ed. Toby Cole and Helen Krich Chinoy. Quotation is by permission of the publishers, Bobbs-Merrill Company.

where today. In all his speaking and writing he stresses the importance of conference and exchange of ideas among the people concerned in the production before going into rehearsal. But I think
before he ever decides to do a play he has a production idea, in
some way with fresh potentiality for the play in the theater, or he is
not interested, and then improvises brilliantly on all the materials
of the theater, which includes the ideas, generously acknowledged,
of those he refers to as his collaborators whenever they meet the
selective process of his own intention and judgment for the basic
unifying idea. Robertson Davies, a member of the board of directors
of the Canadian Stratford Festival with which Dr. Guthrie has been
so significantly associated, has written of him: "I am rarely able to
persuade myself that the theories which he puts forward with so
much cogency and illustrative detail are not evolved *after* the creative
act; he gets his best ideas, and his worst ones, from the source
which every artist knows and cannot name; they rise unbidden from
the depths, and they will not be denied even when they seem to lead
toward destruction." *

Dr. Guthrie himself in the conclusion to his lecture states that the
function of a director of a play "at its best is one of psychic evocation, and it is performed almost entirely unconsciously. Certain
conscious tricks can come in the way or aid the process, but this
evocative thing comes from God knows where. It is completely unconscious."

As has been true of many creative artists, Dr. Guthrie's career
has progressed through phases or periods. Robertson Davies refers
to "the enthusiasm for ritual which is Dr. Guthrie's latest and most
richly productive approach to the theatre." The beauty in power
of his production of *King Oedipus* in masks in the 1954 season at
Stratford, Ontario, was a regeneration of the known roots in ritual
of Greek tragedy; but when Dr. Guthrie writing on Marlowe's *Tamburlaine* refers to that drama successively as "a sort of sadistic con-
certo," "a ritual dance," and "a kind of savage oratorio," † recognition of a distinctive directorial approach is inescapable.

In the lecture in 1952 his central theme is the task of the director

* "The Genius of Dr. Guthrie," *Theatre Arts,* March, 1956, p. 30.
† *"Tamburlaine,* and what it takes," *Theatre Arts,* February, 1956, pp. 21-23,
84-86.

to shape the production into meaningful compositional unity "in predominantly musical and choreographic terms," but at this point he says nothing of ritual. By music he means the vocal quality of speech: "Supposing you are an actor who is playing Hamlet. 'To be or not to be: that is the question: whether 'tis nobler in the mind to suffer . . .'—those infinitely familiar lines. You have to find the inflection, that is to say the tone, to which they are sung or spoken, the pitch, the pace, the rhythm and the color. That is, in fact, very highly creative." By choreography he means all the movements and positions of all the actors in any play. "That is particularly where the co-ordinating hand of the producer is required," he says, "joining up the various songs that are being sung and making them into a unit; and similarly, joining up the various patterns that are being danced, because even in the simplest realistic comedy, in the most ordinary kind of realistic set—the actors have to move, and their movements have to tot up to some kind of choreographic design which expresses the play, which has some meaning over and above the common-sense position in which one would pour tea or put sugar into it."

Earlier, in 1944, in an article "Some Notes on Direction," * even though he opened and closed on the analogy of the director of a play to the conductor of an orchestra, mostly to point up the differences, Dr. Guthrie made no reference to the production of a play as song or dance. At that time he was administrator of the Old Vic and Sadler's Wells Theatres in England, launching a new repertory policy for the coming season, and had just himself directed *Peer Gynt* with the full Grieg score. A year later he came to this country to stage *He Who Gets Slapped* for the Theatre Guild in a new English version by his wife, Judith Guthrie, which he had shortly before staged in England. In contrast to the Theatre Guild production in 1922 directed by Robert Milton the crowded scenes of backstage of a circus were more emphasized and in their handling showed something of that choreographic mastery of large group scenes which has been increasingly prominent in his productions. Richard Bennett as He in 1922 died at the end of the play standing isolated in center-stage; from a position with face upturned, arms raised straining to clenched hands as though by power of will to lift himself into the beyond, his body collapsed to the floor abruptly

* *Theatre Arts,* November, 1944.

inert as though a rope had been cut suspending a heavy sack. In the Guthrie production Dennis King, starting near center-stage, staggered in the death throes of the poison in a revolving movement to nearly rear-stage and fell backward, arms outspread, onto a mesh of backstage ropes which caught and held him suspended as on a huge spider's web. Both renderings were illuminating of the content of the play as a conflict between aspiration and life but gave a different tone and emphasis. One ended the play on a lift in the defiance and projected the conflict from earth into infinity; the other brought the previous course of the play of an aspiring man entangled in the web of life to a point of poignant realization. The pattern of the great ropes dominated the background of the stage throughout the play as a symbol to the unconscious mind of the audience; in the death scene they suddenly became a conscious symbol. At a near-dress rehearsal at which the ropes had been arranged for their general scenic effect but were not secured to receive the body of the actor, Dr. Guthrie explained, "What I'm aiming at is the most effective death-fall you have ever seen." Actually, of course, the whole matter was a manifestation of that flair for originating striking and expressive visual effects which has become known as a characteristic of his work.

Farther back, in 1936, at a rehearsal of *Measure for Measure* for the Old Vic, I experienced a transformation from the conventional that was psychological and wholly in terms of the actor. It was the scene of Isabella and Angelo in which he offers her brother's life on the condition she submit herself to him. The scene was run through and was flat and unmoving. Dr. Guthrie went up on the stage and spoke briefly and quietly to the actor and actress. *Measure for Measure* has been one of the "difficult plays" of Shakespeare for modern production. Isabella has become a not particularly congenial person but the tradition from the nineteenth century exalts her as the heroine. In the first run-through the focus was on Isabella, a situation of spotless heroine and black villain. What happened in the second run-through after the director's words was an effect so absorbing that I found myself caught up in one of those memorable experiences of theater that occasionally come upon one unawares in the isolation of a rehearsal. The actor of Angelo projected with an altogether fresh intensity the inner conflict of the austere repressed man confident in the security of his virtue caught off-guard by a sudden irresistible flare of passion. The scene was enriched and complicated by the interplay of two foci of inner conflict. The horror of Isabella further incited the unruly passion in Angelo, and the power of his passion as revealed shaking itself free from rigid habits of virtue made more fearful the plight of Isabella. One could justify the approach to the scene on the grounds that Angelo, as freshly developed into a man of mixed good and bad involved in psychological conflict, makes better contact with the audience of today than Isabella. Shakespeare's text hardly provides the lines for such a development but leaves room for it in the acting. But the point is that playing Angelo up did not play Isabella's part down, it strengthened it rather, and the total effect was a theatrical change into a more complex and interesting scene. I suspect that Dr. Guthrie today, if not at the time, might explain what he did by saying he simply changed a melodic line with bass accompaniment to counterpoint.

Tyrone Guthrie is sometimes criticized as an overly "theatrical" director. He certainly does not present the function of the director as a sacred custodianship of the script. In the lecture before the Royal Society he refers to the script as "the raw material" of the director's work, and in the article on *Tamburlaine* he remarks that "one is always grieved to find how scholars refuse to regard a play as raw material for the theater." There is constantly implied, however, both in his words and his work, a profound devotion to drama. The energy of his imagination is applied to penetration of the texts of drama as for the theater. For the most part he has chosen to direct the classics of dramatic literature, both because of the theatrical scope they offer, and by the desire to make them live in the theater today. He is most fully aroused by the challenge of a work that has long been relegated from its origination in the theater to purely literary respect as difficult or impossible for the contemporary stage, such as Marlowe's *Tamburlaine*.

Not only do different directors have their individual styles, each bringing to the service of theater the special quality of his own background, intelligence, and imagination, sometimes genius, but they follow radically different procedures of preparation for and conduct of production. As we have seen, Tyrone Guthrie works from his head rather than paper. Max Reinhardt in advance of rehearsals prepared a huge *Regiebuch* of thousands of entries for every minute detail of production. Neither André Antoine nor Otto Brahm used a written production plan. Brahm had no use for detailed advance preparation because rehearsals were the instrument by which he arrived at the shape of a performance. Harold Clurman and Elia Kazan keep notebooks of analysis and reactions during a period of study of the play, something quite different from a prompt-book of directions. Mr. Clurman writes: "Such notes set down for my own use when I have read a play at least a half-dozen times are never communicated to the actors in the form which they take in my little book. They would be unintelligible to actors in this form as well as practically useless. . . . With these notes as a basis I am able to approach the actor." *

There follow two illustrations of aspects of direction which were put on paper and thus may be included in a book. By the courtesy of the respective directors, Sir John Gielgud and Elia Kazan, two scenes from the stage manager's script for *The Lady's Not for Burning* by Christopher Fry, with a photograph of the stage, and excerpts from Mr. Kazan's notebooks in preparation for directing *Death of a Salesman* by Arthur Miller, are presented.

Two scenes from Acts I and III from the stage manager's prompt-book for Sir John Gielgud's staging of *The Lady's Not for Burning* by Christopher Fry.†

The London production staged by John Gielgud; *décor* by Oliver Messel; stage manager, Alison Colvil, with the English cast, was brought to New York by Atlantis Productions (the Theatre Guild, Tennent Productions Ltd., and John C. Wilson) and ran at the Royale Theatre November 8, 1950, to March 17, 1951. The production, directed by the leading actor of the cast, was especially enjoyable for its continuously harmonious and balanced effect.

Sir John Gielgud wrote with reference to notes for production: "I

* *Directing the Play,* Cole and Chinoy, p. 319.
† Reproduced by the courtesy of Sir John Gielgud.

very rarely keep notes of details of the performance, though, of course, they are incorporated into the script by the stage manager as the rehearsals go on. I find it very difficult to remember afterwards the way in which the production has gone, and I hardly think it is fair, either to the author or to the actors, to take credit for points and direction, which may have been suggested by them and not by me."

The stage manager's prompt-book, from which the two scenes are printed here, consists of the text of the play with insertion of stage directions as worked out in production for the movements, positions, and principal business of the actors. The reader should compare the scenes with the corresponding scenes in the published text of the play (Oxford University Press, 1950, pages 31-35 and 90-93.) It may be noted that the first of the two scenes in the published text contains five stage directions totaling twenty-three words, while the stage manager's script contains fifty stage directions totaling four hundred eighty-six words. In the theater the visual effect indicated by the prompt-book directions is received simultaneously with the lines; yet such a multiplicity of stage directions would be disruptive to reading the play. At the same time, reading the play needs to be vitalized by some such visualization running simultaneously in one's mind's eye. By cultivation of theater background a degree of visualization will occur unconsciously on first reading of plays, but the pleasure in a play that is worth it will grow in successive readings. It is especially true of Christopher Fry's plays that the flow of his verse with its luxuriance of language and imagery is immediately easier to follow and more clear in the theater than in first reading because of the punctuation by the actors' movements and stage business, and especially by the pauses and inflections of the actors' delivery. *The Lady's Not for Burning* is so packed with beauty and wit of imagery and verbal felicity that the experience of production at theater pace makes one want to reread the play thus vivified.

The published text of *The Lady's Not for Burning* referred to is stated inside the dust jacket to be "the acting version as it was produced in London." In addition to the prompt-book stage directions some variations in the text from that of the published version will be noted. Sir John refers in his letter to "the development of this production as it was changed and simplified through the rehearsals

and six weeks tour in England." He also points out that what may be
final for one production is not definitive for another: "The handling
of every production differs of necessity, according to the personalities and limitations of the cast."

A photograph of Oliver Messel's set for *The Lady's Not for
Burning* can be seen opposite page 86. When reading these two
scenes, follow the movements and positions of the actors in the
stage directions on this illustration of the stage. Right and Left in
the directions are stage right and left, actors' right and left, not that
of the audience. The three acts of the play take place in a single
room but with a change of furnishing for the third act. The photograph is from Act III. In Acts I and II in place of the littered table
on the left side of the rostrum as in the photograph there was a
desk with a chair back of it. There was a bench at stage right, a
chair center-stage, and a small stool right center. The two scenes
from the prompt-book are from the first and third acts. Stage directions to the ramp Right refer to the corridor leading to an open
outside door. It can perhaps be discerned in the illustration that
the floor of the corridor is canted, or a ramp, which, with the
heavy shadow on the floor just outside the door and other details,
produces the illusion of a corridor of some length when actually the
door is in the same plane as the central window.

In visualization from the stage directions a first recognition will
be a sense of life added to the play in the mere fact of motion. One
may next recognize the fact of pattern, which is necessary to motion
in the theater, a pleasing balance in the disposition of the actors in
movement and location. The pattern of movement derives, however,
from the actors as living persons and should have expressiveness
and meaning. The greater proportion of the movements of the actors
are not doing something but are a part of the being of the characters.
The motivations are in the text. In the scene from Act I as the
household is called together for prayers, Margaret, the placid fulcrum
of domesticity, seats herself at once in the chair Center and does not
move from that position except to rise once and sit down until she
leaves the stage. Nicholas and Humphrey in their animal energy
circumnavigate and cross the stage. Richard, whom Alizon addresses on going to him as "Quiet Richard, son of nobody," takes
his initial position to one side of the stage, behind the bench Right,

and remains there except to sit on the bench when it is vacated until
he is given an action to perform by Tyson at the end of the scene.
Thomas, not a member of the household but an intruder of character, moves about a good bit with frequent and dominating incur-
sions to center-stage and to the rostrum. The Chaplain, a little old
man with the naturalness of a child in his long clerical robe, characteristically sits on the edge of the rostrum. The interlocking of stage
pattern and dramatic significance can be traced farther by the reader
in this first scene and through the scene from Act III.

The process of finding stage movement frequently produces one
of those perfect revealing actions, in some way as Shelley said the
search for the rhyming word seemed often to flash into consciousness
the ultimate word for meaning. The business of the Chaplain crossing to shake hands with Thomas on first seeing him is one of those
telling strokes, a moment that remains in memory from production:
the simple spontaneous action, the cherubic face puckered with age
peering up at Thomas in unaffected universal good will. It should
be noted also that so far as the printed text goes the triumphant
comedy business in the scene from Act III of trundling Skipps off
in the wheelbarrow, daffodils on his chest, was pure production
creation.

From Act I

(THE CHAPLAIN *enters down the ramp from U.R. carrying his viol
and music.*)

CHAPLAIN (*Speaking as he enters, and coming to chair C.*):
I'm late for prayers, I know; I know you think me
A broken reed, and my instrument too, my better half,
You lacked it, I'm afraid. (*Sits chair C.*) But life has such
Diversity, I sometimes remarkably lose
Eternity in the passing moment.

(TYSON *rises, raps on desk, and motions all to get ready for
prayers.* NICHOLAS *and* HUMPHREY *cross to bench R.* JENNET *rises.*
THE CHAPLAIN *crosses to right of lectern and arranges his music,
then sits on edge of rostrum.*)

                                Just now
In the street there's a certain boisterous interest
In a spiritual matter. They say . . . (*Sees* JENNET)

TYSON: I know what they say.

CHAPLAIN: Ah yes, you know. Sin, as well as God

Moves in a most mysterious way.

(*All are now in their positions for prayers.* MARGARET *in chair C.*
ALIZON *on small stool R.C.* RICHARD *behind bench R.* HUMPHREY
and NICHOLAS *sitting on bench R.* TYSON *motions them to stand,
and starts to count for the opening hymn.* JENNET *is on steps
D.L. Before they can start the hymn the* CHAPLAIN *speaks.*)

CHAPLAIN: It's hard to imagine

Why the poor girl should turn Skipps into a dog.

NICHOLAS (*Crossing to R. of chair C.*):   Skipps? Skipps into a
dog?

HUMPHREY (*Cross to R. of* ALIZON):   But Skipps is . . .

THOMAS (*To centre of stage on rostrum C.*):

Skipps trundles in another place, calling

His rags and bones in gutters without end,

Transfigured by the spatial light

Of Garbage Indestructible.

(MARGARET *sits on chair C. again, and* ALIZON *on stool.*)

                                                          And I

Ought to know since I sent him there. A dog?

Come, come, don't let's be fanciful. (*Goes down to stool L. and sits*)

TYSON (*Sits*):   They say one thing, and another thing, and both
at once.

I don't know. It will all have to be gone into

At the proper time. . . . (*Tries to start hymn*)

HUMPHREY (*On centre step of rostrum*):   But this is a contradiction . . .

(RICHARD *sits on bench D.R.*)

CHAPLAIN (*Rise and move towards* HUMPHREY):   Ah, isn't that
life all over.

(HUMPHREY *goes up to desk.* CHAPLAIN *to* THOMAS.)

                                                          And is this

The young assassin? (*Shakes hands with* THOMAS)

                                    If he is the doer of the damage

Can it be she also? My flock are employing

Fisticuffs over this very question. (*Sits L. end of rostrum*)

HUMPHREY: But if he could be the Devil . . .

THOMAS (*Rise*):   Good boy. (*Cross upstage centre on rostrum*)
                        Shall I set
Your minds at rest and give you proof? Come here.

(HUMPHREY *crosses to* THOMAS. THOMAS *takes the prayer book
out of his hand, whispers in his ear, and gives the book back to
him.* HUMPHREY *backs to above desk.* RICHARD *rises.*)

HUMPHREY: That's not funny.

THOMAS: Not funny for the goats. (*Cross
below desk and sit on rostrum*)

HUMPHREY: I've heard it before. (*Close to* TYSON) He says the
Day of Judgement
Is fixed for tonight.

(NICHOLAS *rises*, ALIZON *moves to R. of stool.* JENNET *rises D.L.*)

MARGARET: Oh no. I have always been sure
That when it comes it will come in the autumn.
Heaven, I am quite sure, wouldn't disappoint
The bulbs.

JENNET *sits steps D.L.*

THOMAS: Consider: vastiness lusted, Mother;
A huge heaving desire, overwhelming solitude
And the mountain belly of time laboured
And brought forth man, the mouse. The spheres churned on
Hoping to charm our ears
With sufficient organ music, sadly sent out
On the wrong wave of sound. But still they roll
Fabulous and fine, a roundabout
Of doomed and golden notes. And on beyond,
Profound with thunder of oceanic power,
Lie the morose dynamics of our dumb friend
Jehovah. (*Look at* CHAPLAIN, *look away, and back again*)
Why should these omnipotent bombinations
Go on with the deadly human anecdote, which
From the first was never more than remotely funny?
(*Rise to U.C.*) No; the time has come for tombs to tip
Their refuse: for the involving ivy, the briar,
The convulutions of convolvulus,
To disentangle and make way
For the last great ascendancy of dust,

Sucked into judgement by a cosmic yawn
Of boredom. The Last Trump
Is timed for twenty-two forty hours precisely.
>   (ALIZON *sits on bench D.R.*)
>   TYSON: This will all be gone into at the proper . . .
>   THOMAS (*Turning towards* TYSON):   Time
Will soon be most improper. Why not hang me
Before it's too late?
>   MARGARET (*Looking at* THOMAS, *rises and crosses L.*):
I shall go and change my dress:
Then I shall both be ready for our guests
And whatever else may come upon the world. (*Exit upstairs L.*)
>   (ALIZON *rises and goes half way up ramp R.* CHAPLAIN *moves
>   towards desk.* NICHOLAS *and* HUMPHREY *join* TYSON *at desk, mak-
>   ing a group.* THOMAS *leans on chair C. back to audience.*)
>   HUMPHREY: I'm sure he's mad.
>   CHAPLAIN: And his information, of course,
Is in opposition to what we are plainly told
In the Scriptures: that the hour will come . . .
>   NICHOLAS: Do you think
He means it? I've an idea he's up to something
None of us knows about, not one of us.
>   (JENNET *rises.* ALIZON *comes down to* RICHARD.)
>   ALIZON: Quiet Richard, son of nobody.
>   RICHARD: It isn't always like this, I promise it isn't.
>   (RICHARD *moves prayer books for* ALIZON *to sit on bench R. She
>   does so, and he sits beside her.* JENNET *looks at* THOMAS, *as she
>   crosses to centre of rostrum, faces desk.* THOMAS *moves R.* NICHO-
>   LAS *sits on window seat.*)
>   JENNET: May I, Jennet Jourdemayne, the daughter
Of a man who believed the universe to be governed
By certain laws,
>   (THOMAS *tries to stop her speaking.*)
>   be allowed to speak?
>   (CHAPLAIN *sits on rostrum below desk.*)
Here is such a storm of superstition
And humbug and curious passions, where will you start
To look for the truth? Am I in fact

An enchantress bemused into collaboration
With the enemy of man? Is this the enemy,
This eccentric young gentleman never seen by me
Before? I say I am not. You say perhaps
He is. You say I am. You say he is not.
And now this eccentric young gentleman threatens us all
With imminent cataclysm. If, as a living creature,
I wish in all good faith to continue living,
Where do you suggest I should lodge my application?

    TYSON: That is perfectly clear. You are both under arrest.

    (JENNET *moves to above chair C. The* CHAPLAIN *to above desk.*)

    THOMAS (*R. of* JENNET):   Into Pandora's box with all the ills.
But not if that little Hell-cat Hope's
Already in possession. I've hoped enough.
I gave the best years of my life to that girl,
But I'm walking out with Damnation now, and she's
A flame that's got finality. (*Sits chair C.*)

    (TYSON, CHAPLAIN, NICHOLAS *and* HUMPHREY *confer at desk.*)

    JENNET (*To* THOMAS *R. and kneels*):
Do you want no hope for me either? No compassion
To lift suspicion off me?

    THOMAS: Lift? Compassion
Has a rupture, lady. To hell with lifting.

    (*Chat from group round desk.*)

    JENNET (*Going towards desk*):   Listen, please listen to me.

    THOMAS: Let the world
Go, lady; it isn't worth the candle.

    TYSON (*Hands bunch of keys to* RICHARD, *who takes* JENNET'S
hand and pulls her D.L.):   Richard, take her away, down to the
cellars.

    THOMAS (*Rise, to above chair*):   You see, he has the key
To every perplexity. Kiss your illusions
For me before they go.

    JENNET (*Turning back at cellar opening*):   But what will happen?

    THOMAS: That's something even old nosedrip doesn't know!

    (RICHARD *and* JENNET *exit D.L.*)

    TYSON (*Indignantly, motions to* NICHOLAS *and* HUMPHREY *to take*

THOMAS *away*):   Nicholas! Humphrey!

(HUMPHREY *and* NICHOLAS *move down, one on each side of*
THOMAS, *who breaks away from them, throwing the chair on its
side, and facing the desk.*)

THOMAS: Mr. Mayor, hang me for pity's sake,
For God's sake hang me, before I love that woman!

(HUMPHREY *and* NICHOLAS *force him towards the cellar as the
curtain falls.*)

From Act III

TAPPERCOOM (*Entering from U.L.*):   What's all this I'm told?
I was hoping to hang on my bough for the rest of the evening
Ripe and undisturbed. What is it? Murder
Not such a fabrication after all?

(JENNET *rises and looks at* THOMAS.)

JENNET: Who will bother to hang you now? (*Exit upstairs*)

(THOMAS *crosses the stage after her.* HUMPHREY *who has entered
after* TAPPERCOOM *stops him from following her.* TAPPERCOOM
moves to below chair L.)

RICHARD (*Entering from U.R. with* SKIPPS):   Come in, Mr.
Skipps.

(NICHOLAS *rises to L. of buttress.* SKIPPS *enters unsteadily, trailing his rags and bones and old saucepans. He comes to the foot
of the ramp and leans against the buttress.* HUMPHREY *sits chair
L.*)

SKIPPS: Your young gentleman says Come in, so I comes in.
Youse only to say buzz off and I goes, wivout argument.

TAPPERCOOM (*Crosses to* SKIPPS):   It looks uncommonly to me
as though someone has been tampering with the evidence. Are you
the rag and bone merchant of this town, name of Matthew Skipps?

SKIPPS: Who gave me that name? (*Comes on to stage level,
near* TAPPERCOOM) My grandfathers and grandmothers and all in
authority undrim. Baptised I blaming was, and I says to youse
(*Points at* RICHARD *D.R.*) baptised I am, and I says to youse (*Points
at* NICHOLAS *left of buttress*) baptised I will be, wiv holy weeping
and washing of teeth. (*To* TAPPERCOOM) And immersion upon us
miserable offenders. Miserable offenders all . . . no offence meant.

(TAPPERCOOM *backs away from* SKIPPS, *who follows him round in a circle, ending as they began.*)
And if any of youse is not a miserable offender, as he's told to be by Almighty and mercerable God, then I says to him Hands off my daughter, you bloody minded heathen!

TAPPERCOOM: All right, all right . . .

SKIPPS: And I'm not quarrelling mind, I'm not quarrelling. Peace on earth and good tall women. (*Moves on to rostrum C.*) And give us our trespassers as trespassers will be prosecuted for us.

(TYSON *opens the study door and enters to* SKIPPS *who shakes hands with him.* TYSON *exits to study quickly.* SKIPPS *leans against the study door.*)

(*Shaking hands with* TAPPERCOOM) I'm not perfect, mind. But I'm as good a miserable offender as any man here present, ladies excepted. (*Leans against door*)

(TAPPERCOOM *sits on stool D.R.*)

THOMAS (*Up to lectern*):   Here now, Matt, aren't you forgetting yourself?
You're dead. You've been dead for hours.

SKIPPS: Dead am I? I has the respect to ask you to give me coabberation of that. I says perishing liar to nobody. But I seen my daughter three hours back, and she'd have said fair and to my face, Dad, you're dead. She won't stand for no nonsense.

NICHOLAS (*Slight move toward* SKIPPS):   The whole town knows it, Skipps, old man.

HUMPHREY (*Rises and crosses to* SKIPPS' *left*):   You've
Been dead since this morning.

SKIPPS: Dead. Well, you take my breaf away. (*To* HUMPHREY) Do I begin to stink then?

HUMPHREY: You do. (*Moves behind* SKIPPS *to study door*)

SKIPPS: Fair enough. That's coabberation! (*Puts his hands together as in prayer*) I'm among the blessed saints! (*Goes up to window seat L.*)

TAPPERCOOM (*Rise*):   He floats in the heaven of the grape. Someone take him home to his hovel.

SKIPPS (*Singing*):   Allelluia! Allelluia! Allelluia! (*Leans out of the window singing*)

(RICHARD *puts rags and bones beside the buttress.*)

TAPPERCOOM: Now stop that, Skipps. Keep your hosannas for
the cold light of morning or we shall lock you up.

SKIPPS (*Rudely*):   Allelluia!

(NICHOLAS *and* HUMPHREY *join* SKIPPS *at the window. During
the next speech* RICHARD *beckons to* ALIZON, *who rises and joins
him, and they exit up the ramp U.R.* RICHARD *waves to* THOMAS
as they go, and he waves to them.)

TAPPERCOOM: He'll wake your guests and spoil their pleasures.
They're all sitting half sunk in a reef of collars.

(*The* CHAPLAIN *enters from U.L., rather drunk, he carries his viol
in one hand, and a lighted candle in the other. He sees the company, and totters up stairs L. and exits.*)

Even the dear good Chaplain has taken so many glassesful of re-
pentance he's almost unconscious of the existence of sin. (*Has
crossed to* MARGARET'S *left and sits on chair L.*)

(NICHOLAS *and* HUMPHREY *bring* SKIPPS *down to stool R. where
he sits.*)

SKIPPS (*On the way down*):   Glory, amen! Glory, glory, amen,
amen!

MARGARET: Richard will take this old man home. Richard . . .
(*Rises and crosses U.R.*) Where is Richard? Where is Alizon? Have
they gone again?

NICHOLAS (*Runs up ramp, looks off stage and comes back again*):
Yes, Humphrey's wife blown clean away.

MARGARET: Yes; that's all very well;
But she mustn't think she can let herself be blown
Away whenever she likes.

THOMAS: What better time
Than when she likes?

SKIPPS: As it was in the beginning,
Ever and ever amen, Al-elluia!

MARGARET: Take this old man to his home. Now that you've
made him
Think he's dead we shall never have any peace.

(NICHOLAS *moves wheelbarrow from R. to nearer* SKIPPS.)

HUMPHREY: Nor shall we when he's gone.

(HUMPHREY *and* NICHOLAS *lift* SKIPPS *by the arms towards the wheelbarrow.* HUMPHREY *kicks stool upstage.*)

NICHOLAS: Spread your wings, Matthew, we're going to teach you to fly.

SKIPPS (*As they get him to the wheelbarrow*): I has the respect to ask to sit down. (*Sits*)

(HUMPHREY *places stool upstage by buttress, and picks up the rags and bones.* NICHOLAS *gets the hat and daffodils, and goes to handle of wheelbarrow.*)

Youse blessed saints don't realise; it takes it out of you, this life everlasting!

(*They start to wheel him out.* NICHOLAS *has put the hat on his head, the daffodils on his chest, and* HUMPHREY *gives him the rags and bones, and pushes the barrow up the ramp,* NICHOLAS *pulling it.*)

(*As they go*) Allelluia! Allelluia! (*They exit*)

(MARGARET *goes to foot of ramp.*)

TAPPERCOOM: That's more pleasant!

MARGARET (*Crosses to chair C.*): That poor child Alizon
Is too young to go throwing herself under the wheels
Of happiness. She should have wrapped up warmly first.
Hebble must know in any case. I must tell him.

(HEBBLE *enters from the study, and shuts the door. He is blowing his nose. Meets* MARGARET *C. on rostrum.*)

Oh Hebble, I'm afraid you'll have to come out of your handkerchief.

(*Snatches the handkerchief from him*)

The Day of Judgement seems to have been postponed,
And this gentleman didn't murder old Skipps, and old Skipps
Isn't a dog after all, but he thinks he's an angel.
You may notice the odour of sanctity still in the air.

(TYSON *crosses* MARGARET *and goes towards stairs L.*)

But Hebble, there's something else . . . Alizon Eliott
Has run off with Richard . . .

TYSON: That will all have to be gone into at the proper time.
(*To* TAPPERCOOM) Good night. (*Exit upstairs L.*)

MARGARET (*Calling after him*): You'll have to saddle Timothy
and go after them.

(TYSON *disappears grumbling.*)

TAPPERCOOM: Yes, get him on a horse; it will do him good.

MARGARET (*At foot of stairs*):   Hebble on a horse is a man
Delivered neck and crop to the will of God.
But he'll have to do it. (*Exit upstairs*)

Excerpts from the notebook kept by Elia Kazan in preparation for
directing *Death of a Salesman* by Arthur Miller.*

The first page is headed "Sept. '48"; occasional dates occur
through the 124 pages of notes, but for the most part the entries are
undated. The last entry is dated "Dec. 17, '48." *Death of a Salesman*
opened in New York Feb. 10, 1949, after a two weeks' tryout in
Philadelphia.

Death of a Salesman

Basic: The play is about Willy Loman.

Basic Style: It is a tragedy, in a classic style, with the drive of an
inner inevitability that springs from a single fatal flaw. Willy is a
good man. He has worth. But he is a Salesman with a Salesman's
Philosophy. Therefore he dooms himself.

Basic: This is a story of love—the end of a tragic love between
Willy and his son Biff.

Basic: He built his life on his son—but he taught his son wrong.
The result: the son crashes and he with him.

Basic: The whole play is about *love*—Love and Competition.
The Boy loves him. The only way Willy can give him anything back
is thru the $20,000.

Basic: What the audience should feel at the end of this performance is only one thing: Pity, Compassion and Terror for Willy.
Every dramatic value should serve this end. This Willy is a fine,
tender, capable, potentially useful human. He is just socially mis-
taught. Society, our present society, is the "heavy"—its current philosophy.

* Reproduced by the courtesy of Elia Kazan.

NOTES ON WILLY LOMAN

1) Willy is one vast contradiction, and this contradiction is his downfall. He is a nicer guy than Charley. He is so nice, as someone said once, he's got to end up poor. This makes Charley untroubled and a success, and Willy contradictory, neurotic, full of love and longing, need for admiration and affection, full of a sense of worthlessness and inadequacy and dislocation *and a failure.*

2) Anxiety, the pressing unrelieved sense of worthlessness and insufficiency for which the salesman compensates, hides and covers up with his line of blarney.

3) Why doesn't he take the job Charley keeps throwing at him? He's got to be employed by a big-shot firm. He can't admit of the humiliation of working for someone who lives next door, and who started just as he did. Everything must be the biggest and the best, and I mean the biggest and the best in terms of beating the other guy.

4) He is torn between an absolute need to believe he is *"vital in New England"* and an absolute knowledge that he is not.

5) His fatal error (this is an Inevitable Tragedy . . . *our* Greek tragedy) is that he built his life and his *sense of worth* on something completely false: the Opinion of Others. This is the error of our whole society. We build our sense of worth not within ourselves but thru our besting others and at the same time having their constant perfect approval. A boy, Biff, must be both pre-eminent and still adored, conquering all and still loved by all. An impossibility!

6) Consequently, he both hates and loves the same people and can neither really love nor really hate anyone. If they perfectly approve of him, they are great. If, on some issue they don't, they are his enemies. . . .

7) A "personality!" Willy has that magical thing with which some people are born. It makes them both pre-eminent, beating all others, and still liked.

Willy: Daydreams. A person "talks to himself," in this case has imaginary conversations with other people, because of some compulsive reason. Usually to defend himself, re-enact some scene to prove himself, to *attack* someone that he failed to defend himself against properly in the real world. The FICTION behind each of these imaginary conversations should be found.

Suicide is his only and last desperate means to success . . . also revenge on all people who demeaned his dignity. Suicide solves his problem in the way that he wants it solved. It is his way of proving himself to Biff too, living up to (as he imagines it) the boy's hero-worship of him.

Also the suicide is "an angle," it's the action of a "smart cookie." He's finally in control. It's his way of beating the world that beat him. . . .

Willy is not a retiring, quiet, timid, shrinking man. *N.B. His ideal is Pre-eminence.* His ideal is not to be a little guy. His ideal is to rule the world by selling it. The man himself was violent, tough, loud, fearless (he could handle a meddling cop). He was not a "little man" in the Milquetoast sense. He was explosive. He could raise the roof. Look what he teaches the kids! Self-reliance, Enterprise, Conquest, Beat your neighbor . . . Adventure, Win, Win, Win by your personality, i.e., your natural jungle strength, etc.

And at the end, he wins, *at all costs.* He would and does sacrifice everything to his *ideal.* He really believes it as does all our middle class, and he lives by it.

Willy is haughty, proud—he is dominated by the dream of aggression, competition, pre-eminence. *To end up on top* is a proud thing —even if it seems to be a losing fight with only subjective values.

CHARACTERS IN THE PAST

Ben, *Altogether is in the Past,* is entirely subjective as Willie sees him: the embodiment of Success, Authority, Daring, Manliness, Enterprise, Fearlessness, Self-sufficiency. He is romanticized in Willy's memory and by Willy's necessity—into a God-like figure. He takes his success for granted. He laughs over it, keeps chuckling. Willy talks frantically, a compulsive ardor—then suddenly when Ben touches his arm, he stops, in the middle of a sentence as it were, and then, in due time, Ben speaks his mind in quietness.

Ben (by Willy's romanticized and necessary motive) keeps his own counsel—his mind is always somewhere else on Big things, etc. Ben is amused about his success—Willy is impressed. fierce! frantic, compulsive.

Biff in the Past, is again romanticized in Willy's imagination. Confident, easy, gorgeous, all the kids fawning on him, trying to steal the spotlight from him and no one succeeding. Again, like Ben, self-absorbed with Big things, secret Big things, all in his own mind, contained. Again, when he speaks others are silent. Biff in the past is a stylized figure. Not *as he was* but as Willie sees him retrospectively.

None of these dream figures are actually in the past! They are as much in the present. They are as Willy *needs* to think of them for his own reasons of personal dignity, self-esteem, etc., etc.

Charlie in the past is convenient too for the necessities of Willy's psychology. It's the way he *likes* to think of Charlie, needs to think of Charlie. Not in the past, necessarily, but as much in the present— Just Charlie! So Charlie in the past is an embodiment, a comic embodiment, of all the careless, ambitionless . . . .

Linda in the past is a figure fashioned out of Willy's guilt. Hard working, sweet, always true, admiring. "I shouldn't cheat on a woman like that!" Dumb, slaving, loyal, tender, innocent. Patient with him. Always available for sympathy or even pity.

Actually, i.e., in life, she is much tougher. She has consciously made her peace with her fate. She has chosen Willy! To hell with everyone else. She is terrifyingly tough. Why? She senses Willy is in danger. And she just can't have him hurt.

THEME

Competition is the central fact of our civilization. Willy is competing with Charlie not only directly but through his sons. He both admires Bernard and resents hell out of him. Even *hates* him. After he meets Bernard in Act 2 he goes off talking to himself, asking: what happened to my boys?

The Problem of Modern Man. The problem is: modern man is *Always Anxious!* Because he is between two opposite fatal pulls: to best his neighbor, his brother vs. to be loved by his brother. These are mutually exclusive, an impossible contradiction. Inevitably it will end disastrously.

Again this play is about Love and Competition—the two opposing forces, good and bad, creative and malignant in one Society. Willy Loman's tragedy is that he is pulled to pieces by these two opposites.

Willy's competitiveness was his *own* which he projects and extends and tries to achieve thru his son Biff. Thus he ruins Biff's life by pledging him to an ideal that does not work. Willy should have let Biff become what he was!!

The Suicide is the last logical piece of competition—his only way of combining the two opposite principles. He thinks that he fades out at a moment of love and wins more of Biff's love and at the same time *bests them all* through giving Biff $20,000.

Willy built his son's life to lay at rest his own anxiety (success-anxiety) about himself. He used his son to lay at rest his own fears . . . and it is this "bad" and selfish need of Willy's that Biff "betrayed." Willy is not and never is aware of this—he would be left with nothing if he faced reality (as Biff suggests at the end of the play).

DIRECTING

It is essential to stick, in your emotional feeling through the play to Willy. Find Willy in you . . . it is the portrait of the soul of a man, at the crash-end of a tragic love for his son Biff, one which leads up (in terms of inner emotional events) to his suicide.

In this play, all movement must come from *Character* impulse. No crosses, etc., with *Energy Substituted for Emotion*. General energy instead of particular emotion. This play has a line which is all down the inside of Willy's spine . . . . this man goes crazy—right before your eyes—and commits suicide and Miller shows you the logic behind this series of acts.

This play takes place in an Arena of people watching the events, sometimes internal and invisible, other times external and visible and sometimes *both*. The world is the world of Willy and the way he sees it. In the end it is completely in his world and his eyes get more and more *glazey* as he talks to the people who exist only within his own mind. The people watching have an emotional relation to Willy, a reaching out to him. But by the end of the play, there is no one there for him to reach out to and he is living entirely within himself. The people watching this spectacle are horrified. The *man* simply isn't with them any more.

Direction and Style

This play is essentially about Willy. Biff's importance is only as the love-object which "failed." But the play describes the *Process*— dramatizes the *Process in Willy's mind*. In doing this all the elements of theatre Magic are *necessary*. Tricks—music—disappearances. That's why the coming down out of the beds is right.

Style

There are no flashbacks!

The only laws of these scenes are the laws of Willy's own mind. And all the figures in Willy's mind are distorted by Willy's *hopes, wishes, desires*. (All these figures are different in Willy's imagination than they are in life. Charley more foolish.)

What they are: DAYDREAMS. And daydreams are an action. What Willy is doing in these daydreams is justifying himself. He knows he's failed and he's living his life over in these daydreams in order to justify himself.

Style: must be an activization in physical equivalents of the events of Willy's mind for the last 24 hours of his life. So it is *all* unrealistic, since it all happens *Willy's way*—as Willy feels it, experiences it.

N.B. The last act of Willy's life is a perfect example—it is a piece of action—not an emotion—it is a *deed,* not a feeling. So all through translate his "suffering consciousness" into *acts*.

Directing: Willy's Actions

It seems to be hard to find actions for Willy. What is a man who is anxious, worried, and swimming in guilt, who is frustrated in his search for pre-eminence, etc. *Doing?* He is defending himself from imagined accusations and insults. He is justifying himself for sins real and imagined. ("I'll make it up to you.") He is excusing himself for things he did and couldn't help. He is overwhelmed by sudden feelings of helplessness and seeking refuge in the sure and unmerited security of his wife. Then he is asserting himself by insulting others. Mocking others, berating others, condemning others and accusing others—all defense through attack! Then suddenly aware of this—"building" himself by generously excusing people who have treated him badly (Biff)—showing off how *big* and generous he is! He is all in all so fragile of self-confidence that he can't stand contradiction on anything—considering it or fearing it a lessening of his position or of his pre-eminence.

Directing: Finding Willy's Actions

Another thing he does is once he gets with someone he lies ("I'll be right up") to get off by himself and "think"—for, finally, the only world where he'll be beyond challenge is in a world of his own making. He feels safest alone.

Directing

This play has to be directed with COMPASSION, which simply means with a quick and intense realization of the PAIN of each of the characters . . . and the real meaning of the "SPINE," which means the living and emotional meaning of the "SPINE."

The reader should keep in mind that the excerpts from Mr. Kazan's notebook presented here are a small proportion of the total entries. There is much more on Willy Loman, on all the other characters, on the thematic analysis of the play, and on the approach to its direction. Toward the end of the notebook preliminary thoughts appear with increasing frequency on the physical and technical aspects of staging—setting, lighting, properties. The selection made here is intended to be representative in a way that will contribute most to the development of reading plays. Particularly significant is progression: the notebook is a record of advance through thoughtful, energetic, and directed reading and rereading into experience and understanding of the play. The last entry is announcement of further work to come.

From Elia Kazan's notebook, entry dated Dec. 17, '48

This play is a dramatization of the process in the mind of Willy—an interior crisis that takes about twenty-four hours and ends in a suicide. The play dwells within the interior process. All its values and meanings are Willy's. It is time, therefore, to go thru the play with Willy—his processes: his compulsions, defenses, assertions—and get clear the action of this play in the locale where it happens: Willy's consciousness.

Then go thru and match stage activities for the actors, *behavior,* the physicalizations of mental and ideal events, the props, the physical equivalents, the stunts, the active dramatizations of the scene—*all the stage life* which will be the "play" of the *Inner Arena,* the externalizations of the inner life—everything that will make this hidden story lie before our eyes on a stage.

A scene from Mr. Kazan's annotation of the playscript of *Death of a Salesman* by Arthur Miller.*

With the notebook as preparatory background, Mr. Kazan annotated the entire playscript in detail. The script is bound in a cover with a page of notes opposite each page of script. The notes are a running analysis of situation and motivation leading into manner of delivery of lines and stage business. The pages are divided into three columns, the first for general situation, the second for more particular and internal analysis, the third for stage business. The notes are arranged opposite the lines to which they apply, with an asterisk used to indicate an exact point for business within a line. A representative scene from the annotated script follows. For practicality in printing, the arrangement in columns has been omitted, and for clarity to the reader the correlation between notes and lines has been indicated by corresponding numbers.

* Reproduced by the courtesy of Elia Kazan.

Annotation of Playscript, Act II, pages 23-28

[1] Willy as he seems to the "outside world!"

[2] Bernard is revealed listening to the commotion in the hall. Bernard—a Big Man—looks at his watch all thru. At this moment he is polishing his glasses. Dressed smoothly.

[3] A moment of silence plus traffic sounds.

[4] Bernard and Willy haven't seen each other for years. Last time their relationship completely different. Both therefor soon begin wondering—what happened—examine each other, etc., etc., etc.

Both men loved Biff.

Bernard—behind all his mask can still be touched. He tries to help—has always been *curious,* too, as to what happened to the Boy he loved—and has also had some unanswered questions to ask—if Willy wants to talk "candidly."

Willy, too, is examining something with a *naive* intensity—but something that is vital to him—touches on something that is killing him with guilt.

[5] The way a Salesman is supposed to behave with a girl secretary.

[6] Willy picks up the tennis rackets.

[7] He puts them down guiltily.

[8] *Inspect* each other.

[9] *Willy recovers!*

Willy wouldn't like to be seen by Bernard that way.

Willy has a *whole drama* in his head and in his past with Bernard —he's insulted him 47,000 times behind his back, etc.—and the Boy is a Success! How? Why?

[10] *Bernard:* Put him at his ease. A simple social putting someone at his ease; he is light, swift, and social.

[11] A gesture similar to Ben's with the watch.

[12] *Willy:* Figure out what happened!!??? Bernard is to Willy a mystery, an affront, an insult, a living humiliation.

Bernard: Put him at his ease, help him in a nice simple way. Bernard is proud to be known as the modest fellow.

Bernard offers him a cigarette case. Willy takes it, examines it with awe, hands it back. Bernard opens it, offers cigarette, he shakes his head.

[13] Mystery.

Light rises, on the Right side of the stage, on small table in the
reception room of Charlie's office. BERNARD, *now mature, sits whis-*
tling to himself. A pair of tennis rackets on the floor beside him and
an overnight bag. He is a quiet, earnest, but self-assured young
man. [1]WILLY'S *voice is coming from Right, Upstage now.* [2]*Hearing,*
he lowers his feet off the table and listens towards upstage. Now
JENNY *comes in, his father's secretary.*)

JENNY (*Distressed*): Say Bernard, will you go in the hall
and . . . .

BERNARD: What *is* that noise? Who is it?

JENNY: Mr. Loman. He just got off the elevator . . . .

BERNARD (*Gets up*): Who's he arguing with?

[3] (WILLY *is no longer heard.*)

JENNY: Nobody. There's nobody with him. I can't deal with
him any more, and your father gets all upset every time he comes.
I've got a lot of typing to do and your father's waiting to sign it.
Will you see him?

[4] (WILLY *enters.*)

WILLY: Right under the goal post, boy—
(*Sees* JENNY, *gathering his wits.*)

[5] Jenny . . . Jenny . . . good to see you. How're you? Workin?
. . . or still honest?

JENNY (*Nervously*): Fine . . . how've you been feeling?

WILLY: Not much any more, Jenny. Ha, Ha! [6]

BERNARD: Hello, Uncle Willy.[7, 8]

WILLY (*Almost shocked*): [9] Bernard! Well look who's here!
(*Comes quickly, guiltily to* BERNARD *and warmly shakes his*
hand.)

BERNARD: [10] How are you? Glad to see you.

WILLY: What are *you* doing here?

BERNARD: Oh, just stopped by to see Pop; get off my feet until
my train leaves. I'm going to Washington[11] in a few minutes.

WILLY: Is he in?

BERNARD: Yes, he's in his office with the accountant. Sit down.
(*They sit*) [12]

WILLY: What're you going to do in Washington?

BERNARD: Oh, just a case I've got there, Willy.

WILLY: That so! [13]

¹⁴ How did the little schmuck do it?

¹⁵ *Willy* invests all these things (a private court) with great drama, mystery, and wonder.

¹⁶ *Bernard:* changes subject. Bernard always feels a little uncomfortable squirming under Willy's amazed admiration.

¹⁷ *Both* are now figuring out what happened.

Bernard keeps playing with his Phi Beta Kappa key, his glasses, his watch. They smoke, cigarette case, etc.

¹⁸ *Willy:* redemption, make it up.

¹⁹ *Bernard:* find facts. Bernard knows Willy is lying. Now he begins to wonder the source of it.

²⁰ They are *not talking to each other*. They are *examining each other*. No particular cues—as if speeches are entirely unrelated.

²¹ What is he *really* doing?

²² Change subject.

²³ Willy is *not* a grandfather. He wants it desperately.

²⁴ Offers cigarette here.

²⁵ Change subject.

²⁶ Bernard takes cue—goes behind Willy to get matches, etc.

²⁷ Change subject.

²⁸ *Willy* is bleeding inside. Suddenly can't stand it. Bernard conceals that he thinks Willy is a pathetic fake.

Bernard bows his head and shields his eyes as if he is embarrassed for Willy.

²⁹ *Willy* tries to speak of it. *Can't.* About to cry. Can't speak! Can't speak!

³⁰ *Willy* tenses in his chair and turns out.

³¹ *Bernard:* to help—he's full of pity.

³² *Willy:* forcing it out.

N.B. He thinks it's some secret. Some magic formula of success! "Sentences that sell," some advice he has failed to give.

³³ *Bernard:* help. Gently. Bernard really knows. He *can't look at* Willy, sits on desk with head bowed.

³⁴ *Willy:* just stands there with head bowed . . . he can't look at Bernard and ask what he's asking.

³⁵ *Bernard:* avoid. You can't tell a man like Willy the truth . . . it would be too cruel.

[*Continued on page 56*]

(*Noticing the rackets*)

You going to play tennis there? [14]

BERNARD: I'm staying with a friend who's got a court.

WILLY (*Wonderously*):   Don't say.[15] His own tennis court. Must be fine[15] people, I bet.

BERNARD: They are, very nice.[16] Dad tells me Biff's in town.[17]

WILLY [18] (*Big smile*):   Yeah, Biff's in. Working on a very big deal, Bernard.

BERNARD: [19] What's Biff doing? [20, 21]

WILLY: Well, he's been doing very big things in the West. But he decided to establish himself here. Very big. We're having dinner.[22] Did I hear your wife had a boy? [23]

BERNARD: That's right. Our second.[24]

WILLY: Two boys!—what do you know?

BERNARD: What kind of a deal has Biff got?

WILLY: Well, Bill Oliver—a very big sporting goods man—he wants Biff very badly. Called him in from the West. Long-distance, carte blanche, special deliveries. [25] Your friends have their own private tennis court.

[26] BERNARD: [27] You still with the old firm, Willy?

WILLY: [28] I'm . . . I'm overjoyed to see how you made the grade, Bernard—overjoyed. It's an encouraging thing to see a young man, really . . . really . . . looks very good for Biff . . . Very . . .[28]

[29] (*He breaks off. Then . . .*)

Bernard. . .[30]

(*He is so full of emotion, he breaks off again.*)

BERNARD: [31] What is it, Willy?

(*Pause*)

WILLY (*Small and alone*):   [32] What . . . . What's the secret?

BERNARD: [33] What secret?

WILLY (*With an embarrassed smile*):   [34] How . . . how did you . . . ? . . . why didn't he ever catch on?

BERNARD: [35] I wouldn't know that, Willy.

WILLY (*Quietly, confidentially, desperately*):   [36] You were his friend, his boyhood friend—There's something I don't understand about it. His life ended after that Ebbets Field game. From the age of seventeen nothing good ever happened to him.

[36] *Willy:* PLEAD. Suddenly direct . . . craving to be liberated from his guilt. "I beg you free me from this hell of my guilt." Keep up the "What is it?"

[37] *Bernard:* He's always been curious to find out himself.

[38] *Bernard* walks to window to decide whether or not to tell Willy.

[39] *Willy:* Pain!!!

[40] *Bernard:* still looking out window.

[41] *Bernard:* Proceeding, he knows it will hurt. Trying to do what is necessary—a tough gentleman.

[42] *Willy:* pop off—defend by attack. But even this far away from his guilt, as Bernard approaches it from a distance as it were, it already is intolerable for Willy. He can't stand it and he defends, as usual, by attack.

[43] *Bernard:* cutting right thru—"don't defend yourself! Please!"

[44] *Willy:* beginning to rear defensively.

[45] *Bernard:* Point Willy to the truth. So Willy can really look at it.

[46] *Willy: defending himself.* Guilt!

[47] *Bernard* pinning him to it.

[48] *Willy:* disliking him.

[49] *Willy:* blames Biff to clear himself. Guilt!!—off again like a rocket!

[50] *Bernard:* wishes he were out of it.

[51] *Willy:* insisting. Demanding.

[52] *Bernard:* trying to get out of it. Starts to get away—the watch.

[53] *Willy:* insisting. Forces Bernard to speak. Very violent, very dangerous, wild-eyed. He wants to know yet can't face it!! Willy is CRAZY!!!

[54] An accusing crazy violent gesture.

[55] *Bernard:* telling the truth—there's no way out of it now. laying it on the table—lawyer-like.

BERNARD: He never trained himself for anything.

WILLY: But he did, he did. After high school he took so many correspondence courses. Radio, mechanics, television. God knows what, and never made the slightest mark.

BERNARD: [37] Willy, you want to talk candidly? [38]

WILLY: [39] I regard you as a very brilliant man, Bernard. I value your advice.

BERNARD: [40] Oh, the hell with advice, Willy. I couldn't advise you. [41] There's just one thing I've always wanted to ask you. When he was supposed to graduate, and the math teacher flunked him . . .

WILLY: [42] Oh, that son-of-a-bitch ruined his life.

BERNARD: [43] Yeah, but Willy, all he had to do was to go to summer school and make up that subject.

WILLY: [44] That's right, that's right . . .

BERNARD: [45] Did you tell him not to go to summer school?

WILLY: [46] No! I begged him to go. I ordered him to go!

BERNARD: [47] Then why wouldn't he go?

WILLY: Why? [48] Why! Bernard, that question has been trailing me like a ghost for the last fifteen years. [49] He flunked the subject, and laid down and died like a hammer hit him!

BERNARD: [50] Take it easy, Kid. . . .

WILLY: [51] Let me talk to you, I got nobody to talk to. Bernard . . . Bernard, was it my fault? Y'see?—it keeps going around in my mind, maybe I did something to him. I got nothing to give him.

BERNARD: [52] Don't take it so hard. . . .

WILLY: [53] Why did he lay down? [54] What is the story there?— you were his friend.

BERNARD: [55] Willy . . . I remember, it was June . . . and our grades came out. And he'd flunked math.

WILLY: That son-of-a-bitch . . . .

BERNARD: No, it wasn't right then. Biff just got very angry, I remember, and he was ready to enroll in summer school.

WILLY: He was?

BERNARD: He wasn't beaten by it at all. But then . . .

(*Slight pause*)

Willy, he disappeared from the block for almost a month. And I got the idea that he'd gone up to New England to see you. Did he have a talk with you then?

⁵⁶ *Willy:* to warn Bernard. Willy very defensive.

⁵⁷ *Bernard:* forcing himself to once and for all get the whole damned truth out and finish it. He walks around behind through this speech.

⁵⁸ Proof he is really determined to keep it on the table.

⁵⁹ Bernard loved Biff. He is almost crying.

⁶⁰ Not asking it, just saying it.

⁶¹ *Bernard:* sees the attack coming—"Don't blame me. You made me tell."

⁶² *Willy:* Attack Bernard—only way out—Mad!!

⁶³ *Bernard:* kid him out of it—a very poor attempt. Miserable. Can't look at him.

⁶⁴ *Willy:* attack, almost physically.

⁶⁵ *Bernard:* to calm him. He's beginning to get scared and he certainly regrets the whole thing.

⁶⁶ *Willy:* same angry challenge. He literally would be fighting him in a moment.

⁶⁷ *Charley:* has heard, comes in to save the situation.

(WILLY *stares in silence*)

Willy?

WILLY (*Now with the strong edge of resentment against Bernard*): [56] Yeah, he came to Boston. What about it?

BERNARD: [57] Well, just that when he came back . . . [58] I'll never forget this . . . it always mystified me. Because I'd thought so well of Biff, even though he'd always taken advantage of me. [59] I loved him, Willy, y'know? And he came back after that month and took his sneakers—remember those sneakers with "University of Virginia" printed on them? He was so proud of those, wore them every day. And he took them down to the cellar, and burned them up in the furnace. We started to fight . . . punching each other down the cellar . . . and crying right through it.

(*Slight pause*)

I've often thought of how strange it was that I knew he'd given up his life . . . . What happened in Boston,[60] Willy?

(WILLY *looks at him as at an intruder.*)

[61] I just bring it up because you asked me.

WILLY (*Quite angrily*): [62] Nothing . . . what do you mean, "what happened?" What's that got to do with anything?

BERNARD (*Tries to laugh, touches Willy's knee*): [63] Well, don't get sore.

WILLY: [64] What are you trying to do, blame it on me? If a boy lays down is it my fault?

BERNARD (*To calm him*): [65] Now, Willy, don't get . . .

WILLY: [66] Well don't . . . don't talk to me that way! What does that mean—"What happened?"

(CHARLIE *enters, in vest.*)

CHARLEY: [67] Hey, you're going to miss that train.

The long and intensive application to the understanding of the play is, of course, a road to a single end for the director, the work in the theater with the actors. The interpretive process is more tangibly relevant to the reading of plays; on the other hand, the reader's actors are in his head and he must develop the skill of focusing all the elusive, fleeting images that gather around his interpretation into the sharp picture of the play. Mr. Kazan at work in the theater was described by Arthur Miller in an article in the New York *Times* for February 5, 1950, the week of the first anniversary in the initial run of *Death of a Salesman*. Remembering a rehearsal, Mr. Miller wrote of "the marvel of the actor"—"How utterly they believed what they were saying to each other!"—and continued:

> And Elia Kazan, with his marvelous wiles, tripping the latches of the secret little doors that lead into the always different personalities of each actor. That is the secret; not merely to know what must be done, but to know the way to implement the doing for actors trained in diametrically opposite schools, or not trained at all. He does not "direct," he creates a center point, and then goes to each actor and creates the desire to move toward it. And they all meet, but for different reasons, and seem to have arrived there by themselves.

The purpose of the study in this chapter of the functioning of the director has been to give some introductory idea both of the kind and amount of work he does. The emphasis has been on his preparation for that final period in the theater with which the idea of director is most readily associated. Detailed consideration of the range of his technical knowledge and activities belongs to other studies, and nothing can bring within a book more than a glimpse of the attribute which distinguishes all great directors, what Robert Edmond Jones called his capacity as "animator," the power to energize, to animate, the creativity that is in actors.*

Analysis, organization, and visualization corresponding to that, first of the director, then of the scene designer and of the actors, is the basis of experiencing a play. To make a special study of a few plays, or one, will add to the experience of other plays in reading

* *The Dramatic Imagination,* Duell, Sloan and Pearce, New York, 1941, p. 37.

and to critical appreciation in the theater. No production, by whomever directed, is final. One may reject the interpretation in the theater or find the execution faulty and yet gain stimulus to one's own thought and imagination; the experience in the theater of a previously read play is sometimes totally convincing and satisfying fresh illumination, or one may prefer one's own vision of the play. Acquaintance with the work of directors leads to a more strenuous pleasure in reading plays. The expenditure of time, energy, thought, and imagination a director devotes to experiencing and understanding from script a play of magnitude suggests that a theater in the head can challenge a reader's mental faculties to their highest pitch of action and awareness.

4

In the Theater : The Scene Designer

The reader of plays who gives his attention to the work of the scene designers may be reminded of Wordsworth's familiar tribute to his sister Dorothy, "She gave me eyes." The work of the director is inextricably interwoven with the whole of that evanescent art, the production of a play, and has no enduring record except in rare instances of the preservation of premonitions and echoes of the theater in their notebooks and prompt-books. The art of the scene designer, too, in its completion, unlike that of the easel painter, the muralist, or the sculptor, is blotted out with the lowering of the curtain. But there is a tangible record: most scene designers preserve their drawings and paintings for sets and photographs from production, and they have been generous of these materials to the public in an array of books on scene design magnificently illustrated. These are rewarding and instructive to the imagination if one remembers that a static picture is not a stage set. As the scene designer Jo Mielziner points out:

> The theatre artist employs the fourth dimension of time-space. No matter how pictorially compelling a stage set is when the curtain is raised, it only has life when it continues to develop in relationship to the continuing movement and theme of the play. This may be accomplished by a change of lighting as the mood of the

drama fluctuates. It may also change in pure composition by the relationship and movement of actors on the stage. In some cases the scenery itself changes shape before the spectator's eye. In other words, there is nothing static in a really dramatic stage setting. To be a perfect foil for living actors in a vibrant drama all the arts of the theatre must be combined to accomplish the ultimate aim.*

Alfred Roller, Viennese scene designer, is quoted as refusing to lend his sketches for exhibition with the statement: "The only place to exhibit a stage setting is in the theatre." †

Very well, experience scene design in the theater at every opportunity, but for the reading of plays two things are to be gained from the books and pictures: the photographs of the actual sets and the technical designs give an expanded understanding of the potentialities of the stage, and in the sketches and paintings there is often something more of the artist's vision of the play beyond the stage than in the sets themselves, however well executed. Also, as artists in another medium scene designers have shown remarkable verbal freedom and facility and have given us writing that is both expositorily clarifying and stirring to the imagination.

Playwrights created realism as a demand which was met by the theater. Scene designers, shortly thereafter, created the possibility of a nonrealistic theater as an invitation to playwrights. The early galaxy of modern directors, Antoine, Brahm, Stanislavsky, were inspired by the realistic-naturalistic drama and its emphasis on the determination of character and fate by physical and social environment. They undertook to offer a staging of direct and solid illusion of physical reality in place of theatrical convention and obvious imitation. Ever since that time the great scene designers, from Appia and Craig to Robert Edmond Jones, Lee Simonson, and Jo Mielziner, have been releasing the stage from physical literalness to creation visually of spiritual environment, projection of the inner meaning of the play by suggestion, and opening of the way for the imagination of the audience to reach the play beyond the stage. Robert Edmond Jones wrote in *The Dramatic Imagination:* "A good scene . . . is

* In "Death of a Painter," *The American Artist,* Nov., 1949. Copyright by *The American Artist*. Quotation by permission of *The American Artist*.
† Lee Simonson, *The Art of Scenic Design,* Harper, New York, 1950, p. 35.

not a picture. It is something seen, but it is something conveyed as well: a feeling, an evocation." *

Realistic staging came to the theater by way of the new playwrights and was largely exercised by the directors, since reproduction of external reality does not require an artist. In the early flush of enthusiasm Antoine sought not even reproduction of reality but the object itself and went so far as to bring the carcasses of a butcher shop into a scene. At the end of the movement David Belasco manifested his love of beauty and his perfectionism as a director by carefully selecting valuable art objects rather than use theatrical substitutes when such objects were true to the corresponding room in life. The new stagecraft, the countermovement to realistic staging, came to the theater by way of painting, architecture, and fresh knowledge and awareness of theaters of other times and places. The symbolist and impressionist schools in painting had developed conceptions and techniques of simplification and suggestion, and understanding of the nature of light as an enveloping atmosphere and a dramatic force. Lee Simonson asserted in 1950 in *The Art of Scenic Design:* "Almost every form of design used by designers and directors in the last fifty years has embodied the kind of composition that we associate with Impressionism and which Degas summarized in a remark to George Moore apropos of a painting in one of the official French salons, 'You make a crowd with five people, not with fifty!' " †
From architecture came the concepts of the stage as space and form, three-dimensional. From the Greek and Elizabethan stages, and the Nō stage of Japan and the classical opera of China, came reawakening to theatrical theater, presentation of drama through conventions and on architectural stages without illusionary scenery. Out of such varied influences came symbolism, stylization, expressionism, theatricalism, and formalism in staging, and the rise of the modern scene designer.

The new stagecraft was preceded by a few isolated symbolic dramas—*Peer Gynt* by Ibsen, *The Sunken Bell* by Hauptmann—and by one symbolic dramatist, Maeterlinck. Strindberg wrote symbolic dramas in the latter part of his career and himself pioneered in scene design for their staging. Wagner's symbolic operas, or music

* Page 26.
† Page 38.

dramas, not only preceded the new stagecraft, but it was Adolphe Appia's view of the inadequacy of their production at Bayreuth that set the first of the new designers on his course of becoming a scenic artist. In an over-all view, however, one sees the new stagecraft as opening the floodgate to what was certainly a gathering momentum in the playwriting consciousness. Mordecai Gorelik in *New Theatres for Old* mentions as writers of symbolist drama in some of their work, Ibsen, Strindberg, Dunsany, Synge, Yeats, Maeterlinck, D'Annunzio, Pirandello, Molnar, Ostrovsky, Evreinov, Andreyev, and among American dramatists, Eugene O'Neill, Maxwell Anderson, Paul Green, Martin Flazin, Philip Barry, John Howard Lawson, Clifford Odets, Irwin Shaw, and William Saroyan.*

Of these the symbolic plays only of Ibsen, Maeterlinck, D'Annunzio, and Ostrovsky predate 1900, the approximate dividing line of the old and the new stagecraft. The whole sequence of German expressionists may be added: Toller, Kaiser, Hasenclever, Wedekind, Werfel; the Czechs, Karel and Josef Čapek; the Americans, E. E. Cummings and Elmer Rice, and more recently, Arthur Miller and Tennessee Williams; in France, Giraudoux, Sartre, and Camus; and in England, Christopher Fry.

Some of the developments of the new stagecraft tended to merge the scene designer and director, as the constructivism of bare scaffoldings for the actors on an open stage of Meyerhold, and the fixed architectural stage designed for Jacques Copeau's *Théâtre du Vieux Colombier*. If nonrealistic drama were to have any prevalence, it was inescapable, however, that it must occupy the already existent theater of stages enclosed behind a proscenium arch. Some of the concepts of the successive developments of the new stagecraft belonged within this frame, some could be accomplished only by a transformation of the stage within the frame. Either way the work of an artist was required, of a versatile artist, painter, draftsman, plastic artist, and man of the theater with an elaborate and specialized technical background. Scenic design became a separate profession from that of the director. As stated by Lee Simonson, the scene designer's "extended range of technical control . . . makes him an essential collaborator of the play's director in interpreting a script and bring-

* Samuel French, New York, 1940, p. 201.

ing it to life, and makes his settings an integral part of theatrical production." *

The modern working scene designer is typically not a devotee of a theory, a school, or a movement. That has been gone through. He is an eclectic artist staging realistic and nonrealistic plays according to the truth and needs of each. Selective, often stylized realism has displaced literalness, thereby incorporating realism into art. The enthusiastic excesses of early symbolism of imposing arbitrary and sometimes private symbols of the designer upon the play, are avoided, while symbolic means of true communication have become so common as hardly to be noted, unobtrusively performing their function. The lessons of impressionism, the art of suggestion and the values of light, have become stock in trade.

Whether it is Simonson, scene designer, or Clurman, a director, writing, the collaborative relationship is emphasized along with the primacy of the director for the basic approach to the script. Harold Clurman has stated: "The director writes the 'score' or 'notes' of the theatrical production; the others play them," but "In the playing of the director's 'notes' each of his collaborators—actors, designer, costumer, etc.—brings something of his own individuality or talent to bear." † He illustrated the relationship from his direction of *Montserrat:* "After what I may call the private work on the script, I began conference with the scene-designer. The play's locale offers the designer ample opportunity to make his setting a riot of Spanish and Italian motifs. Since I was seeking a 'classic' style for the play, my first instructions to the designer emphasized that local color would have to be made entirely subsidiary to the structural elements of the setting, so that the characters, each one of whom represents a different approach to life as projected in the dramatist's philosophic scheme, would stand out beyond the accidents of their environment." ‡

Simonson makes a corresponding statement: "The director's general conception of a performance, its rhythm, tone, tempo, and pattern of movement, determines the essential design of a production. A designer's scheme of setting the stage and lighting it determines how a play can be performed. A director's suggestions may be gen-

* Foreword to *The Art of Scenic Design.*
† "Footlight Chat, No. III," *The New Republic,* Mar. 7, 1949.
‡ "The Director's Job, No. II," *The New Republic,* Aug. 15, 1949.

eral or concrete or incomplete. Many may be given to the director by the designer." *

Simonson gives examples of ideas from the director: "The wheat field seen through the barn door of the last act of 'The Power of Darkness' resulted from Emanuel Reicher's plea that somewhere the beauty of the outside world must break in on the moment of redemption. Most of the structure of 'He Who Gets Slapped' grew out of Robert Milton's insistence that he must have a post or a column somewhere near the center of the stage about which to build certain 'business.' The brainstorm in 'The Adding Machine' was the result of a remark of Moeller's—'If the whole scene could go mad, blood you know, something to show what's happening inside the man . . .'" Simonson goes on to indicate the designer's activities following a directorial inspiration such as Moeller's: "Our electrician, Mike O'Conner, two electrical supply companies and myself . . . experimented for several weeks with gauzes, spot lights and revolving discs, and approximated his intuition." †

In *The American Artist,* Nov., 1949, Jo Mielziner has given a clear view of the work of the designer in one of the most successful theater collaborations, Arthur Miller's *Death of a Salesman.* The playwright's script in its demand for a coalescence of diverse scenes in the unity of a single character's consciousness, implicit in the substance of the play itself and in the stage directions in general terms without suggestion of specific stage solution, was a tribute of high respect to our theater in its resources of direction and stage design. Miller has described the origins of the conception as follows: "It came from structural images. The play's eye was to revolve with Willy's head, sweeping endlessly in all directions like a light on a sea, and nothing formed in the mist was to be left uninvestigated. . . . There were two undulating lines in mind, one above the other, the past webbed to the present moving on together in him and sometimes openly joined and once, finally, colliding in the showdown which defined him in his eyes at least—and so to sleep . . . Above all, in the structural sense, I aimed to make a play with the

* *The Art of Scenic Design,* p. 31.
† From Simonson's contributed chapter to *The Theatre Guild: The First Ten Years,* ed. Walter Prichard Eaton, Brentano's, New York, 1929, p. 198.

veritable countenance of life. To make one the many, as in life . . . The image of a play without transitional scenes was there in the beginning. There was too much to say to waste precious stage time with feints and preparations." *

Collaboration does not lack its shades of rivalry. Donald Oenslager is quoted by Norris Houghton from an interview as feeling: "From the very beginning of a production the designer should be one step ahead of the director. He should be prepared to show the director the plans of the settings, should be able to indicate the most workable schemes for mounting the production, the logical color spots, lighting effects, before the director, out of his preconceived ideas, is able to dictate to the designer how these things should be ordered." †

We have seen from Elia Kazan's notebook the penetration of a director's response—"There are no flashbacks!" Mielziner presents the designer's relation to the script: "Miller stated that he wanted the 'simplest possible scenic solution' to the play, but in his first draft the script implied the need for some nine or ten separate settings or locations. In several cases, two and three of these areas were to be used simultaneously. The author and Elia Kazan, the director, agreed with me that even the most rapid mechanical method of scene changing might impair the flow of the action and the unity of the play." Mr. Mielziner devised and presented in rough pencil-and-pen sketches for approval of author and director the now familiar plan of "a symbolic frame of a Salesman's house" through and above which the overshadowing apartment houses would be visible and in which the several rooms required as acting spaces and the back yard could singly or simultaneously be exposed by lighting. "Another vital acting area, as finally devised, was a forestage where by the use of a few simple properties, such as a round table and a couple of chairs, scenes from the past life of the family could be re-enacted."

One of the most effective elements for communication of feeling in the visual experience of *Death of a Salesman* originated according to Mielziner in his concern for clarity to the audience in following Willy Loman's daydreams into seeing the house as it had

* Introduction to *Collected Plays of Arthur Miller,* Viking Press, New York, 1957, pp. 30-31.
† "The Designer Sets the Stage IV, Donald Oenslager," *Theatre Arts Monthly,* Nov., 1936, pp. 879-891.

appeared to him twenty-five years ago: "Miller referred in the manuscript to the fact that the house once had been surrounded by living trees but at the time of the opening scene of the play the trees had been cut down and in their place were ugly apartment houses crowding up and around the house. This was a clue to a scenic effect devised to assist the audience in making the transition with the Salesman. The effect was achieved by covering the entire stage with green leaves projected from numerous magic lanterns. As the projection was slowly brought up on the dimmer and the leaves became visible, the painted apartment houses on the backdrop slowly faded from sight, in a sense visibly liberating the Salesman's house from their oppression and giving the stage a feeling of outdoor freedom.*

The published form of the play, in which the stage directions of the original script are expanded in specific terms of Mielziner's design, incorporates the direction for the transition of scenes: "The apartment houses are fading out and the entire house and surroundings become covered with leaves." Now the imagination of the reader who has never seen the production may be stimulated to seeing and feeling the house, the yard, the people bathed in leaves and air and light.

Death of a Salesman has had and will have many amateur productions in which limitations of space and facilities, or the fresh ideas of a scene designer, will lead to departures from the original staging, but always on a foundation of essential illuminations of meaning from that production which have become a part of the text. Sometimes a scene design is not only so true to meaning but so flexible in practical adaptation that it becomes almost ineradicably associated with the play. Such a design is that of Lee Simonson for the railway viaduct scene in *Liliom,* as produced by the Theatre Guild. Simonson has analyzed the design as follows:

> At the railway viaduct where Liliom plans his holdup, the lighting of the sky must evoke space as infinite as the designer can make it in order to suggest "the magic of strangeness and distance," the lure of the world beyond the horizon that Liliom feels, and again expresses only inarticulately as he watches an express train disappear. The arch of the viaduct becomes a trap where the

---

* "Death of an Artist," in *The American Artist,* Nov., 1949.

cashier can be quickly cornered by Liliom, and Liliom in turn by two rural policemen. The massing of shadow must not only accent the bulk of the viaduct, but also, by its gloom, give a premonition of danger and so heighten the dramatic suspense of the scene. At the same time a few carefully focused spotlights must illuminate the faces of Liliom, his accomplice, "The Sparrow," and the cashier, but must seem to be no brighter than the light that might be cast by the semaphore of the railroad track.*

The design does speak with all the unobstrusive symbols of suggestion Simonson proposes and its means of suggesting space by a simple outline of a single bulk, a part for the whole, is perhaps the only effective means for a small stage as it is usually the best for a large stage. Every amateur production of *Liliom* that remains in my memory, however different other scenes of the play may have been from Simonson's designs, followed in the tradition he set for the viaduct scene. My visualization as I read the play is always close to Simonson's design for that scene except that I see the railway track running on for miles into distance beyond the stage—as Simonson intended we should.

Through much of the nineteenth century the scenic artist was a painter of backgrounds against which the actors spoke, moved, postured and gestured, and scenery was often identified with spectacle. Plays were not infrequently advertised for the number and picturesqueness of the scenes, all newly painted for the current production. The numerous newly painted scenes referred to were, of course, canvas backdrops. Today scene designers characteristically disavow creating pictures or focusing audience attention on their work. They are giving life to the play and creating an environment in which actors can act. Simonson's summary statement is, "The process by which a stage can be made the world of the play is the art of the theatre." † Mielziner speaks of the "requirements of a setting in which this drama could live freely and expressively." ‡ Robert Edmond Jones, a great poet of the theater and meticulous workman,

* *The Art of Scenic Design,* p. 29.
† Foreword, *The Art of Scenic Design.*
‡ "Death of a Painter," in *The American Artist,* Nov., 1949.

made what has become the classic statement of self-abnegation of the scene designer:

> The designer creates an environment in which all noble emotions are possible. Then he retires. The actor enters. If the designer's work has been good, it disappears from our consciousness at that moment. We do not notice it any more. It has apparently ceased to exist. The actor has taken the stage; and the designer's only reward lies in the praise bestowed on the actor.*

One of Jones's favorites of his own sets was for a travel scene in *Lute Song,* for which he hung strips of gray cloth along a batten down-stage, filling the entire proscenium-arch space. The actress moved across stage from one side to the other in and out of the strips of cloth as through the trees of a forest, singing her travel song. Lighted and at audience distance the strips of cloth looked neither like strips of cloth nor like trees. What they did do was to give the feeling of the long, lonely, weary way of the Wife seeking the Husband. The set did not even seem to say to the imagination, "This is a forest," but that the journey of the Wife was as though she were almost lost in a dense and endless forest. The set never returns to my mind's eye in itself but always with the figure of the actress moving in and out of view, her floating song now near, now remote. That was what Jones said that set should be: take the actress out and it was nothing. Perhaps one should add as a parenthesis or footnote that *Lute Song* in another scene gave him opportunity for the gorgeous eye-filling spectacle he also loved.

Our object is visualization of the play in reading. We have gone behind the scenes with the scene designers to some slight degree, but touching lightly on the technical means and processes of their effects. Their own writings are available for such detail. I have found that without some idea of the potentialities of staging, readers of plays are often distracted from the visualization beyond the stage, at which the theater itself at its best aims, by wondering if or how what they find in the text could be done on the stage. For example, Sidney Kingsley's *Darkness at Noon,* a dramatization of Arthur Koestler's

---

* *The Dramatic Imagination,* p. 27.

novel. An introductory note reads: "The action of the play oscillates dialectically between the Material world of a Russian prison during the harsh days of March, 1937, and the Ideal realms of the spirit as manifested in Rubashov's memories and thoughts moving freely through time and space." Stage directions run in such fashion as, while Rubashov paces his cell, "The vague outline of ghostly faces hover above him" . . . "The luminous face of a young woman appears in space" . . . "The young woman materializes. The cell becomes the office of the Commissar of the Iron Works." The scenes of Rubashov's memories and thoughts might appear in the mind's eye in any of several ways, framed in a balloon attached by a string to Rubashov's head like the speeches in cartoons, or blotting out Rubashov's head and hanging in space in place of his head, or interchangeably with the scenes in the cell like colored photograph slides in a viewer. Actually the theater created exactly the right visualization: the memory scenes materialized in space in a frame of darkness in which there remained a shadow of reminder of the prison cell as an opposition. In this instance, according to John Chapman, editor of *The Best Plays of 1950-1951,* the stage setting was devised by the playwright, Sidney Kingsley, who with some difficulty found a scene designer to undertake it: "Finally the stage artist Frederick Fox agreed that Kingsley's notion might be made to work. Fox did make it work, and his settings were among the best of a stage season that was scenically notable." *

Without elaboration into detail, the basic principle was a fairly shallow front-stage space for the prison cell occupied by Rubashov, the back wall of the cell a gauze curtain on the front side of which the huge blocks of gray stone were painted in transparent colors, behind the curtain a raised rear stage. For scenes in the cell the curtain lighted only from in front appeared as solid wall. For the memory scenes the cell space was darkened, light came up behind the curtain, the transparent painting of the cell wall disappeared, and the scene on the rear stage was visible through the gauze. An elaboration of this treatment of a gauze curtain was used with notable effect by Mielziner for atmospheric transitions of scene in *South Pacific.* A gauze traveler, or curtain on a trolley, with design appropriate to one scene painted on the front in transparent colors

* Dodd, Mead and Company, New York, 1951, p. 73.

and for the succeeding scene on the back in opaque colors, was drawn across the stage screening a rapid set change. Then as light faded on the front of the curtain and came up from behind, one design merged into the other as a transition for drawing back the curtain on the new scene. Another example of frequent question is the change of the bare branches of the tree in a field of snow to "the form of a skeleton" in Scene Three of Kaiser's *From Morn to Midnight*. The problem is different as the locale and lighting of the scene remain the same. In the Theatre Guild production in 1922 the designs of the tree and the skeleton were superimposed one on the other on the same piece of scenery in paints of different composition, one of which becomes visible only under one color of light and the other under another. Changing the color in a spotlight on the tree-skeleton produced the effect.

To further appreciation of the technical as well as artistic requirements of scene design, photographs are reproduced preceding page 87 of two of Jo Mielziner's color sketches for a famous set of a famous scene, the crap-shooting scene in the musical, *Guys and Dolls,* together with a photograph from the production. The preceding scene is a street at night, with a rail guarding an open manhole beside which stands a light-company repair wagon. The scene ends with Sky Masterson demanding of Nicely, "Where's the crap game?" "About ten minutes from here. . . . This way," answers Nicely and vanishes down the manhole. The lights black out and come up in the realm beneath the streets of the City of New York. Reliable Nathan Detroit, operator of the "oldest established permanent floating crap game in New York," in desperation for a retired spot has moved his game to a sewer. The players are in a cavernously vaulted space of overpowering solidity. There is a steel ladder on a great central pillar, gigantic pipes and valves on either side. The pipes are orange from the color of protective metal paint, the walls bluish green, a suggestion of steel and of underground. Behind the men two circular tunnels and huge pipe-lines stretch away into the distance in misty greenish light. The effect is startlingly realistic and at the same time romanticized, beautiful, exotic in abrupt contrast to the street above. The setting is Wagnerian and the dwarfed men are completely unaware of it, of surrounding vastness and strangeness. The intensity of their self-absorption is pre-

cisely the same as it would have been in the back of the cigar store or
in Joey Biltmore's garage, and the focus of the setting is both comic
in effect and dramatic. The contrast which is achieved in this scene
essentially by the stage set is integral to the unity of the entire
play. Brooks Atkinson remarked something to the effect that these
people are at once comically incongruous and dramatically engaging
because in their determined effort to remain outside the responsibilities of society they all individually pursue harassed and desperate
lives.

The photograph from production was a publicity photograph, not
a display of the set, and it is unfortunate for the purpose here that
no full-stage view was taken. However, the close-up of the gamblers
in their concentration projects more clearly one aspect of the total
effect of the set in action, and by applying the scale of the pipe and
valve on stage-left to the men, and expanding the scene from the
photographs of the color sketches, the full scale of the setting to its
human occupants can readily be imagined. The color sketches for
two separate pieces of scenery, a "framed hanger" and a "translucent backdrop," will suggest something of how the foreground solidity, space, light, distant perspective, and dwarfing scale were
achieved. It also should be noted that the set had three-dimensional
effectiveness from any angle of view in the house.

It would be well to turn to the illustration of Oliver Messel's
stage setting for *The Lady's Not for Burning* (page 86) and to
consider it as stage design. The introductory stage direction in the
printed text simply says that the scene is the house of Hebbel Tyson,
the Mayor of the little market town of Cool Clary, and that the
appearance is "as much fifteenth century as anything." The stage
design as a locale for the action presents a pleasant harmonious suggestion of fifteenth century, nicely varied and balanced to the eye.
The floor plan with its main floor space, narrower raised level of the
dais, the focus of the window seats, the ramp exit stage right and the
flexible structure of steps stage left is an admirable instrument for
the movements, groupings, and physical relationships of the actors.
The vista and light through the windows and door suggest a wider,
freer, more beautiful world than that of the various human limitations which are given a gay drubbing within the confines of the room.
The play ends at night near dawn and, at the moment, the world

looks "frozen and forbidding under the moon" to Jennet, but the recollection to the audience from the first two acts of sunshine and distance outside gives a welcoming quality to the wide world into which Jennet and Thomas are about to depart, like Adam and Eve at the end of *Paradise Lost,* possessed of their freedom and each other.

Costume design is inseparable from scene design. The figures of the actors in their costumes are a part of the scene. Some scene designers, as Robert Edmond Jones, Norman Bel Geddes, and Donald Oenslager, have also been costume designers. Costume, however, is a field of extensive technical and historical knowledge, and skilled craftsmanship as well as artistry, and more often the costumer is a specialist who works with the scene designer as the scene designer with the director. The basic artistic principles of the two fields of design are the same: the costume should express both the play and the part, and should be such that the actor when in the part lives naturally in the costume. For the theater in one's head it is probable that the characters will be clothed somehow. For modern realistic plays in contemporary setting it is likely the reader will be acquainted not only with the general mode of dress of the social background but with characteristic expression of personality. There is the whole area, however, of what are commonly called costume plays, plays set in other times and places, whether a modern play in an historical or foreign setting or a play written in another background, as an Elizabethan or a Restoration play, or a Chinese play. Adequate experience of such plays through reading requires knowledge beyond that with which we grew up. Dress is both an expression and a molder of the background to which it belongs. Not only are dress and manners inseparable, but dress and inmost thought and feeling. In the eighteenth century, Shakespeare was played in tie wigs and knee breeches and was so much the less Shakespeare. *King Lear* was also performed in the eighteenth century in a version rewritten to a happy ending. For a unified dramatic expression, harmony of costume with character, speech, and action is necessary, not for pedantic historicity of detail but with the freedom of an artist to grasp the expressive essentials. The harmony of play and costume is not always a matter, as in English Restoration comedy,

for example, of the social dress of the period. There are the conventionalized theaters, such as the Greek, and the Chinese and Japanese, in fact, most Oriental theaters, in which costume was purely
theatrical, created as a part of the conventionalized expression, like
the masks or mask-like make-up, and never worn in life. The elaborate and beautiful costumes of Chinese and Japanese theater are
the most important element of scenic effect and a determining factor
in every aspect of the dramatic expression. The Elizabethan stage
presented a curious blend of contemporary dress, theatrical convention, and a rather freely imagined and anachronistic suggestion of
historical costume in plays of earlier times such as the Roman, all
expressive, however, of the Elizabethan age and its drama. The conventional theaters present another area for consciously acquired
knowledge for enhancement of reading of plays. Fortunately, acquaintance with costume as with scene design is bountifully available
in richly illustrated books, some by theater costume designers and
some by historians of costume which the theater designers use as
their source books.

Lighting the stage in conception belongs to the scene designer.
Light has become so much a part of modern painting and of dramatic effect in the theater that it has been called the scene designer's
second brush. The conception has to be executed, however, in
greater or less degree by technicians. Theoretically the designer can
state the effect he wants and illustrate it with his color sketches and
then leave it to the lighting engineer and electricians. But light is so
subtle and elusive a thing the more a designer knows of the relations
between color of light and the color upon which it falls, the effects
of material and textures upon received light, the difference in the
technique of producing effects of light in painting and by reflection
and absorption of light thrown on a painted surface, the more
nearly what happens in the theater will correspond to the painting
in the studio. Some of the finest achievements in staging are in the
lighting, and some of the most distressing disparities between what
the designer conceives and the audience sees. Sometimes, too, compromises are compelled between lighting for mood and meaning and
projection of effective expression of the actors to the reaches of a
theater auditorium. Here, in lighting, the reader of plays is most free.

He need make no compromises; the theater in his head can be in bifocal vision. He needs no technical knowledge, and fears no defects of execution. All that he needs is—imagination and the eye of awareness for all the varied effects of light daily given by the world in which we live.

5

In the Theater : The Actors

There is an expression of the human countenance I have seen many times. It is a beautiful expression, unself-conscious, rapt, beatific. It is the face of a young playwright at an early rehearsal of his first production. He is lost in the wonder of hearing his lines spoken by actors. He is not in the least critical—not yet—either of the actors or of what he has written. The words sound new to him as though they were originating at that moment, and they are astonishingly expressive. The actors give life to a play and it is they alone, not a director, not a designer, nor a super-theater artist such as Gordon Craig dreamed of, who can give body and voice to the words of a playwright.

The designer creates the world in which the play come to life can move and breathe most freely; the director gives order, harmony, and proportion to the life of the play. The initial fallacy of Gordon Craig in *The Art of the Theatre* which led to the final extravagance of *The Actor and the Ueber-Marionette* was his identification of the theater with a temple and his desire to return drama to its origin in ritual. The life in ritual is the living though unseen presence of the god, and ritual has power to bring the presence of the god only by the unified faith of the audience in its object. Without the faith and the object ritual becomes, not drama, but spectacle. And that is where the work of the great European *régisseurs* who most nearly approximated Craig's super-theater artist ended, in spectacle. Reinhardt finally submerged the individual actors not only in scenic and costume delights but in mass effects, and Meyerhold carried his theatricalism of staging on to mechanization of the actors into an approximation of puppets. Spectacle can make an impact on the senses or on the nerves. "When Reinhardt's chorus let loose, several housemaids fainted," commented the critic Herbert Ihering on the production of *Oedipus*.* Spectacle controlled to that end may even produce some kind of aesthetic experience appropriate to itself, but it is not that of drama. When in ancient Greece the leader of the Dionysian chorus emerged as an individual speaker, the actor and drama simultaneously were born, and the drama which developed out of ritual came to be defined as character in action.

Perhaps because the actor is so central to the theater, when the actors, except actor-playwrights as Shakespeare and Molière, have been in control the theater has gone out of balance. Not that actors are inherently incapable as directors. Quite the contrary. It is a matter of theatrical climate, an actor-oriented theater in the eighteenth and nineteenth centuries and a play-oriented theater in the twentieth. In our theater some of the finest directing, in balanced and perceptive regard for the play and concern for the best possible casting and playing of all the parts for ensemble effect, has been by actors—Nazimova's direction of *The Cherry Orchard* and of *Ghosts*, for example; Sir John Gielgud's approximately equal distinction as actor and director; the contribution to our theater of Katharine Cornell as producer. The character of the modern theater, however, in general is maintained by a division of functions. The director is the author's representative, the balancing force, the objective point of view, and as such is recognized and valued by even the greatest actors. In the view of Helen Hayes, to cite one, as summarized from Morton Eustis' interview, "The director must integrate the performance, put the actor straight, guide him in the proper expression of the conception he has formed. . . . If she plays a scene badly, if she speaks a line out of key, if she fails to project the authentic emotion, she expects the director to tell her that she is wrong and try to set her right. That's what he's there for." Miss Hayes also expressed

* Mordecai Gorelik, *New Theatres for Old*, Samuel French, New York, 1940, p. 218.

the limit she placed on the function of the director. He can give her, "in words, the key to the emotion, the suggestion of movement and gesture compatible with the emotion, but never by speaking the line himself or making the gesture. The moment a director starts to act out Miss Hayes' part for her, she becomes self-conscious: she is incapable of copying his action." After relating how a good gesture was "lost forever" from *Victoria Regina* because Gilbert Miller "unfortunately" showed her the gesture he wanted, Miss Hayes went on to relate how a scene that was "a hit every night," because she "spontaneously, felt that it was right—'though actually, it was no more correct than Mr. Miller's lost gesture,' " resulted from a collaboration of director and actress:

> In the scene in which Albert is shaving. . . . Mr. Miller, in a moment of inspiration, said: "You are young, romantic. You have just been married. You have never seen a man shave before. You are interested, intrigued. Why don't you walk around and watch his face?" He didn't tell her how to walk, or where to walk. He simply suggested the emotion and its physical expression. Instantly Miss Hayes grasped what an excellent piece of stage business could be made of the idea, and worked it out for herself.*

Alla Nazimova in interview with Mr. Eustis, more drastically than Helen Hayes limited the director's guidance to the actor to correction: "The director . . . should tell the actor only what *not* to do. If he attempts to read lines, to show the actor the gesture he should use, he is a murderer—or he realizes, unfortunately, that he has to deal with an actor devoid of brain and imagination, and therefore must drill him as he would a parrot!" †

Robert Edmond Jones wrote of the director: he "must never make the mistake of imposing his own ideas upon the actors. . . . The director energizes; he animates." ‡ Actually the great actors have

---

* Morton Eustis, *Players at Work, Acting according to the Actors,* Theatre Arts, Inc., New York, 1937, pp. 23-25. Previously published as a series of articles, "The Actor Attacks His Part," in *Theatre Arts Monthly,* Oct., 1936 to March, 1937. Quotations from *Players at Work* are by permission of Theatre Arts Books.

† *Ibid.,* p. 55.

‡ *The Dramatic Imagination,* p. 37.

always been self-animated. There is no suggestion from Nazimova or Helen Hayes of any need felt for energization from a director, and from the descriptions of the performances of the self-directed star actors of the eighteenth and nineteenth centuries there was no lack of energy or imagination, but a need of balance and restraint and correction of mannerisms. However, with a sprinkling of great actors and presumably some "devoid of brain and imagination" the theater is primarily made up of many competent actors and many immature or inadequately trained actors with latent capacities. The most effective directors today—as was true of Max Reinhardt in his better phases—possess as one of their conspicuous talents the ability to stimulate awareness of their own resources in actors—as Robert Edmond Jones put it, to address themselves to the actors' highest powers and to fuse them "into a white energy."

The creative art of the actor is peculiarly individual, in a way mysterious because the actor uses himself as his instrument, his medium of expression. Actors have written a great deal about their art.* Certain related questions appear repeatedly which the actors have difficulty in answering for themselves, but which for that very reason they attack over and over: the relation between technique and inspiration, emotional identification with the role and detachment, the significance of the actor's personality and loss of identity in the part. The answers are different for different actors, but the norm for the process of the best acting might, perhaps, be summarized as follows. The actor trains himself rigorously in the techniques of expression, his body, face, and voice, making of himself a flexible instrument. He studies the part by an interplay of mental analysis and progressive imaginative penetration until at some time in the course of preparation he experiences complete emotional identification, the loss of his personal consciousness in that of the character, an understanding as from within. From this foundation he comes back to mental analysis of another kind, determining the technical means of projecting the character in theatrical terms, the pieces of business, the movement, gestures, facial make-up and expressions, vocal inflections, pitch, timbre. In this way the role is

* The volume *Actors on Acting,* edited by Toby Cole and Helen Krich Chinoy, Crown Publishers, New York, 1949, provides a very full selection as well as guide to wider resources of the literature on their art by the actors themselves.

created. Then it is rehearsed until what the actor has determined is mechanically perfected until he can recreate the role in performance, and successive performances for audience after audience. In performance the actor becomes typically a split personality, one part becomes the character he is playing, the other remains the actor in detached technical control. It is this final experience in performance which the actors themselves find most difficult to put into words, the sense of ceasing to be themselves, of literally becoming the part that is played, yet of never being carried away into losing the detached self-observation, the technical control, the awareness of interplay with the audience. Of course, the whole process is much less orderly than the kind of composite picture set down here, varying with the individual, not only for the same actor but, from part to part.

The variety of elements that can enter into creating the illusion and the power to the audience is extremely well illustrated in a description by Mrs. Katherine Goodale in her book *Behind the Scenes with Edwin Booth* of Booth's playing of the "Curse of Rome" scene in Bulwer-Lytton's *Richelieu*. Mrs. Goodale's book is a memoir of a season when as a young actress, Kitty Molony, she toured with Booth. She relates that Booth had his cardinal's robes authentically built abroad by an ecclesiastical tailor—"real lace, genuine ermine, heavy corded silk of a color, of a quality, that clinched for the eye their authoritative beauty." In the Curse of Rome scene, Richelieu appears for the first time in his official robes, the cardinal red against a background of "the black velvet mourning of the assembled courtiers—mourning for his own supposed death." Mrs. Goodale continues:

> With the left hand, he snatched away the ermine border—that hindered by falling over his right hand—even as he raised this hand and drew the imaginary circle about Julie, but without taking one step toward her. He faced her, but spoke to Barados, who stood below him (right).
>
> "Mark where she stands. Around her trembling form, I draw the awful circle of our solemn Church. Set but a foot within that holy bound, and on thy head—yea, though it wore a crown—I'll launch the Curse of Rome!"

As Mr. Booth hurled this speech he threw his right hand up above his head and raised himself on tiptoes—an unseen movement, for the train of his robe lay stretched out before him on the stage floor. It hid his feet, and that long red line guided the observer's eye to the very tip of his two high-held fingers.

. . . In the same instant that Richelieu rose upon his toes, all the actors on the stage . . . quickly knelt, bowed heads low, and shrank with terror. As they seemed to descend, Mr. Booth appeared to ascend, and the optical illusion that Mr. Booth suddenly became seven feet tall was produced.

Mrs. Goodale goes on to observe, that "this carefully planned, smoothly rendered business" was Booth's "mountain-peak climbing paraphernalia," but no more than that, for the superb climax of the hypnotic force of his acting:

In this Curse scene his voice held the blasts of Hell. His eyes blazed, in the finality of wrath. His gesture—his posture—was doom to souls. He was not Time; he was Eternity. No one who saw him—heard him—give that curse doubted he could damn a soul.*

There one has it all, the cool calculations of the actor, the trained natural endowments, and finally the vitality and power. Coleridge wrote of Edmund Kean, "Seeing him act was like reading Shakespeare by flashes of lightning." Thomas Davies wrote of David Garrick as Lear: "He rendered the curse so terribly affecting to the audience that, during the utterance of it, they seemed to shrink from it as from a blast of lightning." †

This flashing about of lightning and curses may suggest that acting to be impressive depends on great characters and great passions, but the power of acting is in the absoluteness of the illusion of the reality of a character, or of the truth of a moment of feeling revealed to an audience. Fanny Burney after seeing Garrick as Lear was obviously impressed by him as Abel Drugger in Ben Jonson's *The Alchemist*: "Never could I have imagined such a metamorphosis as I

---

* Houghton Mifflin, Boston and New York, 1931, pp. 23-25.

† *Dramatic Miscellanies,* 3 vols., Printed for the Author, London, 1785, vol. ii, p. 281.

saw; the extreme meanness, the vulgarity, the low wit, the vacancy of countenance, the appearance of *unlicked nature* in all his motions." *

In a play recently on Broadway, *The Entertainer* by John Osborne, Sir Laurence Olivier plays the part of a third-rate music-hall entertainer. He appears not only as the character in his home, but, in front of a tawdry curtain and facing the audience, he performs Archie in his cheap act of banal patter, song, and dance. The part could easily be a tour de force for the actor so identified with classical roles; but even in Archie's act Sir Laurence Olivier is doing more than a skillful imitation, he is playing from inside the character and communicating the man at the same time that he is rendering his vaudeville performance. The part is on the whole unrewarding in the writing. As chosen by Mr. Osborne, or as limited by Mr. Osborne's perception, the character is of such level emotional mediocrity, a man who has "never cared a damn about anything," as to be uninteresting. Mr. Osborne has, however, given Archie one submerged caring about something and one brief moment of the emergence of a substantial emotion. What Sir Laurence Olivier does with that moment strikes one like a blow between the eyes. Archie is talking with his daughter late at night and getting drunk. Sir Laurence hurtles himself bodily out of the stage set, over to the side of the proscenium arch, and leans there panting. "Don't worry about your old man—he's still a bit worried about young Nick," he croaks. His voice slides down to flatness: "At least, I suppose he is. I told you, nothing really touches me." He slumps with heavy violence to the floor, his glass flies from his hand slithering across the stage. By the sudden and unexpected change of perspective, the breaking out from the frame of the set into a close-up, the actor enlarged the character to more than life-size and isolated the emotion.

All art is an intensification of life. Acting is not mimicry of life, nor delivering the lines of the dramatist. The art of the actor is to create out of himself to an audience the intensification of life which the dramatist has suggested in the power of his writing. It is a very great thing. As Colley Cibber wrote in 1740 of the actor in relation to Shakespeare's characters, he "calls them from the grave, to

* Quoted by Mrs. Clement Parsons in *Garrick and His Circle*, G. P. Putnam's Sons, New York, and Methuen and Company, London, 1906, pp. 77-78.

breathe, and be themselves again, in feature, speech, and motion." *
Denis Diderot referred to Garrick as "this famous man, who in
himself is as well worth a visit to England as the ruins of Rome are
worth a visit to Italy." † Thomas Campbell, Mrs. Siddons' contemporary biographer, described her as having on the stage a
"power to magnify one's conception of the heart's capacity for
tender, intense, and lofty feelings," and to make the spectator feel
as if he "were witnessing some god-like soul from the heroic world
pouring forth its sensibility." ‡ Of the part of Lady Macbeth, he
wrote: "It was an era of one's life to have seen her in it. She was
Tragedy personified." § Coquelin, the pre-eminent actor of the latter
nineteenth century in France, described the height of the art of
acting as "transfiguration." // Of his contemporary, François-Louis
Lesseur, as Don Quixote, he wrote:

> When he entered the stage in this last part, although he was really
> a small man, it seemed as if there were no end to his stature, he
> seemed to draw himself out, like a telescope, till he was as long as
> his lance. It was indeed the hero of Cervantes in all the melan-
> choly of his interminable leanness.¶

It is perhaps easier to recognize the power of acting in the preceding centuries than today. Drama and acting was conceived of in
the neoclassicism of the eighteenth century and its heritage into the
ninetenth century in terms of portrayal of the passions, or emotions.
When romanticism in the nineteeth century introduced focus on
creation of individual character it was at first in terms of picturesque,
exaggerated, or in some sense extreme characters of extravagant
emotions. Working in those traditions, "The older actors," as Sir
Cedric Hardwicke recently stated, "were spellbinders. They were

* *An Apology for the Life of Mr. Colley Cibber,* J. M. Dent and Sons, Ltd.,
London, and E. P. Dutton and Co., New York, 1914, p. 59.
† Trans. from Diderot's *Paradox sur le Comedien* (cir. 1773) by Walter
Herries Pollock, Chatto and Windus, London, 1883, p. 38.
‡ *The Life of Mrs. Siddons,* Harper and Brothers, New York, 1834, pp. 255-
256.
§ *Ibid.,* p. 123.
// "Actors and Acting," in *The Art of Acting,* Fifth Series, No. 2, of Publica-
tions of the Dramatic Museum of Columbia University, Columbia University
Press, 1926, p. 20. Originally published in *Harper's Weekly,* May, 1887.
¶ *Ibid.,* p. 15.

true to something bigger than life." * Modern realism and naturalism, however, when it is truly art, if not larger than life, is more concentrated than life. Willy Loman is more intensely and completely the salesman than any single salesman anyone has ever known, which is the reason he seems so true to every person in the audience—he embraces the sum of their individual experiences, and more. Antoine, at the beginning of naturalism, stated: "In acting as in all the arts, sincerity, passion, conviction, that peculiar fever which shakes the soul of the interpreter, are his most precious gifts." †

Shakespeare has actually been best served by a blending of the forceful projection of the old school and the modern style of psychological, or spiritual realism. Shakespeare created directly characters, not passions, except as they arose from the characters. But he gave the theater its greatest passions because he created characters capable of them in situations that called them forth. The old actor-managers by the combination of cutting the text and acting style tended to keep only the passion. When Leslie Howard and John Gielgud played *Hamlet* in the same season, 1936, a notable difference was that Howard, with bodily grace, vocal beauty and range, and sensitivity of feeling, performed the great scenes magnificently but much in between was connective tissue. Gielgud created an alive Hamlet in a continuous line of vitality from beginning to end of the performance. His Hamlet as a psychological entity was at once distinctively modern and a restoration of Shakespeare, and certainly one of the great Hamlets in the history of the part.

Mme. Nazimova, who brought to the highest level possibly of any actress in this country the modern style of spiritual realism, said: "First, last, and always, a player must have imagination. Without imagination he might as well be a shoe-black as an actor. Imagination kindles the feelings, steers the actor through the character into emotion, enables him to reproduce feelings he himself has never experienced." ‡

The greatest demand on the imagination in the reading of plays is

---

* "An Actor Stakes His Claim," *Theatre Arts,* Feb., 1958.
† From a condensation of a brochure issued by Antoine in May, 1890, *Le Théâtre Libre. Saisons 1887 à 1890,* in *Antoine and The Théâtre-Libre* by Samuel Montefiore Waxman, Harvard University Press, 1926, p. 131.
‡ Interview with Morton Eustis, in *Players at Work,* p. 58.

Oliver Messell's setting for *The Lady's Not for Burning*, by Christopher Fry.

Set by Jo Mielziner for the crap game in the sewer scene from Act II of
Guys and Dolls.

Color sketch for Underground Framed Hanger, design by Jo Mielziner, for the same scene.

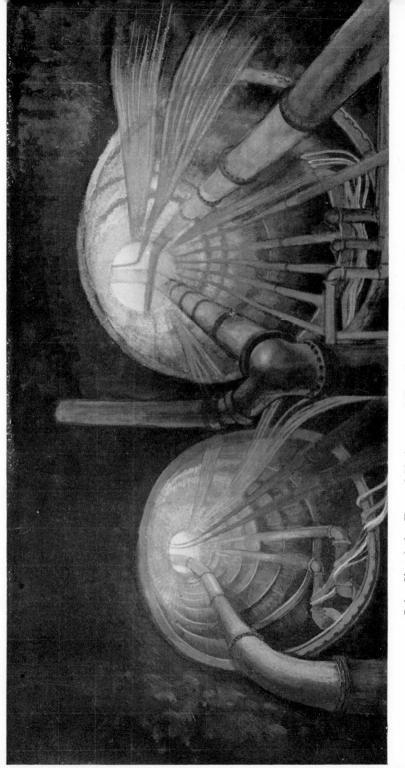

Color Sketch for Face of Underground Translucent Backdrop, design by Jo Mielziner, for the crap game scene in *Guys and Dolls*.

for the full mental creation of the characters. Robert Edmond Jones, whose consistent desire as a designer was "to carry the audience into that other region where the ideal play takes place," with his enthusiasm as a designer could still say: "Is this simplest, broadest, grandest way to carry the audience out of reality always and necessarily to be found in the scenic decorations? Need it, indeed, ever be the designer's way? May it not quite as probably be acting, even in an empty space, which uplifts the spectators?" *

One of Robert Jones's attractive characteristics was his tendency to go all the way in enthusiasm for the idea of the moment. I, for one, prefer for the theater in my head to keep a *décor;* but in a final balancing up it is nevertheless true that, except for a very limited body of stylized and theatrical plays, by far the greater part of a truly theatrical experience of reading plays exists in the mental projection of the characters in their being and in their action.

The visualization of the characters of a play as we read comes from what one has experienced, from all the faces, forms, postures, and movements one has seen from life or from pictures, from earliest childhood to the present moment, the total well of conscious and subconscious memory. There may be a conscious identification, or a face may move into a play sharply etched, mysteriously out of limbo, like the vivid faces in our dreams which on waking we cannot place in remembered experience. By the playwright's summoning to our imaginations, the materials of experience may be broken up and recomposed and modified into freshly created forms and faces fused with the inner being of created character; and we come to know as we read how such a one—rather that single and unique being—will speak and move, what fleeting shadows, what grimaces, what contortions and transfigurations will pass over that face in the created situations of the play.

Some people think they find it helpful to visualize known actors in the parts as they read a play, just as some playwrights do in writing. In playwrights it has seemed to me usually an indication of weakness, a crutch, and so for reading. Rather the reader should study the work of actors to set free his own creativity. What the

* Interview with Norris Houghton, "The Designer Sets the Stage, V, Robert Edmond Jones"; VI, Mordecai Gorelik, *Theatre Arts Monthly,* Dec., 1936, pp. 966-975.

actors have written about their art reveals how much study of the play and the part and exercise of imagination can go into realization of a playwright's character. The techniques of projection, of the deepest concern to the actor, are of secondary interest to the reader as he does not have to perform the part, only to imagine it. Descriptions of acting from audience experience are of great value, and listening to recordings, now so popular, can contribute materially. It is interesting, however, that John Gielgud, at least in 1937, had far more faith in the power of language toward recreation of a performance than in that of mechanical reproduction either by cinema or gramophone. He wrote:

> Some idea of an actor's performance may be conveyed to a third person by a brilliant and expert description or critique, written or told by an eye-witness, but I do not believe that any mechanical reproductions can create an acting performance that one has never seen (although it may be an interesting reminder or a valuable curiosity) whereas a description may suggest it most vividly and encourage those who come after to use it creatively without any spirit of imitation." *

An idea of Gielgud's own playing of Hamlet has been preserved by such a description by Rosamond Gilder in *John Gielgud's Hamlet,* the fullest account of a performance of a part with which I am acquainted. With the text of the play Miss Gilder presents on opposite pages a detailed running description of the playing of the part. The book also includes extensive notes by Gielgud on the costume, scenery, and stage business of the production. Whether or not one saw the performance, the book is a uniquely stimulating experience for the reader of plays.

Above everything, of course, one will want to see plays acted as often as possible for development of the penetration, the inventiveness, the range, and power of one's own creative imagination in reading. And remember always that fact of power. If the playwright is worth his salt, he has created characters in some way larger than life, or intensified in relation to life, and his final dependence on the actors goes beyond their capacity to understand his characters and

* In *John Gielgud's Hamlet,* by Rosamond Gilder, Oxford University Press, New York and Toronto, 1937, p. 42.

to become like them in lineament, to their capacity for superhuman vitality when before an audience. Lynn Fontanne, asked why acting a play is so tiring, answered: "Being the focus of thousands of eyes produces an hypnotic magnetism which makes the actor physically stronger than he is himself, so that when the eyes are withdrawn and the current is switched off he feels like a pricked balloon." * Miss Fontanne hit upon what is probably one of the essentials in the make-up of an actor, the capacity to respond to audience stimulus by pouring his reserves of energy into filling out the more-than-life magnitude and intensity of dramatic character.

It also must be admitted that an actor can occasionally create more than is in the script. On successive readings of the text of *Born Yesterday* I have never been able to find Billy Dawn, as Judy Holliday created the character, except by remembering Judy Holliday. The actress did not falsify anything in the part as written; she simply as an accomplishment of imagination and artistry created more, much more. That is not the function of the reader of plays for his own pleasure, although it may sometimes be fun to do for some readers, if they are capable of it. In general the reader is critically interested in discovering the limitations as well as the accomplishments of playwriting. The problem is to be able to place the limitations correctly, on the playwright or on one's self, and that is a reason for developing one's powers of theatrical imagination. To return to Miss Fontanne's statement, the reader may protest he does not have the enlarging power of the audience upon him. But he has the power of the play. It is not that the actor before an audience goes beyond his imagined conception of the part, but his ordinary human faculties are expanded by aid of the audience to encompass that scope. The imagination is limitless, and reading a great play is a step toward inner enlargement.

Now that reading plays has been identified with a theater in one's head, furnished by the fullest possible exercise of a cultivated and developed imaginative energy with direction, scene design, costume, lighting, and actors, it should be remembered that the theater in one's head and going to the theater are not the same thing. Neither takes the place of the other, but they do enhance each other. Theater is not

* Interview with Morton Eustis, in *Players at Work,* p. 39.

just the bringing to life and presentation of the author's play; it is a group experience for the audience, for each as part of the whole, and it is a living interplay between audience and the actors. An audience-filled theater in its semidarkness, all attention focused on the little but limitless world of the stage, can be a warm and vibrant and exciting place. Love of the theater is love of the occasion, the place, the actors, as well as of the play. Every veteran theater-goer has cherished memories of times when an audience, by those rhythmic waves of continuous applause, brings curtain call after curtain call as though they could not bear to lose the bond with the actors who have given so unstintingly of themselves, and of the sense already of nostalgia with which one has watched the curtain finally fall on a beautiful stage. No, reading plays is not that kind of theater, but imaginative reading of plays does give heightened alertness and response to exactly such experience. An interplay of attending theater and reading plays also develops appreciation and distinguishing awareness of the parts played by the several arts in the theater. Especially, one learns to see the play in the production. For the contributions of director, scene designer, and actor, we have seen the areas that belong in general to each, but also that theater production is so intricate and varied a collaboration that one should be very cautious in assignment from an audience view. Whoever may have been responsible for each detail, there is pleasure in the heightened perception of more facets of the total effect.

Just as positively, the reading of plays is no mere substitute for attending theater. Great plays are literature as well as theater. It is the play as written and read that is enduring, if it has the worth to endure. And let there be no mistake about it, in the play by a mind of magnitude and distinction the dramatist has communicated more of thought and imaginative penetration into life than can be grasped in any one theatrical interpretation or caught at theater pace. The total value of a great play is for reading and study, but reading and study illuminated by understanding of the form chosen by the author, a play for the theater. Finally, no other kind of reading offers to a comparable degree creative experience, almost limitless opportunity for exercise of imaginative energy. The theater in your head may be less splendid than some the world knows, but it is your own.

Understanding
the Play

6

The Meaning of a Play

" 'Freedom at any cost!' that was its meaning for me," Stanislavsky wrote of Gorki's *The Lower Depths* in the course of preparing the production by the Moscow Art Theatre with himself in the role of Sahtin. Harold Clurman found the total significance of the divers elements of Clifford Odets' *Golden Boy*—popular story motifs, the prize-fight world, effective melodrama, scenes and passages of brilliant dialogue—to be an allegory: "The story of the play is not so much the story of a prize-fighter as the picture of a great fight—a fight in which we are all involved . . . What the golden boy of this allegory is fighting for is a place in the world as an individual." * Arthur Miller stated in an introduction to *A View from the Bridge* that "its aim is to recreate my own feeling toward this tale—namely, wonderment. It is not designed primarily to draw tears or laughter from an audience but to strike a particular note of astonishment at the way in which, and the reasons for which, a man will endanger and risk and lose his very life." William Saroyan has written of Samuel Beckett's *Waiting for Godot:* "Beckett is fiercely funny in the midst of perhaps the most abysmal anguish ever put into a play or performed upon a stage—pure, inconsolable, bleak anguish." †

* Introduction to *Golden Boy* in *The Plays of Clifford Odets,* The Modern Library, Random House, New York, 1939, pp. 429-30.
† "Ionesco," *Theatre Arts,* July, 1958.

Paul and Miriam Mueschke put aside familiar critical views of Congreve's *The Way of the World* as a play of refined cynicism and immorality with plot of slight significance and wit, "his be-all and end-all," and develop the meaning of the play in identification with the satiric tradition of Horace and Ben Jonson: the plot of "a struggle of two pairs of adulterers for control of three legacies" is integrated with castigation of vice "by contrasting the punishment of a pair of transgressors on the way to reformation with that of a pair on the way to degradation"; and the wit in its "depth, variety, and subtlety" emanates from repudiating, not condoning, the way of the world.*

Louis Kronenberger sums up the quality of Oscar Wilde's *The Importance of Being Earnest* as follows: ". . . an element of fantasy and an atmosphere of elegance produce an effect of controlled high farce . . . there is a complete sense of the joke for the joke's sake, a scrupulous avoidance of meaning. *The Importance* is all surface, even in its satire; all prankishness, even in its fantasy. . . . It is all trivial; but because it is *all* trivial, it is also art. It is sternly true to itself, it makes a stubborn fetish, an absolute ideal, of triviality and artifice. And that, of course, is the only way of envisaging or enjoying it." †

All these brief statements of the meaning of plays come as introductions or conclusions to more detailed analysis. It is evident that the meaning of a play is complex, although it may sometimes be usefully reduced to a word or phrase, like Stanislavsky's "Freedom at any cost," which serves as a symbol, a key with which to reopen the door of recall of one's experience and analysis of the play. It is also evident that for the many kinds of plays meanings may lie in many different areas, a feeling or emotion of identification or of contemplation, a social problem, an attitude toward or consciousness of life, the pleasure in wit integrated with moral philosophy and purpose, the pleasure in a *jeu d'esprit* unentangled with any other meaning than the purity of its own caprice. And it is evident that the meaning of plays occasions disagreement—when viewed with scholarly detachment as well as in highly personalized response.

---

* *A New View of Congreve's Way of the World,* University of Michigan Press, Ann Arbor, 1958, pp. 7-9, 13.
† *The Thread of Laughter,* Alfred A. Knopf, New York, 1952, p. 223.

Understanding a play, or determining its meaning, is the product of conscious analysis of the experience of a play. In experiencing the play one is the paddler in the bow, leaving the steering to the playwright. Then one looks back and surveys the journey for its destination in meaning. The term *meaning* in connection with a drama, or other work of art, must be approached warily because it has had so many partial and limited applications derived from other spheres, as philosophy, morals, sociology, linguistics, crafts, shows and games of amusement, often from positions of repute. The Congress of the United States is accused of barbarism for inclusion of plays in an amusement tax, but Eugene Scribe was the arbiter of French dramatic criticism as well as leading playwright when he pronounced any other purpose than to entertain a violation of dramatic art. The demand for a moral lesson as justification for a play or other work of imaginative literature in the American society of our parents and grandparents is looked upon as naive, but the history of the Horation principle "to teach with delight" or "give pleasure and edification" by no means belongs to literarily unsophisticated minds, with such adherents as Sir Philip Sidney, Ben Jonson, John Dryden, and Samuel Johnson, to say nothing of Minturno and Scaliger, Ronsard and Boileau. Yet deep in the nature of art is the concept of totality: a work of art is a unified organization of imaginative experience and insight, the creation of a world self-contained and self-justified. The meaning of a work of dramatic art as its ultimate significance, what the play is for, must reside in the play as a whole and be sought in a unified experience of the play.

We are led at once to a common misconception about meaning, that of the "first fine careless rapture," that there is nowhere to go in search of meaning beyond the first emotional impact of the play, that analysis—or dissection as proponents like to put it—will distort or kill. There would be truth in this if we were to stop with the analysis, but understanding grows by an alternating process of critical analysis and dramatic experience. The validity of perceptions from analysis must be tested by reexperience of the play as a whole by reading or in the theater. If they are true perceptions there will be again the fusion of total consciousness, but in an enlarged, enriched, clarified experience which may in turn become the foundation for further analysis, which may lead again to expanded dramatic experience—and so *ad infinitum* except as limited by the resources of the play or reader or both, or time. Nothing is more dangerous to literary criticism than to fail to frequently return to this fountain of restoration. How many fair, towering structures of interpretation of *Hamlet* or *Measure for Measure* have filled one with admiration— until one rereads *Hamlet* or *Measure for Measure*. The entire process of analysis of meaning from previous experience of a play and a return with a fusing imaginative energy for deeper penetration into that meaning is in John Keats's sonnet, "On Sitting Down to Read *King Lear* Once Again":

> . . . *once again the fierce dispute,*
> *Betwixt damnation and impassion'd clay,*
> *Must I burn through; once more humbly assay*
> *The bitter sweet of this Shakespearean fruit.*

Perhaps the most common misconception today about the meaning of plays, and the most difficult from which to free the mind because it is derived from the social milieu into which we were born, is that of looking for a thesis. If our grandparents were overly prone to look for a moral message, we are equally inclined to seek a social message. The development of modern drama was deeply rooted in the rising social consciousness of the later nineteenth century, the reformatory impulse toward the evils of society in place of the sins of the individual. Marxist influence accelerated and gave more specific direction to the tendency, and the depression of the thirties in this country led to the drama of economic criticism and revolt, the proletarian drama, as the strongest dynamism in our theater of that period. The thesis play is only one kind of drama, and one of the more limited and more likely to be ephemeral kinds. In such a play the central significance may be in the thesis: Ibsen's *A Doll's House,* the responsibility of individual self-realization for women in marriage; John Wexley's *They Shall Not Die,* equality of treatment before the law of Negroes and whites, with a sub-thesis that communism is the way to get it; Clifford Odets' *Golden Boy,* the competitive economic system of our society warps the lives of individuals and drives them to spiritual death. Even in this area one must be wary not to oversimplify and miss larger or deeper meaning than the overt thesis. In *A Doll's House* Nora's awakening to and demand for self-realization is embedded in and justified by another aspect of Ibsen's thought, a concept of moral beauty which was present in Nora and absent in Helmer, her capacity for love in contrast to his egoism; and responsiveness of the audience to Nora and the appeal of the play depends precisely on that. The association of the thesis of *They Shall Not Die* with communism is not permanently integral to the meaning of the play; the identification with a passion for social justice and a capacity for indignation are, and give larger meaning to the play. Harold Clurman, one of the representatives as a director and critic of the social movement of the thirties in drama, in his several fine introductions to plays by Odets notes more than once with regret and as a mark of immaturity that the revolutionary intent is somewhat peripheral and generalized. Yet Clurman also noted that it was Odets as the playwright of the middle class with a deep identification with and love for his background, not his theses, which a few years ago made his plays of the thirties seem somewhat dated, that makes them come freshly alive today with warmth, vitality, and truth.

Strindberg's *The Father* has the earmark of a thesis play on the destructiveness of women to man in the relationship of marriage, the generalizations beyond the particular characters and story of the play—"love between the sexes is conflict"; "That is what makes it dangerous, this very unconsciousness of their [women's] instinctive dishonesty"; and so on. Except to misogynists, however, the play has lived as a great drama in spite of its thesis. The marriage in *The Father* is an institution within the play, not in the world, and the Captain and Laura are imprisoned within it. Strindberg transmuted the self-torture of his private obsessions into universalities of agony and torment, like Dante's pictures of the damned. Strindberg's thesis is, of course, still there, a part of the total meaning of the play, but insofar as in its integration with the play it leads to distortion rather than intensification of life, it is a limitation when one comes to evaluate the play.

We are led now to the question: are authors' own statements of the meaning of their plays finally determinative? Not always, even when appearing as a thesis statement within a play. Ralph's rousing speech of confidence in and challenge to the future at the end of Odets' *Awake and Sing* seems superimposed, and was. He added it to the play with other revisions as he came under the influences of revolutionary social program in the Group Theatre. The play of a poor Bronx family during the depression was originally entitled *I Got the Blues,* and the meaning as a convincing effect of the play as a whole remained tied to the earlier version even when the author's conscious intention altered.

Some playwrights have been excellent interpretive critics, of their own plays as well as of others, but what a playwright says of his play is subject to the same test of validity as what anyone else says of it: how does his interpretation bear up under reexperience and reexamination of the play. In an essay in the New York *Times* during the publicity period for the production of *The Rose Tattoo,* which he included as an introduction to publication of the play shortly afterwards, Tennessee Williams wrote: "The great and only possible dignity of man lies in his power deliberately to choose certain moral values by which to live as steadfastly as if he, too, like a character in a play, were immured against the corrupting rush of time," and "plays in the tragic tradition offer us a view of certain moral values in violent juxtaposition." The implication certainly was that the essay related in some way to what he had intended to write or thought he had written in *The Rose Tattoo,* perhaps something he wanted to write, but no choice of moral values is visible in the play, only instinctual action, and the play does not remotely suggest tragedy. The essay has its own intrinsic value, but it is not illuminating to the meaning of *The Rose Tattoo.*

Eugene O'Neill frequently made explicit statements of intentions for his plays in letters or for the press at the time of writing. The intention was not always perfectly realized, notably in *The Hairy Ape* because the play left to itself is one of O'Neill's more powerful and effective accomplishments. *The Hairy Ape* tells the story of Yank, a stoker on an ocean liner, who glories in "belonging" to the world of coal and steel, power and speed, which makes everything else go, until an interaction with the world outside the stokehole causes him to lose his sense of belonging and go beserk in an attempt to find a new identification. After successive rejections by society he ends up in a zoo at night in front of a gorilla's cage, tries to shake hands with the gorilla and is crushed to death. O'Neill explained in an often quoted statement for the press that he regarded the play as a "symbol of man, who has lost his old harmony with nature, the harmony which he used to have as an animal and has not yet acquired in a spiritual way . . . Yank can't go forward, and so he tries to go back. This is what his shaking hands with the gorilla meant. But he can't go back to 'belonging' either. The gorilla kills him. The subject here is the ancient one that always was and always will be the one subject for drama, and that is man and his struggle with his own fate. The struggle used to be with the gods, but is now with himself, his own past, his attempt to 'belong.' " *

Here there is no question about the unity and clarity of the playwright's intention, but there is a question whether he succeeded in writing the play he intended. As the play progresses from the opening realism of the scenes in the firemen's forecastle and the stokehole into expressionistic abstraction, Yank clearly becomes a symbol, but it is doubtful that the play in itself without the author's explanation provides for recognition of Yank as the symbol Man in his relation to nature. It does lead readily to seeing Yank as a symbol of the Worker or Proletariat in modern industrial society, and can be highly meaningful on those terms. As a play of the Worker, however, the final scene with the gorilla is left dangling as to its part in the meaning of the whole, while its significance is precise in relation to the author's intended theme. O'Neill knew the world of the forecastle and stokehole and created it with power and fundamental truth through his lyricism and abstraction, but he was always more interested dramatically in the ultimate problems of man and his fate than in the problems of society. Here we have a nicely suspended question of meaning: is the meaning of the play that which is consciously intended by the author but not communicated by the play itself? Or is it that of his unconscious creation, imperfectly realized because confused by the avowed intention? One may say the play is what it is and is to be experienced only as self-determined, but in this instance a fresh and valid reexperience of the play proves possible in the light of O'Neill's statement. In general one finds, as here, that when there is a disparity between an author's candid statement of intention at the time of writing and the play as directly experienced, the play is imperfect, although it may be of high value.

* New York *Herald Tribune,* Nov. 16, 1924.

What an author may say subsequent to the time of writing has no such authority as an immediate statement. Once a play has been written, the author's thoughts and intentions while creating become a memory and subject to memory's changes, and possibly to adjustment to the experiences and thoughts moving the author at the later time. Gorki in "The Unfinished Letter" on the occasion of Tolstoi's final illness and death which he wrote in 1910 indirectly included an analysis of the character of Luka in *The Lower Depths:*

> All Russian preachers, with the exception of Avvakum and perhaps Tikhou Zudonsky, are cold men, for they did not possess an active and living faith. When I was writing Luka in *The Lower Depths,* I wanted to describe an old man like that: he is interested in "every solution" but not in people; coming inevitably in contact with them, he consoles them, but only in order that they may leave him in peace. And all the philosophy, all the preaching of such men is alms bestowed by them with a veiled aversion, and there sounds behind their preaching words which are beggarly and melancholy: "Get out! Love God or your neighbor, but get out! Curse God, love the stranger, but leave me alone! Leave me alone, for I am a man and I am doomed to death." *

He had written the play eight years before when it was immediately produced by the Moscow Art Theatre. The actor Kochilov described an incident during Gorki's reading of the play for the company. He read beautifully, wrote Kochilov, and continued:

> When he began to read the scene in which Luka consoles Anna on her death-bed, we held our breaths, and a wonderful stillness reigned. Gorki's voice trembled and broke. He stopped, remained silent a moment, wiped a tear with his finger, and tried to resume his reading, but after the first few words he stopped again and wept almost aloud, wiping his tears with his handkerchief. "Ugh, devil," he mumbled in embarassment through his tears, "Well-written, by God, well done." †

* *Reminiscences of Maxim Gorki,* Dover Publications, New York, 1946, p. 35.
† Quoted by Alexander Kaun, *Maxim Gorki and His Russia,* Jonathan Cape, London, 1932, p. 378.

Gorki's recollection of his intention in the creation of Luka was clearly a radical alteration of his sense of the character in 1902.

The occasion, who is addressed, and extraneous circumstances are affecting conditions. Chekhov's many letters on his plays in connection with their production by the Moscow Art Theatre reflect considerable inconsistency and include statements difficult to reconcile with experience of the plays. Without extensive and detailed study of the surrounding factors Chekhov's letters can as readily be misleading or confusing as illuminating for the meaning of his plays. He wrote differently on the same topic and occasion to different people; he wrote at times in a state of irritability arising from the severe and declining condition of his health, his consequent enforced absence from Moscow and separation from production and from his wife, an actress of the company; and, in addition, the extreme interpretive approach of the directors of the Moscow Art Theatre to his plays as revealing the melancholy soul of Russia led Chekhov to exaggerated and at times exclusive emphasis on the comedy of his plays.

Some playwrights sometimes, under today's journalistic and publicity pressures, write outside the discipline of their function of creating plays, like an old-fashioned clock with the pendulum removed, racing noisily back and forth to no useful end. With all the limitations and dangers lying in acceptance of authors' pronouncements at face value and out of context, they are frequently important as well as interesting accessory documentation for the meaning of a play, subject always to the fact that the play itself is the only document of final authority.

The play as a literary form offers one special problem to determination of meaning, the fact of dramatic dialogue as the basic mode of expression and communication. Must the speeches be taken entirely as responses of objectively created characters in dramatic situations, or can they ever be assumed as expression of personally held thoughts and attitudes of the author delivered through his characters? There is no single or simple answer. The extreme view that no speech has meaning except as part of the dramatically created character, that a playwright reveals himself only through the total organization of the play, the functioning of the characters within an action, is logical as a theory of playwriting, but it does not correspond to the facts of the human activity, as anyone who has been much around playwrights knows. The absolute theorists, however, do point a right direction to the degree that every speech should be carefully considered in its dramatic context of speaker and situation. Playwrights are people of verbal power and they give to characters whom they condemn by the total organization of the play ideas which they condemn in speeches of such striking and memorable phrasing that sometimes the author and his play come to be identified with the ideas they repudiate. If *The Way of the World* has been misunderstood, it is in part because Congreve gave such felicity of expression to his witwouds, second only to that of his truewits, as to create a subtlety of distinction easily overlooked by readers prepossessed by the reputation for immorality and cynicism of the preceding Restoration stage. As Louis Kronenberger remarked, Witwoud is "a good kind of second-rater, really, whom we must almost admire till we see him come up against someone better." *

On the other hand, there have been dramatic modes which included the device of a formally recognized spokesman of the author's sentiments, as the *raisonneur* of the latter nineteenth-century French plays of Dumas *fils* and Augier. Less formally, in the sentimental drama of the eighteenth century in England and its successors in the United States in the nineteenth century, with the popularity of the delivery of good sentiments and the clear demarcation of heroes and villains, good and bad people, speeches could be unquestionably identified with the author as well as with the dramatic character. Good modern dramatists often create characters as their spokesman, but in subtle rather than obvious ways. Trofimov in *The Cherry Orchard* in his speeches on the backward state of Russia and its need and hope for the future is clearly a spokesman for Chekhov's ideas, yet when he concludes the longest and most serious speech in the play with "I'm afraid of serious conversation. We should do better to be silent," Chekhov just as clearly is holding him up to ridicule. Every word Trofimov has said about the need for more work and less of theories and talk expresses Chekhov's thought, but Trofimov talks and despises Lopakhin, who is practical and inarticulate and works, and as a character represents Chekhov's ideas for the future of Russia although it is the satirized intellectual Trofimov who verbalizes them. Shaw, who wrote comedies in part for the effectiveness

* *The Thread of Laughter*, p. 143.

of the theater as a forum for his ideas, used his characters as his spokesmen in complex ways: he might divide his ideas between antagonists each of whom represented something he criticized and something he approved; or he might explode an idea like a bomb in the midst of a group of characters and develop it by the variety of responses.

Plays are often enigmatic in their relation between the attitudes of characters and the intention for the play as a whole. John Osborne was promptly identified with the violent speeches of Jimmy Porter in his play, *Look Back in Anger,* and labeled one of the "angry young men" of England but the identification is disputable and his attitude toward Jimmy and his intention in the play open to question. It may be that he was fascinated by Jimmy as Shakespeare by Richard III or Falstaff, or Dickens by Mr. Pecksniff or Mrs. Gamp, and that he reveled in creation of the opprobriousness of characteristic speech for him as Shakespeare and Dickens certainly did for their characters, all without self-identification. He may quite possibly have created Jimmy Porter out of critical observation. What is the relation between Sebastian Venable's "Well, now I've seen Him!"—God—in the spectacle through the blazing equatorial day of the sky filled with black carnivorous birds hovering, swooping down, and devouring the just-hatched sea-turtles in their race for the sea, to the thought and feeling of Tennessee Williams in his play *Suddenly Last Summer*? The play is an unmasking of Sebastian, but it is also an unmasking of life. It is Sebastian's mother, Mrs. Venable, who justifies his perception and the young doctor, who represents a detached point of view through the play such as might be the author's, who protests it. Yet the doctor's closing speech for the play can be understood as recognition of the possibility that the truth of life is as horrible as Sebastian's perception of God.

The greatest enigmas are the plays of Shakespeare because he could express all thoughts with the verbal felicity of proverbs, yet within the sense of characterization of the speaker and of the situation. Hamlet's speech on drunkenness and his advice to the players are not only in character but each is a bright small piece in the mosaic of the total characterization; yet almost without doubt we feel each of these speeches also as an expression of views held personally by Shakespeare. But what of Hamlet's speech to Rosencrantz and Guildenstern of the glory of the universe, reduced to "why, it appears no other thing to me than a foul and pestilent congregation of vapors," and the wonder of men to "And yet, to me, what is this quintessence of dust?" Did the ecstasy before life express Shakespeare's feeling and the disillusion belong only to the dramatic character? Did the ecstasy which he has lost and the disillusion both belong only to Hamlet? Or did lost ecstasy and disillusion together express Shakespeare's feeling in writing *Hamlet*? As I experience and analyze the play, disillusion is presented by Shakespeare as the destroying evil over which Hamlet triumphed in his dying moments, but many critics have found in *Hamlet* expression of a state of disillusion in Shakespeare. In *King Lear* the Duke of Gloucester's exclamation, "As flies to wanton boys are we to the gods. They kill us for their sport," when blinded and cast out from his castle he is wandering in despair seeking his own death, has been treated by some critics as the key speech to the mood in which Shakespeare wrote the play. The outcome of the play in the death of Cordelia by the accident of a message arriving just too late with the irony, then, of Lear's death by heartbreak at the point of restoration of daughter, kingdom, and the beginning of mental health, certainly has a harmony with the view of life expressed by Gloucester. On the other hand, in the context of Gloucester's speech there is developed a rejection of despair as contrary to the divine relation to man, and to many *King Lear* is the greatest of tragedies because in its total effect it achieves catharsis and transcendence of despair over such enormity and bitterness of evil and suffering. Shakespeare's plays were in the most impersonal dramatic mode, without thesis, without *raisonneur* or corresponding formal character, and without obvious informal spokesmen, to the highest degree written completely within the structure of dramatically conceived characters. It is nevertheless possible at times to detect with assurance the voice of Shakespeare the man. In *King Lear* the attribution to Lear and to Gloucester alike, each in the extremity of his suffering, of the thought that those with superfluity should give heed to the poor and wretched and distribute out of abundance to their need can hardly be explained except as reflecting a thought prominent in Shakespeare's mind when writing the play. The positive and social character of the thought bears against identification of the meaning of the play with a world ruled by the careless cruelty of caprice. More often ascription of speeches in Shakespeare's plays to expression of his personal thought or feeling is intangible. One of the most famous speeches and one most frequently referred to Shakespeare's personal philosophy is that of Prospero in *The Tempest* on the evanescence of life which concludes, "We are such stuff/As dreams are made on, and our little life/Is rounded with a sleep." It is written with authoritative truth to the character and mood of the speaker, an old man whose work is about to be finished, looking toward the end of his days. There is no reason to associate the speech with Shakespeare's personal feeling about life except that there is such heart in it, and that may be dramatic illusion. The organization of the play bespeaks the cycle of life; it ends on the passing of one generation and the continuance of life in youth.

The complications and uncertainties involved may begin to make the meaning of a play seem like a will-o'-the-wisp. The question arises, is there a meaning of a play, or many meanings? Close to the fallacy of the first impression as the final and total truth of a play is that of meaning as entirely relative, that there is no single right interpretation or understanding of a play, but a different meaning for each member of an audience. People say, isn't interpretation a matter of opinion, each person's opinion right for himself? Certainly there is not one exact set of words, like a scientific formula, for the statement of the meaning of a play. Interpretive criticism is the art of writing illuminatingly of literature. Nor has there ever been, perhaps, of any significant work of literature a formulation of meaning that is complete and final, leaving no room for a fresh perception. Nevertheless, a play exists, it is there; it is something in itself of tangibility and substance, not the iridescent surface of a soap bubble. Whatever the peripheral variations, there is a center toward which to work in our understanding of a play. The experience any person can gain from a play is within the limits of his apperceptive background from previous experience of drama and of life. As no one embraces within himself all experience, theoretically anyone's understanding of a play may always be an approximation. The meaning of a play is neither an absolute nor a matter of anarchic relativity. The play does not change and its meaning is not reduced by the incapacity or passivity of the member of the audience who has least that is relevant to bring to it. To contend for equality of opinion is simply wrong-headedness or a self-defense for indifference or laziness. One may gain an awakening to a play from another person's interpretive response, but of first importance is to activate one's own perceptions. What should be sought in plays is not affirmation of previous experience, but new awareness, expansion, growth.

It is not that the meaning of a play is relative, but that apprehension of the meaning may be incomplete without being wrong as far as it goes. If the play is rich there may be any number of different right responses, those not mutually exclusive or contradictory, each catching the light from a facet of the total meaning, each representing the capacity of the person experiencing the play. Just as truly, there may be misinterpretation, and there is also the ultimate complete perception. Again, in the plays of greatest richness and scope complete identification of any other mind with that of the dramatist in his creation may be a point in infinity to which closer approximation is indefinitely possible. That is finally the challenge and the pleasure of the great plays, the pull they make upon us for growth, and the reward they hold out not only through study but through the passage of years and ripening in experience.

For analysis and understanding of a play there are several converging routes to that center which is the point of fusion of all the elements into clarified reexperience of the play as a whole. By the nature of drama, the first analysis to be made is that of the structure, the foundational organization of the play in its individual development of the form that makes it a play. Second is the temper of the play, a unifying, pervasive, and distinguishing quality, less tangible than structure, just as real, sometimes as significant for meaning. The temper of a play resides especially in the quality of the language, imagery, and recurrent sentiments or attitudes, but it has no bounds; the sense of the temper of a play may arise from something in the nature of the plot, the structure, the kind of characters the author chooses to write about or the manner of characterization. Third is the dramatic climate of the play, possible effects on the creation of the play of conjunction with one of the traditional modes of function, such as that of tragedy, of satire, or more recently, of social drama; or of writing within the influence of one of the modern movements of drama such as naturalism, expressionism, symbolism, or theatricalism. Finally, one considers individual speeches, overt expressions of attitude or idea, but always in relation to the total scheme of the play. All the elements of the play, of course, interact. Practically, I am impressed with the difficulty of visualizing such a pattern, but abstractly, all the roads to meaning intertwine as they converge to a center.

Before leaving the subject of meaning, there is one large area of study which should be pointed out and recognized as introducing a true element of relativity, that of social background. A play written in an earlier period, as an Elizabethan or a Restoration play, inevitably had shades of meaning for its author and audience which escape us today. The whole complex of contemporary events and institutions, the state of knowledge, ways of thinking, and the meaning of words of the earlier period make it so. I remember Professor Edwin Greenlaw's remarking some thirty-odd years ago that the most pressing problem, at that time, of literary scholarship was recreation of the mind of the Renaissance. There is no limit to the degree of penetration into and identification with an earlier period which may be achieved by absorption in its documentation and delivering one's mind to the engagement, but it is still an approximation; a twentieth-century man cannot become a Renaissance man. Furthermore, there is no precise distance at which the past becomes the modern world; even in contemporary plays the different social background of a foreign country may introduce the same problem, and in one's own country remoteness of the social background of the author and the subject matter of his play from one's own experience is possible. The entire problem becomes one of degree, and whether it is a play by one of Shakespeare's fellow dramatists, a modern French play, or a play of the Bronx or of New Orleans, the responsibility is to reach as far as one's resources permit into the author's perception of the society reflected there.

The question of relativity that arises for the play of an earlier period is: may not the perspective of advances in knowledge and changes in attitude of a later time reveal new and valid meaning beyond that of the author's consciousness? For example, may not the character of Hamlet be better understood in the light of modern psychology than by the Elizabethan psychology of Shakespeare's knowledge? It is quite true that the meaning of the character and the play today and for Shakespeare's audience cannot be entirely the same. It is also true that for the greatest plays, such as *Hamlet,* there is no fundamental difference. What makes the great plays live beyond their time is the power of the dramatist, in some way, to transcend his immediate temporal audience. Modern psychology did not create the human experiences which it labels. It assists our communication concerning *Hamlet* to use terms Shakespeare did not know, but that does not mean we are reading into the play experiences for Hamlet of which Shakespeare was unaware. Similarly, how much fundamental difference does the modern democratic consciousness make to the meaning of *King Lear?* Shakespeare, for all his background of the divinity of kings, quickly reduced and exalted the king to a symbol of humanity.

The meaning of a play, properly understood, is not a simple matter of statement of a subject, theme, or thesis. It is complex because it belongs to the whole of the play and a play is a complex organization. Meaning, however, is not something esoteric or mysterious. Playwrights sometimes go airy or arty before the question of meaning: the play has no meaning, it simply is, it exists. And some modern critical theory would limit discussion of meaning for any work of literature to its techniques, reducing criticism to a field for specialists and a technical terminology. A play, however, is a communication. In action, it is something experienced by an audience; the experience can be analyzed, described, defined, and that is the meaning of the play.

7

Through Structure to Meaning

Nothing more assuredly establishes plot structure as the foundation of drama than the attempts of playwrights of highly original talent to deny it. Eugene Ionesco has written: "I detest the reasoning play, constructed like a syllogism, of which the last scenes constitute the logical conclusion of the introductory scenes, considered as premises." * Never has a play moved with more relentless syllogistic logic from scene to scene to its resolution than his play *The Chairs* which was something of a sensation at the Phoenix Theatre in New York in the 1957-58 season. Ionesco says that he is trying to create a primitive theater, to restore theater to itself and to free it from the tyranny of literature and of messages: "How, and why, translate into logical language a content that should be expressed only in images, in scenic events, antagonisms, dialogues, silence itself used as dialogue; a content that is only that image, that event, that absence or that presence, that form." He breaks down the coherence of language in the course of the play, and that fact itself becomes a part of the coherence of the plot.

The play opens on an old man and an old woman in a room empty except for two chairs down-stage, a symmetrical room with a double door at center rear, a window either side opening black on the sea, other windows and doors down either side of the stage. They are

* Essays by Eugene Ionesco," *Theatre Arts,* June, 1958.

waiting in great tension for the arrival of guests; everyone has been invited to hear his "message for all mankind," his philosophy for the Universe, before he dies. He has engaged an Orator to speak for him. The guests begin to arrive but are invisible to the audience. The old couple greet the unseen presences, bring chairs, seat them in pantomime. This goes on acceleratively until there is no time for words: the bell is ringing, the doors opening and closing ceaselessly, the old couple rushing about overwhelmed with chairs. Ionesco writes in a stage direction, "The movement on the stage has reached a climax." The action subsides, the stage is filled with empty chairs. The Orator, a visible presence, arrives. All is ready for the momentous delivery. The old man and the old woman, after a century together, "after long years of labor in the cause of human progress," resolve to die together in their moment of glory, to become legendary, and leave the scene to the Orator and the message. They leap simultaneously from the two windows at the rear. The Orator tries to address the invisible crowd: ". . . he uses sign language; desperate efforts to make himself understood; then from his throat come moans and groans and the sort of guttural sounds made by deaf mutes." Hopelessly, he goes out: "the stage is empty, with the chairs. . . . The door at the back is wide open, gaping black."

In the opening scene of dialogue between the old couple all coherencies are broken down and fragmented, of language, of the course of their personal lives and relationship, of history, precise premises for the total withdrawal of the hope of coherently communicable meaning to life in the resolution of the play. The story of the play is a struggle for communication of spirit to spirit. From the crisis, or major turning point of the play, when the anticipation of eagerly listening people turns into a climax of physical activity, the old couple overwhelmed with chairs, things, matter, the struggle is doomed to defeat. The continuing address of the old man and old woman as to human presences becomes wholly an irony and increasingly incoherent and empty. The play is resolved in the climactic impasse of the Orator revealed as deaf and dumb, and the scene is left to the chairs.

The practice of Ionesco is an affirmation of Aristotle's dictum in the *Poetics* over twenty-two hundred years ago: "The Plot . . . is the first principle, and, as it were, the soul of the tragedy." Aristotle also stated that a good drama depended on proper development of Character, Thought, and Diction, but without the plot there could be no drama at all. Consequently: ". . . most important of all is the structure of the incidents. For Tragedy is an imitation, not of men, but of an action and of life."

Actually it is not the basic structure of drama which has been protested by a whole line of more and less revolutionary dramatists, but worn-out or mechanical applications of that structure inadequate to new meanings. As one studies Ionesco's essays in detail in conjunction with his plays, one finds that he does not deny causal sequence, but against a causal sequence of events as drawn from the externalities of life he affirms a causal sequence originating entirely in projection of the meaning of the play: ". . . the cohesion that gives a structure to emotions in their pure state corresponds to an inner necessity, and not to a logic of construction imposed from the outside; there is no subjection to a predetermined action, but exteriorization of a psychic dynamism, projection upon the stage of internal conflicts, of the inner universe." The incoherencies of the opening dialogue, the image of the rising tide of chairs overwhelming two human beings, the deaf and dumb Orator, with all the connecting details, each in themselves make no sense outside the play. As a play they are a logical sequence, a structure of meaning.

Eugene O'Neill was a playwright who from the beginning opened up new paths from the theater of his time. When queried by his friend George Jean Nathan whether the experience in the theater with his father's company had been of value to him as a playwright, he answered that he supposed it was a help to know what one was trying to depart from. O'Neill appeared for a time to some critics to be shattering the norms of dramatic structure. In the year that he spent in the playwriting course known as the "47 workshop" at Harvard, George Pierce Baker encouraged him to go on writing but told him that *Bound East for Cardiff* was not a play. *Bound East for Cardiff* has now been studied in many introductory courses in playwriting for illustrative analysis of basic structure. O'Neill himself never confused basic structure with its particular modes of development; the Greek tragedies had entered too deeply into his consciousness for that. He was constantly seeking new ways of applying structure to the endeavor, as he said, to get beneath the banality of surface.

The basic structure of drama has developed out of the simple fact that the first business of any play at any level is to get and hold with final satisfaction the attention of an audience in a theater. People respond to a story, not to any story in the sense of a simple chronological sequence of events, but to a story of a conflict with its generation of suspense and tension as to outcome. For the purpose of a play a unified conflict within the compass of the play is necessary. If the attention of the audience is to be arrested and drawn forward, not thrown back, the conflict will not be under way when the play opens; rather, the play will open on a situation in which the audience is led to see the potentiality of conflict. Then something happens which precipitates the potential conflict, sets it in motion. The course of the conflict follows as a unified sequence, one situation giving rise to the next, until the conflict is resolved, the tension and suspense satisfied by answer to the question of outcome. Thus we have Aristotle's beginning, middle, and end. At the simplest level of drama, that is, melodrama, the only concern is the attention of the audience, creating and sustaining suspense for the outcome of events to a resolution. When we move into the more complex levels of drama of communication of the mind or inner experience of the author, or revelation of life, suspense and tension expand from focus on the events to the meaning of the events in their nature and sequence, or the effect of events on the characters, and their responses. Tension acquires revelatory function. Under tension surfaces break and what is beneath is exposed. Under the tensions of the situations in which they are involved in the play the characters are revealed. Especially, in dramatic conflict the characters are confronted by situations of choice, and what a man chooses or avoids, as Aristotle notes, is the basis of revelation of character. As plot grows out of interaction of character and situation the question of outcome, the suspense, for the audience can become focused not on the event or what will happen to a character, but on what the character will do in the situation that has arisen. Just as powerfully, the inner consciousness of the audience is opened and exposed to itself in response to the tension of the play.

In order to talk conveniently about the structure of drama it is necessary to adopt some terminology. A play opens on a situation of unstable equilibrium. We recognize, more or less definitely, that the status quo of someone on the stage, the principal character or protagonist, is vulnerable. Then some new element enters, something happens, which precipitates a conflict. The protagonist is confronted by a choice: either some desired end seems to become available against obstacles, or something undesirable will happen to him except as he opposes it. If he does not choose to fight, there is, of course, no play. Assuming that the character undertakes the conflict, he must exercise his will and faculties against an opposing force to avert disaster or gain a desire. From now on a dramatic movement is inescapable. The question of outcome for the play as a whole, the answer to which will end the play, has been opened. This question is most commonly termed the *major dramatic question.*

The point of inception of the conflict has been designated in various ways: initiation of the conflict, precipitation of the conflict, projection of the question, inciting moment, and attack. Attack is the most generally recognized and the most inclusive and convenient. The *attack,* then, is the point of precipitation of the conflict and projection of the major dramatic question. It is the point at which an inescapable action becomes evident to the audience, and a question of outcome demanding an answer is created in their minds. It should be noted that, while the playwright knows where he is going from the start, the audience does not. Consequently, while the person experiencing the play for the first time will feel the grip of conflict and a significant question of outcome at the attack, he does not necessarily realize at that moment that it is the *major* dramatic question, the over-all question of the play. There may be introductory *minor* dramatic questions leading up to the attack. Also, as the play advances the major dramatic question may undergo development, a rise to a higher level of intensity or of more significance to the character, so that the member of the audience sometimes may even not be situated to formulate by analysis precisely what is the major dramatic question on which the author has constructed his play until he has experienced the final outcome, the resolution.

The *resolution* of a play has now been frequently referred to: it is the best general term for the point at which the major dramatic

question, either in its initial or a developed form, is answered, satisfying the tension of the audience. "Catastrophe" and "denouement"
are sometimes used in the general sense, but the one is so widely
applied specifically to tragedy and the other to comedy that it is
better to keep them so and to use *resolution* as the general term.

There is a third principal point of basic structure, the *crisis,*
which is fully as significant as the attack and resolution for opening
the way to meaning. The plot of a play from attack to resolution
progresses by successive *complications*. A complication is any new
element that enters the situation after the story starts and affects
the way the conflict will go. New element does not mean extraneous.
The conflict itself either determines what is a complication or generates the complication. In the former case the element is there and
revealed as relevant by the conflict as a touchstone. In the latter, as
plot grows out of the conjunction of character and situation, what
a character does in response to one situation creates a new situation
which in turn becomes a complication. Each complication is a
dramatic unit around what is called in relation to the play as a whole
a *minor dramatic question* with its attack, tension, and resolution.
The entire course of an effective play from attack to resolution is a
climactic movement, rising in tension to the culmination of the
resolution. The rise is not a smooth rise but a rhythmic advance by
the series of climaxes of the successive complications, each gathering
momentum from and rising higher than the preceding, and together
constituting the over-all climactic movement of the play. Mechanically this structure corresponds to the necessities of audience attention, which would break under a continuous line of tension but can
be carried forward by the rise and fall of a succession of minor
climaxes, and which similarly would weaken if the over-all movement were not climactic, each complication carrying the play higher
in tension than the preceding. However, the same principles work
inwardly and this is the structure for generating the highest degree
of revealing tension within the play.

The background has now been laid for understanding the nature
and significance of the *crisis* of a play. Characteristically somewhere
past the middle of the play there is a complication with a stronger
impact and which generates a higher individual peak than any other
of the complications. It sharply steps-up the tension of the play,

lifting it to a higher level of significance from which it makes its continuing rise to the resolution. This is the crucial complication, the situation that results from it, the *crisis,* the major turning point in the development of the plot. Again, this structure is a mechanical practicality. I once heard a very experienced playwright-producer tell a group of young playwrights the crisis was that extra punch you gave the play along about the end of the second act when the seats were beginning to get hard to the audience after an hour or more, and that jolted them and carried them on to the curtain. He also told them that how to build to a crisis was one of the most important things for a young playwright to learn. I should add that his view of dramatic structure was not so narrowly limited, but at the moment he was trying to impress the practicalities, the craftsmanship, of play construction.

In terms of a play as an organic structure of revealing tension the crisis is a development of the conflict inherent from the beginning but unforeseen by the protagonist at the time of making his choice of engaging in the conflict precipitated by the attack. The crisis reveals the conflict to the protagonist as having an unforeseen direction of more serious or ultimate significance. In other words, he is reconfronted by the problem of choice in more difficult terms. To return to *The Chairs,* confronted by the crisis of the proliferation of chairs, the old man takes up again his delusion of the possibility of communication, by which he is doomed to defeat, an ironic defeat since he and the old woman in their suicide-leap escape facing it, awareness left only to the audience. To illustrate further from among the most familiar of plays of radically removed types: In Goldsmith's farce-comedy *She Stoops to Conquer* Charles Marlow, a young gentleman of excessive shyness in the presence of women of repute although at his ease with wenches, is sent by his father to the home of his old friend Mr. Hardcastle in the country in the hope that the visit may culminate in a marriage between his son and Mr. Hardcastle's daughter. Marlow is led to mistake the house of Mr. Hardcastle for an inn, his host for the innkeeper, and his daughter for the barmaid, and conducts himself accordingly. His discovery of his error is the crisis. In Sophocles' tragedy, King Oedipus has been informed by an oracle that only removal from Theban soil of the man who has killed his father and married his mother will lift the plague from Thebes. Oedipus undertakes to find and banish that man and pursues the quest against all opposition. His discovery that he himself is the man, having performed the acts unwittingly, is the crisis.

The crisis as an element in dramatic structure has unfortunately been frequently termed the climax, which is thoroughly misleading, suggesting a rising tension to that point and a falling off to the resolution. If the association has been acquired, it is important to rid one's mind of it. The entire play is a climactic movement, with the resolution the climax of the play, and the crisis an intensification of the movement from there on to the resolution. The major dramatic question as perceived by the audience often undergoes a change at the crisis to a form of more ultimate significance than at the attack; for example, the focus of interest often shifts from a question of external plot to a more inward question of character reaction. It should be noted that every play does not have a crisis and sometimes the crucial complication immediately precedes the resolving complication. Such forms are of rare occurrence, but if such a play is soundly conceived its unusual structure has significance for meaning.

The attack, crisis, and resolution have been referred to thus far as points in the structure of a play, and they are in a diagrammatic sense, but in the written play, while any one of these developments may be accomplished sharply in a single speech or a line, more often some space is required for the projection of an attack, crisis, or resolution.

The aspects of dramatic structure presented here are introductory, a necessary introduction because they constitute the foundation of dramatic form. Drama has developed in different times and places, under differences in physical staging, theatrical conventions, and social background, such differences in dramatic movements and modes, and such differences in the individual temperament of dramatists, as to represent in its total history infinite variety in the details of form and the manner of application of the basic structure to meaning. The process continues, as we have examined in the work of a contemporary *avant-garde* playwright, Eugene Ionesco. But wherever there is drama, however the over-all effects may differ, one finds at the core the conflict, the question, the attack, the complications, usually a crisis, and the resolution. The starting point in the search for the meaning of a play is a scrutiny for these basic elements of its structure. From that starting point one goes on into analysis of the distinguishing ways in which the basic elements are developed, their significance in detail, and the refinements of form in integration with idea.

To make what has been said of basic structure immediately more concrete, Ibsen's *A Doll's House* will be summarized with analysis of the principal points of structure and their relation to meaning. The play is useful for a first analysis because it is widely familiar, rather simple and clear in its outline, and in terms of what one is accustomed to today in drama, conventional in form, although when written it represented a radical departure in some ways from the surrounding theater.*

The play opens upon a situation of potential drama. Nora and Torvald Helmer have been happily married for a number of years. They have three small children. It is the day before Christmas and the future looks especially bright: Torvald has received an appointment as manager of the bank which will mean much more financial freedom than they have known before. Underneath this situation Nora's fate is revealed as delicately poised, in a state of unstable equilibrium. She is maintaining a secret from her husband, revelation of which would be disruptive, she believes, to the happiness of their relationship. Early in their marriage Torvald became seriously ill and his life was endangered if he could not have a change of climate for which they did not have the money. It was important that he should not realize how ill he was, he had a rigid principle against borrowing, and Nora led him to believe she received a gift from her father for a trip to Italy for her own pleasure. Actually, Nora borrowed the money from a Nils Krogstad on the condition of her father's signature as surety for the note. Her father was seriously ill and died just before the note reached him by mail for his signature.

* With the permission of the publishers, Funk and Wagnalls, I have drawn on the chapters "What a Play Is" and "Building the Play" in my earlier book *Write That Play* (1939) for the presentation of basic structure in this chapter, and on Chapter X for analysis of *A Doll's House*. In *Write That Play* the entire text is printed on the left-hand pages with a detailed analysis of the whole process of construction and technique running on the opposite pages parallel to the text.

Nora forged her father's signature and inadvertently dated her sign-ing on the actual date, three days after her father's death. Nora has maintained concealment from her husband through the subsequent years while paying off the note by saving out of the household allow-ance, spending less than Torvald gave her for new dresses, and earn-ing money by getting copying to do for which she locked herself up till late at night and devised stratagems to account for her time to Torvald. Nora feels great pride in having saved her husband's life, and also in having sustained what she thinks of as a business respon-sibility and in having earned money like a man. At the same time she enjoys and feels nothing wrong in being treated protectively by her husband as an irresponsible child, his "skylark" and "little squir-rel." She confides her secret to an old school friend, Mrs. Linde, whom she has not seen for years, and states the basis of her conceal-ment from her husband: "A man who has such strong opinions about these things! And besides, how painful and humiliating it would be for Torvald, with his manly independence, to know that he owed me anything! It would upset our mutual relationship alto-gether; our beautiful happy home would no longer be what it is now." The fact of the forgery, in her ignorance, weighs not at all on her mind. Nora's happiness in her home, in which she feels secure, is clearly vulnerable.

By a converging set of circumstances Ibsen precipitates the attack. Krogstad holds a subordinate position in the bank of which Helmer has been appointed manager. He ascertains that his position under Helmer is precarious and comes to Nora with a threat. He reveals that he has known all along of her forging of her father's signature by the discrepancy of the date with that of her father's death. He will reveal the forgery to Helmer unless Nora will secure his position in the bank. To Krogstad the forgery is the significant factor. To Nora it is that revelation of her cherished secret of having saved her husband's life—and for Helmer to learn it from Krogstad "in such an ugly, clumsy way"—would be disastrous to the happiness of their relationship. Nora is forced to fight for preservation of her home, and potential drama becomes actual, the attack of the play.

The forgery in itself is material for the simplest sort of drama, perhaps melodrama. In the attack by the character of Krogstad, Ibsen prepares for movements in the direction of a drama of character relation and development. Krogstad is not an ordinary blackmailer. By an indiscretion years before he had acquired a shady reputation and is trying, for the sake of his sons, to rehabilitate himself; the position in the bank was his first step up, and, as he says to Nora, "I am prepared to fight for my small post in the Bank as if I were fighting for my life."

The major dramatic question of the play is, will Nora preserve her happy home; but the question undergoes radical transformation at the crisis. As Nora sees the conflict at the attack, her problem is to prevent revelation to Helmer of her secret because it would make their relationship a less happy one, and because for him to learn of it in such a way violates her sense of beauty in human relationships. Nora's successive efforts to prevent knowledge of her secret from reaching Helmer constitute a series of complications following the attack, rising in intensity as each fails until revelation to Helmer is recognized by Nora as inevitable. Nora has also finally been made aware by Krogstad of the significance of the forgery as a criminal offense. Out of her own love for Helmer and his protective airs towards her she becomes convinced that Helmer will attempt to save her by taking the guilt upon himself. To prevent harm to Helmer at any cost she determines to commit suicide as proof that the guilt was hers. She looks forward, however, with a kind of joy to the "wonderful thing" that is going to happen in which she has implicit faith: the moment when Helmer will learn how great was her love for him and will manifest his corresponding supreme love for her, by saying, let the guilt and the consequences fall upon him, he will affirm that she acted for him by his influence. Then she will slip out to take her own life and save Helmer from his love for her.

The letter from Krogstad is in the mailbox. Helmer brings in the letter and reads it. In a melodrama the revelation of the fact of the forgery would be the crisis. Ibsen was writing a play of a theme of human relationships. The crisis is still to come, a few speeches later. Helmer thinks only of himself, breaks into a tirade of accusation for the disgrace Nora has brought upon him and ruin of his career. This, with Nora's recognition that Helmer's character and relation to her are not as she had believed, is the crisis of the play. Nora is confronted by an entirely different conflict and problem of choice than she had foreseen at the attack of the play, or at the point just preceding the crisis. Her former decision of suicide is no longer a solution; she is under the necessity of a new and final decision. The major dramatic question goes through three phases for the audience: Will revelation of the forgery be averted? What will happen when it is revealed? Finally, what will the effect be on Nora of the revelation of Helmer's character and what will she do about it?

Ibsen clears the movement from crisis to resolution of everything but the theme of human relationship. By a plausible development of a previous connection between Mrs. Linde and Krogstad and of his character, Ibsen has Krogstad influenced by Mrs. Linde to return to Nora the note bearing the forged signature. Almost immediately following the crisis the second letter is delivered by messenger. Nora gives the letter to Helmer to read. Helmer has one last chance to show some thought for Nora, and what follows is his most absolute expression of self-centeredness, "*I* am saved!" Krogstad, Mrs. Linde, and a subsidiary character, Dr. Rank, have all been removed from contact with or effect upon the final scene of the play, Helmer and Nora isolated in clarity of view to work out the problem of their marriage. It was this long concluding scene of *A Doll's House,* a man and woman sitting quietly across the table from each other with their minds meeting in conflict, with no physical activity or other theatrical adjuncts on the stage, that was a radical departure from familiar form in the theater at the time the play was written. The scene is the most tense part of the play.

Helmer tries to go back, to erase all that has happened. Nora faces the illusion on which their lives together have been built. She penetrates past the immediately destroyed illusion of Helmer's character and depth of love for her to the false foundation of their marriage based on the illusion of masculine superiority and a wife treated as a lovable, irresponsible child. This is the first serious conversation as equals they have ever had in eight years of marriage, she observes. She decides to leave Helmer, not because she does not still love him, but because she has experienced an awakening to her own deficiencies of development and the responsibility to arrive at a mature self-understanding. Against Helmer's pleading that they work out their problems together, she recognizes that they would soon be submerged again by the habitual relationship.

This scene is a discussion scene in which Ibsen brings out thematic ideas toward which the play is constructed from the beginning: every person's first responsibility is to self-realization as an individual; a marriage which subordinates the mind and will of one to that of the other is destructive to both. Helmer has been blinded to his own deficiencies and has expanded in his self-centeredness; Nora, around her great virtue of selfless love, has had a mind limited to the little circle of her happy home, herself and the objects of her love, and she depends on small lies and deceptions and the exercise of feminine charms and wiles to get what she wants. In her one assumption and maintenance of mature responsibility, which she has concealed from her husband, is revealed the inner capacity with which she meets her great crisis. The discussion is a dramatic action and not merely an argument because the emotions of the principals are deeply engaged and their fates are at stake; it is a movement toward an outcome in Nora's and Helmer's lives.

When Nora packs her bag and walks out of the house that night the play is resolved; the over-all major dramatic question through its successive phases, will Nora succeed in preserving her happy home, is answered. The question is answered negatively in the terms of the initiation of the conflict, but by the turn at the crisis the defeat has become a positive assertion. Just as the potential for melodrama of the motif of revelation of a forgery was transformed in the crisis into a drama of human relationships, fine shadings of characterization and dramatic and emotional involvement in the resolution transform the simple wife-leaves-husband ending into thematic significance. When Helmer asks for some hope for the future, Nora in her weariness and disillusion, having believed in and waited for the wonderful thing that did not happen, says: "Ah, Torvald, the most wonderful thing of all would have to happen," and in response to Helmer's eager question: "Both you and I would have to be so changed that—Oh, Torvald, I don't believe any longer in wonderful things happening." Helmer is able to reply: "But I will believe in it. Tell me? So changed that—?" Nora answers: "That our life together would be a real wedlock. Good-bye." She goes, and Helmer, out of the first reaction of despair before emptiness and finality, says with "a flash of hope": "The most wonderful thing of all—?" That Helmer should conceive of need of change in himself means that change has already begun. Whether or not the process of change in both ever progresses to "the most wonderful thing of all" and reunion, Helmer as well as Nora has been set on the path of self-realization. Actually, in the discussion scene there is thematic statement only of the wrong that has been done to Nora by the nature of their marriage. That the relationship was destructive to Helmer as well as to Nora is essentially brought out most clearly as a part of the theme by the precise details of the resolution without overt statement anywhere in the play. We move here through structure to meaning. *A Doll's House* is a play with a social thesis, that subordination of women to men in marriage is destructive of character; but it is not a "feminist" play, the thesis grows out of a total philosophy of the responsibility of each individual to self-awareness and realization of fullest capacities, and the resolution of the wife's leaving the husband is not offered as a generalized solution but is particular to the dramatic characterization of the two people involved.*

A Doll's House is a social problem drama with the structure built around a thesis as the center of meaning and pointing directly at the meaning. It will be well to look briefly at some plays representing quite different kinds of drama and meaning to see how the basic structural analysis is just as pertinent. *Life With Father,* by Howard Lindsay and Russell Crouse, for example, is a play of light entertainment which was phenomenally successful with an initial Broadway run of 3,216 performances through eight seasons, and corresponding success on the road, in revivals, and in noncommercial theater production. *Life With Father* is a character comedy. The interest and pleasure is not primarily in the plot situations, as in farce comedy, but in being in the house with Father. It is exciting, living with Clarence Day, Sr., not for what he does but for what he is. His family also is a pleasure, particularly as engaged in interactions with Father, and there is a nostalgic enjoyment of the bygone era in which for the considerable class who had a cook and a maid a man's home was a castle of security and comfort, and in which husbands made large noises of dominance while a loved and femi-

* The idea represented by the word translated "a wonderful thing" is important to the meaning of *A Doll's House,* as clearly indicated in its recurrent use. For clarification of possible misunderstanding from mistranslation in some texts of the play, see *Write That Play,* pp. 333-35.

ninely intelligent wife nearly always got her way. The meaning of the play lies in these pleasures. *Life With Father* had an unusually large repeat attendance. People returned at intervals to enjoy another evening with Father.

The basic plot structure of the play is perfectly conventional. The attack comes at the end of Act I—when Father is reminded of the fact and casually remarks that he has never been baptized. Vinnie, his wife, is terribly shocked with the conviction that Father will not get to heaven with her. She determines that Father is to be baptized; he determines that he is not, he would feel a fool at his age. The major dramatic question is, will Father be baptized? The crisis comes at the end of Act II when Father, frightened by his wife's illness, promises if she will get well he will be baptized, and immediately regrets it. In Act III Father endeavors to retreat from his promise; the resolution is at the end of the act when he leaves the house to be baptized. Comparatively little space is given to the conflict over Father's baptism. The play is filled out with numerous minor incidents which also give view to the character of Father and of his family. Some of them, not all, are lightly and loosely integrated with the main plot-line. Quite clearly the play is built around the baptism as an episode revealing in itself and which has enough continuity and duration to hold the play together as a light plot-line on which to hang the revealing incidents. In this play the lack of dominance of the plot structure indicates where the meaning really lies.

Rostand's *Cyrano de Bergerac* is a romantic heroic drama. The structural outline of the play is a love story. Cyrano, accomplished poet and swordsman who fears no woman can love him because of his enormous and grotesque nose, loves his cousin Roxane. Near the end of Act I, he confesses his love and his fear to his friend Le Bret, and almost immediately a message is brought to him from Roxane requesting a meeting. This is the attack of the play, with the major dramatic question, will Cyrano's love for Roxane be fulfilled? It turns out that Roxane loves Christian, a handsome young recruit to the Gascon company of which Cyrano is a member, and the meeting is to ask Cyrano to protect him. Cyrano swears to do so. For Roxane's happiness and as an outlet to his own love, he gives the inarticulate Christian words with which to woo Roxane, a lady of

literary cultivation; and he stands guard over their marriage ceremony against interruption by de Guiche, a powerful noble and rival
for the hand of Roxane. Immediately upon conclusion of the ceremony de Guiche delivers orders to Christian and Cyrano to report
at once to the siege of Arras. During the siege Cyrano writes twice
daily to Roxane in Christian's name without his knowledge, and each
night slips through the Spanish lines for delivery of the letter. Roxane
is so moved by the letters that she makes her way through the lines
by a stratagem to be with Christian. Cyrano warns Christian not
to show surprise that he has written more letters than he supposed.
Roxane reveals to Christian that it is his soul in the letters she loves
and that she would love him if he were not handsome but ugly.
Christian reports to Cyrano and insists that he reveal the truth to
her and declare his own love, which Christian now recognizes. The
marriage, unconsummated and without a witness, he says, can be
annulled. Roxane must have opportunity to choose between them.
Cyrano protests, but Christian leaves him alone with Roxane. At
the moment that Cyrano is convinced of hope for himself and is
about to speak, battle has begun and Le Bret brings word to Cyrano
that Christian is dead, shot in battle. Cyrano exclaims, "I cannot
ever tell her now . . . ever . . ." This is the crisis of the play,
close to the end of Act IV. Act V opens fifteen years later. Roxane
has retired to a convent and for fourteen years Cyrano has come as
a friend every Saturday afternoon to cheer her with news of the outside world. Cyrano has made many enemies by his independence
and his fearless writings attacking every kind of fraud. On the Saturday of the last act he has received a mortal blow on the head by a log
dropped from an upper story of a building as he passed in the street.
Knowing he is dying, he comes to sit with Roxane in the garden of
the convent for the last time, concealing his condition from her.
Roxane asks him to read to her Christian's last letter which she
always carries. Dusk falls and he continues to read aloud the letter
he himself had written after there is no light by which to see the
words. Roxane recognizes the truth, and that the soul she has loved
is Cyrano's. She speaks her love to him and brings him to admit his
love for her, the resolution of the play. The major dramatic question
is answered, Cyrano's love for Roxane is fulfilled—briefly, for he
dies a few moments later.

In *Cyrano de Bergerac* the meaning of the play is less directly in the principal points of the basic plot structure than in the associated actions released in Cyrano by each of those three points. The romanticism of Rostand's play is not that of escape, but a highly sophisticated, disciplined, ethical romanticism, a challenging assertion against the rising tide in society and literature of the naturalistic philosophy of biological determinism minimizing the human will and moral responsibility, a recognition of individual will and of ideas of virtue such as love, honor, loyalty, courage, rejection of compromise. He performed the tour de force of making ideas theatrically visual, picturesque, glamorous, forceful and appealing by setting his play in the France of the seventeenth century, an age in which chivalry in decadence elaborated the outward gestures of honor without the content, and by creating as his hero, based on an actual Cyrano de Bergerac, a man with the imagination and the physical and mental faculties to out-gesture his age together with a largeness of soul to fill with meaning the most grandiose gestures he could conceive. In the opening scene at a theater preceding the attack of the play, Cyrano has been introduced in his salient characteristics of capacity for gesture, his independence, and his fearlessness, and he has announced to Le Bret his choice of purpose in life—"To make myself in all things admirable!" The message comes from Roxane. Cyrano is beside himself:

> *I—I am going to be a storm—a flame—*
> *I need to fight whole armies all alone;*
> *I have ten hearts; I have a hundred arms; I feel*
> *Too strong to war with mortals—*
> (He shouts at the top of his voice) *Bring me giants!*

Immediately his opportunity comes. Lignière, a poor drunken poet, a friend of Cyrano's, comes to him for protection. His verses had offended a man in high place and he has been warned that a hundred men have been placed to set upon him at the Porte de Nesle. Only a hundred, cries Cyrano; Lignière shall go home, conducted by Cyrano. In a magnificent act-ending Cyrano goes out with Lignière, the actors and actresses still in costume with the remnants of the audience forming a procession behind him. (It should be mentioned that the feat of single-handedly putting to rout a hundred men, readily assumed as one of Rostand's exaggerations of life in the idealization of his character, happened to be one of the items in the play drawn from the life of the historical Cyrano.)

Following the crisis at the end of Act IV Cyrano turns from mourning the dead Christian with Roxane to lead the surviving Gascons from an almost hopeless situation into a desperate charge, flamboyantly standing erect in the hail of bullets declaiming the song of the Cadets of Gascoyne before he rushes forward. At the end of the play, after the mutual realization of love between Roxane and Cyrano, the play reaches it climax and the meaning of the play is brought to final sharp focus. Cyrano, dying in delirium, fights his last, his most desperate and triumphant combat alone, shaking off the hands of friends, standing with his back to a tree lunging with his sword at the phantoms of the enemies he has fought all his life— Falsehood, Prejudice, Compromise, Cowardice. Then in clarity of mind—he has lost many things in life, yet,

> *There is one crown I bear away with me,*
> *And to-night, when I enter before God,*
> *My salute shall sweep all the stars away*
> *From the blue threshold! One thing without stain,*
> *Unspotted from the world, in spite of doom*
> *Mine own!*

He falls into the arms of his friends, and to Roxane bending over him he speaks the answer to her question, "My white plume!"—the white plume worn in the wide-brimmed hat of the seventeenth century, the symbol of each man's personal responsibility to the whole concept of chivalric honor. In *Cyrano de Bergerac* each of the three peaks of the plot structure, the attack, the crisis, and the resolution, is like a signpost pointing to one of Cyrano's great fights and great gestures. The last is all gesture and it is all meaning.

Structure and meaning are two aspects of one whole. The structure grows out of the meaning of a play; it is also the way in which the meaning is developed. The structure of *A Doll's House* is comparatively simple because the meaning is developed through the isolation of just two characters, and neither of these characters, as human beings go, is a very complex individual. The relation between structure and meaning is also direct. The basic structures of *Life*

With Father and *Cyrano de Bergerac* are similarly simple and clear, as is the integration with meaning, although in each of these plays, in different ways, it is indirect.

Maxim Gorki's *The Lower Depths* is an example of a difficult and complex play in which to determine the structure. It has been generally recognized as a play of originality and strength, a play to be taken into account in modern drama, but with such opposed views of its meaning that it must be considered a widely misunderstood play. Either it is confused and badly organized or critical method has been faulty and inadequate. When the play was first staged by the Moscow Art Players in 1902 it was an overwhelming success with the public, but the critics were divided, generally favorable in Moscow and unfavorable in St. Petersburg. The critic of a Moscow monthly previously reserved on Gorki wrote that "a sincere hymn to love sounded triumphantly" in the play, and that "the picture of human misery was illuminated by faith in the human soul, and it was the combination that acted irresistibly on the audience." On the other hand, a St. Petersburg critic declared that never before had he "felt a more humiliating sensation than in the contemplation of Gorky's *Bottom*,* a sensation of being forcibly ducked in a cesspool." † Subsequent criticism has been as contradictory: the play has been cited for indestructible optimism, faith, and love of mankind, and for pessimism, moral anarchy, and misanthropy. In the former group attention is generally focused on what is referred to as "the hymn to man," delivered by Sahtin in the fourth, the last, act. In the latter group these lines are either disregarded or dismissed as extraneous. Alexander Kaun's statement, ". . . that note sounded accidental in the play, and Sahtin was drunk, besides," is typical, in conjunction with his summing up of the play: "These men and women . . . are doomed to wriggle in hopeless nothingness." ‡ Synopses of the plot without mention of Sahtin are frequent.

Synopsis without Sahtin runs as follows. The play opens on a

---

* The title has appeared in English as *At the Bottom, Submerged, In the Depths, From the Depths, Down and Out, A Night Shelter,* and *A Night's Lodging* in addition to the most familiar form, *The Lower Depths.*

† Alexander Kaun, *Maxim Gorki and His Russia,* Jonathan Cape, London, 1932, p. 381.

‡ *Maxim Gorki and His Russia,* pp. 555, 556.

lodging house of the lowest sort and its inhabitants, a thief, a pros-
titute, a pimp, an alcoholic, rogues, tramps, down-and-outers. They
squabble, drink, dream and boast, each of a better past. An old pilgrim, Luka, enters who tries to do good to people, preaches brother-
hood and faith: if a man believes there is a God, He exists; a man
can achieve anything, if he only will. He eases the dying moments
of Anna, a sick old woman; he rouses the alcoholic actor to hope for
cure; he stirs a general unrest; and especially he concentrates on
Pepel, a young thief, and Natasha, younger sister of the landlord's
wife, in whom by youth and character there is most promise.
There has been an affair between Pepel and the older sister, Wassilissi, which Pepel is trying to break off as he sees she wants only
money from him, or to use him to rid her of her old husband,
Kostilioff, by murdering him. Pepel is attracted to Natasha and Wassilissi is jealous and making trouble. Luka suggests to Pepel in Act
II that he take Natasha away with him and start a new life. In
Act III he talks to them together and seems to have persuaded
them. Wassilissi overhears them and shortly afterward Natasha's
screams are heard from the room of Kostilioff, the landlord. Wassilissi is beating Natasha and fighting with Kostilioff; a samovar is
overturned and Natasha scalded. Pepel rushes in to protect Natasha,
strikes Kostilioff a blow that accidentally kills him, Wassilissi accuses
him of murder, and Natasha, hysterical with pain and thinking Pepel
and Wassilissi have plotted together, joins in the accusation. The
police are about to arrive as the act ends. The fourth act opens on
the scene as at the beginning of the play. Luka is gone—"He took
flight before the police, as a fog before the sun." Natasha was taken
to a hospital and has since disappeared; Pepel and Wassilissi are
to be tried for murder. The lodgers sit about squabbling, drinking,
drifting in dreams of the past. Nothing has changed. A song is pro-
posed. The Actor goes outside and hangs himself; the discovery spoils
their song.

If the synopsis without Sahtin is complete, *The Lower Depths* is
an extraordinarily badly constructed play, as some of the critics who
disregard Sahtin have affirmed that it is. Either Luka or Pepel
would be the protagonist, with Luka the better candidate, and we
have the resolution at the end of the third act and the disappearance
from the play of the protagonist, with an extended last act which is

only a commentary. We also have Sahtin's speech on man in the last act, which is evidently a major conception and effort in the writing of the play, unprepared for, unsupported, and isolated from the play's structure. But Sahtin is the protagonist of the play. *The Lower Depths* is built on three elements: there is a full background of minor characters, incidents, and details in the naturalistic manner; there is a minimum external plot to hold the play together theatrically in the story of Luka's attempt to better the lives of Pepel and Natasha; and there is an inner or philosophical plot, a struggle within the mind of Sahtin, which gives the unifying direction to the entire play.

Without Sahtin *The Lower Depths* is a badly ordered play of hopelessness in degradation. Trace Sahtin through the play and it assumes an entirely different structure and meaning. Sahtin emerges early in the first act as a man of mind among his lodging-house associates:

SAHTIN: I love the incomprehensible rare words. As a young man I was in the telegraph service. I have read many books.

BUBNOFF: So you have been a telegraph operator?

SAHTIN: To be sure. (*Laughs*) Many beautiful books exist, and a lot of curious words. I was a man of education, understand that?

He is now a cardsharp, a superior activity in the background. He lives in detachment from his surroundings with a dominant and free poise above the general bickerings and complaints. Morally he is a cynic. Early in the act he good-humoredly suggests to Pepel that he finish off Kostilioff, marry Wassilissi, and be their landlord. Pepel sensibly dismisses the idea: "You, my guests, would soon guzzle up the whole place, and me in the bargain." Pepel appears to look up to the older man; after Sahtin has gone out, he quotes him in an argument: "Sahtin says: every man wants his neighbor to have some conscience—but for himself, he can do without it . . . and that's right." At this moment Luka, pilgrim's staff in hand, a sack on his back, and a small kettle and tea boiler at his girdle, enters with a "Good day to you, honest folks." In the theater the visual conjunction of Luka's appearance with the statement of Sahtin's cynical philosophy is the inception of interaction between them. In the course of the act Luka's philosophy of concern for others emerges at intervals. In Act II Luka warns Pepel against Wassilissi's schem-ing to involve him in ridding her of her husband. He proposes that he go away and start a new life and, if he loves Natasha, take her with him, a countering of Sahtin's earlier suggestion. At the end of the act, when Luka is out, Sahtin and the Actor enter together, drunk. The Actor is looking for Luka, who has given him hope of a place to go to be cured of his alcoholism. Sahtin is shouting at him that the old man has deluded him, there is no such place, ". . . there is nothing at all!" As turmoil rises, Luka appears in the door as the curtain closes the act. Again there is the visual juxtaposition of opposed ideas, this time with Sahtin and Luka directly before each other.

In Act III Pepel, in Luka's presence, tells Natasha that he loves her and tries to win her to go away with him as his wife and start a new life together. Luka helps to lead Natasha out of her hopeless-ness to acceptance. Later in the act Sahtin is again discouraging the Actor in the hope Luka has aroused in him, and Luka turns directly to influence upon Sahtin—"You are a lusty brother, Constantin . . . a lovable man. . . . How have you gotten so far afield?" He draws from Sahtin his story. After four years and seven months in prison, he came out, a discharged convict, and found his old course in life shut out. In prison he learned the art of card playing. He went to prison because of a man he killed in a passion, who had deceived his sister, ". . . an old story . . . my sister is dead . . . nine years have gone by . . . she was a splendid creature . . . my sister." Sahtin abruptly tries to push back Luka's questioning, but he is moved: "Tell me, what shall I now begin to do?" They are inter-rupted by Natasha's screams from Kostilioff's room. In the episode that follows Sahtin, the hitherto detached cynic unconcerned about himself and others, identifies himself with Natasha and Pepel; in the phrase that has become current from Jean-Paul Sartre's existentialist philosophy, he becomes engaged. It is he who starts first for Kos-tilioff's room calling on Luka to come with him. As the scene breaks into wild confusion, Natasha, Wassilissi, Kostilioff, and the lodgers all bursting from different directions into the main room, Sahtin is in the thick of the action, the dominating figure. He gets in a couple of blows on Kostilioff himself before Pepel's fatal blow, holds the furiously struggling Wassilissi back from Natasha, tells Pepel he will be a witness for him that Kostilioff's death was the accident of a row, and tries to make Natasha hear sense when in her hysteria she accuses Pepel.

In Act IV Luka is gone, and all his works, except in the mind of Sahtin. Luka's preachment of hope for each individual man has been discredited, but something has been stirred in Sahtin that will not let him rest: "The old man . . . worked on me like acid on an old, dirty coin," he says. He remembers Luka's words and sees in them, not the whole truth, but the beginning of truth—there is a meaning in men's lives . . . don't injure others . . . mankind is of worth. When Luka is spoken of with contempt he strikes the table with his fist: "Be still! Asses! Say nothing ill of the old man." He recognizes that Luka told lies, out of sympathy, to comfort people. Sahtin's mind is driven by question and now demands an answer that will give meaning to life and dignity to each man, but it must be truth, no glossing over the facts of the life that surrounds him. Bubnoff, a lodger, says in Act I, "When a clever man drinks, he doubles his wit." Sahtin holds out his glass for beer, a health to Luka: "The old man—he lived from within. . . . He saw everything with his own eyes. . . . I asked him once: 'Grandfather, why do men really live?' . . . (*He tries in voice and manner to imitate* LUKA.) Man lives to give birth to strength." Sahtin has found his answer: this is the beginning of what has been so frequently referred to as Gorki's hymn to man. Sahtin elaborates in a long speech. People live in each trade, noisy, miserable, and suddenly in their midst one is born who changes the whole trade, in a single impulse advances it twenty years. And so of every class. "Every one thinks that he for himself takes up room in the world, but it turns out that he is here for another's benefit—for someone better . . . a hundred years . . . or perhaps longer." Sahtin's answer is in accord with Gorki's faiths—science, reason, and labor. It is an evolutionary view of progress for mankind, the race, by which even the most degraded and hopeless of men possess a dignity as a part of the whole, and one never knows what any man's part may be: "For that reason," says Sahtin, "we must respect everybody. We cannot know who he is, for what purpose born, or what he may yet fulfill . . . and especially we must respect the children." After some interrupting talk during which he becomes a little more drunk, Sahtin continues to the culmination of his thought:

> Man—that is the truth! But what's man? Not you, nor I, not they—no, but you, I, old Luka, Napoleon, Mohammed . . . all in one . . . is man. (*Draws in the air the outline of a man's form.*) Comprehend! It is—something huge, including all beginnings and all endings . . . all is in man, all is for man. Only man alone exists—the rest is the work of his hand and his brow. M–a–n! Phenomenal. How lofty it sounds, M–a–n! We must respect man . . . not compassion . . . degrade him not with pity . . . but respect.

Sahtin's mind has come to rest. He accepts his present lot for himself, relaxes into becoming again one with the group around him. There is more talk and drinking, a song is called for. One of the lodgers rushes in with the discovery that the Actor has hanged himself. The play ends on Sahtin: "(*Softly.*) He must spoil our song . . . the fool." The Actor did not understand the truth, was caught between the error in Luka's message and hope enwrapped in himself.

The hymn to man is Sahtin's, not Luka's. When Sahtin imitates the voice and manner of Luka it is not to quote Luka, but to pay respect for what he has received from him, not enough, but a beginning, and to take up where Luka left off, to assume to himself the role of preacher. What follows does not correspond to anything Luka has spoken in the play; it is at once a contradiction and an extension of his words. If this point is misunderstood, the structure and meaning of the play are thrown out of alignment. Unfortunately one of the most effective translations as a whole, that by Jenny Covan, obscures the point by beginning the speech as follows: "And he replied: Why, my dear fellow, people live in the hope of something better!" instead of "Man lives to give birth to strength," as in the translation by Edwin Hopkins. On Russian linguistic authority there is nothing in the original text for the phrase "And he replied" which identifies what follows as quotation from Luka; and literally Gorki's words which are translated by Miss Covan, "People live in the hope of something better," and by Mr. Hopkins, "Man lives to give birth to strength," would be either "They live for a better man," or "They live to make a better man." * Miss Covan's translation again suggests the personal hope of Luka's philosophy, while that of Mr. Hopkins gives a free but accurate rendering of the original. The other principal English translation, that of Alexander Bakshy and Paul S. Nathan, represents the passage with essential accuracy.

The attack of the external plot of Luka's attempt to better the lives of Pepel and Natasha is Luka's proposal to Pepel in the second act that he take Natasha with him and go away. The crisis is the death of Kostilioff; the resolution of defeat is determined when Natasha in her hysteria turns upon Pepel at the end of the third act. The attack of the inner plot of Sahtin may be considered as coming at the end of Act II in Sahtin's contradictions to the Actor of the hope Luka has been giving him. It is brought to a focus when Luka addresses him directly in Act III and Sahtin asks, "What shall I now begin to do?" The defeat of Luka's exercise of his philosophy on Pepel and Natasha, the resolution of the external plot, constitutes the crisis of the Sahtin plot. Sahtin's achievement in the fourth act of an answer to the pressure that has grown in him to find meaning and dignity in man is the resolution. The Sahtin line is truly a plot, not merely a thematic development, because it is an action, a conflict, with a protagonist and a major dramatic question: will Sahtin find a meaning in life? It begins when he is aroused out of his detachment into opposing his cynicism to Luka's efforts, swings to a beginning of responsiveness to Luka, and then rises to positive expression in his engagement with the lives of Pepel and Natasha. Confronted by a crisis in the apparent exposure as false of the philosophy with which he has newly identified himself, by a struggle of will and mind he triumphs in the formulation for himself of an answer that meets his inner need. The external plot of Pepel and Natasha gives the propulsion to the inner plot of Sahtin and for the brief period of the row at the end of Act III the two lines are identified in external action. Gorki has built the entire play on a sound plot structure to his culminating object, the hymn to man by

---

* I would like to express here appreciation for the translation of this point some years ago by Mrs. Lila Pargment, professor, now emeritus, of Russian literature at the University of Michigan.

which the play expresses his respect as well as his love for his fellowmen.

In a book of reminiscences Gorki wrote: "To me man is always the conqueror, even when he is mortally wounded and dying. Splendid is his longing to know himself and to know Nature; and although his life is a torment, he is ever widening its bounds, creating with his thought wise science, marvellous art. I felt that I did sincerely and actively love man—him who is at present alive and working side by side with me, and him, too, the sensible, the good, the strong who will follow after in the future." *

The structure of *The Lower Depths* is not obvious, both because it is complicated and unusual, and because so deeply embedded in the full development of background. The background was necessary to Gorki's purpose, the solid foundation for his expression of faith: he felt a love for men at their lowliest, even their worst, and he established a respect for man that would include all by starting in the depths which he himself knew. By the age of fifteen he had worked for a land surveyor, a shoemaker, an icon painter, a ship's cook, and a gardener, later in a bakeshop, as a longshoreman on the Volga, and a railway watchman, and he had been one of the tramps of Russia. In the Czarist police files he was recorded as "a highly suspicious character—well read, wields a good pen, and has covered practically the whole of Russia (mostly on foot)." † Many critics have questioned the freedom of philosophizing granted to characters such as those in *The Lower Depths,* not only to Luka and Sahtin but to the lodgers as a group. Alexander Kaun, however, in describing the life among the workmen in the icon painting shop which Gorki experienced as an apprentice wrote: "Occasional drunken orgies and fist fights climaxed the habitual outlet in philosophizing and song. The more unlettered the common folk in Russia, the more vehement is their articulation in discourse on God and life." ‡

---

* *Reminiscences of Maxim Gorki,* Dover Publications, New York, 1946, p. 145.
† Alexander Roskin, *From the Banks of the Volga, The Life of Maxim Gorky,* tr. from the Russian by D. L. Fromberg. Philosophical Society, New York,
‡ *Maxim Gorki and His Russia,* p. 107.

In the conclusion to *Fragments from My Diary* Gorki himself wrote: "I . . . see the Russian people as exceptionally, fantastically gifted, original. Even fools in Russia are foolish in an original way, in a peculiar manner, and as to loafers—they are positively geniuses. I am sure that by their fancifulness, by the unexpectedness of their twists, by the significant form, so to speak, of their thoughts and feelings, the Russian people are the most grateful material for an artist." *

Gorki came of the life of which he wrote and had little formal education, but he was no unlettered genius writing with the force of spontaneity. Although *The Lower Depths* with another play completed in the same year was his first undertaking of drama, he was already an accomplished and well-recognized writer of short stories, and a skilled and conscientious craftsman. Letters to friends while writing *The Lower Depths,* and the accompanying play, *The Smug Citizen,* show his full awareness of the problems of form and structure in drama, and it is no accident that the meaning of *The Lower Depths* through structural analysis represents what one should expect from his attitudes as revealed all through his several books of autobiography and reminiscences. The meaning of the play may be experienced simply as an impression, but impressionistic response is highly subjective, as has been particularly evident in criticism of *The Lower Depths.* If the impression of a play is in accord with the author's intention, structural analysis clarifies and reinforces; if at odds, analysis may be the means to a rapprochement. By some practice in such analysis an unconscious recognition of structure is cultivated which is carried into direct response.

* Robert M. McBride and Co., New York, 1924, p. 320.

8

The Dramatic Climate of a Play : Traditional Modes

To penetrate to the meaning of a play it is necessary to understand what the author is aiming at and the means by which he undertakes to accomplish his aim. To a degree each play is unique in its object and means. However, by the mere fact that the author chooses the dramatic form his objective and method are brought within a circle defined from the whole broad area of literature, that of dramatic structure as discussed in the preceding chapters. Within drama certain traditions of division of function have developed, as tragedy, comedy, satire, farce, melodrama, social drama, and heroic drama, with their subdivisions and composite forms such as romantic comedy, high comedy, low comedy, farce comedy, tragi-comedy. Ordinarily, the competent playwright is fully aware of the direction he intends for his play in terms of these traditional divisions. Ideas such as the comic or the tragic change with the temper of the times and vary according to the individual temperament of the playwright, but the basic concepts remain. Flowing through the traditional classification of drama by function, there are in modern drama the successive movements of dramatic form, the method of projection, such as realism, naturalism, symbolism, expressionism, theatricalism, which are themselves expressions of function. These movements arise as self-conscious theories, even crusades, and the playwright may consciously ally his play with one form or another. They also be-

136

come diffused into the theater as influences to which the playwright may respond more or less unconsciously by temperamental congeniality. Together the tradition within which the play moves by function and the form or forms to which it is allied in method constitute its dramatic climate, the environment within which the idea of the play develops.

The traditional functional divisions of drama will be considered first. The simplest functions of drama are those of farce and melodrama. A farce is a play of ludicrous situations for the purpose of producing laughter. A melodrama is a play of situations of suspense for the purpose of producing thrills. In both, great latitude is allowed as to plausibility of events and of characterization. Neither farce nor melodrama is concerned with truth of life or a view of life. The purposes of farce and of melodrama, though narrowly limited, are laudable in themselves; laughter and thrills within proper bounds are healthy releases to natural human responses. Farce easily moves over into satire. It is inevitable for the purpose of farce that the object of ridicule, the butt of a situation, will often represent undesirable human traits. Folly is blind and leads into pitfalls. It is a matter of purpose. So long as the sole object is laughter with the emphasis on the ludicrous situation we have farce. As soon as the purpose becomes to castigate by emphasis on the folly as the cause of the ludicrous situation we have satire. Satire, like farce, deals in types rather than individualized characterization, in farce for the freedom of creation of situations, in satire because it is the folly rather than the individual that is held up to ridicule. Satire, however, is not limited, like farce, to drama of situation. Satire flourishes at the level of drama of manners, of social behavior, in which the follies of conduct are made ludicrous by a touch of exaggeration whether or not they lead to ludicrous plot involvement. One commonly meets the term farce comedy. This is a play which plot-wise consists of farcical or ludicrous situations but founded on characterization and truth to life, and which, in consequence, may engage the emotions to some degree as well as arouse laughter. Comedy represents a way of looking at life; farce is not concerned with life. That life is like a farce is a possible view of life, but such a view could not produce farce; it could lead to expression either as comedy or tragedy.

Farce readily merges with other more complex and, in a sense, higher forms of drama. Melodrama has a more precarious foothold, which is the reason it is so often unjustly used as an opprobrious term. So long as melodrama remains detached from truth to life and maintains the thrills of suspense around the grosser dramatic ends such as life or death as its object, it is a legitimate if lesser dramatic form. When melodrama pretends to life and also enters the area of the tenderer emotions we have sentimental drama, the tear-jerker instead of the thriller. Drama is sentimental when emotions are generated for their own sake, for the sensation, rather than for truth of life. Drama of sentiment which is concerned in truth to life with the gentler and admirable expressions of character and human relationships and their appropriate emotions, a play such as John Van Druten's *I Remember Mama,* is an entirely desirable form of drama. In a sentimental play the presentation of life is either shallow or false and the emotions are inappropriate to or exaggerated beyond the situations of their occasion. The business of melodrama is with the suspense of fear and its release and a tacit understanding of detachment from life between stage and audience is necessary for such emotion to be healthily pleasurable rather than morbid. Sentimental drama deals in tears and pathos, which requires identification either by the actuality or the pretension to actuality of life, and it is the distinction between truth and pretension which separates sentimental drama from drama of sentiment. Sentimental melodrama, like Lottie Blair Parker's *Way Down East* and Eugene Walter's *Paid in Full,* and plays that were just sentimental, abounded on the American stage in the latter part of the nineteenth and early twentieth century. Farces and straight melodrama also flourished.

Pure farce and melodrama have been largely taken over from the stage by the motion pictures and television, in part because of the relation between the broad appeal of those forms and the functioning of the motion pictures and television as mass media, and in part because of the scope the screen offers to the basic material of farce and melodrama: vigorous external action. The American theater has tended to become shy even of the terms farce and melodrama as unsophisticated, although George Abbott has sturdily and properly announced plays such as *Three Men on a Horse* as farces and has been notably successful with them. Farce comedy both as label and fact has become more characteristic of our theater and many farce comedies, such as George S. Kaufman's *You Can't Take It With You,* are termed simply comedies. Melodrama has become largely limited to the mystery murder play and in that genre the pure action thriller such as Mary Roberts Rinehart's and Avery Hopwood's *The Bat* has been displaced either by a strong injection of psychological interest as in Emlyn Williams' *Night Must Fall* or of comedy as in Joseph Kesselring's *Arsenic and Old Lace,* or has been intellectualized as in Frederick Knott's *Dial "M" for Murder.* That sentimental plays are frequently to be found in our theater is suggested by J. M. Lambert's remark on theater in the United States: "There seems to be, in that great country, an enviable supply of good, middlebrow, soft-centered plays depositing kindly sentiments over depressing situations, like imitation amber over real flies." *

So wary have many critics become of sentiment that it is quite possible that in some of the plays of the English reviewer's stricture the kindly sentiments are not artificial amber. It is, however, a regrettable tendency in our theater for playwrights to have the courage to present depressing situations without the courage, or insight perhaps, to cope with their full implications. In the plays of William Inge, for example, *Come Back, Little Sheba* was a play of sentiment, the sentiments and emotions proportionate and appropriate to the characters and situation; but in all of his subsequent plays, *Picnic, Bus Stop,* and *The Dark at the Top of the Stairs,* there is a flaw of sentimentality, most disturbing in the last play precisely because it is his dramatic undertaking of greatest seriousness and depth.

When one turns to drama that represents a way of looking at life for truth to be found there and revealed, one meets tragedy as a basic and continuous form from the Greek theater of the fifth century B.C. to the present. Most simply, tragedy isolates one aspect of the total truth of human existence, that man in a universe of forces beyond the finiteness of his faculties and will is subject to defeat and suffering. It is also true that there is a large area in life of the attainment by men of the objects of their will, of happiness and joy. One aspect or the other may be isolated in drama as pure tragedy or pure comedy for intensification of perception and comprehension.

* *International Theatre Annual,* Doubleday, New York, 1957, pp. 49-50.

In the highest type of tragedy there is a tragic mood which unifies the drama and communicates a sense of impending catastrophe from the beginning. The audience knows where it is, what the play is about, and is maintained in a state of appropriate high seriousness. The full tragic force of life is not communicated by accidental catastrophe, but by sustained conflict between a human will and fate. The greater the will and faculties involved, the stronger the awareness of the defeating power. It follows that tragedy reveals at once man's vulnerability and his highest capacities. Only the point of defeat summons the last reserve of strength, and tragedy has traditionally been identified with the fullest sense of the dignity of man. Tragedy, then, is concerned with the ultimate metaphysical fact of suffering in life. If a social utopia could be conceived as in operation, suffering would still be inherent in life by the finiteness of man in an infinite universe and by the imperfections of his human nature. Tragedy looks the truth of suffering full in the face and in the process reveals the supreme dignity available to man, his capacity to transcend catastrophe which his powers cannot avert or escape by the maintenance of his own identity, the integrity of his will.

The core of traditional tragedy is personal identity. Antigone is impelled by what she is in character to perform the burial rites for her rebel brother in defiance of the edict of the state forbidding the rites and to maintain her defiance to death. Because Medea is a barbarian princess she slays her fiercely loved children to avenge the contumely their father Jason has brought upon her and through her upon their children. Because of what he is as a military man of honor, with the egocentricity of that conception of honor, Othello kills Desdemona when he believes her to be unfaithful; and by the stern sense of justice of that idea of honor he takes his own life when he discovers his error. The first action is terribly wrong but not ignoble; upon the second action Cassio pronounces, "This did I fear. . . . For he was great of heart." Webster's pathetic Duchess of Malfi is almost nothing as a character except in her love for Antonio and the strength of that love for which she suffered unimaginable horrors and accepted death with calm dignity. Willy Loman in *Death of a Salesman* lived by a false dream, but it was the only dream he had, and he died to maintain it. The plot of *The Crucible* converges upon the isolation of John Proctor with the choice of putting his name to a lie or a martyr's death for which he feels himself unworthy. Under the final pressure of giving up his identity he finds the goodness in himself to maintain his name and die. Tragedy begins and ends in choice of values, independent and self-determined.

Aristotle in his *Poetics* defined the function of tragedy as an emotional effect, "through pity and fear affecting the proper *katharsis* of these emotions." What he meant by *katharsis* in this context has been a discussed topic ever since. He was using a term of medicine metaphorically. The Greek word continues in the modern English "catharsis," both in its medical sense, and from Aristotle, as the technical term in aesthetics for the emotional effect of tragedy. *Katharsis* in the *Poetics* has been translated as purgation and as purification, both terms justifiable from the original medical signification of the word. Purgation in its metaphorical application to tragedy would mean the consciousness emptied of fear and pity. Purification would mean a cleansing of the emotions of pity and fear of destructive elements, a transformation to a constructive state. There is indication that the latter was Aristotle's intention; but the *Poetics* is a collection of notes, not a finished work, and more important than the pursuit there of implications beyond what can be established is one's own experience of tragedy. Many people have found in their own response to the great tragedies from Greek to modern a consciousness at once of peace, of serenity, and of enlargement and exaltation of spirit. In the contemplation of suffering properly organized as tragedy we realize suffering as universal to human existence; ultimate catastrophe may come to any man, therefore we fear. Suffering may come unmerited, therefore we pity. We experience both fear and pity before the tragic waste, life robbed of the strong, the good, the beautiful. But we are drawn out of self-pity, one of the most painful and the most unconstructive of emotions, which has its origin in the narrow and self-centered consciousness: why did this have to happen to me? We are drawn out of rebellion into peace by the awe before that which is universal and inevitable. On the foundation of peace we are lifted out of despair into exaltation before the capacity of the human mind to transcend all that may happen from without, to maintain itself in integrity and self-determination. We are expanded into identification with humanity at its highest levels of will, of moral choice, of strength. This landscape of dark valleys and lofty storm-swept peaks is the environment of his dramatic idea for the playwright who elects to move in the tradition of high tragedy.

There are lower levels of tragedy, one of which is that of simple purgation. The audience is in a state of tranquillity, not of exaltation, at the end of the play—numbed, passive, drained of the emotions of pity and fear by the expenditure of their capacity for such emotion. Actually such drama usually deals more in pity and horror than the higher tragic fear. Many of the Elizabethan "tragedies of blood" were of this kind, including Shakespeare's early *Titus Andronicus*. John Webster in *The Duchess of Malfi* raised the tragedy of purgation by pity and horror to its highest dignity. Charles Lamb's brief comment remains not only the best characterization of Webster's play but of the potentialities of the tragedy of purgation:

All the several parts of the dreadful apparatus with which the death of the Duchess is ushered in, the waxen images which counterfeit death, the wild masque of madmen, the tomb-maker, the bellman, the living person's dirge, the mortification by degrees,— are not more remote from the conceptions of ordinary vengeance, than the strange character of suffering which they seem to bring upon their victim is out of the imagination of ordinary poets. As they are not like inflictions of this life, so her language seems not of this world. She has lived among horrors till she is become "native and endowed unto that element." She speaks the dialect of despair; her tongue has a smatch of Tartarus and the souls in bale. To move a horror skilfully, to touch a soul to the quick, to lay upon fear as much as it can bear, to wean and weary a life till it is ready to drop, and then step in with mortal instruments to take its last forfeit: this only a Webster can do. Inferior geniuses may "upon horror's head horrors accumulate," but they cannot do this. They mistake quantity for quality; they "terrify babes with painted devils"; but they know not how a soul is to be moved. Their terrors want dignity, their affrightments are without decorum.

It should be noted that the catharsis of tragedy may involve both the purgation and the purification. In *King Lear,* the greatest of tragedies, it seems to me the first sensation at the moment of the close of the drama is the peace of exhaustion; there has been so much of suffering one feels emptied of emotion, all of one's emotional resources have been expended. Then slowly the full catharsis of transcendence, of constructive emotion, flows in. The catharsis of tragedy is only a general concept, the experience differing in exact character for every tragedy. With the catastrophe of *Hamlet,* as Harley Granville-Barker has noted in his *Preface to Hamlet,* there is an element of triumph, of the romantic hero. Hamlet has accomplished his purpose, although he suffers death in the doing and a great waste lies about him. At the end of *Othello* there is a moment of direct personal admiration for Othello; but at the end of *King Lear* there is nothing but heartbreak, and the transcendence of suffering and evil depends completely upon a renewal in one's consciousness of the entire course of the play in its totality.

There are also the tragedies of villain protagonists like Richard III, completely and premeditatively villain, and Macbeth whose character disintegrates before our eyes. A. C. Bradley in his essays on *Macbeth* in *Shakespeare's Tragedies* analyzes such tragedies as producing the effect of catharsis, but a limited catharsis. The pity is for the tragic waste of potentialities misdirected by a powerful will. The catharsis is limited because the emotional response is divided between the protagonist and his victims, and because the expanding identification with human capacity in the protagonist is partial, for the strength of his will and great faculties, while identification is repelled by their direction.

In modern drama there has been a tendency toward tragedy of limited catharsis, not by powerful evil in man, but by a view of man's weakness and spiritually inchoate state as the tragic aspect of existence. Eugene O'Neill aimed at tragedy in *Desire Under the Elms* with immediate thought, by his own words, of the great tragic tradition of the Greeks and Elizabethans.* Eben and Abbie are com-

---

* In an interview published in the Philadelphia *Public Ledger,* Jan. 22, 1922; quoted by Barrett H. Clark, *Eugene O'Neill, the Man and His Plays,* Robert M. McBride, New York, 1929, pp. 146-47.

paratively weak people with spiritual lives stunted and warped by
environment. In a relation founded in lust and greed they grow into
love for each other, inchoate, distrusting. That which is spiritually
best in them, their love, produces the crime of Abbie's killing of
their child. Out of their crime they grope forward in spiritual growth
to a moment when they stand together at the end of the play in
clarity of love which embraces suffering and transcends the future
before them of trial for murder. The future may destroy them. They
are limited in strength, in intelligence, in foundations of spiritual
experience. The play achieves the catharsis of tragedy, pale, but
assured. The moment of spiritual awareness may be only a moment,
but by being enclosed within a work of dramatic art it is indestructible.

More severely restrictive in recent contemporary drama, although it
has roots in Strindberg and in post-World War I German expressionism, is the assumption that the tragic aspect of human existence is that
there is no core of character, personality, will, or identity. The individual human being is a flux of experiences, impulses, and memories, conscious and unconscious, personal and racial, in a body of
declining physiological functions. Psychology, psychoanalysis, brain-
washing, and cerebral surgery have left not even the comparatively
firm outline of a complex of hereditary and environmental factors
of the biological view of humanity which arose in the nineteenth
century as naturalism. This man is a microcosm of the universe, a
play of impersonal, purposeless, meaningless forces in the dark. This
is the man who subsides into non-existence in Samuel Beckett's
Endgame and leaps into darkness in Eugene Ionesco's *The Chairs*.
This view of life is tragic in having to do with suffering, but it is a
negation of the traditional meaning of tragedy as a form of dramatic
art, the foundation of which is individual human identity. Ionesco
escapes into comedy of the grotesque. *Endgame* produces a kind of
bleak catharsis. It is not that distinctively of tragedy but of aesthetic
experience as such. By the unity and intensity with which Beckett
organizes and projects his view of life the consciousness of the audience is unified within the bounds of the idea of the work of art.
Rebellion or conflict is allayed not by enlargement but by closing
in of the consciousness. There is no purification from destructive

to constructive emotion but purification only as elimination of everything but one element from the consciousness.

It is characteristic of much contemporary thinking about tragedy that playwrights are identified with and identify themselves with a total tragic view of existence rather than a perception of the tragic aspect of existence. In the two great periods of tragedy, the Greek and the Elizabethan, the tragic fact was seen as a part not the whole of life, and the same men who wrote the great tragedies wrote comedies. The unity of the play was not understood as representing the playwright's total awareness of life, but an artistic unity. Aeschylus, Sophocles, and Euripedes are generally identified in our minds with tragedy, but by the origins of the Greek theater in the worship of Dionysus and its organization around the festivals of Dionysus, each dramatist who entered a trilogy of tragedies in the competition for production was required to submit with them a satyr play, and in the day-long theater presentations of the festival a trilogy of tragedies was followed by the accompanying satyr play. These satyr plays were robust comedies, by their origin in fertility rites positive and life-asserting. Less regarded as literature than the tragedies or the later Aristophanic comedies, only one, the *Cyclops* of Euripedes, has survived. Shakespeare's writing career intermingled tragedies and comedies about equally and, as the Elizabethan critic Francis Meres affirmed in his *Palladis Tamia,* he was "the most excellent in both kinds." His greatest tragedies were written close together, but not too much credence can be given to their identification with a tragic view or mood as a period in Shakespeare's personal life when one finds *Twelfth Night* and *The Merry Wives of Windsor* adjacent to *Hamlet.* Other great Elizabethans, such as Heywood, Jonson, and Chapman, although not all, wrote both comedies and tragedies. The function of the theater as a whole was recognized both in the Greek and Elizabethan backgrounds as a balance of the two modes. It is reasonable that the fuller the sense of joy in life the more profound is the awareness of its tragic aspect.

In *The Modern Temper,* published in 1929, Joseph Wood Krutch questioned the possibility of tragedy to modern man. "We read but we do not write tragedies," he wrote. "The tragic solution of the problem of existence, the reconciliation to life by means of the tragic

spirit is, that is to say, now only a fiction surviving in art." * In
the chapter, "The Tragic Fallacy," Mr. Krutch states two requirements for tragedy, the assumption that the soul of man is great, and
that the universe concerns itself with him, "That he is, in a word,
noble." † Advancing realistic intelligence has made these assump-
tions untenable, Mr. Krutch continues. To contemporary minds
"man is relatively trivial. . . . The best that we can achieve is
pathos and the most that we can do is to feel sorry for ourselves
. . . from the universe as we see it both the Glory of God and the
Glory of Man have departed. Our cosmos may be farcical or it may
be pathetic but it has not the dignity of tragedy."

Mr. Krutch's book was a crystallization of widespread thought
and feeling of its time. Ten years later in *American Drama Since
1918* he wrote of Eugene O'Neill's *Desire Under the Elms* and
Mourning Becomes Electra, and Maxwell Anderson's *Winterset* as
tragedies accomplished and of several other plays as approaching
the tragic spirit. In the interval between books the plays discussed,
with the exception of *Desire Under the Elms,* had been written and
had been experienced by Mr. Krutch (apparently he had reexperi-
enced *Desire Under the Elms*). He considered *Mourning Becomes
Electra* to be the best modern tragedy in English because of the
strength of the characters and magnitude of emotions, and its meaning to be the same as that of *Oedipus* or *Macbeth:* "that human
beings are great and terrible creatures when they are in the grip of
great passions and that they afford a spectacle not only absorbing
but also at once horrible and cleansing." Actually in *The Modern
Temper* he had ascribed much more to *Oedipus,* namely, nobility;
and all that he says of *Mourning Becomes Electra* limits it to tragedy
of simple purgation rather than purification. For myself, I find
Mourning Becomes Electra somewhat grandiose, the frame larger

* Harcourt, Brace, and Company, New York, pp. 142-143.
† Mr. Krutch states early in the chapter that "a tragic writer does not have to
believe in God, but he must believe in man," but he disregards this statement
throughout the development of his thesis: "The Tragic Fallacy depends ultimately upon the assumption which man so readily makes that something outside his own being . . . be it God, Nature, or that still vaguer thing called
the Moral Order . . . confirms him in his feeling that his passions and his
opinions are important. . . . he is never strong enough in his own insignifi-
cant self to stand alone in a universe which snubs him with its indifference."

than its content, and both *Desire Under the Elms* and *Winterset* more significant for the potentiality of tragedy in the modern world.

Maxwell Anderson, in the epitaph speech of Esdras over the bodies of Miriamne and Mio in the street at the close of *Winterset*, voices a theory for modern tragedy which embraces purification by contemplation of transcendence of fate in the individual will:

> *this is the glory of earth-born men and women,*
> *not to cringe, never to yield, but standing,*
> *take defeat implacable and defiant,*
> *die unsubmitting . . . .*
> *. . . . . On this star,*
> *in this hard star-adventure, knowing not*
> *what the fires mean to left and right, nor whether*
> *a meaning was intended or presumed,*
> *man can stand up, and look out blind, and say:*
> *in all these turning lights I find no clue,*
> *only a masterless night, and in my blood*
> *no certain answer, yet is my mind my own,*
> *yet is my heart a cry toward something dim*
> *in distance, which is higher than I am*
> *and makes me emperor of the endless dark*
> *even in seeking!*

Desire Under the Elms and *Winterset* reveal man, not as great, but with something of greatness in him, not as noble, but groping toward nobility, reaching out and touching, for a moment, greatness. Belief in God or a universe that is concerned with man, or in anything outside man himself, is not necessary to modern tragedy and never has been necessary to the attainment of the tragic consciousness. In *Desire Under the Elms* Ephraim, the father of Eben, speaks often of a God created in his own image, a hard God, but Ephraim's God has never been Eben's and when Eben and Abbie grow into spiritual stature their only guide is the love that has arisen within themselves. Similarly, in *Winterset* Mio and Miriamne achieve their defiance of an impersonal universe by what they have come to know within themselves. By the love of Miriamne, Mio is awakened from a long dream of revenge and festering hate into forgiveness and, when the challenge comes, sacrifice, and they die for each other. The "cry toward something dim in distance," which is higher than man demands no existence or sanction in the universe other than man's growing vision from within himself of a direction pointing to what he may become. Tragedy and supra-human religious faith are harmonious and readily coexistent, as in the deity-permeated Greek tragedies, but when Oedipus discovers that he is the man, though unwittingly, who has killed his own father and married his mother and brought the plague upon Thebes, his actions of striking out his own eyes and calling for his own banishment are the actions he demands of himself by what he is as a man. Greek tragedy, which developed out of religious rites and never lost the association, became fully dramatic, and tragedy, when it became human. Shakespeare's tragedies are of man in this life. The world of *Hamlet* is infused with awareness of another world: a ghost out of purgatory sets the action in motion; Hamlet's first words on sight of the apparition are "Angels and ministers of grace defend us!"; and when he dies Horatio's farewell is, "Good night, sweet prince. And flights of angels sing thee to thy rest!" But the other-world to Hamlet is "The undiscover'd country, from whose bourn no traveller returns," and the words with which he dies are—"The rest is silence." To Hamlet's questioning mind everything is uncertainty except the obligation which he feels within himself to avenge his father's death, which he finally accomplishes. The majesty of Lear's defiance in the storm scene—"Blow, winds, and crack your cheeks! rage! blow! You cataracts and hurricanoes"—is defiance of the elements of an impersonal universe. When he attains the more profound majesty of humble and compassionate thought of the sufferings and needs of fellow human beings it is an awareness born within himself out of his experience as a man:

> *Poor naked wretches, wheresoe'er you are,*
> *That bide the pelting of this pitiless storm,*
> *How shall your houseless heads and unfed sides,*
> *Your loop'd and window'd raggedness, defend you*
> *From seasons such as these? O, I have ta'en*
> *Too little care of this! Take physic, pomp;*
> *Expose thyself to feel what wretches feel,*

That thou mayst shake the superflux to them
And show the heavens more just.

We turn now to the modern tragedy which, to my mind, to the highest degree attains the catharsis of purification, of transcendence: Arthur Miller's *The Crucible.* It is, like the Greek and Shakespearean, set in a background of supra-human religious faith but is a humanistic tragedy of man's power to be true to himself. When in the witch trials of Salem, John Proctor is one of those accused of witchcraft and is given the choice between life by confessing to lies or hanging, he is so oppressed by the realization there is already a lie upon his life, his brief and rejected infidelity to his wife, that he feels there would be a lie in assuming martyrdom for truth—and he wants his life. When he appeals to his wife, with whom there has come to be full love and understanding, for help in his decision, Elizabeth Proctor says: "Do what you will. But let none be your judge. There is no higher judge under Heaven than Proctor is!" Elizabeth's eye is not on God but on the man John Proctor, and when under the final pressure of signing his name to the prepared confession he turns upon his accusers and tears the paper, he is not thinking of God's judgment but of his own judgment upon himself and the preservation of his own identity: ". . . for now I do think I see some shred of goodness in John Proctor. Not enough to weave a banner wtih, but white enough to keep it from such dogs." When Proctor has been taken out to be hanged and the Reverend John Hale begs Elizabeth to go to him, plead with him, save him in the minutes of time remaining, she answers: "He have his goodness now. God forbid I take it from him!"

There can be no factually ascertainable truth of the universe which bars religious faith to rational minds, because it is rational to recognize the boundaries for the functioning of scientific reason; not to do so is itself a faith analogous to that of religion. A religious faith, however, in beneficence, concern, sanction, or judgment outside of man is not requisite to modern tragedy, and historically such faith has been a social accompaniment to, not the cause of, tragedy. On the other hand, that the universe as erected to our view by science lacks dignity as a stage for the tragic revelation of nobility in man is subjective, an expression of human egocentricity. Impersonal the universe may be, but the spaces and intricacies of the physical world revealed by science constitute not a mean but, to many eyes, an awe-inspiring structure. Even if the universe in its balance of forces or their perhaps blind interplay is seen as inimical to man, that is so much the greater challenge. Cyrano cries: "But one does not fight because there is hope of winning! No! . . . no! . . . it is so much finer to fight when it is no use!" If the mind of man pronounces the universe meaningless, it can do so only as an instrument capable of formulating meaning, and thus, created by and a part of that universe, represents a spark of meaning in it. Even if the mind of man is unique in an otherwise meaningless universe, it is unique then in dignity and the challenge to impose meaning upon chaos. That men seem to feel some kind of contradictory sense of triumph, bleak or gloomy though it be, in describing life and the world in uncomplimentary terms, is because in so doing they are dominating that which they disparage. The human mind is enlarged to what it can comprehend.

All these views of the universe have been linked to the question of the potentiality of modern tragedy and are irrelevant because historic and present-day tragedy has been oriented to man and this life and that which comes from within himself. They are questions of religion or philosophy and do not determine the dramatic experience we have come to know as tragedy, although inescapably as an environment they influence its precise terms. Whether or not there is a mystical moral order preexistent or external to man, a moral order may be continuously in process of racial or social creation as a direction within humanity. If in high tragedies of the past the protagonists sometimes seem to be born in fixed nobility, like Antigone, or to leap to a height of nobility like Oedipus, it has been characteristic of modern tragedies to show us protagonists struggling, groping, reaching toward nobility, attaining "not enough to weave a banner with," perhaps, but enough to reveal spiritual self-determination as the possible direction of humanity and enough for humbling awe and purifying catharsis. The active will is there, and that is the primal requisite to tragedy, the individual will and personal identity as reality. If that is destroyed by any necessary modern view of man, tragedy is lost and man is lost. That this should happen, however, is paradoxical: scientific reason, an activity of individual human minds and wills, cannot reduce the conception of personality to complete disintegration without invalidating itself. The literary expressions of denial of all dignity to man also contain their own contradiction as manifestation again of mind and will, a transcending for the consciousness of the artist of what appears to be the awful truth by exercising upon it the arduous process of organization and control of artistic creation.

The depressed views of the world and human nature are probably as much a reflection of social disillusion as of science. Certainly the most extreme manifestations, such as the plays of Beckett and Ionesco, have come from Europe where there has been so much more basis for social despair out of the bitterness of experience than in this country. On the other hand, out of the period of Nazi occupation in France came tragedies such as Anouilh's *Antigone* and Sartre's *The Flies,* somewhat cold in *Antigone* and barely above the rim of despair in *The Flies,* but nevertheless achieving assertion of human dignity. Tragedy is not a matter of facts but of what is made of them. After all, there is no more bitter expression of disillusion than in *Hamlet* or more savage expression of the vileness of man and the corruption of society than in *King Lear,* not even in *The Flies;* and this darkest awareness on Shakespeare's part is integrated into two of the greatest tragedies of transcendence. In 1928 Mr. Krutch saw the reconciliation to life by means of the tragic spirit, like religious faith, as an inevitable decline before the pursuit of intellectual truth into ultimate death in the future. Eugene O'Neill, in 1928, was writing what proved to be one of his least effective plays, *Dynamo,* "to dig at the roots," he stated, "of the sickness of today as I feel it—the death of an old God and the failure of science and materialism to give any satisfying new one for the surviving primitive religious instinct to find a meaning for life in, and to comfort its fears of death with." For anyone to write at that time without such awareness, he continued, seemed to him "simply scribbling around on the surface of things." *

The conviction expressed by Maxwell Anderson in the introduction to the publication of *Winterset* in 1935, that "An age of reason will be followed once more by an age of faith in things unseen," was

* Barrett H. Clark, *Eugene O'Neill, the Man and His Works* (Revised version), Dover Publications, New York, 1947, p. 120.

similarly spoken from a position of suspension between what seemed
irretrievably lost old faith and an unsatisfactory present: "What faith
men will then have, when they have lost their certainty of salvation
through laboratory work, I don't know, having myself only a faith
that man will have a faith." Since what seemed a cataclysmic disruption to religious faith from modern science millions of common
men and women have found adjustment of faith; and in the twentieth century, increasingly to our present decade, more intellect of the
highest order and of such diverse character and background as
the French Catholic philosophers Gabriel Marcel and Paul Claudel,
the international Albert Schweitzer, and the American Christian
realist, Reinhold Niebuhr, has been applied to sustaining traditional
religion than at any time, possibly, since the days of St. Thomas
Aquinas. Emerson remarked on the desirability of recognizing a
pop-gun for a pop-gun and not the crack of doom, and what appeared to be the wave of the future may turn out to be a splash.
Scientific inquiry examines but does not change human nature, although assuredly the scientific spirit is part of that nature and its
total direction and growth. It does not seem probable that the need
of the human spirit for tragedy, as for religion, will cease to exist
in the predictable future. In the meantime, tragedies are being written today.

The most effective modern tragedies have been, particularly in
the United States, what have come to be termed tragedy of the common man in contrast to Aristotle's dictum and Shakespeare's practice of protagonists of high station. Contrary to a rather general
assumption, I feel no conviction that such tragedy is the inevitable
mode for the future, or even for the present. It does possess an
adjustment to our immediate time that goes deeper than the justification frequently offered, that we live in a democratic instead of an
aristocratic society. There are two requirements for an audience to
experience the catharsis of tragedy: identification of the audience
with recognition of suffering and catastrophe as a universal of human
life; and identification of the audience with the capacity of man to
transcend his fate by maintenance of the integrity of his own personality. Periclean Greece and Elizabethan England were periods of
high confidence in man's faculties, and in his moral capacity. For the
balance of the tragic experience the greater problem was to identify

the audience with the possibility to himself of tragic fate. When catastrophe overtook even a man not only of powerful personal faculties but with all the social support of rank, wealth, and prestige, no one in the audience could escape the awareness: this could happen to me. In our less high-spirited age the audience is prone to awareness of the dire possibilities for everyone, including themselves, and the greater problem is to lift them up to the expanding identification with moral capacity. When the protagonist is a common man like themselves or, as is so often true in our tragedies, in some respects below the typical audience member, and even he can rise to nobility, the audience responds more readily with identification. The important truth of modern tragedy is not so much that a little man can suffer as much as a great man, but that a common man can possess as much nobility as a man in high position. It is also true that the protagonists of tragedy, the old or the new, are uncommon men as individuals whatever their station. Tragedy does not deal in the ordinary levels of experience, but exalts us with revelation of human potentiality. That the heights are rare is no more true to the modern temper than to the consciousness of Shakespeare in *King Lear:* "Thou hast one daughter/Who redeems nature from the general curse." Modern audiences and readers respond to Oedipus and Lear because they were created eternally as men, a part of common humanity, not because they were kings, and I see no inescapable reason why a modern tragedy could not be written of a president, a prime minister, or a head of the AFL-CIO, or even of a man like Hamlet who, more than a prince, represented for his time the highest level of intellectual capacity and development.

Another frequent assumption for modern tragedy is that of the realistic bias, that to make contact with our time it must be contemporary in setting and in prose. The identification of the audience with tragedy for catharsis is with an experience of something larger, above, and beyond themselves, to detach them from themselves for clearer perspective and self-awareness. The use of poetry in the Greek and Elizabethan tragedies and of stories not contemporary but out of the national culture were aids to the detachment and the exaltation. In our own time, Maxwell Anderson's *Winterset,* contemporary in setting, gained by poetry, and Arthur Miller's

The Crucible, set in an historical background of our national culture, is a tragedy of higher effect than the contemporary *Death of
a Salesman.* Although in prose, the detachment of a slightly archaic
speech released the dialogue to a compactness and intensity of
expression through imagery and a unity of rhythm without suggestion of artificiality by which the play is the most poetic in effect
of any prose drama I know since Synge's *Riders to the Sea.*

Theories of whether or not tragedy can exist, or of how it should
be formed for our time and the future, are helpless before the tragedies that are written. Like Maxwell Anderson with his "faith that
men will have a faith," I believe that human nature will continue to
need and create for itself in varying forms the spiritual balance and
expansion of tragic catharsis as purification.

The idea of comedy most readily suggests laughter, but laughter
may be the overflow of joy, it may be the spontaneous response to
the ludicrous, or it may be ridicule of folly—a by-product, an
end in itself, or an instrument of correction. These three divisions
represent the basic directions which comedy has taken from its
origin in the *comus,* a festive pageant of joy and mirth in the worship
of Dionysus as the god of fertility and life-giving in ancient Greece.
In some modes of comedy joy has been forgotten in the sole end of
mirth, and in others the mirth has become purposeful and even grim.
In Greece by the time comedy had become fully developed as a
dramatic form Aristotle defined it in distinction to tragedy simply
as "an imitation of characters of a lower type who are not bad in
themselves but possessed of faults not painful and destructive but
with something of the ludicrous in theme." In other words, Aristotle
did not recognize comedy as joyous, but only as laughter-provoking
with possibly some correctiveness of minor faults by ridicule.

Comedy appears in its most pure and complete form as the balance to tragedy in a total view of life in what is commonly called
the romantic comedy of Elizabethan drama, attaining its perfection
in Shakespeare's *As You Like It* and *Twelfth Night* and Thomas
Dekker's *The Shoemaker's Holiday.* Just as that aspect of life of
man as a creature of circumstance, of fate, subject to forces beyond
his control, is isolated and purified in tragedy, the other aspect
of life, man in freedom and power of will attaining his ends and

desires of earthly happiness, is isolated in comedy. As soon as one
enters upon one of these plays one feels oneself in a good world
as assuredly as in a great tragedy one enters at once into a sense
of doom. We have confidence in the world of these comedies. There
may be evil people in them, as in *As You Like It,* but they are not
terrifying and are converted from their evil in the end. There are
serious situations and obstacles to happiness but they are met in
high spirits. Rosalind banished in the Forest of Arden delights us
with the glow and sparkle of her wit, and Viola pining for Orsino's
love delivers his messages to Olivia with irrepressible gallantry. The
happy endings of such plays are no forced convention but integral
to the truth of life which is their concern. *As You Like It* and
Twelfth Night—with *Much Ado About Nothing* not quite pure in
spirit but essentially of the company—have been grouped under
such descriptions as Shakespeare's golden comedies or his joyous
comedies. Joyousness is the essence of such comedies. Happiness
naturally follows in such a world, but their character lies not in the
attainment of the ends of desire but the spirit in which they are pursued. Neither is laughter for the audience the object of the pure
comedy. Joy easily overflows into laughter, and in the relaxation of
a good world there is likely to be merrymaking and laughter at
one another's expense within the play, all of which the audience
shares. There are human foibles, too, aplenty in these plays which
the playwright holds up to the view and delectation of the audience,
but gently, merrily, without harshness and with no purpose to correct. We can laugh at the troubles of the characters because they
are of the kind for which a sense of humor would be a saving grace
if they were our own; furthermore, the characters often laugh gayly,
like Rosalind, or, like Viola, quip ruefully at their own trials. The
mood which releases laughter, not the laughter, is the end. Pure
comedy expresses awareness of all the good things of life, and its
philosophy is in Sir Toby's challenge to Malvolio in *Twelfth Night:*
"Dost thou think, because thou art virtuous, there shall be no more
cakes and ale?" The virtue of Malvolio was merely a solemn and
self-righteous sobriety and Sir Toby's zest was not only for cakes
and ale to the physical palate but for the accompanying merriment
and fellowship.

Romantic comedy is an unfortunate and misleading term for

what I have called pure comedy, an expression of the bias that there can be only a tragic view of life rather than perception of the tragic aspect of life. From this bias life is tragic and the only serious alternative to suffering with man is to laugh at the absurdity of his futile posturings, gestures, and scramblings about. The implication of romantic is that the comedy so designated is unreal, an escape from life into wishful thinking. Yet it is Sean O'Casey who could write what Brooks Atkinson has called "the theatre's most memorable cry of agony"—Juno Boyle's speech at the end of *Juno and the Paycock:* "Sacred heart o' Jesus, take away our hearts o' stone, and give us hearts of flesh! Take away this murdherin' hate, an' give us thine own eternal love!"—who can protest today against those who write "as if life never had time for a dance, a laugh or a song," and say "I always thought that life had a lot of time for these things, for each was a part of life itself." * It has been one of the distinguishing accomplishments of Sean O'Casey's genius to mingle the two parts of life in the same play, from his early plays to *Cock-a-Doodle Dandy* receiving its first production late in 1958. Pure tragedy is a long established phrase and pure comedy would seem the most accurate description of the complementary form. The synthesis of the total nature and meaning of man and the universe belongs to philosophy and religion and is beyond drama, the essence of which is conflict, but the white light broken into its spectrum becomes in its darker range the material for pure tragedy, with its lighter range for pure comedy.

Pure comedy is of rare occurrence in modern drama and has reached no such heights as the Elizabethan, in part because, like pure tragedy, it needs the imaginative heightening of poetry. Christopher Fry's *The Lady's Not for Burning* possesses the rare commodity of poetry in modern drama and comes near the tradition, but underneath lies the modern realistic pressure for the admixture of the good and bad in life in each play. Love wins by a hair's breadth. Thomas Mendip, the disillusioned hero with his deathwish, comes at the end to say to Jennet, "I shall be loath to forgo one day of you, Even for the sake of my ultimate friendly death"; but it is by way of:

* "O'Casey's Credo," New York *Times,* Nov. 9, 1958, Section 2, p. 2.

> *Girl, you haven't changed the world.*
> *Glimmer as you will, the world's not changed.*
> *I love you, but the world's not changed. Perhaps*
> *I could draw you up over my eyes for a time*
> *But the world sickens me still.*

Mr. Fry seems to declare by the play that bad as the world is, it is worth living through for the love and beauty, the romantic mystery, strangeness, and wonder, that are part of it also. The quality that allies the play most closely to pure comedy is the humorous zest for the whole of life with the strangeness of its juxtapositions of the sordid and the beautiful, the dull and the wonderful. The exuberant flood of words and imagery in which flights of fancy are abruptly deflated by a flat phrase is an expression of the sense of excitement before the total spectacle.

Lennox Robinson's plays for the Abbey Theatre, *The White-headed Boy* and especially *The Far-off Hills,* attain, to an exceptional degree for the limitations of pure realism, the spirit of pure comedy. From the latter play one goes out from the theater with the warm sense of having spent the evening with fine people. One's laughter, of which there has been much, is the tender laughter engaged by those we love, such as members of one's own family. In contemporary American playwriting the nearest approach to pure comedy has tended to appear as only an element in farce comedies, our most successful area of comedy, as in Bella and Samuel Spewack's *Boy Meets Girl.* The play ostensibly is a satire on Hollywood, but what holds one's memory is something of warmth and serene joy around the ineffable Susie, the girl who lives according to nature and finds it good. John Patrick's *The Teahouse of the August Moon* is a not very robust follower in the footsteps of the great tradition. The Okinawa of the play is a good world in which the Okinawans are all charming and fine people and the Americans sent by Washington to convert them to modern civilization all succumb to the Okinawan way of life. The play is pleasant and enjoyable but does not possess distinction of imagination or writing. Had Sean O'Casey chosen separation of tragedy and comedy as his way of playwriting, he possesses the Elizabethan imaginative strength of the twofold vision of life and the feeling for language as the instru-

ment of power to have written pure comedy more worthily, perhaps, than any modern playwright has done. Possibly the closest
approximation to the spirit of Elizabethan pure comedy in actual
achievement in modern drama is the Rodgers and Hammerstein
musical *Oklahoma!* The new American music drama which is dis-
placing the old modes of musical comedy, with imaginative heightening by music and dance taking the place of poetry of language,
holds future potentialities in this direction.

The second major division of comedy, that of laughter for its own
sake, has been the most continuous and universal. People enjoy
laughter, laughter makes them feel good; it is a pleasure and end in
itself needing no justification. The basis of such laughter is, in general, perception of incongruities of some kind. In farce the characters
are involved exaggeratedly in situations of absurdity and embarrassment, commonly but not necessarily physical. There has always
been particular delight in the incongruity of dignity disrupted—
the traditional example of the temptation of a top hat to the small
boy with a snowball—but self-assurance meeting embarrassment
with aplomb is also an incongruity and is one of the sources of
laughter in comedy of manners. In the university of my under-
graduate years the commencement procession was led by the president of the university and an eminent scientist of majestic girth
whose academic gown was the scarlet robe of the British Royal
Society and whose cap was the black Oxford tam. One year as they
proceeded down the central walk in full view of the commencement
guests a wind caught the cap from the scientist's head. It alighted
on its edge and rolled. Its owner immediately broke into pursuit,
ample scarlet robe flying. Each time he overtook his cap and
stooped for recovery the wind whisked it away. At last, without
pausing to stoop for it, he extended a foot in his stride and brought
the cap to earth. The action of the wind introduced farce and
brought laughter from the impromptu audience. When the protagonist chose in defiance of all dignity to pursue, and after successive
defeats, chose again in defiance of dignity to exercise a triumphant
strategy the situation was advanced to comedy of character, and the
audience responded with climactic laughter. When the gentleman
with supreme unself-consciousness replaced the cap upon his head,
walked with unpompous calm back to the head of the procession,

turned and fell into step with the president, a second climax was enacted, this time of high comedy, and the audience applauded.

In what is commonly called low comedy we have characters of the lower social order, such as Shakespeare's Bottom with his company of mechanics, and Dogberry and the Watch, who by ignorance and lack of cultivation engage in stupidities and uncouthnesses that are incongruous in relation to an average level of social conduct and intelligence, faults as Aristotle wrote, "not painful, and destructive but with something of the ludicrous in them." The nature of the characters is likely to lead low comedy into the physical situations and horseplay of farce, but the quality of the character is the essential. Such characters are self-absorbed, sublimely unaware of their own deficiencies, in fact, likely to be filled with self-conceit; even when made the butt of jests, verbal or physical, they may be discommoded but not embarrassed. Consequently we laugh at them freely without malice or contempt, cherishing them for the spectacle they provide.

High comedy is a more inclusive term than low comedy, in general designating comedy which depends primarily on finely drawn characterization and wit rather than on situation or physical horseplay. Farce comedy involves characterization but is essentially comedy of situation with the characters fairly simply drawn around idiosyncrasies that give rise to the plot, as in Oliver Goldsmith's *She Stoops to Conquer.* The characters of low comedy are of a simplicity that leads naturally to farcical action and buffoonery and even in their physical appearance are usually laughable. High comedy as comedy of character covers a wide range, but complex characters of wit, whose eccentricities tend to motivate plot, are more likely to belong to the upper strata, although such characters can be found on various levels of society. A notable achievement of Shakespeare in the creation of Falstaff was that he combined the appeals of low and high comedy in one person. High comedy has tended to be associated with the upper levels of society and its most representative form is comedy of manners.

Comedy of manners, otherwise farthest removed from low comedy, corresponds in the detachment of the audience in its laughter. Comedy of manners is comedy of a sophisticated society in which the members by social and economic status have a considerable freedom to flout morality, but not fashion or the correct manner. Louis Kronenburger, who as a critic is particularly at home in the comedy of manners, summarizes the basis of the form in *The Thread of Laughter* as follows:

> Here we have hardly less than a picture of society itself; here the men and women are but parts of a general whole, and what survives—if we have it from the past—is likely to be known as The Restoration Scene, or Regency London, or Victorian Family Life. Here the drawing room is not merely the setting of the play or novel, but the subject and even the hero; here enter all the prejudices, the traditions, the taboos, the aspirations, the absurdities, the snobberies, of a group. The group to constitute itself one, must partake of a common background and accept a similar view of life." *

The sources of laughter in comedy of manners are many: the gauche attempts at fashion of the outsider trying to break in; the affectations of those for whom fashion is the whole and end of life, not its polished surface; the absurdities of fashion held up to view by the mocking rebel within the fold. More than any other form of comedy, comedy of manners, by a natural dramatic intensification of life, is dominated by wit. Wit is fashionable in sophisticated society and its members have leisure to cultivate it. The essence of wit is the imaginatively apt association of ideas that are incongruous or ridiculous to the imagination. Comedy of manners affords to the delectation of the audience the flow of spirit of the truewits side by side with the unconscious incongruities of the badly aimed efforts of the witwouds.

The French have seldom and briefly lost touch entirely with comedy of manners. In English drama Restoration comedy of manners constitutes one of its most brilliant episodes. Amorous adventuring is not inescapably a material of comedy of manners, although there is a natural tendency toward moral license in fashionable society, where social and economic position gives freedom from censure so long as outward decorum is observed. In the period of the Restoration the world of fashion, which was all that

* Alfred A. Knopf, New York, 1952, p. 8.

counted for the playwrights and their audience, was to a particular degree a corrupt society, which provided as plot material in a general background of cynicism and self-interest the pursuit of fortunes by inheritance or marriage and of illicit love affairs. Only second to those fundamental interests was the pursuit of fashion as an end in itself and of wit as a fashionable attainment. The Restoration playwrights were a part of the society of which they wrote, knew it from within, and stripped it bare in their comedies. Because of the unity of the world within the play in its detachment from morality the audience is released to laughter at the undignified postures and embarrassments into which men and women are led in the pursuit of self-interest and self-gratification, and equally at the witty composure with which these men and women of the world frequently carry off their discomfitures. At the same time there is a moral norm outside the world of fashion to which the attitudes and conduct within the play are so gross an incongruity as to provide a further occasion for detached laughter.

All literary forms mingle with those adjacent, and some Restoration comedy becomes satirical, at least urbanely critical, not only of the affectations but of the immorality of its fashionable world. For example, in Congreve's *The Way of the World* Millament and Mirabell are so high-spirited, witty, and charming, with at least moral direction of character, that we are won to identification. They are in line of descent from Shakespeare's Beatrice and Benedick and belong to comedy of character as well as of manners.

In modern drama, especially American, comedy of manners fares badly. The semi-British semi-American practice of Noel Coward, as in *Private Lives* and *Design for Living*, was too self-consciously shockingly risqué and, after all, was too soberly moral. They were plays with the thesis of individual unconventional morality as a higher morality. Samuel Taylor's *Sabrina Fair* in 1953 was a true comedy of manners, set in the society of the Long Island rich (not immoral), and was unified in tone and smoothly polished, if not sparkling, to a degree that made it something of an oasis in recent American playwriting. S. N. Behrman of our playwrights has represented most consistently the graces of comedy of manners, the urbanity, style, and wit; but his best plays, those of fair ladies such as *Biography* and *The End of Summer,* are more plays of individual character and personal problems than of a society. Society is admirably created in so far as it is present, but on the whole Behrman's plays have the manner rather than the substance of comedy of manners. Philip Barry aimed more closely at the substance with far less of the manner in *Philadelphia Story*. Our plays generally, including our comedies down to such exercises in popular appeal as George Axelrod's *The Seven Year Itch,* tend to be plays of individuals, however democratically representative, not of a society except when the society is confronted as a problem.

Still within the area of comedy of laughter for its own sake but involving identification as well as detachment is the complex level of comedy of character—Falstaff the supreme achievement. Falstaff is fully conscious of the incongruities of his person and conduct with the social norm for a gentleman and a knight. He is an individualist who chooses his own values: he is an egoist, a materialist, a sensualist, and a hedonist. He is "the fat knight" because he loves food, sack and sugar, and laughter and engages in physical activity only as necessary. For freedom from social pressures he renounces the court and maintains life by highway robbery and chicanery. He lives for personal enjoyment and is himself. He acts at times like a coward: he will "fight no longer than he sees reason" and runs for his life when in the dark he is surprised and believes himself outnumbered at the Gadshill robbery. And at the Battle of Shrewsbury when he finds himself assuredly about to be bested by a doughty opponent he lies down and plays dead. The groundlings at the Globe Theatre probably saw Falstaff as a low comedy character and laughed at the incongruity of a knight who was a coward. But Falstaff would not have chosen to be a coward and the central fact of his character is self-determination. The incongruity with his knighthood was in the values for which he chose to fight or not to fight, and the undignified conduct, in knightly terms, he was willing to adopt to save himself. He was ready to risk his life in highway robbery with the odds reasonable to the object, money to maintain life; and when there was a war on and his job inescapably was to fight he conducted himself with cheerful fatalism. The incongruity of Falstaff as a knight was not cowardice but deliberate rejection of the whole idea of knightly honor, challenging death for the sake of honor as against preserving life for its enjoyments:

Well, if Percy be alive, I'll pierce him. If he do come in my way, so; if he do not, if I come in his willingly, let him make a carbonado of me. I like not such grinning honour as Sir Walter hath. Give me life; which if I can save, so; if not, honour comes unlook'd for, and there's an end.

Every gentleman in Shakespeare's audience would recognize a more delightful incongruity here than that of a simple coward knight.

The fullness of satisfaction in Falstaff as a comic character is that he is at once a mass of incongruities and at the same time there is such completeness, a wholeness, a consistency about him. There is something of shock, an incongruity, in the agility of his wit coming from so gross a body that makes it the more laughable. At the same time the very unquenchable flow of his wit, embracing humor and fancy as well, is of a piece with his physique in amplitude. Falstaff knows and is at ease with himself. He can direct wit upon himself and revels in the wit his fatness arouses: "I am not only witty in myself, but the cause that wit is in other men." Because of his complete self-awareness we laugh with him as well as at him. Low comedy gives rise to laughter entirely of detachment as does comedy of manners, essentially. Comedy of character, as that of Falstaff, may combine detachment and identification. We laugh at the incongruities at the same time that we like and enjoy the old reprobate as company, but the deepest identification is an experience of release for the time into freedom from the pressures of society with its constraints and responsibilities. We join in laughter like that of Prince Hal who with Falstaff and their comrades, in Hotspur's phrase, "daff'd the world aside and bid it pass."

The third main stream of comedy is that of corrective laughter. The classical tradition as expressed by Ben Jonson and again in the eighteenth century in England is that of attacking follies rather than vices by holding them up to ridicule. Vices are motivated by self-interest or passion and are not readily laughed out of countenance, while follies most commonly spring from vanity, and ridicule cuts at their root. From Ben Jonson's *Every Man in His Humor* to Sheridan's *The School for Scandal,* satirical comedy was essentially a form of comedy of manners with exaggeration and the barbs of wit as the weapons. Jonson was avowedly and vigorously satirical in purpose. In the comedies of the Restoration the witling apes of fashion were assuredly held up to ridicule but whether correctively or purely for laughter is questionable. The degree to which satirical intention was realized in the Restoration playwrights' depiction of the world of fashion, including its cynicism and libertinism, has been a subject of critical dispute. Sheridan in *The School for Scandal,* writing for the more strait-laced audience of the eighteenth century, deals in the suggestion of sin rather than sin. The names of his scandalmongers, Lady Sneerwell, Mr. Snake, and Mrs. Candour, indicate satirical intent and the hypocrisy of Joseph Surface is exposed and the essential goodness of the erring brother Charles revealed and rewarded; but the play is too slickly theatrical, the happy resolution too precisely dovetailed to the sentiments of his audience, to carry moral conviction such as is communicated by Ben Jonson. In comedy of manners, when satirical, there is always a question of how far the ridicule of fops, rakes, and dupes is truly corrective or merely an ego-expansion for an audience which seldom sees itself, but always a neighbor, as the object of aim. Of the moral fervor of Ben Jonson there can be no doubt when in *Volpone* he left comedy of manners and folly behind, except in subsidiary characters, and exposed the vice of avarice as fully to loathing as to ridicule. However, in spite of the meting out of poetic justice in the end to all the knaves, there being no one to be made happy, *Volpone* is so grim as satire that little of comedy remains. Molière remains the greatest master of satirical comedy, to the purpose of which he adapted farce comedy, comedy of manners, and comedy of character. In *Les Précieuses Ridicules* he aimed so directly at the most brilliant level of the Parisian society of Louis XIV in its most extravagant affectation that members were converted and the authority of precious standards of literary taste and social etiquette was broken. In *Tartuffe* he attacked religious hypocrisy as savagely in the presentation of Tartuffe himself as Ben Jonson attacked avarice. The satirical portrait of Orgon whose credulity is duped by Tartuffe is as extreme as that of Tartuffe, but of a folly, not a vice, and is ultimately not harsh. The exposure and discomfiture of Tartuffe at the hands of the women of Orgon's household as attractive comedy characters of audience identification in an exuberant sequence of complications make the play one of the great comedies as well as a great satire.

In the eighteenth and nineteenth centuries in England, Europe, and America, the corrective laughter of satire became lost in comedy of sentiment in which the corrective function was left to the moral lesson of poetic justice in the happy ending, with virtue rewarded and folly and vice punished or reformed.

George Bernard Shaw in our time adopted the stage as the most effective medium for social reform, and comedy as the form with most audience appeal. He exposed human conduct as neither folly nor vice but as irrational; he was concerned with the conduct and attitudes of individuals only as representative of and constituting society, and with society not in its manners but its fundamental morality. The respected and the established were particularly the objects of his exposure to rational questioning. Although the materials and methods of his comedies are various, he characteristically employed lucidity of exposition, pointed with wit, rather than the exaggerations of satire. His plays were motivated by high seriousness of purpose and his reformatory attitude toward the theater itself was to make it a place for intelligent discussion of matters of importance. His plays are not merely palatable but highly enjoyable as comedies because of his masterly revelation of the incongruities of the irrational in the light of the rational with the shock of reversal, of the unexpected. Suddenly it is what has been accepted as rational that is seen to be irrational.

George Bernard Shaw created a unique form of corrective comedy. He has had influence but no worthy follower. The most distinctive development since that of Shaw has been in the use of irony by contemporary French playwrights. Irony as a critical instrument is as old as the ancient Greek origins of comedy. It is a significant element in Shaw's total method and has been especially characteristic in modern drama of French and middle-European playwrights. Irony has, however, been given an emphasis as the basic method of expression of a mood of serious and critical comedy by French playwrights during and since the war to a degree that justifies speaking of contemporary French ironic comedy as a mode. Of such plays that have been produced in English translation or adaptation in this country, Jean Anouilh in *The Waltz of the Toreadors* directly by gross farce and caricature mordantly exposes the high-romantic dreams of a retired French general as illusions and posturings and ironically reduces him at the end from the momentary gesture of suicide to seeking comfort with the new maid in the dusk. The greater irony, however, is the entirely indirect communication of humane pity by Anouilh in his most pitiless exposure of the general. In *Time Remembered* Anouilh ironically shatters the walls of the empty structure of sentiment for the memory of a dead dancer in which a prince has enveloped himself, by the intrusion of a live milliner. More ironically Anouilh undertakes communication of his devastation of romantic sentiment within the mood of a gently romantic fairy tale. This latter irony is not entirely successful; *Time Remembered* is a cream puff which would be the better for some lemon added to the filling. In *Clerambard* by Marcel Aimé irony is heaped upon irony. The Vicomte de Clerambard, an unpleasant tyrant to his family and neighborhood, becomes a worse and more unpleasant rather than a better man when converted to religiosity by the experience of a visitation from St. Francis of Assisi. The visitation proves to have been a delusion and the Vicomte is convinced that the appearance of St. Francis was an hallucination. He is then provided with a real miracle, which everyone sees but the local priest, and the Vicomte resumes his self-appointed mission. In *Clerambard* there are undoubted sharp barbs of criticism ironically projected and there is also in the ending an ironic suspension of meaning. Jean Giraudoux's entire play *The Mad Woman of Chaillot* is a single consistently composed irony. *The Mad Woman* is a droll and happy play. The city of Paris and its common people are threatened with destruction by the exploiters of society for gain. The exploiters are all rounded up in a neat human package and enticed into the sewers of Paris and the door closed upon them forever by a stratagem of the Countess Aurelia, the mad woman of Chaillot, and three other mad ladies, her friends. Paris, or the world, is saved and the common people are released to simple human goodness and happiness. The Countess concludes, "You see how simple it all was? Nothing is ever so wrong in this world that a sensible woman can't set it right in the course of an afternoon." The gist of the play is not in the obvious surface irony that it is the mad people who are sane, but that the entire play is a wistful fairy tale. With no overt sign within the play Giraudoux succeeds in saying clearly: How pleasant it would be if the problems of the world and their solution were so simple, but they *are not*. By the triumph and happiness within the play we are reminded of the bitter truth of life.

In contemporary American playwriting, satire has been most successful as a development of farce comedy: attachment to material accumulation taken off in George S. Kaufman's *You Can't Take It With You,* Hollywood's artificialities and absurdities in the Spewacks' *Boy Meets Girl,* the vulgarities of uncultivated use of money and more seriously the corruption of government and degradation of the individual by money used as power in Garson Kanin's *Born Yesterday.* There is an aesthetic pleasure in the experience of purity of form, the practice of clean-cut isolation of genres, by which a play is sometimes spoken of approvingly as an example of pure comedy of manners, satire, farce comedy, or comedy of character. Such experience is not characteristic of contemporary American playwriting, or of modern drama generally. *Born Yesterday* is as much a comedy of character as it is a satirical farce comedy, with Billie Dawn the center of enjoyment from the beginning and progressively engaging audience identification until she becomes a romantic heroine by the end. There is also injection of social criticism in direct speech as well as by satire, and of democratic idealism. Modern drama has been a free drama with little concern for rules, or for that matter, for aesthetic effect as such. At its serious levels modern dramatists have been concerned with getting any and all essential truth of life onto the stage, and at the lower levels with whatever will attract to the box office. Such drama has its compensations of variety and flexibility, of the unexpected, and of a vital drive. Especially, serious concern with social problems has been so dominant in the development of modern drama as to move into all the forms, even in so light a comedy as *Born Yesterday* or our higher dramas conceived definitely as tragedy, such as *Winterset* and *Death of a Salesman.*

In classical Greek and Roman drama there were only the two divisions, comedy and tragedy. The Renaissance inherited the two great traditions and developed a third major form for which the term tragi-comedy was invented. Shakespeare's contemporary, John Fletcher, defined tragi-comedy in an address to the Reader introducing *The Faithful Shepherdess* as follows:

A tragi-comedy is not so called in respect to mirth and killings, but in respect it wants deaths, which is enough to make it no tragedy, yet brings some near it, which is enough to make it no comedy, which must be a representation of familiar people, with such kind of trouble as no life be questioned [*i.e.,* be put in danger], so that a god is as lawful in this as in a tragedy, and mean people as in a comedy.

What Fletcher was aiming at was freedom from the unity of mood of tragedy and comedy which by classical rules limited the kinds of characters appropriate to each form: for tragedy men and women of the higher orders and permissibly gods, for comedy people of low station. The tragi-comedy was a play of serious situations which did not, however, end catastrophically, as in tragedy. The way was being prepared for the sentimental comedies in France and England of the eighteenth century in which with little humor, if any, the principals were dragged through heart-rending situations to a happy ending of sorts, while excessive misfortunes and even the deaths of secondary characters along the way provided additional pathos to the general orgy of emotion. Oliver Goldsmith's hearty farce comedy *She Stoops to Conquer* was a protest against the lachrymose comedies of his day but the combination of an hour and fifty minutes of situations of overwrought emotion with ten minutes of happy ending survived through the next century. In the latter half of the nineteenth century, however, with the rise of scientific and rationalistic interpretation of human life, realism in literature, and a strong and reformatory social consciousness, there developed a new kind of drama serious in mood which is termed social drama.

Social drama is drama serious in material and treatment in which the outcome may be either happy or unhappy according to the logic of events. Tragedy is man against fate, against beyond-human forces, and is accordingly unified in mood to the inevitability of catastrophe. In social drama man is in conflict with forces in society or within himself, which are closely related as the individual and society are constantly interactive. The forces in social drama are human-size, which precludes the inevitability of tragedy, although in any given instance such forces may be relatively too strong for the individual concerned and lead to defeat. Social drama branches out in several directions. First of all, social drama is a study of humanity in action, in conflict, to reveal truth of human life. The focus may be outward on the interrelations of the protagonist with other people or with social institutions, or inward on the individual to the degree that we speak of psychological or character drama. Ibsen's *A Doll House,* for example, is a story of individualized characters but essentially in their dramatic relation to the institution of marriage, while in *Hedda Gabler,* a character drama, the story takes place within a marriage but the marriage is merely an irritant to a potentiality of conflict that is inherent in Hedda's character. Social forces have entered into the forming of Hedda's character but they are in the background in the play, with the focus on what she is.

Social drama readily becomes the social problem play correctively directed against conditions in society destructive of human welfare and happiness. Tragedy deals with the ultimate metaphysical fact of evil, suffering inescapable to human life as such, and acts only upon the inner spirit of man. Society is within human bounds, created by men and alterable by man. Tragedy releases us from futile, self-destructive rebellion; the social problem play stirs rebellion where it counts. It reveals the effects in human lives of social evils and leads to thoughtful consideration sensitized and energized by emotional identification. Contrary either to tragedy or comedy the ending of a social problem play may send the audience out from the theater with an emotion in part painful injected into the consciousness as a provocation to further thought. Although Ibsen's *Ghosts* in its organization is the closest to tragedy of his plays, with a suggestion of parallel between the scientific facts of heredity and transmitted disease to the idea of fate in Greek tragedy, there is no tragic catharsis in the ending. Mrs. Alving, confronted by the collapse of her son Oswald into the final imbecility of congenital syphilis, is left at the curtain of the play in suspension before the futile choice of administering the poison her son had provided with the injunction that she give it to him when this should happen, or devoting her life to sustaining the empty unlovely physical existence that is all that remains of her son. There is no tragic resolution of an act of will, only the grim, anguished recognition for Mrs. Alving of the truth of past error and present consequence. The ultimate causation of the catastrophe does not have the inevitability of tragic fate because it lies in social hypocrisies and personal timidities and the audience is left with the painful awareness, it need not have been. This is suitable to Ibsen's corrective purpose in *Ghosts*. The limited emotional satisfaction and release in the social problem play, whether the ending is unhappy or happy, arises primarily from the perception of logicality and truth.

In general the social problem play presents the evils of society on a foundation of values for human life held by the playwright and within the bounds of general principles. It gives the audience awareness of the evils and moves to thought which may at some time lead to action. If occasion for action arises the effect is to make the members of the audience more ready to respond and to act more intelligently. The line between the social problem play as such and its limited form, the propaganda play, is not a precisely fixed division, but in general when the play is focused on convincing the audience of a specific solution or to arousing to immediate action, it is a propaganda play. The playwright is a specialist only in human nature and values and in dramatic projection, but the pure social problem play without a suggestion of propaganda can lead to specific as well as general results by its energization to specialists in the field of the problem. On the evidence of a letter by Winston Churchill, then in the Home Office, which has supervision of the administration of justice, John Galsworthy's play *Justice* was directly responsible for a reform in English judicial procedure by which individual extenuating circumstances were admitted to consideration in criminal cases.

What may be called pure social drama and the social problem play of reform blend into one another to such degree that often any attempt to draw a line for classification can represent no more than a fine shade of emphasis. Ibsen affirmed as his dramatic faith that drama should be not only revelative, but redemptive—but to be redemptive it must be truly revelative; and Ibsen's plays are thought of very nearly as the archetypes both for modern social drama as such and the social problem play. The social dramatist also can mold comedy to his serious purpose. Shaw's comedies are meant to be both socially instructive and reformatory, and Galsworthy's only comedy of his better known plays, *The Pigeon,* pleasantly amusing and warmly human in its realistic portrayal of character without satirical exaggeration or wit, is as truly a social problem play as any that he wrote. Modern social drama arose and developed initially in identification with prose realism, and prose realism is generally thought of as its most characteristic form, but in its purpose it has embraced all the successive movements in the modern theater, including symbolism, expressionism, and theatricalism. Ibsen's poetic fantasy *Peer Gynt* is equally a social drama with *Ghosts,* and Ernst Toller's expressionistic dramas *Man and the Masses* and *The Machine-Wreckers* with Hauptmann's *The Weavers.* Thornton Wilder's theatricalist *The Skin of Our Teeth* is a social drama of the broadest sort with a philosophy of the human race as its theme. Symbolic philosophical drama is a distinctive development of social drama among contemporary French playwrights, as in the existentialist plays by Jean-Paul Sartre, such as *No Exit* and *The Flies,* and the plays existentialist in essence if not by avowal by Albert Camus, *Cross Purpose* and *Caligula.*

Although it is in modern drama from approximately the latter third of the nineteenth century that social drama has been defined and isolated as a category and has become the dominating mode, in its purpose it is by no means a modern invention. Euripedes was writing a pacifist play in his tragedy *The Trojan Women* with concern for the immediate relations between Athens and Sparta. Sophocles directed his *Oedipus at Colonos* toward Athenian patriotism and unity, and social problems move variously through others of the Greek tragedies. Shakespeare was concerned with national unity, political theory of kingship, and immediate dangers of civil war in his history plays *Richard II,* the two *Henry IV* plays, and *Henry V,* and with his thought less mature and clearly defined, in the earlier history plays. We see the social element in drama more readily when the plays and problems are immediate. What kind of dramatic content is viewed as social, even, is a matter of what a society believes in. If the modern world has tended to place faith in psychology, sociology, and science generally as most pertinent to the problem of man's state, medieval society possessed a background of belief in a very specific God and a very literal damnation or salvation in a life to come as the most important determinants of how man walked his earthly life; and the mystery and miracle plays of the Biblical story and the lives of saints and the allegorical morality plays, such as *Everyman,* were social dramas of that time.

While modern social drama in its origins and course has characteristically been positivistic in its philosophical foundation, limiting the search for truth to the observable and rationally knowable phenomena of nature, there has been in recent years a renewal of identification of drama with religious consciousness. Actually the atheistic philosophical dramas of Sartre and Camus have a negatively driven religious urgency, and Sartre in *The Flies* after virulently rejecting in the symbol of Zeus both Christianity specifically and all supernatural religion, proceeds to create a Messiah in his existentialist hero, Orestes, when he frees the people of Argos from their guilt consciousness, symbolized in the plague of flies, by assuming the guilt and drawing the flies to pursuit of himself alone. The plays of Paul Claudel, another of the modern French philosophical dramatists, are religious dramas of extraordinary intensity in which within the framework of Catholicism he affims non-materialistic and absolute values. The two most distinguished playwrights in England since Shaw, T. S. Eliot and Christopher Fry, are essentially religious dramatists. Eliot from *Murder in the Cathedral* to *The Confidential Clerk* has been writing about God, sin, and salvation in various manners and guises; and more than half of Christopher Fry's output other than adaptations, *Boy With a Cart, Thor, with Angels, The Firstborn,* and *A Sleep of Prisoners,* are religious in subject. In this country anyone with considerable acquaintance with plays in manuscript is likely to have become aware of a strong trend since 1945 away from the sociological to an ethical and religious approach to the problems of society, a seeking for a deeper motivation and energization for their solution than has been offered, with far from satisfactory results, by the economic, material, and scientific thought which has dominated the modern world. Partially because this direction has been most strong among the young men and inexperienced playwrights and partially because of the specialized character of Broadway and its audience the trend has been far more evident in manuscript than in professional production. In its ethical phase with religious undertones it has appeared powerfully in the plays of Arthur Miller, and in specifically religious terms in Clifford Odets' *The Flowering Peach,* a play of beauty not granted a high degree of Broadway success. The play is a homely elaboration of the story of Noah in which Odets, in contrast to his earlier plays, allegorically faces the world problem in the larger than economic terms of total moral stature. The play expresses belief in God as the height to which man's ideals reach at any given time, humility before man's imperfection as an instrument for carrying out his aspirations, and hope that man will make, not destroy, the world. Especially significant for the conjunction of social drama and religion as forces in the present time is the strong and widespread movement of cultivation of drama by the churches, Catholic, Jewish, and principal Protestant denominations. They all have national boards or other organizations for the fostering of religious drama, broadly and liberally defined, both in writing and production. Some of the strongest drama departments are in church universities; drama institutes and festivals are held; and productions are sponsored in churches, schools, and communities.

Social drama is a broad and flexible form which sprawls amorphously over the terrain of modern drama. By its demand for the truth, the whole truth, and nothing but the truth, so generally at the level of observable facts, both the isolation for intensification of an aspect of truth of pure tragedy and pure comedy and the exaggerations of satire are foreign to it. Comedy of manners, which reflects a direct and exact observation of society, is too limited to surface truth for the spirit of social drama. An emotion, the catharsis of tragedy or the release of laughter of comedy, is not its object. All these highly selective factors which through much of the history of drama have contributed to precision of form and comparatively clean-cut definition of categories are unoperative for social drama. It has pursued its vision of revelative and redemptive truth, freely creating form as it went, drawing upon and invading traditional forms, itself only tangentially concerned with form or tradition.

Social drama has been representative of the most distinctive achievements of the modern world, the search for objective truth and the concern for suffering, also of its limitations. The concentration on man's material existence has intensified humanitarianism and the pressures to remedy social evils, to remove causes of pain, interferences to personal happiness, and restrictions on individual self-realization. Spiritual values, however, have been lost sight of, individualism becomes self-centeredness, and attack on unnecessary evils becomes blind rebellion against all suffering and human limitations, catastrophic or petty. The age of splendid rebellion becomes the age of frustrations. Social drama both climbs to the heights and sinks to the depths of the society of which it is a reflection as well as an examination.

The great emotional releases which are a part of the function of the theater do not belong to social drama. In such drama emotion is not an end but a means to opening and sensitizing the mind to receptivity for perception of the truth revealed, or to energization of response when the purpose is reform. The social problem play may arouse indignation, but at its best, an indignation restrained and guided into thought. The social dramatist should have a passion for truth or a passion for reform which is felt by the audience and gives vitality to his play, but disciplined in the writing within bounds of emotion for the audience which permit of thoughtful perception and consideration. The great overwhelming and unifying sweep of emotion belongs to tragedy or to heroic drama just as the complete release of tension in laughter belongs to comedy. The entrance of philosophic and religious thought and areas of reality into drama opens the way again to primacy of emotions and tragedy, as in Arthur Miller's *The Crucible*. Outside the more specific definitions of religion as belief in God or in some supernatural power or moral authority, philosophy and religion impinge upon one another but with a line of demarcation. Philosophy has to do with the rational processes by which belief as to the nature of things is determined for and made acceptable to the intellect. Even a mystical philosophy represents the reasoning on which the conclusion of a mystical view of reality is founded. Religion in its broadest sense has to do with faith, with the commitment of oneself to a belief, whether it be in God, in man, or oneself, or even a cause or a leader. If the commitment is total of the whole self, it is religious in essence. The faith accepted may have been arrived at rationally, philosophically, though not necessarily so, or subsequently be substantiated by reason. Reason often is a guide to action but for any action of any kind to be taken there has to come a point when thought stops. The commitment to a faith is an action of the most significant sort and contains the potentiality for drama of intensity both in the struggle toward commitment and in the culminating act of acceptance. A faith possessed is that upon which a man will act, by which he will live resolutely, and for which he will die, and is the material for high drama and tragedy.

High drama is drama of man in the nobility of exercise of his will by moral choice in conflicts of magnitude and, unlike social drama, has as its object the release of powerful emotion in the audience. It includes, in addition to tragedy, heroic drama. In history of drama in the terminology of the neoclassicism of the seventeenth century, tragedy embraced all high drama in distinction to comedy and included plays with triumphant and happy endings as well as those of catastrophe and defeat, and the term heroic tragedy was used to express a dignity comparable to that of the admired heroic or epic poems of Homer. In the vogue of heroic tragedy in France and England the play was written in what was considered to be the nearest equivalent of Homer's poetic measure, the heroic couplet in English, the Alexandrine in French. The characters were of high station in settings remote from contemporary society; and the play was packed with strong situations of high passions in which the protagonist and other principals exercised their nobility of character in dilemmas involving honor, duty, loyalty, and love. Essentially the term heroic referred to magnitude. In England the heroic tragedies were extravagant and empty. In France the genius of Corneille created heroic tragedies in which the extravagance had something of magnificence and in which, especially in *Le Cid,* the heroic quality was not merely that of magnitude but true nobility for all time. In universally applicable terms heroic drama is drama of the power of man's will to achieve, not narrowly personal ends, but ends dictated by loyalty to ideals. The emotions aroused in the audience are admiration and emulation. Successful heroic drama has never been common; it has tended to give way to the more ultimate revelation attendant upon defeat in tragedy, or to sink into drama of escape, of vicarious excitements not provided by life for the audience. Shakespeare's *Henry V* is an heroic drama presenting an ideal of kingship. Schiller in *William Tell* wrote a drama of the heroism of the Swiss people in their devotion to freedom as well as of an individual hero. Rostand's *Cyrano de Bergerac* has been called many things, a romantic tragedy, a romantic comedy, a romantic character play, but above all else it is an heroic drama, a challenge to nobility. That heroic drama can be immediate to our own time was proved by Sidney Howard's and Paul de Kruif's *Yellow Jack,* a play on the heroism of medical research as specifically exemplified in the solution of the problem of the carrying of yellow fever by the *Aëdes aegypti* mosquito as the intermediate host. In the play the emphasis was on the heroism of the team of doctors in Cuba who proved their theory to their own minds by acting as guinea pigs, and then called on soldiers to volunteer for the same tests to gain the force of publicity for acceptance of their theory. Characteristically when a motion picture was made of the play the doctors were shadowed by focus on the heroism of the comman man in the soldiers. However, there was enough heroism to go round, and the motion-picture version serves to emphasize the breadth and immediacy of appeal possible to heroic drama. More recently, in *The Diary of Anne Frank* by Frances Goodrich and Albert Hackett, we had the quiet unexaggerated heroism of the thirteen-year-old girl who, in the unnatural confinement of two years in hiding from the Nazis, refused in the strength of her spirit to miss her girlhood and its growth or to lose faith in people. Just as significant is the heroism, presented without mitigation, of the weaknesses and failures of the two families in their struggle with adjustment to group living in confinement, privation, and fear. The dangers of heroic drama are exaggeration and sentimentalization, heroics instead of heroism, but at its best the effect of heroic drama provides an experience of exaltation.

The division of drama into categories could be extended into indefinite multiplicity, but it is the broad lines of distinction of purpose and function that are useful as an aid to penetration to meaning in the experience of plays. Neither are the categories rigidly divided; their definition is a matter for illuminating discussion, not for filing-cabinet classification. The different modes of drama, especially in modern drama, are often mingled in one play and by recognition of the several traditions at work the total complex meaning becomes more clear. Sartre's *The Flies* is notable in this respect. The play is based on the Greek tragedies of the story of Orestes and there is tragic catharsis in Orestes' consciousness of inner freedom transcending anguish. At the same time the emotional impact of catharsis is greatly moderated by the intellectual concentration on the play as a symbolic dramatization of the existentialist philosophy. The play is also a social problem play as the philosophy is one of engagement or identification with society in the problem of its degradation, which is dramatized in the action of Orestes in killing Aegisthus and Clytemnestra. By Orestes' assumption of the role of Messianic savior the play becomes heroic drama.

9

The Dramatic Climate of a Play :
Modern Movements

Equally important with the traditional modes of function and purpose in the climate of a play are the modern movements of form or method of communication. The varied forms have grown out of fresh conceptions of content and purpose for drama and are inseparable from meaning. In approximately the last third of the nineteenth century a revolution in drama occurred which in continuity to the present time has given us what we mean by modern drama. The unifying element in modern drama has been the impetus toward reality, the drive to get truth of life onto the stage. The forms which the pursuit of this purpose has taken can be divided generally into realistic and nonrealistic. In the critical parlance of recent years the terms representational and presentational drama have come into common use and are an accurate expression of the distinction between communicating reality through direct reproduction of the external forms of life and by means of theatrical symbols.

The second most striking characteristic of the modern theater has been variety, an increasing accumulation of forms. As the drive for truth of life has taken the dramatists into different areas of dramatic conflict and has led to creation of new forms for its expression the new movements neither displace what has preceded nor themselves die and pass away. They lose self-consciousness and sharp identity but become diffused into the theater as part of the

total repertory of form and manner upon which succeeding playwrights draw in fresh combination and application, or as influences
which they in part unconsciously follow. In no former theater has
such variety of forms existed in juxtaposition as in the European
and American theater of the twentieth century, an international theater interlocked and interactive by the readiness of modern communication. The character of each of the principal movements: realism,
naturalism, symbolism, expressionism, and succeeding variants of
nonrealistic form, needs to be understood both by definition and in
general temper as a part of the climate of playwriting in the modern
theater.

The revolt in European drama arose first in the movements of
realism and naturalism in such close association that it is often useful
to speak of the realistic-naturalistic movement. The revolt was
against distortion of reality, remoteness from reality, and limitations
on reality in the current theater. In the mid-nineteenth century,
although at a height in the art of acting, the theater was at one of its
low ebbs in the character of its drama. New plays were divided
between a declining romantic drama and a new form that has come
to be designated as the well-made play, both representing essentially
a theater of escape.

Romantic drama is a term much used and so variously and often
so loosely as almost to call into question its continued usefulness. It
is necessary to examine the term with some care before proceeding
further. In the latter eighteenth and early nineteenth centuries in
Germany, France, and England it referred primarily to a freedom of
form and release to strong emotion in rebellion against the emotional restraint and formal rigidity of the preceding neoclassicism.
The total romantic movement, of which romantic drama was a part,
was complex and involved assertion of individualism in thought and
expression against the reduction to rule and order; the sense of
wonder and mystery in life with responsiveness to strangeness and
the picturesque in contrast to the rational clarity of neoclassicism;
and a return to the medieval and renaissance worlds for subjects and
settings and in spirit. Perhaps most fundamentally, in contrast to the
neoclassical stress on understanding human nature by the light of
universal categories and common elements, the romantic movement
represented a turning inward on individual personal consciousness
and experience as the knowable reality and a mirror of the univer-

sal. In retrospect the greater part of Elizabethan drama, including that of Shakespeare, is often referred to as romantic for its freedom of form and expression and variety of content, in contrast to the more limited area of classical unity, order, and restraint, which was represented most forcefully in the precept and practice of Ben Jonson. In the latter part of the nineteenth century romantic drama was identified by the new realists with exotic settings and exaggerations of situation, emotion, and sentiment. Today romantic is sometimes used to indicate plays as not true to life but as simply giving the audience an agreeable period of escape from reality into a world more exciting or pleasantly ordered. Romantic is also used merely for the fact of exotic setting, particularly when in the medium of poetry, without reference to the relation of the play to inner reality, as Maxwell Anderson's *Elizabeth the Queen, Mary of Scotland,* and *Anne of the Thousand Days* have been termed romantic tragedies, and Christopher Fry's *The Lady's Not for Burning* a romantic comedy. However, the term is also used today with varying auras of meaning derived from the whole complex of elements of the historical romantic movement: for the glamour surrounding great historical personages of Maxwell Anderson's group of plays, for the "ever abiding feeling of the strangeness and wonder of reality" to which Christopher Fry ascribes the character of his playwriting, for the taste for the bizarre, the outré, the grotesque, the violently sensational, that is an element in Tennessee Williams' plays. A word that has so many meanings is indispensable, even though we often have to determine its import by the context of its use.

Romantic drama is both an historical form preceding what we commonly call modern drama and a living force in modern movements. John Gassner in his illuminating book, *Form and Idea in Modern Theatre,* traces formal roots of realism in the preceding romantic movement, and also points out and then develops with precise discrimination a connection between the later symbolist drama and romantic drama: ". . . the spirit of symbolist drama and stage production was undeniably romantic. Even in treating familiar scenes of life, symbolist dramatic art sought to evoke mystery and wonder and the pathos of romantic isolation. The romantic drama, however, is *explicit,* whereas the symbolist drama is suggestive." *

* The Dryden Press, New York, 1956, "The Idea of Freedom of Dramatic Form," pp. 7-17, and "A Note on Romanticism and Symbolism," pp. 127-130.

The romantic revolt against the bondage of the neoclassical rules produced a few great dramatic works, those of Schiller and Goethe in Germany and Victor Hugo in France, and prepared the way for the freedom of form of realism. But the genius of romanticism was lyric and meditative more than dramatic, and the constructive impetus in drama was short-lived. In breaking away from the emotional restraint of neoclassicism, romantic drama often degenerated into sound and fury; by leaping backward over neoclassicism to medieval and renaissance inspirations it tended to become imitative rather than progressively creative; and by its exotic settings and pursuit of the spectacular and the sensational in situation, characterization, and emotion it lost contact with truth of life and became a drama of escape.

A new fashion in theater—the well-made play—arose in Paris, originated by Eugene Scribe and further established by Victorien Sardou, and spread over Europe. Scribe, in developing and practicing the well-made play, made no pretensions to any other purpose than to entertain, to get and hold the attention of an audience by a skillful construction of alternating suspense and surprise, and to satisfy them with a happy ending. Nothing that would offend the taste of a polite audience or make them uncomfortable was allowed to enter. Playwriting was reduced to theatrical formulae. The well-made play has been described as the supreme triumph of mechanics over dramatic content. The well-made play also, however, performed a transitional function by bringing drama home from the exotic settings of romantic drama and down from the heights of royalty and the higher nobility to the lower aristocracy and upper middle class for its social setting. The movements of realism and naturalism were a revolt for establishing truth of life fully and freely as the function of the theater. To this end these movements developed specific conceptions as to the nature of truth and its embodiment in dramatic form.

Realism is a broader concept than naturalism and, basically defined, includes naturalism as a specialized form. The aim of realism, as of modern drama generally, is truth of life, inner and universal; but what distinguishes realism is truth to life in external and particular detail. Realism as a method ascertains truth by observation and communicates it by direct representation. The background of realism is immediate in time and place to the author and his audience, specific in locale, and treated with fidelity to physical facts and social manners. An historical background or one geographically and socially remote may be treated in the spirit of realism, but the basic idea of realism is immediacy. The characters are normal to the background, more often than not representative. One or more of the characters, particularly the protagonist, may be in some manner exceptional, but within reasonable limits. The characters are treated with particular truth to individual lives and personalities but by their relation to their background representative truth is revealed. Realism originated as a characteristic depiction of the middle class. Out of the commercial development of the nineteenth century the newly arisen middle class had become the theater audience and was interested in itself, and playwrights of the middle class arose with them and in accordance with a tenet of realism wrote of the background they knew. Philosophically, the middle class was identified with an idea of the mean or average level of human life as constituting its most representative and significant truth. The realistic approach has been extended to all levels of society so that it is now common to use the distinguishing phrase, middle-class realism, for the initial development, particularly in connection with the drama and influence of Ibsen.

Formally the method of realism was an attempt to reduce theatrical conventions to a minimum. All drama depends upon conventions. A theatrical convention is simply any device of communication mutually understood and accepted between stage and audience. Masks were a convention of the ancient Greek theater, as of the Japanese Nō play, and similarly the mask-like make-up of the classical Chinese theater. Facts of age, sex, station in life, and character were communicated by symbolic masks, and probably, in the vast amphitheater of Greek productions, the larger-than-life masks also served for projection of countenance. Greek, Japanese, and Chinese theater all involved non-realistic conventions at almost every point; in costume, in setting, in the use of poetry, song, and dance, and in a variety of devices such as the Greek Chorus and the Chinese travel song for delivery of exposition to the audience. The soliloquy and the aside are familiar conventions of English drama from the Elizabethan to the rise of realism in the nineteenth century. Realism undertook to create an illusion of the actual background of the scene and to provide as nearly as possible the actual furnishings, to dress the characters as in life, and to limit the means of communication to prose dialogue in language essentially natural to life, although admitting of the selective and ordering process of art. First the aside, then the soliloquy, were progressively eliminated as disruptive to the realistic illusion. Exposition must be worked with apparent naturalness into the dialogue, all scenes must have definite locale, and rigid continuity and consistency of time and plot linkages must be maintained. In short, the object of the realistic method is as direct a representation of life externally as is possible to the theater as a medium.

Nevertheless, realism is still dependent upon conventions, of which one of the most absolute in demand upon audience understanding and acceptance is the so-called fourth-wall convention, by which the open side of the stage for the view and audition of the audience is treated by the characters in the play as solid and admitting no awareness of the audience. This convention becomes more radical in the recent development of arena staging, what might be called the four-walls convention. It is a convention that the characters in a play are speaking in ordinary conversational tones when their vocal projection is presumably clearly reaching the rear of the balcony. Representation of wood or stone by painted canvas is a convention. However, by eliminating convention as far as possible realism aims at leading the audience to forget that it is in a theater and to become lost in the sensation of a keyhole glimpse of life. In short, realism as a theatrical method can be summed up as itself a convention, the acceptance by the audience of the illusion that the production is not a play but life.

An impulse toward realism and elements of realism is not new to modern drama. The scenic device, invention of which is attributed to Sophocles, of the *periaktoi,* a perpendicular prism painted on each side with a different background which was revolved for a change of locale, suggests a realistic impulse in the Greek theater. The essence of the convention of poetry in drama is that the detachment from realism of the fact of characters speaking poetry at all, when in life people speak prose, opens the way to acceptance of the further departure from realism of fullness and richness of expression of the emotional significance of each dramatic situation. Similarly by the more extreme convention of opera there is no disruption of the illusion of reality when a dying man delivers an aria for which in life he would lack breath. The inner reality is revealed by waiving allegiance to external reality. In life people characteristically become inarticulate under emotional stress—although anger is rather commonly an exception by its breaking down of inhibition. Love and grief are notoriously inarticulate. The playwright working strictly within the convention of prose realism must at least give the illusion of inarticulateness at the points of greatest dramatic significance. Talent and genius always capitalize on the restraints of form and the playwrights of realism have raised to a high art the weighty pause and the moving and meaningful broken utterance. Yet nowhere in realistic drama does precisely this realistic effect appear more sharply and artfully than occasionally in the midst of Shakespeare's generally poetic method. Othello, in scene two of Act IV, convinced that Desdemona has been unfaithful to him, comes to her room and treats her cruelly as though she were a public woman. He goes out; Iago enters. Emilia, Iago's wife and Desdemona's attendant, cries out:

> *Alas, Iago, my lord hath so bewhor'd her,*
> *Thrown such despite and heavy terms upon her*
> *As true hearts cannot bear.*

Shakespeare breaks the blank verse with a half-line for Desdemona: "Am I that name, Iago?" Desdemona's avoidance of the word "whore" is no delicacy of speech; the Elizabethans were free in such matters and Emilia, also a gentlewoman, has just spoken plainly. Shakespeare by a stroke of realistic inarticulateness has revealed the total inner purity of Desdemona which shrinks from the idea of the word. At the end of Act IV in *King Lear* when Lear is awaking from sleep with his mind almost restored he speaks in bewilderment:

> *. . . . . . . Do not laugh at me;*
> *For (as I am a man) I think this lady*
> *To be my child Cordelia.*

Shakespeare here also breaks the blank verse for Cordelia's half-line, "And so I am! I am!" Again, when Lear cannot understand her tears, for she, unlike her sisters, has cause not to love him, Shake-speare breaks the verse to give Cordelia only the emotion-choked words, "No cause, no cause." There are many entire prose scenes in Elizabethan and Jacobean drama that are essentially realistic reflection both of middle-class and of low life of the author's contemporary England, even though ostensibly set in an earlier time or distant place. There are even entire prose dramas set in contemporary London, as Thomas Middleton's *A Trick to Catch an Old One,* but there are elements of language, of form, and of surrounding facts of production by which the audience would constantly be aware that they were witnessing a theatrical performance, a work of art, not a transcript from life. Not until the latter nineteenth century was realism developed as a theory of drama directed against that consciousness.

It is extremely important to keep the terms realism and realistic sharply distinguished from the ideas of reality and the real. Realism and realistic refer to a theory of drama. Non-realistic forms, past and present, represent as deep a concern with reality and the real as does realism. Realism arose as a reaction against the loss of contact with reality in the immediate theater, but it is a truism to say that revelation of truth of human experience is the basis of the greatness of the non-realistic Greek tragedies and plays of Shakespeare. In modern drama, the realistic-naturalistic movement was only fairly under way before non-realistic movements arose out of the same basic impetus, to reveal significant reality in the theater.

With all the variety of form that has developed in the modern theater since the first rise of realism, realism has remained the dominating force, so much so that in considerable critical writing and a great deal of general thought there is the assumption of realism as the norm of drama and contemporary non-realistic plays are still often referred to as experimental drama. Historically, in terms of over two thousand years compared with less than a century, realism might be looked upon as a theatrical aberration. The danger in realism is that of sinking into the commonplace, the merely reportorial, the superficial, and the literal. Fortunately in practice realism has frequently been modified in directions to which have been applied such terms as artistic, stylized, imaginative, or free realism. Stage setting has generally become selective and suggestive;

and realism has frequently been combined with other elements, from the symbolisms in Ibsen's *Ghosts, The Wild Duck,* and *The Master Builder* to the blending of realistically presented immediate external events in *Death of a Salesman* with the projection of Willy Loman's mind and memories.

Realism in the theater today has become a pervasive attitude toward content rather than a rigid constraint on method, an identification of significant reality with the immediately local and contemporary and with ordinary people of middle or lower than middle background, people with whom the audience can identify directly on a familiar and homely level. A good deal of the bias of realism is revealed with particular clarity in an article in the first issue of *Horizon* (September, 1958) because it is applied to the non-realistic medium of music drama. The author, D. M. Marshman, Jr., writing on the development of the new type of musical play, states: "So far, it has brought about only a limited revolution in the musical theater —one confined to form, technique, craftsmanship—which may be summarized as a revolution of *method*. Still to come is an equivalent revolution in respect to matter." He finds one exception, "perhaps a beacon light for the future progress of the musical play—*West Side Story*." "This show," he points out, "is a musical play practically lifted from newspaper headlines. Its story—written specifically for the show . . . dramatizes a juvenile gang war in New York City." He concludes: "What is significant is that *West Side Story,* the first musical play whose theme, setting, and characters are realistically drawn from contemporary life, succeeded in every way. It lifted the musical play to its highest standard yet, and playgoers followed it upward. If, in the next few seasons, new musical plays continue to be produced in contemporary dimensions, an American artistic achievement of high importance will be upon us."

There is a deeper level of realism, however, than regard for the immediate, the commonplace, and the reportorially available, which is more universal than the modern movement and its particular technique; that is the concern for psychological truth to character. When Macbeth speaks longingly of "sleep that knits up the ravell'd sleave of care," or Romeo responds to Juliet's calling his name with "How silver-sweet sound lovers' tongues by night," like the hundreds of most quoted passages from Shakespeare, the lines have been caught up out of context for their poetic intensification of common truth of life. In dramatic context, however, such lines are not true to life in the realistic sense as language which anyone would use in life; they are natural only to the dramatic character in the poetic drama. On the other hand they are psychologically true to a realistic sense of what the character might feel in the situation. More significant is the connected and intricate psychological consistency of the characters in Shakespeare's plays. For the poetic drama of the Elizabethan stage it is reasonable to imagine at least a considerable element of stylization in the acting, yet the whole tenor of Hamlet's, and presumably Shakespeare's, advice to the players is realistic in this deeper sense: "Suit the action to the word, the word to the action; with the special observance, that you o'erstep not the modesty of nature: for anything so overdone is from the purpose of playing, whose end, both at the first and now, was and is, to hold, as 'twere, the mirror up to nature." Acting and dramaturgy are so interrelated that one might expect from these words to find in Shakespeare's plays the profound psychological truth to character which prompted Oscar James Campbell to say on Shakespeare's treatment of the plot for Othello which he found in an Italian novella:

> He . . . gives each figure just those qualities which will explain in terms of human character the actions which the plot requires of him. In other words, he psychologizes them. . . . A penny-dreadful tale is thus miraculously transformed into an absorbing tragedy of human beings more vital and credible than we, who watch them move to their inevitable doom.*

Naturalism, most completely differentiated as a special form within the larger movement of realism, is distinguished by application to human life of a philosophy of scientific determinism, identification of the function of the dramatist with a scientifically objective investigation and documentation of human life, emphasis on the minute and cumulative detailing of environmental factors, and insistence on the slice of life or fragment of life as the formal principle of drama: in all, a more extreme revolt than that of general realism against the

---

* *Shakespeare: Richard II—As You Like It—Othello—Antony and Cleopatra,* ed. Oscar James Campbell, Charles Scribner's Sons, New York, 1931, p. 241.

artificialities of dramatic form. These characteristics were fixed upon naturalism by definition. Two other characteristics developed in practice and became as firmly a part of the naturalistic movement: a marked tendency toward selection of the lower levels of society and lower human types as subject matter, and emphasis, with brutal frankness in presentation, on the physical, sordid, and unpleasant.

The terms realism and naturalism have unfortunately been used interchangeably and synonymously. I remember in a lecture a good many years ago Robert Frost said the poetic idealist would present a potato washed, while the realist would offer it with the dirt on; and that he preferred his potato washed. Now a potato washed or un-washed is honest realistic fare, but leaving the dirt on would represent the naturalistic kind of realism. W. H. Buford in a book on Chekhov defines his drama as "psychological naturalism," but what follows in no way differs from general realism: "a drama which should be content to make the spectator fully aware of complicated states of mind in a group of invented characters, without asking whether the result fitted in with any accepted notion about comedy or tragedy, so long as it interpreted convincingly the general sense of life as we know it." * On the other hand, N. Efros in "Tchekhov and the Moscow Art Theatre" wrote that Chekhov "is an artistic realist; no other definition can be applied to him." † John Galsworthy, in his essay "Some Platitudes Concerning Drama," divided the prospective course of English drama into naturalism and a new poetic drama, perhaps in prose, but a prose of fantasy and sym-bolism, and described naturalistic technique as the aim of the dramatist, with "imagination, construction, selection, and elimina-tion—the main laws of artistry, . . . to create such an illusion of actual life passing on the stage as to compel the spectator to pass through an experience of his own, to think, and talk, and move with the people he sees thinking, talking, and moving in front of him." ‡ In England the term naturalism has been used to the present time as by Galsworthy, essentially as equivalent to realism and in place of realism for drama that is true to life and natural in manner. Although

* *Anton Chekhov,* Yale University Press, New Haven, 1957, pp. 43 and 45.
† In *Literary and Theatrical Reminiscences,* tr. and ed. S. S. Koteliansky, George H. Doran Company, New York, 1927, p. 118.
‡ In *The Inn of Tranquillity,* William Heineman, London, 1912, pp. 199-201.

the English realists were fully aware of French naturalism they were much more influenced by Ibsen and Chekhov, and the English theater and playwrights have had too much of gentlemanly good taste for full-blown naturalism. Now that John Osborne and the "angry young man" have entered the theater English reviewing lacks a properly distinguishing term for them.

Naturalism as a theory of literature for the novel and stage in its fullest and most precise form was launched by Émile Zola in the famous Preface to the second edition in 1868 of his novel *Thérèse Raquin*. For the next twenty years accompanying his enormous output of novels and a number of plays he maintained a crusade for naturalism in prefaces, journalistic writings, and correspondence.* Zola had precursors both in the novel and drama, but it was precisely his function to call attention to what had already been done, and it was he who formulated the theory of naturalism, gave it a name, and did most of the fighting for it. His own works for theater, mostly dramatizations of his novels, were unsuccessful but he exercised a great deal of influence on other playwrights and powerfully supported André Antoine in the founding and conduct of the *Théâtre Libre* as a center of revolt against romantic drama and the formulae of the well-made play.

Zola announced naturalism as "a consequence of the scientific evolution of the century," "the literature of our scientific age." Man was to be understood biologically, physiologically, as an animal, subject in his "passionate and intellectual acts," "like all the phenomena of living bodies," to "the laws of scientific determinism." The function of the novelist or dramatist is to study man "under the influences of heredity and environment" and, finally, "in the reciprocal effect of society on the individual and the individual on society," to "analyze all his physical and social causes that make him what he is." Writers are "to put themselves resolutely under the schooling of

---

* His dramatic criticisms for periodicals from 1876-1880 were later put into book form under the titles *Le Naturalisme au théâtre, Le Roman experimental,* and *Nos Auteurs dramatiques.* The first two of these books with a number of other items from Zola's journalistic writings were published in a single volume in English in 1893 under the title *The Experimental Novel and Other Essays,* in which may be found his entire philosophy of drama. (Translated by Belle M. Sherman, Cassell Publishing Co., New York.)

science. No more lyricism, no more empty words, but facts and information."|

The initial theory of naturalism does not necessitate concentration on one level of society or human types more than another, but in practice the naturalistic school did concentrate on the lowest levels of society, character, and conduct. There were several reasons for this. Zola himself criticized the editors of the journal *Le Realisme* published in 1856 and 1857 for advocating a realism that was "exclusively bourgeois. . . . We must admit the depicting of all classes." Regardless of his theory of objectivity, however, he possessed the highly individualized response of creative genius to life. He was obsessed with the physical, the tangible. His biographer Matthew Josephson came to the conclusion that "Zola got an authentic inspiration out of holding his notebook in one hand, and feeling, smelling, seeing, the REAL THING"; and on his preparation for *La Curie,* a novel outside his area of familiarity, "It is not to be doubted that he experienced an authentic scientific rapture in finding out from a dozen carriage builders all the mechanism of the princely equipages of his time." * While the theory of naturalism stressed the commonplace in the accumulation of factual detail, in his choice of subjects Zola showed an imagination drawn to the exceptional, to the extremes of life in animality and in violence of passions, especially of sex. In *Thérèse Raquin,* based on Zola's novel of the same title and his best play, Thérèse and her lover throw her husband into the Seine. They are free to marry, but they are so oppressed by the horror of their deed, the torment of mutual recriminations, and the accusing eyes of the paralytic mother of the victim pursuing them in fiendish joy in their suffering, that they take poison on the night of their marriage. The play failed when produced in 1873 but was subsequently praised and became one of the models of drama of the early naturalists, although it was far from an exemplification of Zola's theory. Jules Le Maître, after defining a poet as "a writer who by virtue of his idea, or vision of an idea, notably transforms reality, and then makes it live again," affirmed that Zola was no naturalist, but "the brutal and sad poet of blind instincts, of carnal love, of repulsive humans." †
Ferdinand Brunètiere, from a condemnatory point of view, wrote:

* *Zola and His Time,* Macaulay Company, New York, 1928, p. 176.
† Quoted by Josephson, *Zola and His Time,* p. 375.

"With his brutal style, his repulsive and ignoble preoccupations he has gone further than all the other realists. Is Humanity composed only of rascals, madmen, and clowns?" *

Zola apparently was not self-deluded on the relation between his theory and practice. Matthew Josephson recounts how at one of the gatherings of Flaubert, Zola, Daudet, and Goncourt, Flaubert burst out against the nonsense of the naturalistic crusade. Zola replied that Flaubert had a small fortune which permitted him to be free to do anything he pleased, but he had been obliged to gain his living absolutely by his pen, "And by Jove, I say the devil with Naturalism(!) like you; and yet I shall repeat those ideas and go on repeating them." He went on to say, in effect, that he wrote his books to be judged as an artist and that his journalistic crusade for naturalism was what would be called today an advance publicity for his books.†

The influence of Zola's practice was as strong as that of his doctrine. The works of his immediate followers and imitators in the theater, while frequently pursuing the commonplace in characters, situations, and speech to banality, also went to extremes in depiction of depravity, what were called *rosse* plays, and the creation of *grand guignol* horrors without Zola's vitalizing power. Samuel M. Waxman in *Antoine and the Théâtre Libre* quotes the French critic Filon as defining *rosserie* as "a sort of vicious ingenuousness, the state of soul of people who never had any moral sense and who live in impurity and injustice, like a fish in water." Among the *rosse* plays Waxman summarizes *La Sérénade* by Jean Jullien as "a play in which a mother and daughter are mistresses of a family tutor who is finally accepted as a son-in-law by a complacent father." ‡ Brutal horror in the name of naturalism was carried so far that Auguste Linert's *Conte de Noël,* described by Waxman, was hissed at the *Théâtre Libre.* "Even that hardened audience couldn't stomach it." §

A second reason for the concentration of naturalism on the unsavory areas of society was the spirit of social reform, with Zola again formulating the doctrinal justification. Zola was himself a re-

---

* Quoted by Josephson, *Zola and His Time,* p. 205, from "The Realistic Novel of Today," in *Revue des Deux Mondes,* early in 1875.
† Josephson, *Zola and His Time,* p. 244.
‡ Harvard University Press, Cambridge, 1926, pp. 82 and 83.
§ *Antoine and The Théâtre-Libre,* pp. 143-44.

former at heart, as witnessed by his part in the Dreyfus affair, and this aspect of his character no doubt naturally influenced the direction of his work. Certainly he defended his own and other naturalistic writings against the accusation of immorality on the ground of social reform. In *A Letter to the Young People of France* he wrote: "We are looking for the causes of social evil; we study the anatomy of classes and individuals to explain the derangements which are produced in society and in man. This often necessitates our working on tainted subjects, our descending into the midst of human miseries and follies. But we obtain the necessary data so that by knowing them one may be able to master the good and the evil. Lo! here is what we have seen, observed, and explained in all sincerity. Now it remains for the legislators to bring the good and develop it; to battle against the bad, to extirpate and destroy it." * The naturalistic writers exposed the festering sores of society to view; cure was the business of others.

Closely related to the spirit of social reform and more fundamental to the impetus of naturalism was that of artistic reform. In *Naturalism on the Stage* Zola defended the naturalists against the charge of immorality on the high ground of truth: "We accept only nature and . . . we are not willing to correct what is by what should be. Absolute honesty no more exists than perfect healthfulness. There is a tinge of the human beast in all of us, as there is a tinge of illness. . . . We tell everything, we do not make a choice, neither do we idealize; and this is why they accuse us of taking pleasure in obscenity . . . the naturalistists affirm that there is no morality outside of the truth." † Of course, moved by his temperamental attraction, Zola did make a choice: in the Preface to *Thérèse Raquin* he wrote: "I have chosen characters who were completely dominated by their nerves and blood . . . to seek in them the beast, to see nothing but the beast." The promulgation of the naturalistic doctrine opened the floodgates to similar temperament wherever present, but back of it all was the honest enthusiasm for the rising spirit of science with truth as the banner, and a literary rebellion against the falsification of life, not only by the restraints of artificial form, but by

---

* In *The Experimental Novel and Other Essays,* trans. Belle M. Sherman, Casswell Publishing Co., New York, 1893, pp. 102-103.
† In *The Experimental Novel and Other Essays,* p. 127.

idealization and the restraints of prudery. In the spirit of science and truth whatever existed in life was fit subject matter for representation in the novel or on the stage. What was felt to be the most forceful, but actually the easiest, way to make assertion against prudery was to present on the stage to the most extreme degree precisely what had been barred by prudery, or taste. It is characteristic of rebellion to run to extremes. In the spirit of defiance minor naturalistic writers in Zola's time, and since, have hurled what is ugliest and most repellent in the face of what they felt to be comfortable, complacent, blind society and have said, See, this exists.

Finally, regardless of theoretical breadth, it was inherent in the view of man as an animal to seek the most significant truth of human nature in the social levels where man was stripped most nearly to the animal. The early realists sought representative truth at the middle or common level of society; the naturalists felt they were getting at foundational truth by digging down to the base of the structure. They both were influenced to some degree, it is probable, by the associations of words and false analogy. Each found and revealed an area of truth, however, although not necessarily the most ultimate, which may well be conceived as being in the direction of man's growth.

All of these influences which have been described as tending to identify naturalism with unpleasing views of humanity were each in themselves superficial to or contrary to the initial doctrine, although as a cumulative force they might well be expected to be irresistible. Depiction of the lower levels of society and of human nature and conduct with brutal frankness of detail and expression has continued to be one of the associations of the term naturalism in the description of drama to the present time.

Few effective plays embodying complete naturalism have been written. Henry Becque's *The Vultures,* written in 1882, has been regarded as the model of naturalism in French drama. It is an exposé of rapacity in middle-class life, powerful in its objectivity and the exclusiveness of motivation in the characters. A wealthy industrialist dies and leaves his wife and three daughters, who know nothing of business, prey to an assortment of vultures which includes a dishonest partner and the lawyer who ostensibly represents the interests of the family. As the only salvation for the family one of the daughters consents to marry the partner, a senile miser. The only safety is to identify the interests of the fiercest vulture with one's own. Becque followed *The Vultures* with *The Parisian Woman* in which a wife manipulates a *ménage à trois* of herself, husband, and an alternation of lovers purely on motivations of practicality and respectability. It is the perfect unconsciousness of depravity in the wife which gives force to the play. The uniform baseness of motivation in Becque's plays actually represented a temperamental pessimism about human nature rather than scientific determinism, and in that respect they differ from Zola's doctrine. Following Becque in the 1890's and within the fostering of Antoine's *Théâtre Libre* Eugène Brieux and François de Curel represented the other most successful creators of French naturalistic drama. Brieux was moved primarily by the object of social reform in his presentations of the conditions which produced misery and injustice in his contemporary society and he departed from the objectivity of naturalism into direct didacticism. Curel was naturalistic primarily in the scientific detachment of his dissection of unusual emotions. In *The Fossils,* his best-known play, his psychological interest was brought into conjunction with a social idea in his examination of decayed aristocracy.

It was outside France, in Hauptmann's *The Weavers* and Gorki's *The Lower Depths,* that naturalism reached its highest level of representation. In *The Weavers* Hauptmann embodied every tenet of naturalism without any of the distortion from temperament that characterized Zola's own works and those of most of his immediate followers. Hauptmann presents the misery of the home weavers of Silesia brought about by the continual lowering of the price paid for their webs due to the introduction of cheaper production by power looms. In the method of naturalism he accumulates with massive power factual details of environment and the interplay of men and society. There is the brutal frankness of unpleasant detail, as in a man going outside to lose his dinner of dog meat when the family has been reduced to eating their pet. The manufacturer and his man-ager and their associates are presented with objective detachment in their social representation. The rise of the weavers into revolt is presented factually without overt identification of playwright or audience. The action of the weavers is not put in the light of praise-worthiness but of psychological necessity: "Once in a lifetime a man

has to express what he feels," says an old weaver. The impression
derived from the play is that of inescapable cause and effect: if
people are pressed down into misery long enough and hard enough,
revolt follows. Individual leaders to give the starting momentum to
revolt are pressed up out of the mass. Naturalistic in structure, the
movement of the play has no sharp attack but rises gradually out of
a succession of incidents, and comes to an indeterminate resolution.
The revolt is momentarily successful in that the power looms have
been smashed and the soldiers called in have been driven off, but
the weavers are left suspended without further objective or direction.
New power looms will be built, more soldiers called in if necessary.
Out of the complete objectivity of presentation the audience arrives
at strong identification with the misery of the weavers and a sense
that something must be done to prevent such social maladjustments.

Gorki's *The Lower Depths,* often cited like *The Weavers* as an example of absolute naturalism, is naturalistic in background and basic
technique; but in inner thematic content and direction it is a struggle
to find a way out of naturalism's degrading view of man into an
affirmation of dignity. In a Preface written in 1923 for his play *The
Judge,* Gorki paid his respects to naturalistic theory and then stated
what he thought of how it worked out in practice:

> The characters of a drama should all act independently of the
> volition of the dramatist, in accordance with the law of their in-
> dividual natures and social environment . . . it is his business
> cold-bloodedly to describe the manner in which they all behave.
>
> The dramatist who adopts this attitude can write a pure work
> of art, a drama, that is, devoid of personal bias, a picture of the
> struggle of conflicting wills, without betraying the slightest trace
> of his own feelings.
>
> Now, as a matter of fact, I know no play written according to
> this theory in all European literature, and as for myself, I could
> never write one.*

The course of naturalism has been for its elements to divide into
separate streams of influence. Of least importance from the start
except to himself was Zola's great idea of the "experimental" novel

* *The Judge,* trans. Marie Zakrevsky and Barrett H. Clark, Robert M. McBride
and Co., New York, 1924.

or play. He endeavored to draw a parallel to the scientist performing an experiment in the laboratory. The novelist or dramatist selected his characters, placed them under certain conditions in his novel or play, and demonstrated their reactions according to the laws of their being. He labored unavailingly to get around the inescapable difference that the materials of the scientist have an existence and reactions independent of the scientist, but the characters and the situations in the novel or play are created by the author and the reactions determined by the author. The fallacy of a work of fiction as scientific experiment was obvious. The nearest possible approach to science is that the author create the characters, situations, and reactions to the utmost of his ability with truth to life according to his observation and understanding of human nature and of society. This naturalism has largely settled for. Such a standard of scientific detachment could come out either as a disciplined restraint to objectivity as in Hauptmann's *The Weavers* or as a highly subjective appearance of objectivity as in Becque's *The Vultures*. The latter has been more common among the streams of naturalistic influence. A good deal of naturalism has been more a matter of subject and technique than of point of view about the nature of man—the lower levels or unpleasant aspects of life with the naturally accompanying grossness of speech, and avoidance of sharpness of dramatic structure; in other words, extreme manifestations of the freedoms asserted by realism generally in relation to conventional nineteenth-century theater. Antoine frequently used the term ultra-realism. Naturalism as ultra-realism is a continuing force, appearing in all respects, for example, in John Osborne's *The Entertainer*. The battle for freedom of subject matter in the name of truth has, for better or worse, been won, as is evident from such divers dramas as *Tobacco Road, A Streetcar Named Desire,* and *West Side Story.* The proportionate reduction of plot to clinical examination of character and motivation appears in such recent works as Tennessee Williams' *Cat on a Hot Tin Roof* and Eugene O'Neill's *Long Day's Journey Into Night,* although each of these plays contains a great deal that is not naturalistic. The early technique of naturalism of massive accumulation of detail has had less continuance, although it has a late and effective expression in O'Neill's *The Iceman Cometh,* which is not, however, naturalistic in philosophy and contains unnaturalistic symbolism. More frequently than naturalistic plays we find plays representing elements of naturalism.

Of all the elements of Zola's theory it is his philosophy of life, rather than the purely and directly artistic principles or his scientific determinism, which has had most subsequent significance in drama. The real immorality of naturalistic literature was not in the area of the early accusations, which really were directed against offense to what was considered good taste. Zola's defense of the right and responsibility of art to truth was essentially sound, even though the practice misrepresented man as much as did the idealization of accepted literature. The real threat to basic moral consciousness was in the absorption of the individual human will, with responsibility for moral choice, into a total causation of all that a man is, what he thinks, feels, and does, in the complex of hereditary and environmental factors—the philosophy of scientific determinism. With or without Zola the biological view of man and scientific determinism would have entered into and molded drama. The formulation of naturalism was practically prophetic, shortly to be reinforced by the Darwinian revolution in biology, placing man more firmly in continuity with the animal kingdom than before, and later by the revolution in psychology of Freud, with his emphasis on the unconsciousness of motivations, the primacy of the pleasure principle, and man's murderous and sexual drives. It should be noted that popular and literary Freudianism largely lost sight of Freud's own emphasis on the will and reason, with salvation lying in rationally, rather than morally, directed will. The promulgation of the theory of naturalism, however, gave a home and continuity to the development of a literature of determinism and an animalistic view of man. Strindberg was directly influenced by Zola in his earlier period and in *The Father* we find Laura, the wife, in her conflict for supremacy over her husband, acting as she must by her inner nature as a woman without moral concept or conflict. The husband for his side of the conflict speaks in terms of morality, but it is environmentally derived from society, and he too acts as he must. Strindberg's later work became a struggle toward salvation out of the naturalistic morass. O'Neill was influenced by Strindberg, and by Freud, and we find in his dramas motivation by obsessive passions, frequently murderous and sexual, in continuity with naturalism. O'Neill's plays, however, for the most part represent fatalistic rather than scientific determinism. Most characteristically, although not in all his plays, the characters are torn between inchoate or rudimentary aspirations of spirit and obsessive passions in a conflict in which they are fated to destruction. Completely in the naturalistic tradition of human nature, although not in objectivity of treatment, the plays of Tennessee Williams present almost solely instinctual action without moral conduct.

The philosophy of scientific determinism as the foundational distinction of naturalism from general realism is made especially clear by the contrast of Ibsen. Ibsen developed his own revolution against the well-made play and theatrical convention in his new realistic dramaturgy in independence of French naturalism. He also was aware of and stimulated by new advances in science and derived from them his rigid sense of causal sequence, particularly that action arises from character and the past creates the present; and he was possessed by an austere regard for truth. *Ghosts* is often referred to as a naturalistic drama because of the unsavory subject matter of venereal disease in the plot involvement and the emphasis on heredity. But *Ghosts* with all of Ibsen's dramas is built upon a philosophy of the rationally guided freedom of individual will, moral concepts, and the responsibility for, as well as inescapability from, the consequences of choices made and their action. Consequently, in *Ghosts* as in Ibsen's other realistic dramas, in contrast to naturalistic drama, the structure is closely knit and decisive. He rejected the artificially tight plot structure of the well-made play and went back to Greek drama for the more tightly bound construction based on moral choice, action, and causal sequence. Closely examined, the total character, including structure and technique, of both Ibsen's drama and naturalistic drama, can be seen as related to their respective philosophies of human nature, just as the forms of Elizabethan and of seventeenth- and eighteenth-century neoclassical drama reflect the views of man and the universe of their backgrounds. Such generalizations, of course, are subject to variants and exceptions in so individual a matter as artistic creation. Strindberg's *The Father,* for example, although naturalistic in philosophy is even more tight and sharp in structure and spare of detail than are Ibsen's plays.

That naturalism, considered not as a total conception of drama but as continuing in its several streams, is a pervasive influence in immediately contemporary drama is strikingly evident by the presence of several elements of naturalism in so unnaturalistic a work as Archibald MacLeish's *J.B.*, a poetic philosophical drama derived from *The Book of Job*. The play was published early in 1958, produced at Yale University, and given Broadway production in the 1958-59 season. *The Book of Job* magnifies God; *J.B.* magnifies man, and magnifies him greatly in the power of his spirit—to question, to defy, to accept the universe, to endure. Yet this drama of man's highest contention is enacted on a stage in an empty tent at night of "A traveling circus which has been on the roads of the world for a long time"; the parts of God and Satan are taken by two roustabouts, broken-down actors; and the men of dignity, sincerely well-intentioned, howbeit, under pressure, bigoted, who are the comforters of Job in the Bible are represented by three sordid and unlovely types from our contemporary society. A shadow from the cloud of naturalism touches *J.B.* At the same time, the appearance of such a play as *J.B.*, as also those of Arthur Miller, is evidence of a growing freedom from naturalistic thinking in our theater.

Nonrealistic drama returned to the theater as antirealism-naturalism, as a series of conscious revolts—symbolism, expressionism, dadaism, surrealism, theatricalism, formalism, epic theater. The terms overlap, the ideas and forms branch out, merge, and interplay. The movements have lost the identity of initial theory in varied practice but together have become part of the dramatic climate in which plays are written and produced. The drive behind the antirealistic movements has been the same as that which motivated realism and naturalism: the search for more ultimate truth for the stage or, in some phases of the over-all development, for more theatrically effective means of projecting truth. As has been discussed in the chapter on the scene designer, while naturalism originated in playwriting and drew stage setting after it, the nonrealistic movements were active in painting ahead of the theater and came to the theater as much by way of scene designers, from Appia and Craig on, as by playwrights, and developed by a close association of writing and staging. Although Antoine was moved to extremes of realism in stage setting in the *Théâtre Libre* productions by recognition of the importance of environment in naturalistic drama, the fact is, most realistic and naturalistic plays depend primarily on the lines and can be presented in essential communication on a bare stage, while in a large proportion of modern nonrealistic drama stage effects are corporeal to the play.

The reaction against realism came as early as the 1890's with symbolism. A symbol is something tangible which by some association stands for something outside sense perception—an idea, a quality, or a totality of meaning—as an anchor for hope, or the cross for Christianity. Many such symbols have become established and are understood as conventions. More crudely, the symbol may suggest the idea by resemblance, which is allegory—Spenser's representation of Gluttony, for example, in the procession of the Seven Deadly Sins in *The Faerie Queene,* by a man with a fat belly and a neck long like that of a crane riding on a swine. In allegorical narrative the action is symbolic, as in Bunyan's representation of the life of a Christian in a pilgrim's progress from his home to the Shining Gate through such trials and triumphs as sinking in to the Slough of Despond and in the Valley of Humiliation overcoming Apollyon, the fiend of pride with his fiery darts. In a religious background such as that of the Middle Ages, or the intensely religious consciousness of a John Bunyan, the intangible readily takes on concrete reality and produces allegorical literature. A common religious background also develops conventional symbols and basic lines of allegory within which the writer can create the interest of variations while possessing assurance of easy clarity. The medieval morality plays, most familiar in *Everyman,* are drama of this kind. The modern symbolist in art or literature, however, has to create more subjectively and individually and to establish the meaning of the symbols within each work with the danger always of failure of clarity.

Symbolic drama was not new in the 1890's. Ibsen had written poetic symbolic dramas in *Brand* and *Peer Gynt* preceding the development of his realism—from which symbolism was never totally absent—and *The Master Builder* toward the end of his career in 1892 is a complete interfusion of realism and symbolism. Symbolism as a reaction against realism and especially naturalism, however, is particularly associated with initiation by Maurice Maeterlinck. The theater of his time seemed to him "primitive, arid, and brutal." In 1896 in an essay "The Tragical in Daily

Life" * he stated the sense of drama by which he had been writing
plays since 1889:

> I have grown to believe that an old man, seated in his arm-chair,
> waiting patiently with his lamp beside him; giving unconscious
> ear to all the eternal laws that reign about his house, interpret-
> ing, without comprehending, the silence of doors and windows
> and the quivering voice of the light, submitting with bent head
> to the presence of his soul and of destiny . . . motionless as he
> is, does yet in reality live a deeper, more human, and more univer-
> sal life than the lover who strangles his mistress, the captain who
> conquers in battle, or "the husband who avenges his honor."
> . . . Indeed, it is not in the actions but in the words that are
> found the beauty and greatness of tragedies that are truly beauti-
> ful and great. . . . One may even affirm that a poem draws the
> nearer to beauty and loftier truth in the measure that it elim-
> inates words that explain the action, and substitutes for them
> others that reveal, not the so-called "soul-state," but I know not
> what intangible and unceasing striving of the soul toward its
> own beauty and truth.

Against the materiality, concreteness, and logicality of realism
Maeterlinck opposed his mystical philosophy. The most profound
and universal experiences of human life were the intangible aware-
nesses, just beyond grasp, at the outer edge of consciousness
impinged upon by eternity. He concluded his essay with the statement: ". . . there are in man many regions more fertile, more
profound and more interesting than those of his reason or intelligence . . ."
Maeterlinck gave the term "static" to his idea of drama. The
awareness, not action, was significant and his object was the creation of mood, an atmosphere, a feeling of something present but
unseen. His range of themes was limited, with a sense of the presence of death and fate or destiny recurrent. Approaching almost a
negation of drama, what seem to be his slightest works, short one-
act plays, especially *Interior* and *The Intruder,* most adequately
accomplish his aim and are most effective in the theater. In *The*

* In *The Treasure of the Humble,* trans. Alfred Sutro in 1898.

Intruder a family waits together in a room knowing that one of its members is dying in the next room. An unseen felt presence passes through the room. Death has entered the house. In *Interior* through a window we see a family seated together in the light of a lamp while an Old Man and a Stranger, looking in, linger against breaking the news to them of the drowning of a daughter. We see them as the Old Man at last reveals what has happened. Their destiny has entered the room. Except for the light of the lamp as a circle in the darkness where destiny is present and approaches there is no particular concrete symbol in either of these plays. The play as a whole in its characters, situation, and speech, and especially the mood, suggests the idea. Suggestion of the intangible is the essence of the symbolist movement in drama.

Simultaneously with symbolism in the 1890's there was a reaction against naturalism in the form of neoromanticism. The two movements had in common a conviction of poetry and beauty as significant truth—denied, disregarded, or destroyed in naturalistic drama—and of the reality of ideas. The two movements interacted: Edmund Rostand wrote an allegorical beast-fable of modern life in *Chantecler* and the vague medievalism of Maeterlinck's *Pélléas and Mélisande* and others of his plays is romantic. Neoromanticism produced its one significant playwright in Rostand, and one great play in *Cyrano de Bergerac*. Rostand's play is an assertion of the reality of individual will and of the ideas of virtue against naturalistic determinism and amorality. In distinction to the symbolist method of suggestion, in the romantic play the ideas are embodied in a character and his actions.

Rostand had no successors or appreciable influence although his play of Cyrano lived on. Maeterlinck, likewise, was the only important dramatist of the symbolist movement in the French theater, but for a brief period his plays and statements of theory were popular and influential through Europe and America. Symbolism took hold especially in Germany, and amid generally bad results Hauptmann wrote *The Sunken Bell*. In Russia Leonid Andreyev wrote striking symbolist plays, for the most part in the cruder method of allegory, as in the figure of "King Hunger" in the social drama of that title, but more subtly in his last plays, *He Who Gets Slapped* and *Samson Enchained*. In Italy Pirandello symbolized the

relativity of truth to the individual in outwardly realistic form in
Right You Are if You Think You Are and with departure from
realism in *Six Characters in Search of an Author*. In Ireland William Butler Yeats was a poetic symbolist, in his latter plays deriving an additional influence from the Japanese Nō plays.

In England and the United States the influence of Maeterlinck
and symbolism subsided into pretty and pleasant fantasies, as in
James M. Barrie's *Peter Pan, A Kiss for Cinderella,* and *Mary
Rose,* and in this country the innumerable more or less precious
Little Theater one-act plays of Pierrot and similar fancies. Occasionally valid symbolism appeared in this mode, notably Edna St.
Vincent Millay's stern as well as graceful one-act criticism of the
causes of war and human strife generally, *Aria da Capo*.

This is a good point at which to give some attention to fantasy in
drama. Fantasy is nonrealistic but it is not one of the anti-realistic
searches for truth. Fantasy is the creation by the imagination of
forms which have no counterpart in the world of sense. In this general meaning the symbols of symbolist or expressionist drama may
be, and the distortions and reassembling of parts of externally real
forms of surrealism always are, fantasies; but in common usage a
play as a whole is called a fantasy when the primary impulse is
the pleasure of exercise of imagination for its own sake. Fantasies
are an expression of the spirit of play, of whimsy, of caprice. They
may be grotesque or bizarre, or delicate and graceful, but more
commonly drama as fantasy has come to be associated with beauty
and poetry. The introduction of supernatural elements is almost
inevitably one of the most frequent forms of fantasy. The stylized
figures of *commedia dell'arte*—Columbine, Pierrot, Harlequin,
Pantaloon—by the fact of their disappearance from the theater as
a living tradition became a favorite material for revival in fantasy
in the twentieth century. Children spend a considerable part of
their lives in a world indistinguishably made up of fantasy and reality, but for adults fantasy is a separate world. There can be no
sharp and arbitrary line of division, but when a play as fantasy becomes too strongly directed at truth, whether as psychological revelation or as symbolization of ideas, we call it something else. The
value of fantasy depends upon how completely the author can engage and enrich the imagination of the audience. Shakespeare in *A*

Midsummer Night's Dream created a fairy world which did not exist before and which has been the fairy world of English-speaking people ever since. In other words, fantasy when it is imaginatively strong enough can implant a new truth, but it is not the pursuit of truth which already exists.

To return to the pursuit of truth beyond realism, the symbolism of Maeterlinck as a movement passed, but in passing it found Strindberg and at a time when symbolism met the need of a new phase of the spiritual autobiography of all his writing. Following a mental breakdown and recovery Strindberg entered for the remainder of his life into an accentuatedly subjective state of consciousness, further developed by mystical religious philosophies, especially that of Swedenborg, which made naturalism no longer an adequate mode of expression. Independently he commenced his development of symbolic drama in the first two parts of *To Damascus* in 1887 and 1888. With influence from Maeterlinck he wrote *The Dream Play* in 1901-02, the first of a number of symbolic dramas among the plays of the latter half of his career as a dramatist, culminating in *The Great Highway,* his last play in 1909. Strindberg described the method of *The Dream Play* in a memorandum which he desired to have printed on the programs:

> In this *Dream Play,* as in the previous *To Damascus,* the author has sought to imitate the disconnected but apparently logical, form of the dream. Anything may happen; everything is possible and probable. Time and space do not exist; on an insignificant background of reality imagination spins threads and weaves new patterns: a mixture of memories, experiences, free fancies, absurdities, and improvisations. The characters split, double, multiply, evaporate, solidify, diffuse, clarify. But one consciousness reigns above them all—that of the dreamer; it knows no secrets, no incongruities, no scruples, no law.

The Dream Play is a flow of images with little more of plot line than that the Daughter of Indra comes to earth to experience the lot of mankind. The play is a cry of pain—"It is a misery to be man!"— met with the Daughter's reiterated response, "Men are to be pitied!" and a breath of salvation at the end in the promise of the Daughter to carry the plight of mankind before the throne of Indra. Although *The Dream Play* very accurately recreates the character of dreams, it is not about dreaming but about the reality of life through the perception of creative imagination. Objective reality is as unstable to the consciousness as the images of a dream, but its only continuity or meaning is in the consciousness. The following lines are a guide to the significance of the play:

THE DAUGHTER. . . . All this I have been dreaming—
THE POET. It was in one of my poems.
THE DAUGHTER. You know then what poetry is—
THE POET. I know then what dreaming is— But what is poetry?
THE DAUGHTER. Not reality, but more than reality—not dreaming, but daylight dreams—
THE POET. And the man-children think that we poets are only playing—that we invent and make believe.

Maeterlinck's plays are pallid beside *The Dream Play* and its successors, and could never directly as an influence have met the state of consciousness which produced German expressionism. Strindberg was a soul in torment struggling to salvation who did not so much sublimate his personal agonies and visions into identification with humanity as intensify and enlarge them by identifying humanity with his subjective life. Strindberg's symbolic plays were the genetic influence from drama for the rampant movement of expressionism in Germany.

Expressionism had no lawgiver like Zola for naturalism and Maeterlinck for symbolism. The new mode spread among playwrights who made various pronouncements, and critics commenced describing and defining, but the definitions so differed that one contemporary critic refers to Georg Kaiser as on the edge of expressionism, not quite the real thing, while another refers to him as the arch-expressionist. Accounts even differ as to when and by whom the term expressionism was first applied to drama. It already existed in painting to describe the expression of inner experience as opposed to the representation of outer forms. In general terms expressionism arose in drama in Germany in the years immediately preceding World War I, grew through the years of the war in spite of lowered dramatic activity, and at the close of the war burst out explosively, spread from Germany, and flourished through the 1920's.

For the purpose here of examination of a dramatic climate in relation to the meaning of plays, an inclusive description is most useful. The common element was dramatization of the individual consciousness, of the inner conflicts and states for which there was no external equivalent in action or speech and which could not be represented directly on the stage. The problem was to give concrete form in the theater to all that was purely subjective. This led to considerable versatility of experimentation in dramatic method, out of which several developments of form became conventional to expressionism in Germany and its spread to other countries. Interior or stream-of-consciousness monologue, which differs from the old soliloquy in its psychological realism, became one of the most frequently used methods of externalization, often dominating a play. Soliloquies had been psychologically true before in content and even in the sequence of ideas—never more true than in *Hamlet*—but they were cast in the grammar of speech. In the expressionist monologue the playwright undertook to suggest the nature of stream of consciousness as a flow of images rather than rationally formulated thought and the flashing of words and phrases instead of full sentence structure. Stream-of-consciousness monologue appears not only as soliloquy, but in many plays speeches with an ostensible listener on stage were similarly an outpouring of the flow of consciousness. Actual dialogue, then, was sometimes reduced to short crisp exchanges of phrases or broken and unfinished sentences. A second characteristic of expressionist form was a nervous staccato style. The style was derived in part from the broken movement of stream-of-consciousness monologue and in part from the explosive temper of the movement, an eruption of inner tension, often febrile and neurotic, of the individual with his environment. The third formal characteristic of expressionism, so recurrent as to be nearly identifying, is abstraction, characters without personal names representing types, classes, or ideas—The Lawyer, The Poet in *The Dream Play;* The Cashier as protagonist of Kaiser's *From Morn to Midnight;* Mr. Zero, a bookkeeper, in Elmer Rice's *The Adding Machine;* or running down the cast of Ernst Toller's *Man and the Masses*—Workmen, Workwomen, The Nameless One, Officer, Priest, An Official, and Sonia Irene L., who, however, is simply The Woman throughout the play.

Other common formal characteristics were the use of scenes in the dream or vision manner as a part of the play instead of the whole as in Strindberg's drama, and an episodic structure of dramatic "stations" without causal sequence one to another but constituting a succession of events or stages in the progress of the protagonist from an initiating action to the resolution, a form which had its inception in Strindberg's *To Damascus.* The basic problem of expressionism was to find means of making inner experiences and abstract ideas concrete on the stage, and the ingenuity of playwrights, beyond the basic methods of stream-of-consciousness monologue and dream or vision scenes, multiplied devices indefinitely —symbolizations, allegories, masks, characters as automata, groups of people identically dressed and masked or made up and moving simultaneously, and frequently the projection of a sequence in the mind of a dramatic character in an essentially realistic scene. The projection of consciousness in scenic devices—the bare tree which turns into a skeleton in *From Morn to Midnight,* the walls of the bedroom of the bookkeeper Mr. Zero in *The Adding Machine* papered with columns of figures, the brainstorm in which he kills his employer, the askew pulpit in which he stands for his trial in "A Place of Justice"—was so general as to ally expressionist playwriting and scene design inseparably.

An expressionist play might dramatize the playwright's emotional consciousness of life as a whole (Strindberg's *The Dream Play*); or its scope might be a conflict of ideas, of thought, on a specific problem in the mind of the playwright as in Toller's *Man and the Masses,* in which is reflected his own mind torn and disturbed between the claims of Marxism for alleviation of the plight of the masses with the necessity of violence as an instrument, and his innate humanity and feeling for the dignity of the individual man. The conflict is resolved in a rejection of violence and of subordination of the individual to any mass concept—"A leader has no right to sacrifice any one but himself." An expressionist play might also be an objective, detached projection of the consciousness of a dramatic character as imaginatively conceived on a basis of observation. Elmer Rice's *The Adding Machine* is such a play, with the bookkeeper, in the usual manner of expressionism, not an individual but an abstraction of the class of white-collar slaves in modern society. Kaiser's *From Morn to Midnight* is a play of the same type and with the same subject; at the same time Kaiser's dramatization of the experience of the Cashier may be read as a symbolic projection of his own inner conflict of search for meaning and value in life, or in his society. Some expressionist plays were entirely subjective in material; in others on a framework of a realistic situation the inner experience of a character in response was dramatized as the body of the play. The external scenes, however, were usually only semirealistic, drawn by stylization into unity with the expressionism of the play. The entire play might also consist of scenes of external reality, but distorted through the mind of a character or the subjective view of the playwright.

Georg Kaiser's *From Morn to Midnight* (*Von Morgens bis Mitternachts*) is the most readily available in English translation, through anthologies, of the German expressionist dramas. It exemplifies the staccato style, the extensive use of stream-of-consciousness monologue, the episodic structure of stations, characters throughout without personal names, and dramatization of the consciousness of the principal character in response to an initial external situation. The entire play is a symbolic presentation of abstract ideas. The protagonist is a bank cashier, in the opening scene in his cage imprisoned in a colorless life of routine. A glamorous Lady enters and by misleading circumstances is taken to be an adventuress. Stirred by her perfume and the touch of her hand in a transaction through his window, the Cashier seizes an opportunity and absconds with a large sum of money. In Scene II the Cashier presents himself to the Lady in her hotel room and discovers his error, that she is a respectable woman accompanied by her Son. Scene III opens on the Cashier walking through a field in snow. By his action he has burned his bridges. He is free, life before him. The entire scene is a stream-of-consciousness monologue in symbols on the theme of value in life. The money is power to buy what he chooses: "But I must pay. I must spend. I've got the cash. Where are the goods that are worth the whole sum? Sixty thousand and the buyer to boot—flesh and bones—body and soul. Deal with me! Sell to me—I have the money, you have the goods—let us trade." The bare branches of a tree change to the form of a skeleton—the Cashier's thought of death as the inevitable awaiting end. But, "I still have many obligations to fulfill before evening." The skeleton reverts to the tree. The first two scenes are somewhat stylized external reality. The third scene is transitional: there is the external action of escaping from the police, but the content of the scene is the Cashier's stream of consciousness turned by the external situation to the search for value—what does life offer that is worth the giving of the whole self? The four following scenes are stations on the quest, each a dramatization in a semirealistic situation of the Cashier's thought on one value after another, each rejected. In Scene IV he returns to his home and family—domesticity and comfort. That is not enough. He leaves. Scene V is at the bicycle races. The Cashier appears and drives the riders and the crowd to a frenzy by the large prizes he offers. There is an accident: "When life is at fever heat some must die," remarks the Cashier. Sudden silence—His Royal Highness has entered his box. Excitement, intensity, competition, power cannot be an ultimate goal. The Cashier leaves, withdrawing his offered prize. He next appears in a private supper room in a cabaret, Scene VI, seeking the pinnacle of life in the senses. The First Mask who comes to him responds only "Fizz!" to everything he says—no mind. The Second and Third are ugly behind their masks; the Fourth has a wooden leg and cannot dance, is joyless. The Cashier puts a banknote on the table and leaves. An ironic by-product of pleasure—the money is stolen by succeeding Guests, and the Waiter with a wife and children, who will be held responsible, is going to drown himself. Scene VII is a Salvation Army Hall. The Cashier has learned there is nothing of worth that money can buy. The spirit is the goal. He confesses his embezzlement and scatters the banknotes in the hall. The other penitents scramble for the money and become a fighting mass that rolls to the door and out into the street. The Cashier and a Salvation Lass who followed him to the bicycle races and the cabaret and led him here are left standing alone. Religion is illusion—but there is love, the eternal reality: "Maiden and man . . . sense and aim and goal!" The Salvation Lass turns him over to the Police for the reward. The Cashier cries: "Here above you I stand. Two are too many. Space holds but one. Space is loneliness." A tangle of wires at the ceiling is illuminated and forms the outline of a skeleton. The Cashier addresses the skeleton: "From morn to midnight, I rage in a circle . . . and now your beckoning finger points the way . . . whither?" He shoots himself. The only verity found is the awareness by the individual of his own isolated existence, the end of which is death.

The Cashier falls back with arms outstretched, and his last gasp and sigh are like an "Ecce, homo." From an abstract representation of a social class, critical of an economic system which dehumanizes the individual, the Cashier has developed into the symbol of Man whose idealism is denied by the reality of experience. The play goes no further than there is something wrong somewhere. For the curtain, the electric lamps all explode, a Policeman says, "There must be a short circuit in the main," and darkness. The pessimism of the play is relieved only by a kind of exultation in the stripping away of all illusions in the staccato rhythm of the Cashier's final speech.

Kaiser's drama represents not only many of the forms but a spirit that was prominent in German expressionism. Concentration on the realities of inner experience is not necessarily a denial of or protest against the external world, but it nevertheless is true that one of the possible effects of finding the world in which one lives extremely unsatisfactory is introversion. The Germany of the years following World War I, with broken traditions and pride, economic and political disruption, and the recent memory of the violences of war and the immediate violences of strikes and internal revolt, was a society adrift; it was fertile ground for the subjectivity of expressionism, with pessimism as one natural direction. Kaiser's idealistic pessimism of the conflict between human aspiration and the facts of experience was one of the dramatically more productive reactions because a binding tension was maintained between the two worlds of the mind and material reality. That Kaiser's plays are distinguished by a clarity of dramatic form is compatible with, and probably in part a result of the balance of that tension. Many of the German expressionists found no principle by which to discipline their thoughts and emotions and expressed their view of the world as an unordered chaos in a chaotic and formless drama. There was also an area of expressionism which lost the motive of search for and communication of truth and was no more than the unrestrained projection of the emotions and personal fantasies of the dramatist, which were frequently sexually obsessed, violent, macabre, and sadistic. This was the lowest depth of expressionism. The extreme subjectivity of the expressionist movement, within which the playwright Kasimir Edschmidt could state that "the expressionist believes in a reality which he himself creates against all other reality," * attracted neurotic minds destructively stimulated by the social state of postwar Germany. Every mode of drama contains its inherent direction of excess. The excesses of expressionism, like those of naturalism with its biological view of man, were peculiarly repellent. Those of realism are merely dull. That the basic conception of expressionism, however, could furnish a medium for a mind of profound humanity, active social consciousness, clarity of principle against compromise, and self-sacrificing integrity is established in the plays by Ernst Toller, whose *Man and the Masses* is perhaps the noblest manifestation of the movement.

Expressionism is linked with romanticism by its emphasis on the individual consciousness and arose as a recoil from the objective focus of naturalism on rationality, environment, and materiality. Walter Hasenclever, one of the first of the expressionists, declared, "Reality on the stage is of no account; all the persons in the play have only to reflect the Ego of the poet as set down in the principal character." † Nevertheless, the movement as it progressed was influenced by that same force of the dominance in society of scientific thought which produced naturalism. As one of its developments expressionism explored the irrational as an area of significant reality, but explored it, in contrast to the old romantic drama, in the light of modern psychology and especially psychoanalysis, with the closely allied science of anthropology. Sociology also contributed to the abstractions of expressionism with the ideas of classes and social groups and types as dramatic entities. In the wake of expressionism, although by its author's assertion not directly influenced, Eugene O'Neill's *The Emperor Jones* is a study of the irrational fears projected in vision scenes of Brutus Jones as arising from his subconscious memory of his personal past and from his racial past. A considerable part of the stream-of-consciousness asides of

* Quoted by John Gassner in *Form and Idea in the Modern Theatre*, p. 123, from Thomas L. Dickinson, *The Theatre in Changing Europe* (Holt, 1937), p. 23.

† Quoted by Toby Cole and Helen Krich Chinoy, *Actors on Acting*, p. 239.

O'Neill's *Strange Interlude* have a Freudian basis. In stripping away external actions as the material of drama and ruthlessly exploring the raw materials of action in the stream of consciousness and the irrationalities of the subconscious mind, expressionism, like naturalism, asserted the validity of whatever exists in human life as subject matter for the stage. In its scientific phase expressionism was psychological naturalism pushed to a logical conclusion. Its object was to dig for the inner roots of truth in the human being and to present what was found there directly, unobscured by the veil of external action. To this end it was necessary to dispense with realism as a method.

Expressionism did not triumph over realism and as a self-conscious movement did not survive the 1920's. It was expressionism, however, which had the force and spreading power to break the bondage of realism and to change the dramatic climate of the modern theater. It led the way for a succession of antirealistic movements which together have established the sense of freedom for varied inventions of form to meet the needs of fresh subject matter or spirit for communication. Expressionism added to the playwright's repertory of formal devices, but its influence was not superficially on form, but to the end which O'Neill referred to on more than one occasion as his object, to get beneath the banality of surfaces.

Dadaism and surrealism, like expressionism, came to the theater from painting as movements of antirealism, expressionism and surrealism having appeared in art in the first decade of this century, Dadaism not until 1916. Expressionism was generating in drama in Germany from 1910 to 1912, developed during the war, and took a central position in German drama for the decade from 1918. Surrealism entered the theater significantly in France in 1917 with the productions of Guillaume Apollinaire's *The Breasts of Tiresias* and Jean Cocteau's ballet, *Parade*. With Cocteau, a playwright of lively imagination and talent, as its central figure, surrealism developed a considerable vogue in France in the twenties and thirties. Dadaism penetrated the theater to only a minor degree, in France or elsewhere, although there was briefly a Dadaist coterie in Germany following World War I.

Dadaism was essentially an esoteric cult among bohemian art-

ists. It was irreverent, capricious, and destructive. The Dadaists rejected all accepted artistic values and the idea of meaning in
art and occupied themselves with shocking the Philistines. André
Breton, a principal spokesman, wrote: "The main thing is to disturb
the ceremony." * To be antirealistic was not enough; they satirized
expressionism as well. In this country E. E. Cummings' *him* was
produced in 1928 at the Provincetown Playhouse in New York.
Mordecai Gorelik described the production as having "swung diz-
zily through twenty-one scenes of repartee. The environment of
New York City and other places turned like a revolving door, and
the stage was filled with such personages as Me, Him, the three
Weirds, Mussolini, a Blonde Gonzesse, and Six Hundred Pounds of
Passionate Pulchritude." † At the time of its appearance Cummings' play was the pet of college intellectuals, who searched it for
profound symbols of the unconscious. It possessed some imaginativeness and pungency but not enough sense to sustain high regard.
It remains, however, as a point of reference for Dadaism in the
American theater. Gertrude Stein's *Four Saints in Three Acts,* an
opera with music by Virgil Thomson, produced in 1934, has been
classed both as Dadaist and surrealist.

Dadaism was a digression in the line of development of modern
drama. Although its products, in so far as it was productive, superficially resembled surrealist plays, Dadaism made a mockery of the
search for truth. The surrealists were seeking the most fundamental reality of human existence and believed it was to be found
and revealed in the free movement of the unconscious mind, "all
exercises of reason and every esthetic or moral preoccupation being absent." ‡ The stream-of-consciousness monologues of expressionism were too directed and selective for the purpose of the surrealist. The endeavor was to capture from consciousness the fugi-
tive fantasies and images that rise from the unconscious without
premeditation, recognizable origin, or connection. Wherever there
was least intrusion of reason was the hunting ground of surrealism:
the fantasies of children, the aberrations of the insane, and dreams.

* Quoted by Mordecai Gorelik, *New Theatres for Old,* Samuel French, New
York, 1940, p. 246.
† *New Theatres for Old,* p. 247.
‡ From André Breton's First Manifesto of Surrealism in 1924, quoted by
Mordicai Gorelik, *New Theatres for Old,* p. 255.

Even more than expressionism, surrealism relied on images over speech and remained closely allied to painting—to Dali's limp watches sliding over the edge of a table or the branch of a tree, and feminine forms with arboreal decorations; to Chirico's lovely architecture in desert space. Surrealism has produced pantomimes, ballets, and motion pictures as well as spoken drama. Such fabrications as the anachronism of Eurydice receiving letters delivered by a mailman and the fantasy of Orpheus' Passage to Death through a mirror in Jean Cocteau's *Orpheus* are suggested by John Gassner as "especially appropriate if it is believed, with Jung and his disciples, that the unconscious contains in the form of symbols the archetypal emotions of the human race." Familiar reality was rejected as a delusion. Once the façade of reality was destroyed, irrational occurrences would evoke "the anxieties, obsessions, and primitive wishes that constitute the true reality that lies behind the surface of everyday behavior." * During and since the war surrealism has become more a diffusion into the theater, like that of expressionism, than a directly productive movement. The American theater has possessed in William Saroyan a natural and surprisingly cheerful surrealist in the improvisatory manner of his playwriting, with *The Beautiful People, Jim Dandy,* and others of his plays representing essentially a surrealist type of symbolism, the free fantasy of the unconscious.

In addition to numerous sporadic movements in the crusade against realism which failed of appreciable productivity, there was the influential movement of constructivism in Russia with the closely allied futurism in Italy which were essentially modes of staging rather than playwriting. In fact, in expressing their view of the modern world as a process of mechanization, the exponents of these styles subordinated the play, as society subordinated human beings, to production. Actors were made to move like automata; the play was interpreted in lines and balances of force over three-dimensional, bare, and purely functional stage structures. The mechanistic practices of staging were interpretative rather than creative of dramatic literature, but they lent themselves well to and reinforced the abstractions of expressionism.

Simultaneously in the 1920's with the extreme emphasis on the subjective reality of the individual in expressionism and surreal-

* *Form and Idea in the Modern Theatre,* pp. 110-111.

ism, Erwin Piscator as a director and Bertolt Brecht as a director and playwright developed in Germany a fresh approach to emphasis on social reality which has come to be known as "epic realism." The tight structure of Ibsenian realism was too confined, too restricted to private lives, to bring the realities of modern society into the theater. Plays would have to become more loose in structure, more extensively narrative or "epic" again, as they had been in the Romantic and Elizabethan theaters. They were to be given a new principle of unification, the demonstration of a social issue, which could bind together a loose or even episodic structure. The old realism of illusion was discarded for utilization of any and all the instrumentalities of theater and of modern technology for communication of the idea. Soliloquies, direct address to the audience, commentators, choral chants, supernatural interventions, exposed mechanics of staging, and slides, films, recordings, loudspeakers might be mingled in the same play with scenes of realistic characterization and representation. The illusion of actuality was broken by fragmentation of scenes and interruption of the action for comment as a deliberate restraint on a solely emotional involvement. The principle of epic realism as promulgated by Brecht was a presentation of some aspect of social reality simultaneously and in balance to the emotions and the intellect. The Living Newspaper productions and documentary plays on economic themes of the Federal Theatre during the depression years of the thirties were a development from epic realism. Paul Green's pacifist play *Johnny Johnson* showed influence from *The Good Soldier Schweik,** one of Piscator's most successful productions. Brecht himself in the body of his plays is one of the significant modern dramatists. Whether or not his theory of the rejection of emotional identification in order to maintain the audience's critical awareness—a theory that sees drama as a demonstration of reality rather than as a revelation of truth—has either basic artistic validity or the possibility of wide-spread audience appeal, Brecht's epic realism has undeniably added to the resources of theatrical device. This can be seen in, for example, Thornton Wilder's theatricalist play *The Skin of Our Teeth,* which shows the influences of epic realism.

Theatricalism is a broader concept than the specific antirealistic

* Piscator's dramatization of a novel of the same title by the Czech, Jaroslav Hacek, which was unfinished at Hacek's death and completed by someone else.

movements we have been examining. Theatricalism represents, first, the principle of recognition for an audience that they are witnessing a play and not an excerpt from life, the antithesis of the convention of realistic illusion. Secondly, theatricalism exploits the resources of the theater in methods and devices for communication other than direct representation, those which are distinctively of the theater, either previously existent, or newly invented or combined by the playwright. Some *avant-garde* extremists maintain that the object of writing and performing plays is to create theater and nothing but theater—theatrical actions, characterizations, and images. But theater throughout the main line of its history has always been something larger than itself, not a little circle isolated within life, but through its different modes a suggestion, evocation, focusing, or expansion of truth of life. Exactly the criticism of realism is that it says too little beyond what is there before the audience on the stage. Even further, the nothing-but-theater extremists unintentionally ally themselves to what they would most vehemently repudiate, the well-made play of Scribe developed on his theory that the sole purpose of a play is to get and hold an audience's attention agreeably, to entertain in the theater. However, the *avant-garde* playwrights with their enthusiasm for the forms of theater frequently create a lively experience for an audience and contribute active inventiveness of fresh means to the larger ends of theater. For the greater part, theatricalism, rather than an end in itself, has been an instrument of release moving through the antirealist movements of modern theater.

All nonrealistic plays are not theatricalist in the full sense. A surrealist play may be theatricalist in the variety of devices it employs for communication, even though its object may be to draw the audience as completely as possible into forgetfulness of the theater itself. As in a play of external realism, there is created for the audience an illusion of reality—in this case, the reality of the unconscious mind. On the other hand, a surrealist drama, by glaring incongruities with outer reality, may keep the audience constantly reminded that what is before them is—has to be—theatrical communication. Theatricalism served expressionism particularly well and is indispensable to the Brechtian theory of epic realism, of interrupted illusion.

An extreme view of theatricalism has appeared recently and

most familiarly in the plays of Eugene Ionesco, that of pure theater, of reducing to the minimum, if not eliminating, the means of communication that do not belong solely to the theater, by which Ionesco means, essentially, language. He does not do away altogether with language, but he fragments language in its grammatical sequence and even within the word until it loses identity with speech as we know it in life and becomes theatrical image. At the same time he stresses the use of purely visual images, physical objects such as the chairs in the play *The Chairs,* and pantomime. Such a view of theater characterized the production theories of constructivism and futurism, but did not create the writing of plays. Ionesco is writing plays of considerable effectiveness, but so far, and inescapably, limited in scope. In the composite art of the theater, language is the most flexible and intricate of the several media, the one possessing range and power together. And the fact that drama may have originated in pantomime, dance, and song represents just that, primitive origin and not purer drama.

In a sense all nonrealistic drama is theatricalist, but nonrealistic conventions, established with a high degree of unity of practice such as the poetic medium, the Chorus, the masks of Greek drama, and the poetry, soliloquies, and open platform stage of the Elizabethan theater, created a unified artistic illusion without self-consciousness. The audience neither forgot nor were reminded they were in a theater. They experienced it as a familiar fact. Such a theater is conventionalized rather than theatricalist. There is almost inevitably something of self-consciousness in full-fledged theatricalism today. It is antirealistic, and out of all the movements away from realism no single style has emerged as a nonrealistic norm and no particular devices have become completely conventions of our theater. In Thornton Wilder's *The Skin of Our Teeth,* one of the finest manifestations of out-and-out theatricalism in the American theater, the capacity of the human race to advance and survive is presented in the suburban New Jersey family of Mr. and Mrs. Antrobus whose lives encompass the invention of the wheel, the Ice Age, Noah's Flood Atlantic City style, war, and the story of Cain. With this basis and whimsical details throughout, such as a baby dinosaur and a baby mammoth elephant as household pets, the further shenanigans of scenic flats which leap into the air and reassume proper position for no apparent reason or purpose, and obvious remarks about the play addressed by an actress to the audience, are unnecessary to remind us that it is a play. Nevertheless, the caprices are enjoyably humorous and the effect of ingenuousness disarms the audience so that it is caught unawares with identifying emotion.

Aggressive theatricalism has had less productivity and value directly in the American theater, thus far, than as a formalizing influence on realism. Thornton Wilder, without the effect of self-consciousness, blended the theatricalist elements of absence of scenery and properties and a combined stage manager, narrator, and commentator with a foundation of realistic characterization and action in *Our Town*. Tennessee Williams in *The Glass Menagerie* tells his story in the perspective of memory by having the brother Tom move back and forth between taking his part in the action and stepping outside the frame of action as narrator and commentator looking back from several years later. The stream-of-consciousness asides in O'Neill's *Strange Interlude* are a part of an otherwise realistic play. There are other plays of this flexible realism, like Samuel Beckett's *Waiting for Godot*, in which the balance is much more heavily on the theatricalist side. In fact, one could say of *Waiting for Godot* that the realistic element in the conversation between the two tramps is a symbol in the theatricalist organization of the play.

The greatest value in theatricalism and the successive antirealistic movements does not rest in the specific doctrines but in the stimulus to freedom and fresh invention they have introduced into playwriting. Variation from realism is no longer antirealistic, and a playwright does not need the support of a school or movement to be nonrealistic. Today it is hardly pertinent to try to classify strictly such plays as Sartre's *The Flies*, Giraudoux's *The Mad Woman of Chaillot*, Fry's *A Sleep of Prisoners*, Eliot's *The Cocktail Party*, Saroyan's *My Heart's in the Highlands*, Beckett's *Endgame*, MacLeish's *J.B.;* they are to be experienced, analyzed, and understood individually.*

* For those who wish to read further on the modern theater movements: *New Theatres for Old* (French, New York, 1940), by Mordecai Gorelik, one of the group of brilliant scene designers who developed the new theater in staging in

Contemplation of the movements of modern drama in their product of plays *en masse,* as in this chapter, may easily produce an accumulated impression of the macabre, the dismal, the morbid, and neurotic. There is both a valid stricture in such an impression and less than justice to the value and effects of the movements. The clear bright light of the neoromanticism of Rostand, it is true, is isolated and Maeterlinck's feeling for beauty sheds only a misty aura of light over his symbolizations of death and destiny. Realism, as distinguished from naturalism, is the most flexible and varied in its products, but it is the least spectacular of the movements and progressed early from the stage of self-conscious rebellion into familiarity as the norm of the period. By the time realism produced a Chekhov and *The Three Sisters* and *The Cherry Orchard* the plays were not startling manifestations of a new movement, but perfect and beautiful expressions of a rare spirit. It should be noted that a survey of the origin and development of movements in the theater is actually to a considerable degree a review of *avant-gardes.* Conceivably an *avant-garde* of sweetness and light could arise, but the general healthy desire of people for sweetness and light leads to so much popular purveying of the merely sentimental and superficial that to maintain the distinction would call for a refinement of perception hardly to be expected of *avant-garde* enthusiasm. An *avant-garde* is a self-designated advance from the established and the popular with a consequent inherent tendency toward the unpalatable either by obscurity of form or unpleasantness of content or both.

There have been, however, prevalences in the modern temper which have had a limiting effect on drama, identification of truth with scientific fact, social consciousness, and materialism. As has been remarked upon in the preceding chapter, cleansing tragedy

---

this country, offers a thorough survey and analysis from an individual and stimulating point of view with emphasis on the antirealistic movements; John Gassner in *Form and Idea in the Modern Theatre* (Dryden press, New York, 1956) presents an analytic survey from the romanticism leading to the modern movements into the present decade as the basis for a philosophic examination of relation between form and idea, a distillation from his years of historical study and associations as editor and critic with the working theater in significant application to the theater of today.

and the release of comedy have been of infrequent occurrence. The serious dramatic nose was held to the sociopsychological grindstone, and drama of social criticism or of flagellation of the human species took the place of tragic exaltation on the one hand and exuberant comic freedom on the other. Comedy as popular entertainment remained, but partially by the loss of association with poetry and partially by loss of recognition, paradoxically, as a serious expression of the human mind and spirit, comedy at the level of dramatic literature declined. The French maintained comedy of ironic recognition of human frailties and worse, saved from grimness by literary polish and deftness of execution. There was the revival of comedy of manners in the plays of Oscar Wilde. Shaw by the positiveness of his faith in rationality was released to making robust comedy out of irrationality and with the superabundance of his wit produced the outstandingly original and vigorous comedy at the level of dramatic literature of the period.

Within the general limitation of identification of truth with scientific fact, the movements tended to further limitation by adopting a single scientific view: biological, sociological, psychological, or psychoanalytic, like those three blind men each of whom was convinced he knew what an elephant was like by grasping respectively the trunk, a leg, and a tail. Nevertheless, the nobility of the search for truth and the seriousness of investing the theater with the purpose of free revelation of truth must not be forgotten. If great values that had once been in the theater were left out or diminished, areas of truth new to the theater were admitted and, especially, new modes of projection capable of broader and more varied application than that of their invention were created. In the freshness of the several movements, drama of nobility rose out of and above the movements in individual character and great talent, an Ibsen from realism, a Gorki from naturalism, a Toller from expressionism. The theater has received heritages of value from the modern movements, and with changing temper of the times the older values of tragedy have at least reappeared; cheerfulness, too, keeps breaking in. The tragedies of Miller and MacLeish's *J.B.,* and the exuberant comedies, Fry's *The Lady's Not for Burning* and Wilder's *The Skin of Our Teeth,* are modern plays and each owes something of its form to the dramatic climate of modern movements.

10

The Temper of a Play

For understanding a play by analysis of the play itself there is the structure and there is its temper. The structure is the playwright's consciously planned and organized solid foundation for communication of the meaning of his play. The temper is more complex, less tangible, more intuitive. Some acquaintance with the background of approaches to form and function that have developed historically and in modern movements, as discussed in the preceding chapters on dramatic climate or environment, is necessary both to clear understanding of the structural character of plays and to recognition and appreciation of the significance of elements in their temper. Analysis of the structure of a play is like describing a person by his physique; analysis of the temper is like undertaking to describe the quality of the total personality. Personality is affected by physique and is in part revealed in physical appearance, and both are affected and in some respects determined by environmental conditions and influences. The jerky episodic structure and staccato speech of expressionistic drama, for example, as previously discussed, produced an effect more of nervous energy than directed power, and more readily expressed neurotic irritability of rebellion than the drive of a possessed ideal. Yet in Ernst Toller's *Man and the Masses* the structure and style proved capable of communicating the progress of a tearing mental conflict between opposed ideals to rejection of one and assertion of the other.

The temper of a play derives in part from the class of drama within which it is written, such as tragedy, comedy, or social drama and their particular modes, and in part from broad concepts of drama, such as realism, naturalism, and the various antirealistic movements, whether by direct theoretical allegiance or by disseminated influence. The personal temper, however, which gives each play its distinctive individuality, is a composite effect from any and all the elements that go to make up a play. Of these, language is one of the most distinguishing. *Romeo and Juliet* and *Antony and Cleopatra* are both Shakespeare and both tragedies of love, but the unifying poetic tone of one is in the quick bright lyricism of the springtime freshness of young love in the balcony scene, and of the other in the somber autumnal richness of the slow threnody of Antony's and Cleopatra's deaths. In *Macbeth* the unifying mood of foulness and guilt is in the accumulated images of blood, darkness, and animals of the night and of savagery. Although many of Shakespeare's plays have a distinguishing unity of tone in the language, in general the flexibility and range of his verse is applied to individualizing characterization with a consequent focus on psychological interest and truth. Marlowe's "mighty line," on the other hand, especially in *Tamburlaine,* sweeps through the whole play in one tumultuous roll which expresses the reaching of his mind beyond the bounds of human faculties, experience, and will. A great deal of the exhilarating temper and meaning of Christopher Fry's plays is in the fluent verve of his language and imagery.

In modern prose drama, O'Neill's straining for power of language beyond his verbal facility is a revealing fault that becomes a part of the temper of his plays of frustration of man's reach beyond his grasp. There are many plays of prose realism, occasionally one that is very fine, *The Diary of Anne Frank,* for example, in which the language has too little individual distinction for special significance in the temper of the play. On the other hand, in the plays of John Galsworthy the language does not draw attention, yet is intrinsic in its quality to their temper. Galsworthy's plays express his severe regard for truth, sense of good taste, and humane and judi-

cial perception of both sides of a situation and the consciousness
and point of view of the persons involved. The temper of his plays
in the determined naturalness of their language is not weakness or
unimaginativeness, but the strength of restraint and balance, and
corresponds to his most characteristic plot organization of presenting the characters on opposed sides of a conflict in equal perspective to the audience.

The language of Molière in the precision and ease of the verbal
play of his wit, its pungency without excess, is an essential part of
the temper of his comedies, but the most important element is his
choice of characters for ridicule. They are subject to excess of one
sort or another: the *précieuses* who are excessively exquisite, guard-
ians who are excessively watchful of their wards, Alceste in *The
Misanthrope* who expects too much of human nature, Orgon in
Tartuffe who is duped by his overly credulous piety and is saved by
the common sense and wit of his wife, daughter, and serving-maid
who see through, unmask, and totally discomfit the consummate
hypocrite, Tartuffe. The temper of Molière's comedies is an affirmation of rationality, reasonableness, and sense of proportion.

In reading plays, stage directions for translation into theater can
be as meaningful to the temper as the dialogue. In Tennessee Williams' *The Glass Menagerie* the total organization is to the end of
presenting an action in the perspective of memory, but the meaning
of memory in its softening of harsh reality is made most clear in the
stage business and directions at the end by which the transition
from enactment of the story to its memory is accomplished. Tom
Wingfield has been essentially driven from home by a climax in the
habitual, unreasonable nagging of his mother for having committed the blunder of bringing home for his crippled and too-sensi-
tive sister Laura a gentleman caller who turned out to be engaged
to be married. He stands on the fire-escape outside the door and
while he delivers a speech as though looking back on this moment
from the future, an interior scene is played in pantomime, "as
though viewed through soundproof glass. Amanda appears to be
making a comforting speech to Laura who is huddled upon the
sofa. Now that we cannot hear the mother's speech her silliness is
gone and she has dignity and tragic beauty. Laura's dark hair
hides her face until at the end of the speech she lifts it to smile at

her mother. Amanda's gestures are slow and graceful, almost dance-like, as she comforts the daughter." All the elements that go to make up the structure and temper of *The Glass Menagerie* are directed to the meaning of strength which tenderness holds in memory over harsher reality, also not forgotten. The temper of a play, however, can be in part unconscious or involuntary to the playwright. *Cat on a Hot Tin Roof* represents the peak of Williams' playwriting to date in its imaginativeness, intricacy, and scope, in its fullness of life. There is much of corruption revealed in the play and in general it is indicated as such. In a note on the inclusion for publication of his original third act with the third act as rewritten for the Broadway production, Williams refers to the "moral paralysis" and the "state of spiritual disrepair" of Brick. Yet in the temper of the play can be felt a fascinated dwelling on corruption rather than a facing of corruption for the sake of fidelity to truth of life. The effect is intangible and not easy to identify in source, but I think the key to it may perhaps be found in the inclusion in Big Daddy's "talkin' jag" to his son Brick in Act II of the incident of the perverted form of prostitution of a little girl of four or five set on by her mother which he had encountered in Morocco. Big Daddy exclaims, "Jesus, it makes you sick t' remember a thing like this!"—but inclusion of the incident is not only unnecessary but irrelevant and disruptive to the play. It is shocking enough to arrest disproportionate attention and momentarily to break the continuity of dramatic identification. Something of this ambivalence could be felt in the temper of *A Streetcar Named Desire,* it is stronger in *Cat on a Hot Tin Roof,* and *Suddenly Last Summer* definitely breaks down into the temper of decadence when Williams not only creates horror upon horror but decorates the final horror. In Catherine's narrative of what had happened last summer, the unspeakably perverted Sebastian Venable had drawn upon himself attack by the crowd of naked, sun-blackened, starving urchins that infested the beach at Cabeza de Lobo: "Cousin Sebastian had disappeared in the flock of featherless little black sparrows, he—he was lying naked as they had been naked against a white wall, and . . . They had *devoured* parts of him. . . . There wasn't a sound any more, there was nothing to see but Sebastian, what was left of him, that looked like a big white-paper-wrapped bunch of red roses had been *torn, thrown, crushed!*—against the blazing white wall." Verbal felicity, especially compelling of visual images, has been expended on horror and evil throughout the play, but here the horror is irrelevantly prettified. Although there is moral assumption in *Suddenly Last Summer* the temper is that of fascination by evil. Morbid enjoyment of evil requires a moral frame of reference to produce the shock, the thrill in horror. Beaumont and Fletcher's similarly brilliantly decadent *Philaster* following upon the Elizabethan energy embroiders horrors with incomparable verbal felicity accompanied by moral sentiments.

The ways in which the personal temper of a play may be communicated are so individual, various, and often subtle that classification is impossible. Each play must be considered in itself. Chechkov's *The Cherry Orchard* arouses a curiously personal feeling of affection. When Joshua Logan's *The Wistaria Trees* was announced for production some years back as an adaptation of *The Cherry Orchard* the letter columns of the drama sections of newspapers were overwhelmed with expressions of indignation and outrage at the idea of adaptation. While the protests were generally in terms of not tampering with perfection, I think the basis of the strong personal identification is in the sense of Chekhov's affection for all his characters. Yet the method of presentation is objective to the extreme degree, even to the total absence from stage directions of any suggestion of authorial attitude. Furthermore the characters are presented critically with detached clarity, but with no harshness. What creates the quality of affection in the temper of the play is the affection of the people within the play for each other in all the relationships: of family, between family and servants, between neighbors, and even where there is every basis for antagonism, between Lopakhin, the now prosperous businessman who had been a child on the Ranevsky estate as the son of a former serf, and the genteel but now impoverished Ranevskys. They may bicker somewhat, criticize, chide, and twit each other, but they are all filled with sentiment and affection which rises easily to the surface and overflows. *The Cherry Orchard* would be pulled apart by the stress between regret for the passing of a gracious past now gently decadent, and confident anticipation of a future now crude but healthy in direction, and by the critical dissection of the characters as socially representative types, were it not for the binding power of affection among and for the characters as individuals in the temper of the play. The result is a delicately organized unity.

In Norman Rosten's *Mister Johnson,* produced by Cheryl Craw-ford and Robert Lewis in 1956, the central figure is created as so lovable a character that one inescapably feels authorial affection for him, but the affection is not the determinative factor in the personal temper of the play. Norman Rosten is a poet as well as a playwright, and what is felt most strongly in *Mister Johnson* is a poet's response to a bright phenomenon of life. Mister Johnson is a poetic character and his creator has the poet's capacity to give him words that reveal him as such. The story of the play is built around his entanglement between the native African background of his origin and his devotion to being a civilized good public servant in the white man's world. Considerable native background is necessary to understanding of the plot and of Mister Johnson's psychology, but beyond those dramaturgic effects the tapestry of background communicates a poetic impression of colorful phenomena. Mister Johnson could have been treated so as to be comic through the early course of the play, and pathetic in his catastrophe; by the personal temper of the play he is romantic throughout, with poetic beauty and dignity.

Modern music drama presents a new focus of temper. With substantial stories and dramatic integration of the music, the songs through the projection of music may be made the principal statements of meaning, and they do not always come at the structural peaks of plot. In other words, the communication of meaning depends more upon the temper of the play proportionately to structure than is common to straight plays. For example, in *The King and I* Anna's song with the King's wives and children, "Getting to Know You," is poignantly moving and is the thematic center of the play, but is not at a high point in the plot. What the play is about is not the reform of the Orient by the Occident, but people of different backgrounds growing by association into mutual understanding. Even in reading the published book without the music, the place of the song in the temper of *The King and I* is clear by the words of the lyric with the accompanying action. However, with recordings of the songs of many of the music dramas available, the way to read the book of a music drama one has not heard is supplemented by a recording, when possible.

The temper of a play may be in sentiments and attitudes enunciated in the play, the kind of material the author dwells upon, or the light cast upon the matter. It may be in harmony with the general temper of the time or at odds with it. The temper of plays is as various as the personalities that create them and each play by the same author has its own individual character. In some plays structural design is more prominent for the discernment of meaning, in others the enveloping temper, but if the play is all that it should be there will be, of course, harmony between the two. It is often from the quality of the personal temper of a play that the most memorable enjoyment as well as sense of the play's meaning is derived.

Evaluating
the Play

11

Principles of Evaluation

It is not necessary to evaluate a play that one has seen or read, but everyone does. What we are concerned with here is how to perform this familiar exercise worthily. Hippolyte Clairon, a French actress of the eighteenth century, wrote in her *Mémoires:* "the approbation of the critic is in no ways flattering, nor his censure any disgrace, unless he is known to possess those qualities necessary to enable him to form his judgment with accuracy. It is not enough to approve or reject a work; the man who does either, ought to show himself capable of judging." * Anyone who has experienced and understood a play is prepared to evaluate that play for himself; the more plays one has experienced and understood the better qualified he is to evaluate for others. As there are principles and ways of approach for understanding a play or arriving at its meaning, so for evaluation. Eloquent statements of impressions are often enjoyable reading, but analysis is more convincing. In reading plays for pleasure, evaluation, if only for oneself, is the final pleasure, and there is great satisfaction in bringing conviction to one's own mind.

First of all, a play should be judged in its own kind, not for what it is not. One may have a personal preference or taste for

* From excerpts in *Actors on Acting,* ed. by Toby Cole and Helen Krich Chinoy, Crown Publishers, New York, 1949, p. 173.

229

naturalism, for symbolism, for theatricalism, and so on, but every theory of dramaturgy in the hands of congenial talent or genius and in a favorable climate of theater conditions has produced drama of merit, and masterpieces are of many kinds. There has been a recent predilection in criticism in England for theatricalism, but as Harold Hobson has remarked: "Naturalism,* the imitation of the visible and audible surfaces of life, has produced some of the finest things that the theatre has created anywhere in the world. It is not a tradition to be jeered at. It made Ibsen and Galsworthy and the Manchester school of dramatists." † Stanislavsky made the statement that, "Having tried in the theatre all the means and methods of creative work; having paid homage to the enthusiasm for all sorts of productions along all the lines of creativeness . . . I have come to the conclusion that . . . the only king and ruler of the stage is the talented actor." ‡ Similarly, the only king and ruler of dramatic form is the talented playwright. Theories have served as an energization and organization of the talents of dramatists and are to be understood by critics rather than promulgated. Fresh dramatic modes, as naturalism at one time, expressionism at another, are seized upon with enthusiasm by playwrights as a bolder, freer opportunity for communication of more ultimate truth of life. The once-new forms become familiar, become diffused into the theater, each a part of the total repertory of means upon which the playwright may draw for expression. No form becomes so outworn that it may not be reanimated by a playwright who finds in it the right instrument for his purpose, the historical romantic verse drama transformed into sophisticated drama of criticism of their respective societies by Rostand in *Cyrano de Bergerac* and again by Christopher Fry in *The Lady's Not for Burning,* and historical realism given tragic dignity by Arthur Miller in *The Crucible.* Eugene O'Neill at the end of his career wrote his greatest drama in *Long Day's Journey Into Night* completely in the realistic mode which he had once rejected and without even the symbolic undertow of *The Iceman Cometh.* Anouilh and Sartre have built contemporary drama on

* Commonly used in England as synonymous with realism.
† *International Theatre Annual,* Doubleday, New York, 1957, p. 198.
‡ *My Life In Art,* p. 569.

the framework of Greek tragedies. At any time, too, one may be confronted by a play which is the first striking out into a new direction of form. Each play should be judged with openness of mind to the single consideration of how well and at what level it performs the function of drama.

There is another area of theory which sometimes gets in the way of the playwright as well as of the critic, that of current social, psychological, or philosophical doctrines. The Marxian theory of playwriting and of criticism prevalent in the thirties, by which a play was evaluated for its contribution to social revolution, made Clifford Odets' *Waiting for Lefty,* marred his *Awake and Sing* and *Rocket to the Moon,* and was essentially irrelevant to but not seriously disruptive of the enduring dramatic values of *Golden Boy* and *Night Music.* The proletarian plays of the thirties in general have a hollow ring today. Eugene O'Neill's *Strange Interlude* owed some part of its original success both with the public and critics to the Freudianism of the play, but in retrospect *Strange Interlude* compared with *Desire Under the Elms* and now with *Long Day's Journey Into Night* seems empty. It is the difference between a psychological theory of life and life itself. It was O'Neill's most signal failure, *Dynamo,* that was written out of the large conviction that the one big subject for drama in our time was man's struggle to come to terms with his need for a new faith. No theory of content, social, psychological, or philosophical, makes drama. Life makes drama.

There has been complete psychoanalytic interpretation of *Hamlet.* We are told not only that the Ghost is a figment of Hamlet's imagination, but that Hamlet presents an advanced development of the Oedipus complex. The murder of his father is imaginary, a wish fulfillment of his desire for his father's death; his idolization of his father and pursuit of revenge are compensations for his guilt feeling, and his hatred of Claudius a transference of his hatred of his father to another father image. It is easy to see, or should be, that relevancy as dramatic interpretation cannot sensibly be claimed for such a psychoanalyst's parlor game because Shakespeare by chronology could not have been allegorizing a psychiatric case study. But the contemporary *Death of a Salesman* contains a father-son conflict and pseudo-Freudian heads are nodded wisely. Similarly, Willy Loman is callously thrown aside by his old firm when he is no longer useful to it in dollars and cents and the play has been seized upon accordingly by left-wing critics or shied away from by violently anti-left-wing new critics. These approaches are just as dramatically irrelevant to *Death of a Salesman* as to Shakespeare because the kind of truth revealed in the play as written lies in such things as the almost unbearable power of emotion when Biff breaks down and cries and Willy recognizes that his son loves him. The truth of Willy's suicide, the element of the heroic in it, cracked as his mind is, can be lost by analysis in terms of paranoia. O'Neill's *Desire Under the Elms* and *Long Day's Journey Into Night* both contain material as susceptible to Freudian treatment as that of *Strange Interlude* but O'Neill did not write those plays in the manner of *Strange Interlude*. The truth of *Long Day's Journey Into Night* is the hate and love together, and no theoretical analysis makes the fact, the wonder and the poignancy of it, the pain and beauty, so clear as does just its direct revelation from the play as true. The best criticism has a simplicity about it. Reduction to a theory, such as psychoanalysis or a view of the capitalist system, is sometimes called oversimplification; rather, it is simplification in the wrong direction. The simplicity that cuts through to the truth of life in the play, shedding off irrelevant simplifications of dramatically extraneous theories, is the revealing criticism.

The first thing a reader should look for in evaluating a play is internal unity. A play is not life but an interpretation of life, material of life experienced through the temperament and ordered by the mind of the playwright. The edges should not be blurred, the play should not merge with life but be bounded by a clean circle. The play should exist as a consistent world within itself. You may or may not like that world, but the first demand upon a play is that it be a created world, that, as has been discussed in preceding chapters, it have a unified meaning or effect, which embraces the whole of the play. The meaning may be intricately composed of several elements, but if so, they must be an integrated organization, not a loose array, and there should be no spare parts in the play in relation to that meaning. The unity of a play is determined by the meaning for which it was written and includes every aspect of the play, the plot in its basic structure and all the details of its development, all the infinite details of speech and action by which the characters and background are created and the plot is clothed with life, the quality of the language, the dramatic mode which the playwright selects or creates, and the temperament of the playwright which inevitably permeates the whole.

The unity of plot may be single and direct as was characteristic of Greek tragedies, or it may be a complex structure with subplots interwoven upon the main plot as in the plays of Shakespeare and other Elizabethan drama. One writer observed that it seemed as though any good Elizabethan poet could strike out a great scene, but only Shakespeare could construct a great play. The statement does less than justice to some of Shakespeare's contemporaries, but the fact remains that part of what made Shakespeare a great dramatist was the content of his plays, and part was his skill in ordering and controlling the complexities of Elizabethan dramaturgy. In the immensity of the structure of *King Lear,* for example, the unusual expansion of the Gloucester subplot in lesser hands could easily have become unwieldy. It is not just that Shakespeare integrated the Gloucester story plot-wise by having it touch at intervals as a complication on the main plot of Lear and finally converge upon it, but that the broad development of the parallel story of filial ingratitude in the Gloucester household is a structural means by which Shakespeare expands the meaning of *King Lear* beyond a domestic tragedy of a particular family into a sense of the order of things, a symbolic drama of the cosmic conflict of good and evil. Similarly, consider the mastery Shakespeare developed in meeting the practical demand of the Elizabethan theater for the appearance in every play, even in the tragedies, of the low comedy player of the company to satisfy the groundlings. The low comedy scene of the drunken porter in *Macbeth* is famous for the variety of functions of intensification of the tragic situation which it serves. Duncan has been murdered and is lying in his blood in an adjoining room when there comes the sound of knocking at the castle gate. The drunken porter crosses the stage grumbling to himself at the impatiently repeated knocking and imagining himself the keeper of the gate to Hell, quite unconscious of the irony of the actual hell within his castle. The sound of the knocking has already touched the audience with awareness of Duncan lying dead out of view, whose ears cannot be reached by the knocking or ever by any sound again, when the same thought strikes Macbeth with a flash of remorse. The arrival at the gate has come soon upon the murder, leaving Macbeth barely time to compose himself for acting his scene of grief and anger at the discovery of Duncan. The delay of the soliloquy and the consequent repeated knocking builds up the suspense for the impending scene of Macbeth's confrontation by his visitors, and the comic character of the soliloquy creates a grotesque contrast of intensification of the tragic horror. The unity of plot structure and of episodes to the meaning of a play is not always obvious or to be determined by casual examination.

To turn to some modern plays, Strindberg's *The Father* gives the impression of a stark unity of plot line, of characterization, and of dialogue. The characters seem stripped of all action, traits, or speeches except those bearing on the theme of the conflict of the sexes in marriage for power in the home, all slanted to the destructiveness of woman to man in that relationship. Strindberg repeatedly in the play emphasizes the uniqueness of the effect of the marriage relation. The woman who is an unscrupulous and ruthless destroyer to her husband is a kind and amiable friend, and woman in the maternal relationship is beneficent to man. But Strindberg was a mad genius and for all the white heat of his passion which burned out irrelevancies from *The Father,* he was not completely in logical control of his material. When the Captain bursts out against all women in all relationship to man there is a contradiction:

I believe all you women are my enemies. My mother did not want me to come into the world because my birth would give her pain. She was my enemy. She robbed my embryo of nourishment, so I was born incomplete. My sister was my enemy when she made me knuckle under to her. The first woman I took in my arms was my enemy. She gave me ten years of sickness in return for the love I gave her. When my daughter had to choose between you and me, she became my enemy. And you, you, my wife, have been my mortal enemy, for you have not let go your hold until there is no life left in me.

Here the obession of misogyny of the author has broken through the bounding wall of the unity of the play and destroyed the illusion of its inner reality. We lose faith in the play as thematically an intensification of a truth of life and see it as distortion. In contrast, a play by Chekhov, *The Cherry Orchard* or *The Three Sisters*, produces an illusion of casually inconsequential and irrelevant speeches. People break into speech out of context and break off with the thought suspended, unfinished. Actually Chekhov's plays represent a technique of delicate selectivity. The spoken words come from somewhere and the unfinished thought goes on somewhere. They are an emergence into dialogue from the stream of consciousness of the character, and the successive glimpses create by gradual revelation and suggestion the continuum which is the character's total being. It has been said of a play by Chekhov that a single phrase removed would leave an incompleteness in the movement, like the omission of a measure from a musical composition. A naturalistic play such as *The Weavers* by Hauptmann represents another kind of complex unity. The total power of the play grows out of the slowly gathering momentum of the piling up of details of the misery of the weavers until it finally breaks into revolt and violence, from which the play rolls on in freshly gathering momentum until the movement subsides at the end into the realization for the audience that the inevitable has happened and nothing has been gained to the weavers except the emotional release. If the reading of *The Weavers,* or the experience of the play in the theater, were to be interrupted at any point before the crisis at the end of Act IV, when the weavers break into the house of Dreissiger, the manufacturer, and smash up the furnishings, the feeling would be that the play is weighed down with unnecessary and repetitious detail. But when one remains in the slowly gathering wave of revolt through to the end, there comes an experience of unity of effect and power of communication of meaning, the inevitability of revolt when people are pressed down long enough and hard enough with misery. Other plays in basically naturalistic technique such as Gorki's *The Lower Depths* and O'Neill's *The Iceman Cometh* present the same problem of recognition of unity of detail to total effect.

A play may fall short of unity in the quality of the language relative to the meaning of the play. For realism Eugene O'Neill wrote flexible and vigorous speech, but he was possessed by a reaching for poetry and for magnificence which drove him in a large proportion of his plays to conceptions of content and form to which his verbal powers were inadequate. His language was often awkward and meager relative to the demands upon it, as in *Mourning Becomes Electra,* and at his worst he broke into purple patches of straining for effect. With the failure of unity between language and intention in many of O'Neill's plays, other qualities gave something of greatness beyond more perfectly executed plays by dramatists of less boldness of imagination and more constricted vision of the function and potentialities of the theater. The temperament of a playwright subtly rather than overtly revealed may either suffuse a play with a unity of feeling as in Tennessee Williams' *The Glass Menagerie,* or may confuse the unity of effect and meaning as in his *A Streetcar Named Desire.* In the latter play somewhat exaggerated sympathy for broken fragility in Blanche Du Bois seems mingled with a feeling of fascination for the brute virility of Stan Kowalski, her destroyer.

The requirement of unity is quite as rigorous in comedy as in serious drama. In the blend of reality and fantasy of Mary Coyle Chase's *Harvey,* the particular demand upon unity of detail is not that the audience should be induced to believe in Harvey, a six-foot-tall invisible white rabbit which is the pleasant companion of Elwood Dowd,—they do not,—but that they should believe in Elwood's belief in the rabbit. The play requires an unwavering and delicate control of every shade of conduct of Elwood, that it shall always be in accord with the existence to him of Harvey. The reality of Harvey to Elwood and the gradual encroachment of his reality upon the psychiatrist and upon Elwood's sister preserves the rabbit from becoming a symbol, while the precision with which the pleasantness of Elwood—who has committed his life to being pleasant instead of smart—makes gentle conquest of his sister sustains the effect of delightful absurdity. The play has a unity of light comedy which could easily have been marred by an intrusion of the sententious.

The most rewarding area for analysis of the processes of unification to the end of pure comedy is in the early comedies of Shakespeare, the harmony of disparate elements of *A Midsummer*

Night's Dream, the richer and more robust unity of *Twelfth Night* and *As You Like It.* The golden world of *As You Like It* inhabited by the gallantry and wit of Rosalind can even sustain the presence of two villains and several threats to life without ever a doubt as to outcome. Even Shakespeare fell short of unity of effect in *Much Ado About Nothing,* in which the aim seems to be pure comedy. The near-tragic love story of Hero and Claudio is perfectly enclosed within the comedy matching of Beatrice and Benedick by skillful plot organization, but Beatrice and Benedick are perhaps the most realistically created of Shakespeare's romantic characters and Hero and Claudio are lifeless figures of literary convention. Contemporary American comedies frequently fall short of unity, not for lack of organizational skill but by lack of conviction in the function of comedy. Some serious theme, social, psychological, or moral, is drawn in half-heartedly as a kind of apology. On the other hand, our theater has produced a notable line of effective fast-paced farce comedies, such as *Three Men on a Horse, Boy Meets Girl, The Solid Gold Cadillac,* a type of play which depends primarily on mechanical organization for its unity. Such a play starts on a situation somewhat off the norm of social conduct or human behavior and expands and accelerates by a kind of logical syllogistic development into hilarious madness.

A play should have unity in all its elements, and, secondly, they should be well ordered. The ordering of a play is essentially theater craftsmanship, the technique of determining theatrically effective scenes and arranging the material in accordance with the principles of audience attention and response. Response in the theater is different from and more demanding than in reading a novel and the reader of a play can evaluate the ordering of the play only by having summoned to the full his capacity for theatrical imagination. The unity of *The Weavers,* as has been discussed, is enforced by the continuity of experience in the theater, but in the ordering of the material there are two weak points for theatrical effectiveness. Hauptmann was following the naturalistic principle of founding the causation, the inevitability, of the revolt fully in the environmental circumstances of the weavers. The first scene of the weavers bringing in their home-woven webs for sale to the manufacturer presents the situation of their des-

perate state under continued reduction of the price they receive
because of the competition from new power looms. The second
act in the home of one of the weavers presents directly their
miserable starving state. The third act in a tavern through the
talk of people of other classes presents a view of the social structure with the weavers at the bottom—"The weavers are like a
bone that every dog takes a gnaw at." In the fourth act in the
home of the manufacturer the conversation of his guests, a pastor,
a lawyer, and a teacher, makes clear there is no help for the
weavers from any of the institutions represented. Each of these
acts is well-ordered in rising to a climactic propulsion of revolt
at the end, and the fifth act is engaged throughout with the revolt in full swing and is climactic in relation to the preceding
acts. But the third act sags. Acts I and II are concrete with the
weavers in their misery directly before the audience. The third
act is within the unity of the naturalistic philosophy of the play,
but is abstract talk about the weavers until the weavers on the
march enter at the end of the act, and has less theatrical force
than the preceding acts. The principle of holding audience attention and continuously intensifying response by climactic progression from beginning to end of a play is violated. The fourth act is
also abstract to a degree but is sustained in tension by awareness
of the approach of the revolting weavers, the threat to the in-
mates of the house, and expectation of the violence which erupts
at the end of the act. There is again a weak interval when the
fifth act opens on the weavers of another town whom the audience
has not until then seen or heard of, a break in the closeness of
continuity demanded by the pace and time limitation of the theater. With the entrance of the previously known weavers the audience response is caught up again and carried forward to the end.

Right ordering of material as a structural principle extends
throughout the play from the main outline and the building of the
play, scene by scene, into all the minutiae of arrangement of details for climax, significant juxtaposition for contrast or reinforcement, hidden interweaving of plot lines to the illuminating flash
of contact, psychological truth to the movement of mind of a character, the tight and inevitable sequence of causation of each development growing out of what precedes.

The unity of a play and its ordering are inseparable. Determining all the details is the over-all pattern or design which is the playwright's technical solution to communication of the meaning of the play. In Tennessee Williams' *The Glass Menagerie* "the scene is memory," as he states in a stage direction; the perspective of memory is gained by the design of introduction of the scenes by a narrator, the son, in whose memory they live, as well as by the omission of some details and exaggeration of others, according to their emotional value as touched by memory. In Williams' play the concept of memory is that of distance; in Arthur Miller's *Death of a Salesman,* which also involves memory as subject matter, the concept is immediacy, "that everything exists together and at the same time within us," as he wrote in the Introduction to his *Collected Plays.* Miller found his solution of design in the image of "two undulating lines . . . one above the other, the past webbed to the present moving on together" in Willy Loman, the interweaving of memory scenes and present action, all as in the present. In contrast to both plays, "the straightforwardness" of the form of Miller's earlier play *All My Sons* he explains as "in some part due to the relatively sharp definition of the social aspects of the problem it dealt with." A well-ordered play has an architectural design functional to the unifying idea, or spirit, of the play. The baroque efflorescence of decoration on the structural outline of Fry's *The Lady's Not for Burning* is as purposive as the spare Doric weight of design in Miller's *The Crucible.*

An effective play is not only theatrically organized but posseses theatricality of substance, that is, it communicates by visual and auditory images. The bare tree which changes into a skeleton in Kaiser's *From Morn to Midnight,* the growing castle crowned by a bud at the beginning of Strindberg's *The Dream Play* and opening into a gigantic chrysanthemum flower at the end, are brilliantly conceived visual symbols of the kind in which expressionist drama abounded. They belong to stagecraft and the good playwright thinks readily in terms of whatever kind of stage effects the theater for which he writes can supply. However, not only is the actor the most continuous focus of visual attention in any play, but the actor is the most universal element to all stages, and it is in what the playwright does with the actors that

the sense of theater shows most clearly. Simplicity and quietness may have as much power as the strenuously and obviously
theatrical. In Miller's *The Crucible* the hysteria of the girls, in its
dramatic position of deadly import, is a terrific climax to the scene
of the trial for witchcraft, but the moment of confrontation of
Elizabeth and John Proctor in the last act towers above it. They
have both been condemned for witchcraft, although Elizabeth
will not be hanged because of the child she carries. They have
been imprisoned in Salem jail for months without seeing each
other or word between them. On the day John is marked to be
hanged Elizabeth is allowed to see him on the hope of the judges
that she may influence him to save his life by confession. She is
brought in, her clothes dirty, her face pale and gaunt. The heavy
chain is removed from her wrists. She promises nothing, only asks
that she may speak to her husband. "Herrick enters with John
Proctor. His wrists are chained. He is another man, bearded, filthy,
his eyes misty as though webs had overgrown them. He halts inside the doorway, his eye caught by the sight of Elizabeth. The
emotion flowing between them prevents anyone from speaking
for an instant." Two actors, a man, a woman, stand across the
stage from each other. It is a visual image into which and from
which the drama flows, and it remains perhaps the most indelibly
imprinted single moment of the play, visually, in its emotional
impact and its dramatic significance. It is of such things that
theatrically effective drama is made. Indirectly one sees the principle at work in Ophelia's account to her father of how Hamlet
came distraught to her chamber. The scene remains as sharply in
our minds as those actually enacted on the stage because the nar-
ration is all visual images in precise statement of Hamlet's successive looks and movements. Shakespeare was accustomed to
thinking in terms of actors.

Chekhov's *The Cherry Orchard* has one of the most effective
final curtains in modern drama, a summing up of the play in a
blending of visual and auditory images after the last line has
been spoken and all the principal characters have left the stage.
The room is empty, the sounds of departure outside are heard
and fade away. Firs, the old family servant, feeble and ill, enters
and mumbling to himself lies down on the sofa. After a moment
of silence, as he lies without moving, "The distant sound is heard,

as if from the sky, of a breaking string, dying away sadly"—
the sound which has been remarked upon earlier in the play by
the family sitting in the garden, with natural explanation offered,
here becomes a symbol of the dying past. "Silence follows it,
and only the sound is heard, some way away in the orchard, of
the axes falling on the trees," a sound which ushers in a new
way of life. Tennessee Williams demonstrates a more generalized
kind of auditory imagery in his fine sense for use of background
music for mood and thematic reinforcement. In *A Streetcar
Named Desire* the music is given a realistic source, from Negro
entertainers at a barroom around the corner from the Kowalskis'
New Orleans apartment, a "blue piano" which expresses the
spirit of the life which goes on there. In *The Glass Menagerie* the
tune "The Glass Menagerie" which expresses Laura is a delicate
and distant sound introduced as one of the several theatricalist
devices for communicating the nostalgia of memory, which is the
condition upon which the play is constructed.

While some of the most memorable effects in theater come from
auditory images to be executed by stagecraft and constitute an
area for judgment of a play, the most potent, the most universal
auditory theatrical medium is language, language as spoken by
actors. This leads to the quality and command of language of the
playwright as one of the most basic considerations in evaluation
of a play. The value of language as sound in the theater is only
instrumental to its functioning as the principal means of dramatic
expression and communication. However, unless language has theatrical quality it fails as drama, and language for the theater is a
very different instrument from that only to be read. It must be
speakable, words that can be spoken "trippingly on the tongue,"
as Hamlet commanded the players. It must have audible intelligibility, words that can be caught by the ear and their meaning
taken in at the pace of speech. It must have appeal to the ear
as sound, and it must have projection. The theater is larger than
life and of greater intensity. The projection demanded of its language is not only for the physical space of stage and auditorium,
but for the enlargement and penetration of ideas to the mind and
emotions. Finally, language for the theater must be more than
readily speakable, it must be actable; it must give range for the expressive vocal flexibility of the actor. These are the specialized

requirements of dramatic language in addition to the expressiveness of meaning required of all language as literature. George Bernard Shaw found the difference between literary and theatrical effectiveness difficult to analyze but immediately recognizable in practice. He wrote: "I cannot give any rule for securing audible intelligibility. It is not missed through long words or literary mannerisms or artificiality of style, nor secured by simplicity. . . . 'This my hand will rather the multitudinous seas incarnadine' is such a polysyllabic monstrosity as was never spoken anywhere but on the stage; but it is magnificently effective and perfectly intelligible in the theatre." Henry James aspired to the theater and failed there. Shaw continues with reference to Shakespeare's line, "James could have paraphrased it charmingly in words of one syllable and left the audience drearily wondering what on earth Macbeth was saying." *

Actually, all the elements of theatrical effectiveness are combined in Macbeth's speech cited by Shaw. Part of the reason for the audible intelligibility is the easy articulation for speech of the accents, which similarly articulate the words to the ear. The words are arresting in sound and stimulate the ear to alert response, and they have the projection of language that is larger than life. Finally, they are expressive of an agony which is vocally actable. Always one finds oneself returning to Shakespeare for standards of judgment of drama. For development of the sense for the theatrical quality of speech as distinguished from that of literature to be received only through the eye on the printed page, nothing is better than reading Shakespeare aloud. If the voice is given free rein one finds oneself not only speaking easily, but unself-consciously and naturally acting, the voice led into flexibility and range, and one discovers the emotion and meaning in the lines by speaking them.

Our era of realistic prose has misled us into frequent identification of theatrically effective language with plainness and simplicity. But Christopher Fry's language is more intelligible spoken or heard than silently read. On the other hand, there is the extreme of effective simplicity of prose in the language of Samuel Beckett. Read without auditory imagination, the language of *Waiting for*

* "On Printed Plays" (The *Times Literary Supplement,* May 17, 1923), in *Shaw on Theatre,* ed. E. J. West, Hill and Wong, New York, 1958, pp. 165-66.

Godot and more of *Endgame* is flat, even banal; heard in the
continuity of the speeches there is revealed a sensitive poetic ear
and fine craftsmanship of language which does much to lift those
plays out of the merely grotesque and dreary. Tennessee Williams' greatest asset as a dramatist is his facility with language.
The speech given to his characters at once lays bare the hidden
intricacies of nerves and feeling and has the power to hold and
carry on the attention of an audience seemingly indefinitely. The
extreme instances in his later plays of Margaret's monologue in
the opening scene of *Cat on a Hot Tin Roof* and Catherine's extended narrative as a means of revealing the heart of the drama in
Suddenly Last Summer suggest theatrical tour de force and a breaking down of the discipline of soundly dramatic construction. But
this does not invalidate the extraordinary capacity in those speeches
to maintain a rigidly fixed attention in the theater. Another kind of
theatrical power of language is in speeches which depend wholly for
their effect on the dramatic context. When the Reverend John Hale
at the curtain of Act Three of *The Crucible,* starting across to the
door, says "I denounce these proceedings! . . . I denounce these
proceedings, I quit this court!" and slams the door to the outside behind him, his lines represent no intrinsic distinction of writing, but
in conjunction with the character and situation and as an accompaniment to the decisive action they are hammer blows.

The language of a play should not draw attention to itself. All
theatrical qualities are subordinate to, the instruments of, dramatic
integration. The playwright has a story to tell, characters to create
and reveal, ideas to be expressed, emotions to be generated, all
to be welded into a drama. His principal medium and source of
power is language.

Whether a play is realistic or nonrealistic it should possess vitality in the characters. Even in so abstract and theatricalist a
play as Ionesco's *The Chairs* the play is dramatic because of the
intense life of the Old Man and the Old Woman. It is their life
which gives the antagonistic animism to the chairs, and embodied
in actors they become a real old man and old woman. The Cashier in Kaiser's *From Morn to Midnight* has no individuality but he
is electric with life by the energy of his quest and the staccato
rhythm and hard images of his speeches, which to the mind's eye
in reading give a corresponding spasmodic drive to his movements.

Some minor characters, or even all but the protagonist, in an expressionist play may be puppets, but if the play is effective the protagonist is a force. In Toller's *Man and the Masses* not only the protagonist, The Woman, but all the characters outside the abstract groups engage emotional response from the audience; even the miserable old women in the prison cell at the end of the play who scramble for The Woman's possessions when she is taken out to be shot and then at the sound of the volley quietly replace them, are sharp focuses of human animation. In many abstract plays, as in Wilder's *The Skin of Our Teeth,* or even for the opening scene of *From Morn to Midnight,* the effectiveness of the play depends upon a foundation in the characters of external observational reality. Similarly in fantasy and plays of the supernatural the illusion of reality of characters comes from an adaptation of elements of actuality to the laws of the world of the play consistently developed.

In realistic drama characterization is the main substance of the play. Accuracy of external details to the character's social background, status, and individuality; and psychological consistency, and a sense of truth to human nature are the means to the illusion demanded that each character could exist in real life. The audience may or may not be acquainted with the kind of people or situation presented. It is, in fact, hazardous to try to judge too closely on such grounds because the background and people known may be similar but never identical. What counts is that the playwright, by sufficient and sharply delineated concrete details that fit together as a consistent whole within the play, induces the conviction that he knows the background and characters. One may never have been aboard a U.S. Navy cargo ship, but the AK601 with its officers and crew in Thomas Heggen's and Joshua Logan's *Mr. Roberts* are real within the play. From experience of the play one has the sense of knowing one such ship and its occupants, whatever others may be like. That is the end of realistic characterization: creation of a new individual, as life creates, within the laws of humanity one who is different from all others, one who has never existed before.

Most American readers not only do not know the Norwegian background of Ibsen's *Hedda Gabler* but never knew closely a woman like Hedda, yet even through the medium of considerably less than satisfactory translation, they respond to Hedda as one of the most alive characters in modern drama. That so many dramatic characters are strongly alive in translation points to how much of the playwright's communicating power of language rests in the creation of content for the speeches, and also to how much of dramatic characterization is in action, what the characters do.

To speak of dramatic characters as possessing vitality means more than that they are recognizable as corresponding to life. It means that they are alive with intensity, not necessarily by being drawn from a type in life possessed of vivid or strong personality, but with an intensity created by the playwright. It may derive from the zest the author feels for his characters, as in the very simple people of Saroyan's *My Hearts in the Highlands;* it may gradually emerge from the subtlety, precision, and completeness of delineation as in Chekhov's *The Cherry Orchard;* at the highest level, it is the enlargement of life by the author for revelation of essential and universal truth, from whatever level in life, that which becomes a Willy Loman, a Cyrano de Bergerac, or an Othello. Poetic drama, with its unrealistic conventions, is often psychologically realistic and heightens characterization by the poetry. Satire, based directly on life in society, animates type characters by exaggeration. Whatever the basis, source, or method, vitality of characters furnishes the most common bond between play and audience.

There are many good plays in our realistically minded theater today, of which the principal merit is warmly created recognizable ordinary characters, and it goes far to engage an audience. It is a more common capacity than distinction of organization or of language, or of mind. William Inge's plays stand high within this order; one feels his identification with his characters and the audience is drawn into identification. Plays move from the level of good plays toward greatness when there is more than warmly identified penetration into what the characters feel, there is depth of penetration into their total being and origins, movements, and significance of what they feel and do; when the characters are not merely alive and recognizable by their accurate ordinariness, but possessed of some extraordinary and revealing vitality; and when the characters are not the end of the play, but fill their part in a total drama which throws some light upon life out of a comprehension distinctive to the mind of the playwright. Possessed of extraordinary vitality as each of the characters is in *Long Day's Journey Into Night,* one remembers them less individually than in inseparable interrelation which reveals the mind of O'Neill and enlarges our comprehension of life.

Distinction of mind in the playwright is essential for appreciable merit in a play. High distinction is rare, and should be valued accordingly. Run-of-the-mill plays of theater entertainment often show technical skill, facility with language, and superficial truth of characterization; but the plays we return to are those in which there is life seen through a temperament, life interpreted or experienced in the light of a distinctive mind. The play has a quality that is different from that of a play by any other author. Through it we experience life differently than we have before. Even the gentle touch of freshness of point of view that pervaded Truman Capote's fantasy about people escaping from the world by living in a tree house, *The Grass Harp,* in 1952, was enough to arouse a minority of reviewers to strenuous acclaim of a generally not well-regarded play. It is a vigorous individuality, although restricted and of doubtful quality, that has arrested attention to John Osborne's plays. Distinction of mind can go a long way in atonement for other deficiencies; its presence can also sometimes be less obvious than other merits. There is a fine distinction of mind in Lillian Hellman's plays, especially in *Watch on the Rhine*—a hard rationality and moral clarity, that is sometimes not fully recognized because of the very apparent workmanlike craftsmanship in conventional form and her exact rather than electrifying use of language of direct communication. Distinction of mind is not the patent originality of creation of startlingly new forms, unless a fresh form is inescapable to expression of the mind of the author, as with the plays of Samuel Beckett. Nor is it originality in plot inventiveness; no story or situation is so old or worn that it cannot be seen and treated in a new light. Shakespeare borrowed plots and characters, in the Elizabethan fashion, and transformed them; he took up theater vogues and transformed them, the revenge tragedy to *Hamlet,* the romantic tragi-comedy of Beaumont and Fletcher to *A Winter's Tale* and *The Tempest.* Shakespeare overshadows his contemporaries, but he worked in a theater of dramatic minds of magnitude and distinction: Marlowe, Webster, Jonson, the greatest among others, each uniquely himself, each play immediately distinguishable as his own. In our theater of recent years, from at home and abroad, Sartre, Giraudoux, Eliot, Fry, Brecht, O'Neill, Miller, Williams, Beckett, and Ionesco come readily to mind as possessing this distinction, a strongly personal outlook on life. We may be attracted or repelled, and in final analysis give high or low value to what each contributes to our experience; but without the strong individuality interest is not engaged, we are little aroused, and evaluation becomes a mild matter indeed.

In drama as in all art, energy of imagination is a primary measure of value. Ibsen is quoted as saying that it was a long time before he fully understood that "to make poetry is to see, but—mark this—to see with energy," and thus be able to compel the readers and spectators to see it all, as the poet had seen it.* The distinction of mind which looks upon the same thing that others look upon and sees more or differently, penetrates below a surface, isolates and defines one aspect, brings to bear upon it associations remote but pertinent, is the initial exercise of a trenchant imagination. When the energy becomes creative, gives form to the perception, it then can compel readers and spectators also to see. Van Gogh saw rhythms everywhere in landscape. He struggled with technique until he made the spectator see, not the rhythms abstracted, but the landscape itself filled with rhythm, vibrant with life instead of static. Eugene O'Neill saw life in terms of division and stress, between man's actuality and his delusions of himself, between his positive and destructive impulses, between his spiritual yearnings and the answers life offered. Because he found no resolutions adequate to the magnitude and universality of his sense of division and had too much integrity to settle for easy or half resolutions, his plays seldom come to rest. When his imaginative strength for creation of form was lowest, his plays are strained and turbid, when high they communicate stress as his awareness of life. The farthest degree of resolution and integration of form and content is in *Long Day's Journey Into Night* which comes to rest in a static ending of clarity of recognition of absence of hope for the Tyrone family's future through the mother, and for the larger theme, to an equipoise of love and hate existent

* Francis Bull, *Ibsen, the Man and the Dramatist* (The Taylorian Lecture, 1954), Oxford, at the Clarendon Press, 1954, p. 13.

together. In the personal turbulence in O'Neill's plays there is far more than ordinary imaginative energy. Shakespeare's power to see and transcend, what Keats called in a letter his enormous possession of "negative capability . . . when a man is capable of being in uncertainties, mysteries, doubts, without any irritable reaching after fact and reason," represents a much greater energy of imagination. Sophocles with Shakespeare possessed supremely the power of at once living within and above the storm which makes the force expended in the greatest art unobtrusive.

Energy of imagination is a quantitative measure. It begins with what the playwright sees, how much of the magnitude and infinite scope of life, the universe, his mind encompasses. It determines the intensity of his awareness and depth of his perception, and it enters into every phase of his technical creation from structural solution to power of language. There is energy of imagination in Tennessee Williams' first speech for Margaret in *Cat on a Hot Tin Roof,* as she opens and kicks shut drawers of the dresser: "Well, I!—just remarked that!—one of th' no-neck monsters messed up m' lovely dress so I got t'—cha-a-ange." It is not only that Margaret's designation of her husband's brother's children is striking verbiage, but that the speech immediately launches the characterization. By imaginative energy the individual voice of John Proctor in the closing lines to Act III of *The Crucible*—". . . we are only what we always were, but naked now. Aye, naked! And the wind, God's icy wind, will blow!"—is swept up into the total symphonic voice of the drama.

Imagination is the fusing principle of art which brings separated elements together into creation of a new reality. Not only did Shakespeare's imagination give first existence in *A Midsummer Night's Dream* to a fairy world of delicacy and grace quite beyond the homespun imagination of the folk sources on which he drew, but the fusing imagination is also notably present in the harmonization of such disparate elements as the young lovers, the fairy world, the earthy company of mechanics, and the court of Theseus into a total unity of effect. In all its aspects and details the play is perhaps as flawless as mortal creation can be. Yet with all its perfection it is not a great play because in its material and function Shakespeare's imagination is operating within the limits of a romantic fantasy farce comedy, a type of play which corresponded for the Elizabethan theater somewhat to the musical comedy (old style, not the new) in the modern American theater. No great complexities of human character and depths of experience, no profound conflicts, struggles, and reconciliations, are within its scope. The energy of imagination required to fuse into the single dramatic character of Hamlet and the revealing structure of a play all the idealism and disillusion, the doubts, hesitations, self-torments, and reintegration of humanity's moral sensitivity and intellectual acuteness, was infinitely greater. *Hamlet* has probably engaged intense identification of more people individually through succeeding generations than any other play, and has become practically a symbol for great drama.

A play may be a good play, a fine play, by perfection, but a great play only by magnitude and intensity. Intensity alone is not enough for the measure of greatness. The consciousness of the playwright may be confined to a limited area or drawn to a sharp point of perception with such efficacy of projection that the consciousness of the audience is drawn for the time into the completely unified identification which is the object, the nature, the function of art, its intensity. Samuel Beckett's *Waiting for Godot* in the "bleak, abysmal anguish" which Saroyan ascribed to it, is such a play. The question then arises, how much of life has been encompassed in the perception, how much of the potential consciousness of the audience has been shut out. A great play not only intensifies awareness but expands, stretches the mind and emotional capacity. Because man is in part a rational being, the great plays have a balance of reason with imagination and in the scope of their vision engage the rational powers. Even a good play requires rational discipline combined with imagination for achievement of effectiveness of form. A play to be great does not have to be flawless. Distinction of mind, energy of imagination, intensity, and magnitude can accumulate a power not to be disrupted by minor flaws of execution. *King Oedipus* and *Antigone* in their close symmetry give the impression of flawlessness, *Hamlet* and *King Lear* do not; but who is concerned with minute perfection in experiencing any of these plays? Sound evaluation starts with a capacity for positive response and in analysis rests on a sense of proportion. There are also kinds as well as degrees of greatness, massive power and refined power; Saladin's scimitar

which cut silk in mid-air and Richard Coeur de Lion's two-edged
sword which severed an iron bar were both great weapons. Each
play should be measured for its distinguishing qualities and function.

The common end to which all the elements of every play as a
work of art of whatever level or kind are fused by the energy of
imagination under rational control is power—power to penetrate, to
move, to expand, to unify. The object of a work of art is to communicate the truth which the artist sees and as he experiences it,
not life but the interaction of the consciousness of the artist with
life. This is all that he can do in integrity, and integrity is one of
the first demands, perhaps the first, which we make upon the artist. The way to integrity is hard, especially in drama, the most
public at least of the literary arts and most subject to extraneous
pressures. Absolute integrity is integrity to the limitations of the
artist's consciousness of life as well as to the utmost reach of his
capacities. It is the sense of assurance from his drama of this kind
of integrity that has commanded such enormous respect for the
plays of Eugene O'Neill within their limitations, and is one of the
sources of their power. The object of a drama is not only to communicate, but to communicate in the way of art, which is by revelation, by embodiment in a unified whole, not by logical analysis
from mind to mind. A work of art arouses the fusing energy of
imagination of the reader or spectator to a unified identification
of consciousness with the artist's truth. Fusion in nuclear physics
has been found to release more energy than fission, and the bomb
is cleaner of by-products. A drama is measured by its transmission
of power from the imagination of the dramatist to the imagination
of the audience.

Power, however, within the limits of integrity and successful
communication, is not the end of estimation of a play. There remains evaluation of the awareness of life which is communicated.
The freedom of the artist to the integrity of his vision of life has
so often been oppressed by narrow, transient, and irrelevant considerations of morality that a fear, in all sincerity, seems to have
arisen in many critics today of passing judgment on the content
of drama. It is quite right that nothing should impinge upon the
dramatist's freedom of creation—it is a freedom of conscience as
well as of art. But equally there should be no constraint on the

freedom of the critic to perform his final responsibility, to evaluate what the dramatist creates as well as how successfully he creates it.

From one point of view, once the play, or any work of art, is created it belongs to life as a whole, something is there in life which was not there before, and it is subject to all the social and moral considerations by which we try to formulate values and determine what is good for people. On the other hand, from an ultimate moral point of view all art that is truly art, that is, created with integrity, is permitted and of value. For moral formulation we do not shut our eyes to any aspect of life but confront it, and every artist's perception is a part of the whole and an extension of the experience of life. But all this is not dramatic criticism. Another area which is not dramatic criticism is that of uncultivated and unanalyzed response. Anyone has the right certainly to his likes and dislikes, his merely personal impressions. His enjoyment of plays will be extended if through examination into principles and experience of their application he develops an habitually immediate response which can be supported by analysis. Furthermore, a great deal has gone into the creation of a play, even a mediocre one, which merits more than casual like or dislike; it deserves estimation of its worth on grounds of dramatic criticism.

By reference to the principles of evaluation that have been set forth, what may be called constructiveness of content is properly a measure of a play. Constructiveness of content does not refer to what is presented but how it is presented, to whatever ideas, attitudes, emotions, and total revelation energize, give poise to, and unite mankind as against those which debilitate, disrupt, isolate, divide, and destroy. Through the history of drama one finds as fundamental among such ideas and attitudes courage in the quest for and facing of truth; faith that life and the universe have meaning, or that meaning can be created; that there is dignity and worth in man at his best, whatever his worst, and common to man in his potentiality; that the individual man in his proper nature is an entity and possessed of will and responsibility, however limited and conditioned; that love is as common to man as hate; and that ideas and ideals are as truly a force and reality as matter and mechanics. A play of constructive content in this large sense is something more strenuous than what is sometimes called a wholesome play, like *Saturday Evening Post* covers, admirable as such art is in its modest way. There is no merit to dramatic art in being either in harmony with or at odds with conventional morality and popular appeal. There is an obligation against conformity or popularity as a motivating end. It is integrity that counts, which makes the relation to the ultimate morality of constructiveness or destructiveness to the human spirit the most difficult area in which to maintain universally valid principles of dramatic art, rather than application of private morality, temperament, or mood. It is, however, possible. In terms of the attributes by which a play approaches greatness, more energy of imagination is represented in a tragedy that confronts man's fate and transcends it than in a play that does not get beyond anguish and despair. There is more magnitude and energy in defiance, with or without hope, than in a whine or a whimper, just as before the absurdities of humankind there is more energy in the sharp laughter of corrective ridicule or even the lusty guffaw of low comedy than in a snigger of contempt. *King Lear* is the greatest of tragedies, as many people find it, not because its scope and intensity of suffering and evil are beyond any other drama, although scope and intensity are measures of greatness, but because of the energy of imagination by which the suffering and evil are transcended. The greater the obstacles to the human spirit that are surmounted by the human spirit in a drama the more power is released.

Nihilistic drama in which meaning in life is denied is actually a giving up of the search for meaning and is minor drama in regard to energy of imagination. Sustained search for meaning, though without attainment, represents more energy than nihilism, and may represent either more or less energy than drama in which life is viewed and interpreted in the light of a meaning. O'Neill's search has more power and distinction of mind than drama of easy acceptance of commonplace meanings, but less than the great dramas of faith, the dignity of the individual will in moral choice in Sophocles, harmony and love as more ultimate than hatred and strife in the nature of the universe in Shakespeare, perhaps the faith in rationality and sense of proportion in Molière. Drama of faith or acceptance of meaning in life is justly to be measured in terms of distinction of mind and energy of imagination, how fully life has been freshly and individually confronted, and of magnitude, how much of life is encompassed.

Drama of compassion has become one of the most frequent phrases of approbation in dramatic criticism of recent years, often as though compassion were the very end of drama, the most appropriate emotion with which to look upon one's fellow men, and a mark of virtue. The compassion of a Savior as the prelude or accompaniment to his office for the plight of man is an emotion of grandeur. Compassion as the scope of revelation in drama is often a small and easy emotion, giving the audience a warm and passive glow of virtue, identifying them with the subjects on the stage in self-pity, or gratifying them with a sense of superiority. Compassion can be patronizing or enervating, and if no more is seen in the subjects than occasion for pity, it is degrading and becomes a palliative to the merely sordid. Sahtin's speech in the conclusion of Gorki's *The Lower Depths,* a play of tramps and down-and-outers, "Man must be respected—not degraded with pity—but respected!" expresses the energy of imagination which molded the entire drama. Arthur Miller does not have Willy Loman's wife say to her sons that their father is a human being and suffering, and they must pity him, but "attention must be paid." Depth of pity is released toward Willy Loman in the course of the play, but in the end the emotion is drawn up into respect. There is greater energy of imagination, intensity, and magnitude of emotion, however, in *The Crucible* when John Proctor in Salem jail stands before his wife, the peak of terrible pity toward which the play has moved, in which pity is lost, transformed into awe before the power to endure.

Drama which denies rationality to man is internally inconsistent and lacking in unity of content with form, since an effective play itself represents a rational discipline and control of imagination. Formulation of the premise for the content of the play that man is an irrational animal is itself an act of reason, although the conclusion may be derived from incomplete data, or represent a fallacy of logic. Dadaism and some of the extremes of expressionist and surrealist theory have at least had the logical consistency of denying the element of rationality to the creation of drama and replacing it with pure subjectivity even to the idea of automation. Pursued to its logical conclusion such theory would arrive at a drama of subliminal suggestion with the scene designer executing the ideas, images, rather, from the playwright's unconscious or—why not—becoming the playwright. Drama which, without overtly denying, merely disregards the rational element in humanity is lacking in scope.

There is enough of negativism in the temper of our time that drama of negation gains a certain critical acceptance, professional and non-professional, less from conviction than from timidity. There have been times when optimism was intellectually respectable and popularly conventional and the embarrassment was to be caught out by the phenonoma or event proving better than the prediction. Today there is considerable tendency to prepare in self-defense against being thought unsophisticated or naive by keeping to the side of foresight of the worst; to guard against being thought lacking in tough-mindedness and courage to face the truth by limiting insight to the unpalatable. In so far as attitudes, optimistic or pessimistic, are adrift with the temper of a time, in society as a whole or in cliques of intelligentsia, as dramatic material they are lacking in distinction.

Drama, response to it, and criticism are all inescapably to a degree subjective, taking their rise from individual limitations and capacities of perception. Five men are sitting on a porch watching the continuous and endless stream of automobiles going by on a highway. One says, "Look at all the poor fools, going, just going, and not going anywhere," although on another day when he was in a car moving on that highway he had a quite definite objective in mind. He goes off to write a play. Another says, "What miserable lives all those people lead, dirt, gasoline fumes, heat, nervous tension for hours every day to get to their homes and back to work, too exhausted when they reach home to enjoy the little time they have there." He writes a play. A third says, "You look at those cars from here like this and it's just a mass of people going by, but imagine yourself in any one of those cars; you would find yourself sitting next to someone in whose life, if you knew all about it, there is a drama," and he writes a play. A fourth says, "There is a microcosm of human life flowing before us, sordid, joyous, tragic, grand. There is a fate in his present journey for each of those people: one is on his way to his death, another to great happiness; one is at this moment contemplating a crime, another is living heroically, though quietly and unsung." He also will write a play. The fifth does some figuring on increase of population and traffic, wear on the paving, and taxes. He does not write a play, but he may be very necessary and useful to those who do.

The plays will be seen and read, enjoyed more or less, estimated more or less highly, and on the part of most readers or spectators the final judgment will be granted on the quality of the vision of life of the playwright. Great critics from Aristotle on have so judged, and all that has been cherished as representing greatness in dramatic and non-dramatic literature, the Greek tragedies, *The Divine Comedy,* Shakespeare's plays, *Don Quixote,* has been so measured for its contribution to the dignity of man in energy of imagination, magnitude, and scope of vision. The end of reading plays is pleasure, a cultivated pleasure of a high order of exercise of mind and emotional capacities, an intensification and expansion of awareness and understanding of life. Our natural response is to content as the end, technique as the instrument. As Samuel Johnson sensibly remarked in defense of certain passages in *Paradise Lost* against theoretical criticism: "Perhaps no passages are more frequently or more attentively read . . . and, since the end of poetry is pleasure, that cannot be unpoetical with which all are pleased."

The best playwrights have themselves set the highest and most comprehensive standards. Chekhov is quoted by a friend as having once said "that a literary production should be gifted, wise, and noble; but with us, alas, it was either gifted and noble, but not wise; or wise and noble, but not gifted; or wise and gifted, but not noble!" * Greatness with perfection is rare in dramatic art, as in all things human. Some touch of greatness with much of excellence is not infrequent, and the critical reader, not unaware of limitations and flaws, will find his enjoyment first in the discernment of merits.

* Vladimir Nemirovitch-Danchenko, *My Life in the Russian Theatre,* trans. John Cournos, Geoffrey Bles, London, 1937, p. 201.

12

Analysis of a Play :
Our Lan', by Theodore Ward

To make more concrete all that has preceded I am presenting the full text of a play with accompanying analysis. The considerations on which the play, *Our Lan'* by Theodore Ward, has been selected are that it is a truly fine play that has been produced and reviewed with high praise, but with a comparatively short run and not hitherto published it offers experience of a new play for most readers.

My first acquaintance with Mr. Ward and *Our Lan'* was at the Theatre Guild in 1945, when on the basis of a draft of the play he was awarded a Theatre Guild scholarship and membership in the playwriting seminar which it was one of my functions to organize and conduct. Mr. Ward rewrote *Our Lan'* in the seminar. In the spring of 1946 at the close of the seminar seven of the ten members organized as Associated Playwrights and arranged for the use of the 400-seat Henry Street Playhouse, of which Edward Mitchell was director, as a theatrical laboratory for production of their plays. In the following season Edmund Hennefeld's *Deputy of Paris,* Nicholas Biel's *Winners and Losers,* and *Our Lan'* were staged for a week's run each with Edward Mitchell directing, and for *Our Lan'* the music arranged and directed by Joshua Lee. Off-Broadway production in the spring of 1947 had not become the occasion for general review attention that it is today, but *Our*

256

Lan' attracted such attention and in such terms that the next week Broadway producers were competing for the play. Brooks Atkinson wrote in the *Times* that *Our Lan'* at the Henry Street Playhouse was one of the best plays of the total New York season. Eddie Dowling opened *Our Lan'* on Broadway at the Royale Theatre the following September. The play ran for five weeks, forty-one performances. There was again high praise from reviewers. There was also some confusion of play and production in comparative references which were more favorable to the play in its original simple mounting than in the more elaborate production, on which George Jean Nathan in his *Theatre Book of the Year* for 1947-48 made the summary statement that a play may "be a better theatrical show in one production than in another, but if the play itself is not still the same play I have lost what critical sanity I once suspected I had." That *Our Lan'* as a Broadway production had a respectable rather than a hit run is simply one of the not infrequent examples of the fact that length of run and the quality of a play do not always correspond, and that opportunity to experience a play is an occasion for individual judgment. It is a pleasure to make *Our Lan'* available for reading.

Brooks Atkinson in *The Times** characterized the play as "a natural and easy narrative . . . What *Our Lan'* has to say might be conveyed with a slicker style. . . . But it could hardly have more warmth of humanity; the simplicity could hardly be more genuine, nor the mass scenes have more strength of character." In an extended article subsequent to the two productions, Isador Schneider made an especially distinguishing analysis:

> Critics have long pondered the phenomenon that well drawn and convincing evil, negative and destructive characters abound in literature but convincing "good" or "positive" characters are rare. We get one in Joshua Tain, the blacksmith who leads the farmers in *Our Lan'*. We have an extraordinary impression of his goodness and strength, an impression that is deepened by the revelation of his moments of weakness. For example, Tain's shock over a disappointment, and his outburst of jealous

* April 19, 1947.

rage make understandable the magnificent act of moral courage and generosity that follows it.

This is true of Ward's feelings for people in general. All his
positive characters have their moments of faltering and backbit-
ing; but we never lose sight of their nobility and strength as
well. And even the negative characters like the landlord and
the cotton buyer and the Yank captain are shown as not evil
in themselves, but evil in their functions. Very few writers have
this natural loving understanding of human beings.*

Joe Pihodna in the *Herald Tribune*† commented on "the
warmth, dramatic power and feeling." Louis Kronenberger, writing for *PM,* with reservations on the form of the drama, responded favorably to the author's "humane yet objective approach
to the story.‡ Reviewers generally remarked on the use of the folk
songs as a natural and integral part of the play to significant effect—
"honestly to hearten and forward dramatic action," "to discharge
emotional tension."

George Jean Nathan summarized his judgment of *Our Lan'*
as follows:

> Ward, a Negro, and his play about Negroes are, however, in a
> class apart. Commingling power with pity, pride with humility,
> and hope with despair, the story, reinforced with song, tells
> simply and affectingly of the Negroes who were given land in
> Georgia by General Sherman after his Civil War operations in
> that territory, of the subsequent decision of the Federal govern-
> ment to take it from them, of their struggle to hang onto it and
> of their final compulsory relinquishment of it, along with their
> trustful but defeated efforts to cultivate it to their economic in-
> dependence. The natural tragic force of the theme is immeas-
> urably greater and much more impressive than the artificial
> soapbox force of all the recent Negro Propaganda plays rolled
> into one.§

* *New Masses,* Oct. 14, 1947.
† The *Herald Tribune,* April 21, 1947.
‡ *PM,* April 21, 1947.
§ *The Theatre Book of the Year, 1947-1948, A Record and an Interpretation,*
Alfred A. Knopf, New York, 1948, p. 48.

To my mind, at the same time that *Our Lan'* gives dignity and stature to the Negro people, the play crosses all barriers of race and culture and gives dignity to humanity.

Mr. Ward was born in Thibodeaux, Louisiana, his father a schoolmaster who sold books, religious, practical, and classical, and patent medicines from his horse and gig to those for whom doctors' offices and libraries were not available. Mr. Ward's first adventures in reading were the sample first chapters from which his father took book orders. He commenced his writing with short stories and poetry. While a student in the Extension Division of the University of Utah, his instructor, Dr. Louis C. Zucker, advised him to apply for the Zona Gale Scholarship, which enabled him to attend the University of Wisconsin for two years, where he turned to drama. Before *Our Lan'* he wrote six plays, two of which were produced, *Sick and Tiahd,* a one-act play written while he was an instructor in dramatics at the Lincoln Center in Chicago, followed by *Big White Fog,* his first full-length play, produced by the Chicago Federal Theatre. *Big White Fog* has had a number of productions since. In 1938 Mr. Ward wrote an article, "The Future of the Negro Theatre," for *New Theatre Magazine* and has continued to write frequently on the subject in a variety of publications. In 1940 he was active in organizing the promising but short-lived Negro Playwrights Company in Harlem, and some years later undertook to establish a similar organization in Chicago.

Following *Our Lan'* Mr. Ward was named "Negro of the Year for 1947" by the Committee of Selection of the Schromberg Collection of the New York Public Library, for his contribution to the American theater. He received two grants from the National Theatre Conference which enabled him to write his play *Shout Hallelujah,* and in 1949 a John Simon Guggenheim Fellowship on which he wrote his play *John Brown,* which was produced for a six weeks' scheduled period by People's Drama and then sold to organized theater groups. His plays, *Throwback* and *Whole Hog or Nothing,* were presented in 1952 at the Chicago Eleventh Street Theatre under the auspices of the Cultural Committee of Arts and the Committee for the Negro in the Arts. Mr. Ward has written in all twenty-odd plays, including eight of full length, and the libretti of two Negro operas, for one of which, *A Grand and Beautiful Thing,* Irving Schlein, former assistant to the late Kurt Weill, has composed a score. Mr. Ward now lives with his wife and two young daughters in one of Brooklyn's spacious-roomed and high-ceilinged old apartments of the late nineties with windows overlooking ivy-hung St. Bartholomew Episcopal Church. He is at present engaged at work on a Negro folk opera.

In approaching, now, the text and accompanying analysis of *Our Lan'* the play should be read through first without regard to the analysis for experience of the play. Some of the best known plays in the literature of American drama, such as *The Green Pastures* and *Porgy,* now more widely known in the musical form *Porgy and Bess,* are in Negro folk speech. Like the Irish dialects of the plays of Synge and O'Casey, Negro folk speech is more than local color; it contributes an inherent expressiveness and beauty to drama. For all such plays part of the spelling is necessarily phonetic, depending on the ear of the author, and is usually not maintained with full consistency, both because the speech itself varies, and for greater ease in reading. It is suggested that enough of *Our Lan'* be read aloud for the quality and effect of the speech to become established to the ear.

TEXT AND ANALYSIS
of
OUR LAN'
by Theodore Ward

OUR LAN' printed by permission of
Theodore Ward

© 1941, Theodore Ward

Our Lan'

An historical Negro drama in two acts
by Theodore Ward

SETS:

I.   A Cave on the Road to Savannah
II. A Forge on the Island

Acknowledgments are gratefully made to Manuel Gottlieb, from whose "The Land Question in Georgia During Reconstruction" many of the important notes were taken; to Elizabeth Lawson, Wm. Burkhardt DuBois, and James Allen, whose works were among the major sources consulted.

The Author
September 16, 1941

CAST OF CHARACTERS

NEGRO:
Joshuah Tain
Georgana, his daughter
Charlie Setlow
Ellen, his daughter
Gabe Peltier
Tom Taggert
Sarah, his wife
Joe Ross
Patsy, his wife
Edgar Price ⎫
Emanuel Price ⎪
Chester ⎬ Young Freedmen
Lem ⎭
Ant Dosia, his mother
Delphine
Roxanna, her young siste₁
Ollie Webster, a young pre-Civil War Mulatto Freedman

Oliver Webster, his father
Daddy Sykes
James, 13
Beulah, 13
Martha, 12
Ruth, 12
Alice, 6
Fred Douglass, 7

WHITE:

Libeth Arbarbanel, a schoolteacher
Captain Bryant
Captain Stewart } Officers of the Freedmen's Bureau
John Burkhardt, a planter
Hank Saunders, his overseer
Rebel Soldier I
Rebel Soldier II
A Cotton Broker
A Sergeant

White Soldiers of the Union Army
Freedmen

ACT I

Scene I

SCENE: A CAVE on the road to Savannah

TIME: Evening, January 1865

[1] (*In silhouette against a fire burning in the Center, are three ragged Negroes—*EDGAR, *and* EMANUEL, *in their early twenties, and* PELTIER, *aged about thirty-six. They are waiting for a couple of sweet potatoes to bake in the ashes. Down-Right, a ledge affords the only entrance and exit*)

EDGAR (*Humming in a low voice as he watches the flickering fire*): "Oh, de blind man stood in de way 'n cried: Oh, Lawd, save me—— (*As he ends the slow, plaintive refrain, he rises and goes down to stand at the ledge, looking out, wistful, bewildered, questioning, as he renews the refrain*) "Oh, de blind man stood in de way 'n cried: Oh, Lawd, save me——" (*Glancing around, he sees* PELTIER *testing one of the potatoes*) How dem yams comin', Peltier? [2]

PELTIER (*Pushing potato back into ashes with stick*):   Dey still hard.

EDGAR: Damn! Dey been in dem ashes long nuff t' be soft ez butter.

PELTIER (*Rising*):   Ah think Ah git some more breish.

EMANUEL: Thas er good idea—We'll need it fore de night's gone. (*He straightens out blanket*)

EDGAR (*As* PELTIER *goes out—seeing* EMANUEL *endangering blanket*):   Look out, Emanuel, fore yuh burn mah blanket!

EMANUEL: The Yanks show up, yuh wish Ah hader burnt it!

EDGAR (*Grunting, as he turns back to ledge*):   Phumph!

EMANUEL: Anybody steal from de very folks what sot 'em free need thar neck broke!

EDGAR: Yank or no Yank, Ah ain't fixin t' freeze mah behind!

EMANUEL: Yuh sing er diffunt story ef Gen'l Sherman ketch yuh.

EDGAR (*Ignoring him and singing*):   "Oh, de blind man stood in de way 'n cried: Oh, Lawd, save me!—" (*Scanning the sky, and suddenly amused*) This Januwery wind risin higher 'n higher—Yes, Sah! (*Ejaculating and going on slyly*) Heh! Wouldn't sprise me if it cut somebody's behind t' er frazzle fore mawnin.

Our Lan'

ANALYSIS

Act I, Scene I

¹ The opening of the play with the figures seen only in silhouette against the light of the fire in the dim cave and the plaintive spiritual low in a single voice is arresting visually and auditorily, has a strong and unified mood, and raises question immediately of who the men are and why they are in the strange situation. Every element of the scene contributes to the mood, the dimness of the cave, the theme of the spiritual, a blind man, and the men unknown, their faces not clearly seen. The cave with a glimpse of sky in strong moonlight outside through the entrance is a visualization of the state of the people who gather there through the scene. They are wandering, lost, as in the dimness of a cave and like the blind man who stood in the way and cried for salvation, until they are led out into light and hope at the end of the scene.

² With the beginning of dialogue and its progression through the scene homely reality is established in the strangeness of the cave. Exposition for the audience of antecedent material, the time in the Civil War, and the immediate dramatic situation, the characters as freed slaves with the background of slavery in their minds, the tribulations and disappointments they have gone through in their freed state, and the glimmering hope of land, all come out naturally and with the pungency of folk speech in the dialogue without any forcing or obviousness of exposition. The background of the people comes alive in the imagery and allusions of their habitual speech—"a nimble-footed mule keep de skin on his back," "de whole shoat or nuffin," "de Yanks aint all candy-sweets 'n gravy," "more company for de Big House," "finger ain't big ez er goose-quill, skinny's honeysuckle stems."

EMANUEL: Don't yuh worry bout me, Edgar Price.

EDGAR (*Joining him*):   Who said anything bout yuh, Emanuel, Boy?

EMANUEL (*Pursuing his own thoughts*):   If it wasn't fer de Yanks, whar'd yuh be?—Still in de Quarters, duckin 'n dodgin ole Marster!

EDGAR: Heh! Thas all yuh know bout it.

EMANUEL: Yeah—! Yuh de one Cuffee old Marster ain't never had t' lose er wink of sleep ovah.

EDGAR (*Wisely*):   A nimble-footed mule keep de skin on his back—But yuh ain't sharp nuff t' kotch de scent of that!

EMANUEL (*Listening*):   Hush! . . . Ah hear somebody.

EDGAR: Must be Peltier.

EMANUEL (*Rising*):   This quick?—It can't be . . . (*He goes to ledge and looking out sees newcomers*) It's a couple of ole folks. Comin up heah—Lawd, Ah wonder if dey got er bite or two?

EDGAR (*Joining him with alacrity*):   Lawd, Buddyboy, heish your mouf!

EMANUEL (*To newcomers*):   Hydy, Folks!

VOICE: Hydy!

EMANUEL: It's kind-er steep, ain't it?

MAN (*Appearing, puffing—a small black man of sixty-five*):   Ah reckon this heah's de tallest hill—(*Entering*) in de whole State of Gawgie!

EDGAR (*Attempting to assist his companion*):   Gimme your hand, Anty, 'n Ah'll pull yuh up.

WOMAN (*In a huff, as she ignores his offer*):   Now hold on, Sonny! (*Brushing by him, she turns and admonishes him sharply*) If yuh want t' git long wid me, don't call me "anty!" (*A huge black woman, she limps to fire*)

MAN (*Meanwhile—Placatingly*):   Now, Patsy; de boy didn't mean no harm.

PATSY (*Emphatically*):   It's time these youngsters learn we's free—(*Parentally, turning to* EDGAR) Ah's titled t' a handle on mah name, Sonny—Ahm Miz Patsy Ross, 'n thas mah husband, Mister Joseph Ross.

ROSS: Jes call me "Uncle."

EDGAR (*Smiling*):   Us glad t' meet yuh, Miz Patsy—Set your

carpet sack down 'n catch your breath.—Ahm Edgar Price 'n this no-mannered rapscallion heah's Emanuel.

[3] PATSY (*Her good nature rising*):   Yuh all brothers, hunh?

EDGAR: No'm. Us ain't no kin. Us jes goes by de name of ole Marster—(*Emphatically*) But us goin change that.

ROSS: This heah's er mighty nice cave yuh all got.

PATSY: De Lawd will provide, hunh, Son?—But lemme set down fore this leg slays me! It's worse'n er prickly pear—(*Sitting*) Too much trampin for mah weight Ah speck.

EMANUEL: Whar yuh all come from, Uncle?

ROSS: Ah reckon us kivvered evvy road in de State of Gawgie, Sonny. But us used t' blong t' Jeb Winters, down in Ware County— few miles jes this side of Waycross, case yuh know whar dar.

PELTIER (*Re-entering with armful of brushwood*):   How de yams?

EDGAR (*Stooping to fire quickly*):   Damn! Ah bet dey burnt t' er cinder! (*He sighs with relief as he rakes potatoes from fire*) Dey all right.

PELTIER: Den les have em.

EDGAR: Drop your wood 'n meet Miz Patsy 'n her husband, Mr. Ross—(*To latter*) This ouah new partner whut jes joined up wid us de udderday—He named Gabe Peltier.

PELTIER: Hydy!

ROSS: Us glad t' meet yuh.

EMANUEL (*To* PATSY):   Yuh all et supper?

ROSS (*Interposing*):   Supper? Sonny, us still waitin fer breakfust.

PATSY (*Admonishing*):   Now, Mister Ross!

[4] EMANUEL (*To his* BUDDIES):   Yuh speck us could let em have tha lil one?

EDGAR: Cose. (*Picking up potato, he finds it too hot to handle*) Doggone!

EMANUEL (*Pushing potato with stick*):   Here yuh is, Miz Patsy —Us ain't got but two or us'd give yuh all more.

PATSY: Gawd bless yuh, Son—It's er shame for us t' take it.

EDGAR: Go long, Mam. Us glad t' split wid yuh. (*Dividing other potato*) Here, Peltier.

PELTIER (*Forlornly, to* ROSS):   Don't look much like Freedom, do it?

[3] As new arrivals to the cave enter the audience becomes acquainted with the characters individually by the natural exchanges of courtesy and curiosity about each other.

[4] The sharing of two potatoes, all the food three people have, with two more, which comes so readily to Emanuel's thought and is agreed to as a matter of course by Edgar, introduces a simple kindliness and concern for one another that belongs to the people of the play generally and has grown out of common experience of hardship and sorrow.

ROSS: Sure don't—But tell me sompen, yuh all—Yuh heayd anything bout Gen'l Sherman givin all de Freedmens rations?

PELTIER: Whar yuh heah dat?

ROSS: Us met er man this mawnin say das what dey tell him.

EDGAR: Ah bet mah freedom gainst er lead nickel; anybody git rations from de Yanks goin sweat for em.

PATSY (*Shocked*):   What—?

EMANUEL (*Explanatorily*):   Edgar de kind got t' have de whole shoat or nuffin.

EDGAR: Pay yuh best t' bank tha fire.

EMANUEL: Oh, sure—Cuz yuh done run outer chips.

EDGAR: Heh! But Ah reckon yuh never will learn no sense, Emanuel, boy. Yuh can't see de Yanks ain't all candy-sweets 'n gravy!

ROSS: Ah think Ah git what yuh mean, Sonny. We can't git nowhar wukin for board. Here tiz de year of Ouah Lawd 1865. Us been free two whole years. But Ah got mah first time t' make er dollar.

PELTIER: Dem Yanks don't mean us nogood, nowhar—Ah wuz t' Missippi—

EMANUEL: Missippi—Yuh been t' Missippi?

PELTIER (*Nodding*):   Hit's wuss thar!

EDGAR: How yuh mean?

VOICE (*Below—Calling*):   Hallo!

[5] EDGAR (*Crossing to ledge*):   More company for de Big House —(*Calling down*) Hallo!

VOICE: Mind if we come up?

EDGAR: Naw, Sah! Us got plenty good room!

ROSS: Evvywhar yuh turn somebody trampin!

PATSY: Ah speck de Lawd must-er got us mixed up wid de Israelites. Looks like we got evvything goes wid de wilderness but de pillar of cloud by day 'n fiah by night.

[6] SETLOW (*Entering—He is a wiry mulatto, quite gnarled and 40. Behind him are his children,* ELLEN, *a good-looking mulatto of 20, and* JAMES, *a lad of 13*):   How yuh all come on?

ROSS: Jes poorly—How's yoursef?

SETLOW: Ahm still lookin up—But lemme make yuh all's

[5] The successive arrivals of newcomers to the cave enlivens the scene and builds up cumulatively the broad background of "Everywhar yuh turn somebody trampin!" which is brought to a focus in the particular group and episode of the play.

[6] The arrival of Setlow with his children Ellen and James completes the company of the first scene, who will join with those following Joshuah at the end of the scene to make up the total company of settlers on the island for the rest of the play. When the full company appears on the island in the next scene, eight are already acquaintances to the audience from the cave, which gives a substantial feeling of continuity, and twelve including five children are new, which enlarges the total group sufficiently to fulfill the impression at the end of this scene of the momentum of a considerable force outside into which the people in the cave are drawn.

quaintance. Mah name Charlie Setlow, 'n thas Ellen, mah oldest, 'n James.

ROSS: Us right glad t' meet yuh.

EDGAR (*Smiling*):   Set your carpet sack down, Miss Ellen, 'n draw up t' de fiah.

ELLEN: Us ain't cold, thanky.

JAMES: Pappy, mah belly feel like er empty croakersack.

SETLOW: Ellen, Ah speck yuh better stir up dem turnips—(*To others*) They's frost bitten 'n Ah's mighty skeered they won't do.

ELLEN: Ah don't think they'll hurt nobody—(*Getting out turnips*) Only us ain't get er pinch of salt!

EDGAR: Us had some salt—Emanuel, whut yuh do with tha salt?

EMANUEL: Yuh de las one had it.

[7] EDGAR (*Discovering salt*):   Oh, heah yuh is, Miss Ellen. (*Joining her, he's arrested by her delicate hands, or pretends to be*) Bless mah soul! (*Teasingly*) Whar yuh git dem lil ole hands?—In de Big House, Ah bet!

ELLEN (*Pleased*):   Now hold your buzzin, Mister Bumblebee.

EDGAR: Fingers ain't big ez er goose-quill; skinny's honeysuckle stems—Blessed me!

JAMES: Pappy, Ellen ain't cookin; she's sparkin!

ELLEN (*Reaching for him*):   Ahma crucify yuh! (JAMES *scurries beyond reach*—EDGAR, *laughing, sits near her*) Gimme de water jug, Pappy. (SETLOW *hands jug, and she begins preparation of turnips*)

ROSS: Brer Setlow, which way yuh all bound?

SETLOW (*Hesitatingly*):   Well . . . Ahm tryin t' make it t' Sawanny.

ROSS (*Interested*):   Yuh got some prospects dar?

[8] SETLOW: Well, t' tell yuh de truth, Ah heard Gen'l Sherman fixin t' give way de lan.

ROSS (*Excited*):   'N yuh do say!

SETLOW: That's what dey tell me.

[9] PELTIER (*Sharply*):   It's talk, Man. Nuthin but talk.

SETLOW: How yuh know?

PELTIER: Year fore las, dey said Gen'l Grant was gwine do de same—'N me, de big fool!—Ah tramped clean cross Alabama 'n

[7] The exchanges between Edgar and Ellen prepare for their having just got married in the next scene, as appears when Edgar is about to leave as a soldier. In Scene Three Ellen tells Delphine how she met Edgar one night and had him at the altar the next morning.

[8] Setlow's information that he is on the way to Savannah because he has heard General Sherman is going to give away land and Ross's quick excitement prepares for Joshuah's company and the climactic excitement of response at the end of the scene.

[9] Peltier is established here as a pessimistic man—by sore experience—and throughout the play a positive reaction from him always has an especial force to it.

The immediate deflation of the hope introduced by Setlow prepares for the dramatic effect of reversal when the same hope is reintroduced by Joshuah and his company so forcefully as to be accepted,

Missippi t' Vicksburg—But Ah wish yuh coulder seed whut Ah found!

EDGAR: What, Peltier?

PELTIER: Dem Yanks wuz herdin everybody like cattle in de camp—Ole folks, women 'n chillun—some sick, some half-naked, with sores from head t' foot . . . Some dyin by de cart loads.

PATSY: Do, Jesus!

PELTIER: But wait. Yuh ain't heard de wuss yit. (*Bitterly*) All dem—like me 'n yuh—able t' wuk. Phey! Dey turn dem ovah t' de planters!

ROSS: Oh, go long!

PELTIER (*Quietly*):   "Leasin," dey called hit—Jes er-nother name for slavery!

SETLOW (*After a moment*):   Well, Ah kin see tain't no use gwine t' Sawanny.

(*Silence.*)

PATSY (*Quietly*):   Sometimes Ah wonder if dese white folks got good sense.

ROSS: Me, too. Dey set er man free wid no job 'n no lan, 'n tell him t' go farge for hissef—But how's he gwine farge?

EDGAR: Dey figger us like de birds, Ah guess.

JAMES: Thas what Mammy said, Christmas.

SETLOW: Whut Ah tell yuh bout buttin in ole folks' conversation?

¹⁰ PATSY (*Laughing*):   Chillun de same evvy generation—(*Soberly*) But whar yuh leave your wife, Brer Setlow?

SETLOW (*Quietly*):   Ah had bad luck bout her, Mam.

PATSY: Oh, yuh don't say.

SETLOW: All this trablin round 'n fust one thin 'n er-nother— Us bury her side de road New Year's Day.

PATSY: Lawdy, jes two weeks ago!

(ELLEN *hides her brimming tears.*)

SETLOW (*Taking out Bible*):   Yes'm.

PATSY: Blessed Jesus!

EMANUEL (*Seeing Bible*):   Is yuh er preacher, Mr. Setlow?

SETLOW (*Sadly*):   Ahm jes er man of Gawd, Son—(*Reading by firelight*) "Then Job arose 'n rent his mantle 'n shaved his head 'n fell down upon de ground 'n worshipped 'n said: Naked came

[10] The discouragement to the hope of land leads into a mood of depression and recalling of past sorrows which subsides into a moment of silence into which comes James's announcement that he hears singing, the beginning of the rising movement to the end of the scene.

Setlow's quiet faith, his familiarity with the Bible, and his recourse to it for comfort introduced here is the distinguishing contribution of his character to be woven throughout the play.

Ah out of mah mother's womb, 'n naked shall Ah return thither; de Lawd gave 'n de Lawd hath taken away; Blessed be de name of de Lawd."

PATSY (*After a moment*):   Well, yuh kin be thankful yuh still got your chillun. Me'n Mister Ross los ouahs fore de war.

ROSS: Yes, Suh. Saw em sold t' one stinkin trader aftuh ernother till de last wuz gone—God knows whar.

SETLOW: They sold two of mine.

(*Silence.*)

ELLEN (*Drying her eyes, she sees* JAMES *going to ledge*):   Come back here, James.

[11] JAMES: Ah heah singing.

EMANUEL (*Joining him*):   Ah b'lieve so, too!

(*They listen.*)   (*Wind.*)

ROSS: Heah anything?

EMANUEL: Naw, Suh. (*Turning back*) Ah guess we's been hearin things.

JAMES: But Ah heard singing.

PATSY: Ah speck it's de wind, rollin cross dese barren hills.

ROSS: Barren is de name for em. (*Preoccupiedly*) Maybe if us jes had somebody us could send t' see Father Abraham, us could show him what er fix us is in. Then us could axe him, if he ain't plannin t' gin us de lan, if he wouldn't sell it t' us, 'n let us pay in er year or two.

(*They appear to dwell on the wisdom of his words, and all is silence.*)

[12] JAMES (*Springing up and rushing to ledge*):   There tiz ergain!

EDGAR: Ah believe yuh right. (*He also goes to ledge*)

PATSY (*Catching sound*):   Somebody singing all right.

JAMES (*Looking out, excitedly*):   There they come!

EDGAR (*Looking*):   It's er whole drove of folks comin round de upper bend.

ROSS (*Scrambling up*):   'N yuh do say!

SETLOW (*Listening*):   Them's ouah folks, too!

(*Sound of singing.*)

ROSS (*Looking out*):   Did yuh ever see such er passel in de moonlight!

SETLOW: Lawdy, it's same's de year of Jubilee!

[11] With James's statement that he hears singing the climax of the scene is introduced lightly, withdrawn, responded to hesitantly, and then moves with swiftly gathering acceleration. The silence while they all listen creates a strong audience engagement—they listen with the people in the cave for any sound of singing.

[12] Joshua's company out of view makes a theatrically effective situation with the excitement of the raised voices of those who go outside to the ledge calling in what they see, and the group in the cave breaking into quick movement as one after another rushes to the opening of the cave. The audience is strongly engaged and hold to the lines by knowing no more than is called in from the ledge.

ELLEN (*Eagerly*):   Pappy, yuh spose they mighter heayd bout de lan?

SETLOW: Praise Gawd, Ellen—They jes might!

13 VOICES (*Led by a powerful baritone, growing rapidly louder*):
"Ah looked ovuh Jordan 'n what did Ah see:
Comin fer t' carry me home—
A band of angels comin atter me:
Comin fer t' carry me home . . ."

ELLEN: Lawdy, thar's somebody thar sure kin sing!

PATSY: Yes, Lawd. They could use him in de Heabenly Choir.

ROSS: He got er baritone won't behave!

EMANUEL (*Excitedly*):   Ahma go down dar 'n meet em.

(*Exit* EMANUEL.)

SETLOW (*Shouting after him*):   See if yuh kin find out if they gwine t' Sawanny!

VOICES (*Singing nearby*):
"Ahm trampin
Trampin
Trampin
Trying t' make Heaben mah home—Hallelujah!"

ELLEN (*Carried away*):   Pappy, us oughter take in behime em!

VOICES (*Singing rollickingly—as the horde of passersby ostensibly move on*):
"Now if yuh git to Heabem
Before Ah do
Tell all mah friends
Ahm comin too!   (*Fading.*)
Trampin
Trampin
Tryin t' make Heabem mah home!"

14 EMANUEL (*Below, shouting*):   Edgar, come on yuh all. They givin way lan!

SETLOW: Great Gawd A'mighty; hit's true!

PELTIER: Can't be!

EDGAR (*Simultaneously*):   Whar, Emanuel?

ELLEN (*Interposing*):   Lawd, Pappy; les go!

SETLOW: Hush, Gal!

[13] Joshuah is introduced to the audience in this scene only by the strong, rich, confident voice which creates a fine anticipation for his first appearance in the next scene. The marching rhythm and joyful exuberance of the song in full-throated chorus with the power of the leading voice, approaching, swelling, receding, creates an effective visualization for the audience and an upsurge of emotional response. The contrast between the spirit of "Ah looked ovuh Jordan" and that of "Oh, de blind man stood in de way 'n cried" is the distance the scene has come.

[14] Emanuel's vibrant shout from outside, "They givin way lan!" comes like the age-old "Land ho!" from the masthead, with all of man's sense of roots in the earth. The scene breaks into wild excitement and confusion of activity, the impetus made more irresistible by the added word, "They say yuh got t' be there in de mawnin' if yuh want t' git yore share!"

MANUEL (*Simultaneously*):   In Sawanny—Gen'l Sherman given everybody lan!

SETLOW: Lawd er mercy—Come on, Chillun! (*He is struggling to gather his belongings*)

PELTIER: Yuh going?

SETLOW: Ah ain't gwine stay!

EMANUEL (*Appearing, excitedly*):   Come on, yuh all. They say yuh got t' be there in de mawnin, if yuh want t' git yore share!

SETLOW: Ellen, will yuh hep me git these things!

EDGAR (*Grabbing up blanket*):   Damn if Ah ain't gwine be thar!

ROSS (*Seeing* PATSY *getting her bundle*):   What yuh fixin t' do, woman?

PATSY: Go—What yuh think?

15 ROSS (*Amazed*):   But yore leg!

PATSY (*Shouting*):   Don't stand thar talkin, Mister Ross! Git on out-er heah down th road!

JAMES (*Anxiously, as* SETLOW *starts out*):   What bout de grub, Pappy?

PATSY (*Pushing* ROSS):   Git on, Mister Ross!

JAMES (*Frantically*):   Pappy, yuh leavin de grub!

SETLOW: Git on—Ah'll git de pot!

EDGAR (*Catching* JAMES, *as others crowd out*):   Come on, Boy. Us gwine t' Sawanny; git ouah Fawty Acres 'n ouah mule! (*Yelling, he disappears*) Whaaaaaaaaaaaaaaaawhooooo!

(*Exit.*)

SETLOW (*Following with pot and bundles*):   De Yanks done blowed de horn! Whoopeeee!

16 PELTIER (*Unable to resist*):   Dey might be right 'n dey might be wrong—But make way for me, Cuffees, Cuz Ahm Comin Long! Yahoo!

(*Exit.*)

17 (*Blackout.*)

[15] The scene ends on the beginning of the note of heroism in these people. Footsore, weary, Patsy with her lame leg, all are going to be tramping through the entire night, joining in the song "Ah looked ovuh Jordan . . . Trampin, Trampin, Trying t' make Heaben mah home—Hallelujah!"

[16] It is both amusing and deeply moving for the end line of the scene when even Peltier goes, characteristically with reservation, "Dey might be right 'n dey might be wrong," but with the biggest shout of all.

[17] This first short scene gets the action immediately under way with the question, Will these people receive land? Although this question is launched with the definiteness and vigor that might well distinguish the attack of a play, it is answered in the next scene and the new question raised, Will they be able to keep the land?—which is the major dramatic question running through to the resolution, and represents in its introduction, I would say, the attack of the play. The first scene, including the question, is entirely introduction, accomplished with notable swiftness, dramatic force, and strong forward projection.

ACT I

Scene II

SCENE: THE FORGE on an island off the coast of Georgia.

TIME: Afternoon, two days later

¹ (*The Lights pick out* DADDY SYKES, *a rusty-black old fellow of 70, who is sitting on the steps of the Cotton House, scratching his crinkled gray head in an attitude of surprise and amazement, as he listens to the sound of* VOICES *singing, some little distance Off-Left.*

In a moment, as the light increases, the whole scene becomes visible and the Spectator notices that an old Storehouse is Down-Left, its porch about a foot above the ground. Beyond it, an old oak with overhanging moss and a circular seat about its roots. A path behind the oak curves off Up-Left. Here a bit of weedy field and open sky. On the other side the Forge juts enclosing the rear and revealing the fire-box set in a niche in the wall, blackened with soot and age. A pathway separates the Forge from the Cotton House on the Right, as the latter protrudes into the scene in a state of near decay. The steps to the latter are further forward, leading up to a narrow porch. A rain barrel, with an angle-iron suspended above it with a rod for striking attached to a cord, are on the upper side of the steps. Remnants of old farm equipment, an overturned anvil, and several tufts of weeds are scattered like dumb witnesses remarking the vanished prosperity of this former slave kingdom in the sea.)

² VOICES (*Singing joyfully*):

"Roll Jordan roll—
Roll Jordan roll—
I want to cross over into campground!"

SYKES (*Puzzled*):   What de debil! (*Seeing a good-looking girl of 16 appear, suddenly, on porch behind him*) Roxanna, whut yuh reckon tiz?

ROXANNA (*Excitedly*):   Ah donno, Daddy Sykes—(*Running down and off Up-Left*) But Ahm sure goin see!

VOICES (*In an outburst of frenzied shouting*):   Whoooooooooo-peeeeeeeeeeee! Here we is, Folks!

(DELPHINE *enters—She is an extremely attractive brown young*

Act I, Scene II

[1] The opening of the scene out-of-doors in the strong sunlight from a spacious sky is an expressive contrast to the preceding scene. An interval between the scenes is necessary for change of set and is desirable for the sense to the audience not only of the passage of time but of the all-night tramping of the company, followed by receiving their "tickets" for the land and the movement to the island. This can be communicated with linkage of one scene to the next for effectiveness of the contrast by continuing the sound of singing through the interval. The singing should not have the smoothness of a set chorus, but should have a touch of natural irregularity, and the rise and fall of progression over a varied terrain. Near the end of the interval the singing should fade down to a few seconds of silence, then be heard again faintly, increasing in volume for a brief interval, then rising strongly as light comes up on the scene and continuing to rise quickly to the entrance of the singers.

The stage setting, which remains as the single set for the remainder of the play, is both pictorially effective and expressive. The front of the Cotton House just projecting into the stage rising on one side and the oak tree with circular bench and the front of the storehouse rising on the other side frame the Forge at the back and to the side nearer the Cotton House. Beyond the Forge the field ends in a low line of trees or bushes in the distance against the high sea-sky rising over a flat island. A large central stage area is left clear as an acting space for the considerable number of people who are on stage together at intervals through the play. The Forge is a massive structure set in a wall of brick or stone with a roof on corner-posts projecting forward, three sides open. The Forge is important: it was the heart of the self-contained farming operation of the period, and it expresses Joshuah, with his strength and his skill beyond the field-hands.

[2] The scene immediately becomes lively and filled with expectation in a succession of swiftly developing stages to the entrance of Joshuah and the full company.

woman of 23, wearing a woolen shawl about her shoulders, and clutching it above her full bosom.)

SYKES (*Seeing her*):   Will yuh listen t' dem fools!

VOICES (*Frenziedly*):   Done crossed ole Jordan at last! Bless Gawd! Bless Gawd!

DELPHINE (*Amazed*):   Goodness gracious me!

VOICE (*In religious frenzy*):   Bless Gawd! Bless Gawd!

ANOTHER (*Calling*):   Beulah! Yuh Beulah! Come back heah!

[3] SYKES: Ole Marster ain't goin like this!

(*A group of children run in wildly only to disappear off Up-Right.*)

DELPHINE (*Attempting to intercept one*):   Little Girl, wait! Wait!

(*The children laugh merrily in the distance.*)

PELTIER (*Entering with* TAGGERT):   Hi, Folks—Kin we git through t' de Quarters dis way?

DELPHINE: Yes, Sah. But who yuh all?

PELTIER: De new owners—

DELPHINE (*Amazed*):   What yuh mean?

TAGGERT (*Going off Right with* PELTIER):   Tell yuh later, Daughter.

(*Exit.*)

VOICES (*Singing merrily, as group approaches*):
"Oh, dem golden slippers!
Oh, dem golden slippers!
Goin' shout all over God's golden streets!"

[4] (*Dancing and prancing, a crowd of men and women enters, filling the area with the rich spectacle of their antics and colorful garments, which for all their bedraggled condition, afford an atmosphere of pageantry.*

ROXANNA, *in complete rapport, dances on the arm of* LEM.)

DELPHINE (*Attempting to catch* ROXANNA):   Roxanna, you come here to me! (ROXANNA *evades her*) All right, Miss! You wait!

ROSS (*Prancing, he waves a ticket above his head, and addresses* DELPHINE):   Shake your foot, Daughter—Us got tickets for the lan! (*Singing in parody*)
"Oh, de golden ticket!
Oh, de golden ticket!" (*Cutting a step he disappears in crowd*)

³ In Daddy Sykes's exclamation, "Ole Marster aint goin like this!" the first note of foreboding and potential conflict is introduced into the joyful scene.

⁴ With the entrance of the joyous crowd of men and women dancing and filling the stage the contrast to the preceding scene is complete.

[5] (OLLIE WEBSTER, *an aristocratic mulatto, immaculate in the apparel of a gentleman of the times, crosses to stand aside on porch of Storehouse.*

EDGAR, EMANUEL, *and* CHESTER *are in crowd wearing Union Army uniforms and carrying rifles.*

[6] JOSHUAH TAIN, *leader of the band, stands protectingly as all swirl about him, his lip puckered slightly in his habitually winning smile. One senses his sincerity and warm-heartedness, which seem to bind him to the others in deep, sympathetic accord. Indeed, he is an expression or symbol, if you will, of the best traits of his people. There is a sure sense of dignity about him and his very physical strength bespeaks something of the relentnessness and courage which characterized the bulk of the vilified black men of the period—a people conditioned by the terrors of ruthless oppression and communicating their spirit from generation to generation; not by precept but by example—now graphic, now more or less obscure; now passive, now insurrectionary, but always passed on; the sons emulating the inarticulate father; the daughter fashioning her life on the pattern offered by her dumb but undaunted mother—in a word, one senses that here is a man!*)

JOSHUAH (*As they swirl to a halt*):   What er ilun! What er ilun!

ROSS: It's de lan of Canaan!

DOSIA (*A raw-boned woman of 50, in grip of religious ecstasy*): True, Jesus—True, Oh Lovely Lamb!

[7] JOSHUAH (*Fervidly*):   Ah no sooner spied her, fore she commence t' seep into mah bones, 'n Ah said t' mysef: Joshuah, look yonder; dar's yo home—At last, yuh 'n yore people got er home!

(DELPHINE *gazes upon him enrapturedly.*)

DOSIA (*Wildly*):   'N it's all on account of yuh, Joshuah!

ROSS: Us got t' gib him er big honor!

PATSY: How bout makin him Gubner?

DOSIA: Das just what!

[8] JOSHUAH (*Lifting his arms*):   Hold on, yuh all. Hold on. (*Indicating forge*) Gimme er fiah yonder, 'n er hammer 'n er pair of tongs, 'n Ah'll make yuh er two-wheel driver. But don't axe me t' be no Gubner!

ROSS: But, Joshuah, us got t' had er gubment—?

JOSHUAH (*Noticing* DELPHINE):   Ah know. But we'll settle dat

⁵ Ollie is not only immaculate in his apparel but ultra-fashionable —long-skirted double-breasted coat with extra wide lapels and extra large buttons, narrow-legged trousers with straps under the insteps, elegantly tapered shoes, extra high stiff collar and a wide cravat fluffed out in front, and a pearl-gray large hat with curled brim and high flat crown flaring at the top.

⁶ Joshuah is a powerful man of middle height with straight flat back and columnar neck on which the head is squarely set, well-molded almost massive features, and ease and freedom as he stands or moves. Standing now in the midst of the band he does not tower above them by height, but is dominant to view because he is straight and still in the surrounding movement.

⁷ Joshuah's first speech, eloquent in simplicity, states the theme of the conflict of the play, to possess a home.

⁸ The gist of the situation—get to work, government and formalities can come later. Joshuah is a leader by being representative of these people, what they are but more completely at a higher level.

later—Set up er Council or sompen—(*Crossing to* DELPHINE)
How do?

DELPHINE (*Bashfully*):   Fine, Suh.

JOSHUAH: Mah name's Joshuah Tain—What might be yores?

DELPHINE: Delphine.

⁹ JOSHUAH (*Smiling*):   Delphine. Thas sure is er pretty name.
But Ah reckon yuh kin wear it!

DELPHINE (*Pleased*):   Ah speck t'wouldn't do t' try to spute yore
word.

JOSHUAH (*Laughing*):   Take a blind judge not t' back me up.

OLLIE (*Joining them*):   I agree with you perfectly, Mr. Tain!

JOSHUAH: This is Mr. Ollie Webster—

OLLIE (*To* DELPHINE):   Had I known you were here, I would've
visited this island sooner.

JOSHUAH (*Laughing*):   Who wouldn't? (*To all*) But Ah didn't
git chance to tell yuh all. His papa was one of de main men what
talked Gen'l Sherman into lettin us have de lan—

ROSS: 'N yuh do say!

¹⁰ JOSHUAH: But not only that. Ah speck through his Papa's
goodness, we goin have er teacher!

PATSY: Lawdy, a teacher!

JOSHUAH: Yes, Mam. This mawnin he sot down 'n writ us er
letter t' de Abolitionists up Norf 'n axed em t' send somebody. Now
ain't that sompen?

OLLIE: Oh, it was nothing, Mr. Tain. We free men are proud to
do all we can to help you climb.

JOSHUAH: 'N yuh kin depend on it; we won't let yuh down!—
But, Delphine, who heah sides yuh?

DELPHINE: Jes mah lil sister, Roxanna, there—'n Daddy Sykes,
here.

JOSHUAH (*Pointedly*):   'N de white folks—?

DELPHINE: They's away—cept'n for de overseer, Mister Hank.
Marse Burkhardt 'n Master Luther, they gone t' war; 'n Miss Burkhardt, she is in Paris. She left me t' take care of de house.

JOSHUAH: Whar this overseer?

DELPHINE: He live in Savannah, 'n only comes over now 'n then
t' keep his eyes on things. But what yuh all mean by callin this
yore home?

⁹ The love story of Joshuah and Delphine, and the intrusion of Ollie, are set in motion at once.

¹⁰ One of the most winning attributes of these people is the meaning to them of a teacher, with legal freedom and the hope in land of economic freedom, the aspiration for freeing of the mind from ignorance.

JOSHUAH: Gen'l Sherman done gin us de whole ilun—

DELPHINE: You don't say!

JOSHUAH: That's bout de Alpha 'n de Omega of it.

11 SYKES: De Alpha 'n de Omega, hunh?—Delphine, yuh better tell these crazy Cuffees sompen.

PATSY (*Sharply*):   What's de matter wid this ole man?

12 DELPHINE: Daddy Sykes, Ah think yuh better hush!

SYKES: But what bout Mister Hank—What he gwine say?

DELPHINE: I donno—and furthermo', I don't care!

ROSS (*Approvingly*):   Thas tellin him, Daughter!

SARAH (*Outside, calling*):   Joshuah!

(*The* GROUP *turns Up-Left.*)

DELPHINE (*To* PATSY—*sotto voce*):   Is you all's leader married?

PATSY: No, chile. Why?

12 DELPHINE (*Stepping off embarrassedly*):   I jes asked.

13 SARAH (*Entering, angrily—bearing a bundle. Behind her is* SETLOW *rolling a barrel of flour*):   Joshuah! Do you know them Yanks ain't gin us er speck of meat?

CROWD: What? No!

JOSHUAH: Dar wuzn't no meat t' be had, Sarah.

SARAH: Den, Joshuah, how us goin live?

JOSHUAH: We gwine draw on de Commissary of de Al'Mighty!

DOSIA: Joshuah, what kind of blasphemin talk is this?

JOSHUAH (*Indicating sea—Off-Left*):   Ant Dosia, yuh see tha ocean yonder?

DOSIA: Cose Ah see it.

JOSHUAH: Well, what yuh think de Lawd put de fish 'n shrimp 'n ister in tha water for?

SARAH (*Appeased—laughing*):   Lawd, Joshuah, leave it t' yuh!

(*Rumble of voices Off-Right.*)

JOSHUAH: What now? (*Turning up, as* PELTIER *and* TAGGERT *enter, angrily*) Yuh come in like de whirlwind.

PELTIER (*Furiously*):   Ah wish yuh could see them huts!

TAGGERT: They ain't fitten fer er dawg t' sleep in!

JOSHUAH: Is tha so?

PELTIER: They ain't nothin but er nest of spiders 'n lizards 'n thousand-legs—

TAGGERT: Not only tha. You ought t' see de roofs.

¹¹ The warning note from Sykes again.

¹² Delphine's identification with the newcomers in general, and interest in Joshuah in particular are immediate.

¹³ The people have arrived in their promised land and the first complications arise, discontent, first with the lack of meat, then with the condition of the huts, then with no mules. These complications are still preliminary, an important function being to introduce Joshuah in his capacities of leadership, his sympathetic understanding, poise, resourcefulness, firmness with flexibility; another function is to establish the actual hardships, how much these people, with a little strengthening from time to time, are prepared to endure and overcome for self-dependence and homes.

JOSHUAH (*Easily*):   Well, if they ain't right, we'll jes have t' fix em.

PELTIER: Take er month t' fix dem roofs. Meantime, whar we goin live?

TAGGERT: Yeah. 'N de nights still frosty, too!

ROSS: De Big House empty ober dar.

DOSIA: Das right. De white folks gone!

JOSHUAH: Tha don't cut no figure. We can't use it.

TAGGERT: How come we can't?

JOSHUAH: Cuz it don't b'long t' us.

SARAH (*Sharply*):   What yuh care? Mah chillun got t' hab er dry place t' stay.

TAGGERT: 'N she don't mean *maybe!*

JOSHUAH (*Gently*):   Gen'l Sherman gin us de lan, Anthony. He didn't say a mumblin word bout de Big House.

TAGGERT: Damn dat.

JOSHUAH: All right. Ah tell yuh what. We'll let de chillun sleep in de Big House till we fix dem huts. Will dat suit you?

SARAH: It's more like it.

ROSS: Yuh all worried bout de huts—But what bout de mules? Howcome us ain't got no mules?

JOSHUAH (*Pained*):   We ain't got none, Brer Ross, cuz de Army ain't had none t' spare!

[13] PELTIER: Fore Gawd, Joshuah! How in de world we goin raise er crop wid no mules?

[14] JOSHUAH (*Sharply*):   Now listen, everybody. There's sompen we got t' git straight right now. We didn't come heah t' have no barbecue. Just yistiddy we had bout ez much chance ez er house-fly in de winter time. But today yuh kickin. Yuh got lan. Yuh got de chance t' look forward t' yore own bale of cotton; yore own ca'iage 'n span. 'N yet yuh kickin! What yuh think this is?—A lil ole measly patch of ground? This is er whole ilun!

SETLOW: Thus saith de Lawd God of Israel. Ah brought yuh up from Egypt, 'n brought yuh forth out of the house of bondage . . . And Ah delivered yuh out of de hand of de Gyptians 'n out of de hand of all dat oppressed yuh, 'n drobe dem out befo yuh 'n gave yuh their lan!

¹⁴ Joshuah's innate assurance in leadership comes to a climax on the petty complications; he checks the complaints with sternness, then lifts the people up with enthusiasm and homely but imaginative eloquence.

DOSIA: Amen! Amen!

JOSHUAH: Yuh ready wid your "Amens." But how many yuh see we got tha chance t' turn dis ilun into de prettiest 'n most bountiful spot in de ocean?—Jes bloomin wid flowers 'n bumper crops?—Lawd, Ah tell yuh, it's like er barrel of hebenly waters! (*Quickly*) Only dar's er few tadpoles in it got t' be fished out fore we kin drink. Cuz dem tadpoles like (*Pointing Off-Right*) dat frozen ground 'n all dem weeds yuh see stretchin yonder. They's dem broken-down huts yuh don't want to live in. But when a man's in de hot sun 'n famished for water, he don't go thirsty just cause de waterboy bring him er bucket wid er few tadpoles in it, do he?

(*Whistle of scow.*)

SETLOW: Deed he don't!

OLLIE (*Stepping forward*):   Mr. Tain, it just occurs to me; I may be able to help you with respect to the huts.

JOSHUAH: Is that so? How?

OLLIE: I think I can arrange for you to get lumber.

EDGAR: Not so us can build?

OLLIE: Yes.

EDGAR (*Elated*):   Hot ziggedy damn!

[15] OLLIE: My father owns a half interest in a sawmill—just outside of Savannah, which has been closed since the outbreak of the war. I think I can persuade him to let you use the steam-donkey and bandsaw—

JOSHUAH: That'd be a Godsend, Mr. Webster.

ROSS: Yes, Lawd! Wid all tha timber yonder, us could build us er town!

JOSHUAH: You speak t' him, Mr. Webster. Tell him we'll come git it, 'n pay him fer his trouble in de bargain.

ROSS: Yeah, Suh. 'N ef he don't care t' wait—maybe us git him one of dem mortgages yuh heah tell of.

OLLIE (*Going—laughing*):   Well never mind the mortgage. I'm sure he'll be glad to do what he can. But I must get aboard. I'll see you again in a day or two.

(*Exit.*)

JOSHUAH: Thanks er lot for yore pains, 'n tell yore Pa we all say de same!

[15] The forward movement set by Joshuah is continued and supported by Ollie's assurance of the probability of getting a steamdonkey and a bandsaw for making lumber from his father. It should be noted, although Ollie conducts himself badly later on with Delphine, he is established first as a sympathetic, likable, character. He is sincere in his interest and efforts to help.

(*Whistle of steam scow, shrilling above ad libs of farewell.*)

[16] JOSHUAH (*To* EDGAR): Thar's de whistle blowin for yuh, boys!

ELLEN (*Suddenly regretful*):   Oh, no! No!

EDGAR: It's all right, Sugar Tit. It's all right.

ELLEN: But, Edgar—Oh, they'll kill yuh!

EDGAR (*Embracing her*):   Kill me! Shucks, Sugar Tit. De Reb ain't born kin settle mah hash!

ELLEN: You don't know, Honey!

PATSY: Shame on yuh, Ellen. Them boys goin way t' fight for ouah freedom. Yuh ought t' be proud to see em go.

SARAH: Tiz er shame though—'n dey jes got married!

EDGAR: She all right—Yuh all, jes look after her, 'n don't forget t' save mah fawty! (*To* ELLEN—*going*) Come on, Honey. 'N cheer up. Them Rebs ain't goin have no more chance wid me then er hen-house full er chickens wid er weasel!

(*Exit, as* EMANUEL *and* CHESTER *also break away and go out, the crowd ad libbing.*)

ROSS (*Shouting after them*):   Eberytime yuh spy er Reb, don't stop t' spit. Jes let him hab it!

JOSHUAH: Remember, this is yore chance t' gain de glory! (*Turning to others*) But come on, everybody. Let's see what kin be done bout dem cabins. (*Going*) Tell dem bats t' git dar carpet sacks 'n move on over t' de Big House—cuz de new tenants heah 'n they takin over—yes, Suh, 'n ain't got no room t' spare!

(*Exit, others following.*)

DELPHINE (*Arresting* ROXANNA):   Yuh wait!

(LEM *halts also.*)

ROXANNA: But, Delphine. Ah want t' go with them.

DELPHINE: You've seen them huts before—(*To* LEM) Scuse us, young man. There's somepen I want t' say private.

LEM (*Going*):   Sure, sure!

[17] DELPHINE: Now listen, Roxanna. You's started sompen I ain't goin have. That boy ain't been here a minute, but already yuh's let him get out of place with you!

ROXANNA: Lawd, Delphine. I ain't did nothing with tha boy but just dance with him.

DELPHINE: And you don't even know his name—

[16] We are reminded here in this isolated new-paradise of the hard fact of the background of war, and the cheerful courage of these people is revealed.

[17] What Delphine has to say to Roxanna establishes substantialness of character in Delphine in her sense of responsibility for her younger sister, prepares for the irony of her own failure with Ollie after all her care for her sister, and reveals Delphine's ambition and not too clear-sighted view of Ollie which prepares for her degree of responsiveness to him later on.

ROXANNA: I was just trying to be nice.

DELPHINE: That ain't what I'm talking bout. I got no objection
to yuh tryin t' be nice. But yuh don't be nice to people by gettin out
of place with em, or lettin them git outer place with you. The boy
ain't in your class. One look should-er told you he ain't nothing but
er field-hand. And from now on I want you t' remember that—you
understand?

ROXANNA: So I ain't sposed t' even speak t' him, hunh?

DELPHINE: Of course you speak t' him. But yuh let him stay his
distance. I promised Mammy I was goin raise you right. 'N Ah mean
to do it. If you make a mistake, it ain't goin be my fault—I want
you t' be somebody. 'N if you listen t' me yuh will. Someday you'll
run cross a man of quality—one like that Mister Ollie was just
here—

SYKES (*Entering excitedly*):   Now us gwine see sompen sho
nuff!

DELPHINE: What're you talking about?

[18] SYKES (*Pointing Off-Left*):   Yuh see de *Gypsy Belle* easin t'
de wharf yonder, don't yuh?

DELPHINE (*Tensing*):   Mister Hank!—Roxanna, run warn em.
Quick. Catch em 'n tell de leader—

(*Exit* ROXANNA, *running.*)

SYKES: Ah knowed us wuz gwine run into sompen. Ah seed de
sign! Bat bumped square into me last night.

DELPHINE: It did?—What's de meanin of that?

SYKES: Somebody round heah in fer bad luck.

DELPHINE: Is yuh sure?

SYKES: De sign say: tarrible luck!

DELPHINE: Oh, Daddy Sykes, yuh jes tryin t' put bad mouth
on em. Tha sign could mean anything.

SYKES: Hab it yore way. Go right ahead.

DELPHINE: Yuh don't reckon he got his gun?

SYKES: Mister Hank alway carry tha forty-four! (DELPHINE
whirls and rushes off—)Whar yuh goin?

[19] DELPHINE: Ahma warn de leader!

(*Exit.*)

SYKES (*Quickly taking seat*):   Ah ain't gwine hab nuffin t' do
wid it mahsef!

18 Following upon the introductory complications of internal discontents which have been triumphantly resolved, with Daddy Sykes' announcement of the arrival at the island of the overseer, ominous preparation for the attack of the play is introduced.

19 There is a sharp thrust of emotion in the promptness of Delphine's thought and action to warn the leader, the realization of the completeness and warmth with which she has so immediately identified herself with the newcomers as her people, and with Joshuah as leader.

DELPHINE (*Re-entering at once with* JOSHUAH *and others*):   He's mean 'n sneaky as de devil. Yuh got t' watch every move he make.

JOSHUAH: Ah understand. (*To others*) Spread out, yuh all. 'N jes leave everything t' me.

ROSS (*Sotto voce*):   Heah he come.

²⁰ SAUNDERS (*Entering—a wiry, leathern-faced white man of perhaps 40*):   By golly, what's going on heah? (*Coming down*) What de dickens yuh Cuffees doin on this island? What yuh call this?

JOSHUAH: Well, Ah reckon, Suh, yuh might say we's jes gittin settled.

SAUNDERS (*Shocked*):   Well, Suh! So yuh walk on the place and make yourselves t' home, eh? (*Kicks barrel*) What's this?

JOSHUAH: Flour.

SAUNDERS: Yuh sure come t' settle all right. (*To* JOSHUAH) But tell me. Who's land do yuh think this is?

JOSHUAH: Ouahs.

SAUNDERS (*Shocked*):   What?

JOSHUAH: Gen'l Sherman told us t' come heah 'n stake out fawty acres er piece, 'n he give us tickets for it.

SAUNDERS (*Laughing*):   He did, eh?

ROSS: He did dat. (*Exhibiting ticket*) Heah's mine right heah— good fer *fawty* any part of this ilun.

SAUNDERS (*Curious*):   Let's see it. (ROSS *exhibits it beyond his reach*) Hand it here.

ROSS: Yuh kin see it from heah, can't yuh?

SAUNDERS (*Authoritatively*):   Gin it to me!

ROSS (*Evading him*):   What fer?

SAUNDERS (*Laughing*):   What's the mattuh, yuh fraid Ah'll keep it?

ROSS (*Restoring ticket to pocket*):   Gen'l Sherman told me t' take good care of mah ticket!

SAUNDERS: Well, Ah suppose the Gen'l must have his little joke. (*Turning to* JOSHUAH) But don't yuh know yuh must have a deed to own land?

JOSHUAH: We git deeds—Gen'l Sherman say atter de war. He told us t' jes go head 'n raise a crop.

SAUNDERS: And how do you expect to raise a crop without stock?

[20] The entire episode between Saunders, the overseer, and Joshuah with his people constitutes the attack of the play, initiating the basic conflict, and projecting the major dramatic question, will these people be able to keep the land? The episode itself is a well-built dramatic unit, advancing climactically through a series of complications to the culminating point of Saunders' threatening departure, "You jes stay heah—(*Laughing*) Yuh'll learn!" and Dosia's recognition, "That aint no good laugh." The sequence is masterly in the insight of its creation in this brief space of Saunders as an understandable human being, no villain, not brutal, but reacting and speaking at every turn as a man with the point of view of a fixed and settled background to which the situation confronting him is completely at odds. The people of the island are just as fixed and determined in their newly acquired point of view as freedmen. Here is the clash, not just of individuals, but of an old and new order. Joshuah's poise and firmness as a leader is further brought out.

PATSY: Ah kin plow lan same as er mule. With these hands Ah raise cotton dis year—buy two mules!

SAUNDERS: By Golly, yuh Cuffees take de cake! (*Looking around, he scratches his head in a quandary*) Yuh make me feel Ah ought t' trust yuh—'n by golly, thas just what Ahm goin do. Ah was plannin t' drive yuh off de place. But Ahm not goin do it. Ahm goin let yuh go t' work 'n start earnin your own living.

JOSHUAH: We ain't wukin fer no white man!

SETLOW: No, Bless Gawd!

SAUNDERS: Where yuh goin t' find work if not from a white man?

JOSHUAH (*Sharply*):   We goin wuk. We goin wuk all right. We goin wuk right heah on de lan what blongs t' us!

PELTIER: Yeah! 'N Ah'd like t' see any man put me off this lan!

SAUNDERS: Mind yore tongue, nigger!

PELTIER (*Quietly*):   Spose yuh make me!

21 SAUNDERS (*Reaching for gun*):   Why, condfound yore black hide!

JOSHUAH (*Simultaneously with two others crowding him, pinning him in vice between them*):   Now jes er minute, Suh! Pay yuh best not t' start nothin here!

SAUNDERS (*Indecisively*):   Ah see yuh all lookin fer trouble!

JOSHUAH: Naw, Suh. We's peaceful folks.

SAUNDERS: Yuh call it peaceful seizing other people's property?

JOSHUAH: Been any seizin done, Suh, yuh must see de 'spute's tween yuh 'n Gen'l Sherman 'n his Army.

SAUNDERS (*Relaxing*):   This land belongs to John Burkhardt, and there ain't a Yankee living who can turn it over t' you. Why, condfound it, there ain't a white man South of the Mason and Dixon Line who wouldn't rather be dead than live under such topsyturvy conditions. By Gawd, it's the same as makin us slaves and yuh masters. But perhaps that's what yuh want?

JOSHUAH: You couldn't pay me t' be nobody's stinkin master. 'N furthermore, Ah'd advise you t' git on way from heah 'n leave us erlone.

SAUNDERS: Ah see yuh one of these smart alecks. But never mind. (*Going*) You jes stay heah—(*Laughing*) Yuh'll learn!

(*Exit.*)

²¹ With Saunders' reaching for his gun the situation could easily have broken into violence. It is restrained by the quality both of Joshuah and his comrades; it comes to a peak of tight hard tension, and relaxes. The episode ends quietly but ominiously for the future.

DOSIA (*After a moment*):   That ain't no good laugh.

PELTIER: The scoundrel, lucky somebody didn' bust his brains out!

ROSS (*Ominously*):   If yuh ask me, this ain't de last of him.

PATSY: De Lawd delivered Daniel!

JOSHUAH (*After a moment*):   We's in ouah rights. This country don't b'long t' his kind no more. (*Suddenly going, cheerfully*) But come. Let's git de grub divided up 'n see what we kin do bout tryin t' git settled fore de night comes down—(*Raising song*) "Didn't my Lawd deliver Daniel, d'liver . . ."

²² OTHERS (*Singing*)

"Daniel!
Daniel!
Didn't my Lord deliver Daniel,
An' why not every man!"

(*Their voices soaring over the island, they all follow* JOSHUAH *out in courage and hope.*)

(*Blackout.*)

ACT I
Scene III

SCENE: The Same

TIME: April, 1865, or three months later.

[1](*The former atmosphere of complete dilapidation has changed to one of thriving improvement. There are no tufts of weeds, and in the rear several furrows of upturned soil show that the land is being plowed, while the presence of a donkey steam engine indicates that the Freedmen are planning to build new homes as soon as the crop shall have been planted. Outside, nearby, the men are singing a work song, which they humorously compose as they bend their backs to the arduous task of breaking the soil without the assistance of an animal.*

VOICES (*Male Chorus singing*):

"Ole Marster sot in de shade 'n he cried:
Hoe, Boy, hoe!
Ole Marster sot in de shade 'n he cried:
Hoe, Boy, hoe!

²² The tension of the company is released in the stirring song of faith and hope—no standing about engaging in song, but everyone singing as they go about the work of getting settled for the first night on the island, with the scene ending on a forward projection in activity as well as spirit.

Act I, Scene III

¹ At the end of Scene Two the major dramatic question of the play, will the settlers be able to keep their land, is introduced sharply in terms of opposing outside forces, but is made no more definite than a vague threat for the future. The threat is then left in the background through the remainder of the act until the last scene. In Scene Three the question of the settlers keeping the land is in terms of their internal effort, a question of their keeping the land by their capacity successfully to work the land and make homes and a future for themselves against the internal obstacles and hardships. The scene is one of strong forward surge and hope.

A play of the type of *Our Lan'* in a number of scenes with considerable passages of time can easily become episodic and jerky in production. Continuity between the scenes is important and the music in *Our Lan'*, the number of scenes which open or end, or both, in singing, provides the means. The strong, fervent "Didn't my Lord deliver Daniel" should continue into the blackout, fade down

[*Continued on page 307*]

Ole Marster sot in de shade 'n he cried:
Git all dem weeds fore Ah tan yore hide!

"Hoe, Boy, hoe!   (*Emerging in pairs, a team of Freed-*
Hoe, Boy, hoe!   *men, drawing a plow to which*
Hoe, Boy, hoe!   *they've harnessed themselves by*
         means of a rope. They are sweat
         drenched. Entering they cross, de-
"Now Ah know ole Marster *scribing an arc to reverse the plow*
 goin be good 'n sore *before disappearing again, as con-*
Hoe, Boy, hoe!   *tinuing to sing, they strike a new*
Ah know ole Marster goin be *furrow*)
 good 'n sore
Hoe, Boy, Hoe!
Ah know ole Marster goin be good 'n sore
Cuz we wuk for oursefs or don't wuk no more!
Hoe, Boy, hoe!
Hoe, Boy, hoe!
Hoe, Boy, hoe!"

(*As their voices fade,* DELPHINE *saunters in. For a moment she halts to gaze at their retreating figures—her mood one of deep preoccupation.*

[2] ELLEN *appears Up-Left. Halting she sizes up the situation, then exclaims in confirmation of her suspicions*)

ELLEN: Ahanh!haaaaaaaaaaanh! (*Seeing* DELPHINE *turn with a guilty flush*) No wonder yuh can't spend no time at de net!

DELPHINE: Why—what yuh mean?

ELLEN (*Laughing*): Never mind. Yuh ketch on!

DELPHINE (*Lamely*): Why—Ahm on mah way t' de net right this minute.

ELLEN (*Teasingly*): Shame, shame on yuh!

DELPHINE (*Embarrassed, knowing the drift of* ELLEN'S *insinua-ations*): But Ah don't understand—what's Ah got t' be shame bout?

ELLEN (*Laughing*): Ah's had my eye on yuh all winter, Girl. Yuh ain't hangin round dis forge for nothin.

DELPHINE: Lawd, a pusson can't even walk out de house widout being cused of being up to sompen!

and out, and be immediately followed by the sound of the work song of the opening of Scene Three coming in as from some distance away, then rising as light comes up on the empty stage and reaching full-voice with the appearance of the men on the plow. The work song is heavy in rhythm and communicates the panting effort, especially in the aspirant of "hoe!" Its function is to keep the men together on each forward step and pull by the accents of the verse. At the same time there is a rollicking overtone in the spirit of delivery. The stage setting with just the front of the cotton house on one side and the storehouse on the other projecting onto the stage leaves almost the full width of the stage in view beyond the forge for the crossing of the men drawing the plow, which gives time for full realization to the audience of their straining effort. As practical staging, a low cut-out screen representing the line of weeds that would be left at the edge of a field could cross the stage immediately behind the forge. The heavy property of a complete plow would be unnecessary, as the plowshare would not be in view, only the handles held by one man, the other men leaning into the ropes around their shoulders. With a sky-dome, the perspective of the field stretching away to a line of trees and bushes would be painted on a flat with a cut-out top against the sky-dome; without a sky-dome, the field, trees, and sky all on a backdrop.

[2] The opening sequence of the men on the plow singing establishes the group and its progress. Against this background the progress of the personal story of Delphine and Joshuah is introduced in the meeting between Delphine and Ellen. The story of Delphine and Joshuah is a personal love story; at the same time it is integrated with the story of the group not only in the interweaving of plot but in significance. To each of them their love means a home, which is the significance of the entire play for the group.

ELLEN: Yuh needn't try t' throw me off, Girl. Yuh got yore cap set on Joshuah, er mah name ain't Ellen.

DELPHINE: Yuh so smart!

[3] ELLEN (*Disarmingly*):   Now ain't no use rufflin up yore feathers, Delphine—specially not wid me. Ahm wid yuh, Honey!

DELPHINE (*Surprised*):   Yuh wid me?

ELLEN: Cose—but tell me—Ahm jes dyin t' know how yuh makin out?

DELPHINE: But ain't nothin tween me 'n Joshuah.

ELLEN (*Coaxingly*):   Oh, come on, Honey—why be like tha? Yuh kin tell me!

DELPHINE: But ain't nothin t' tell.

ELLEN (*Matter-of-factly*):   Oh, there must be somepn!

DELPHINE: Ahm *tellin* yuh now.

ELLEN (*Seriously*):   Wid all de looks tween yuh 'n him these last three months— (*Convincingly*) Yuh can't tell me that. (*Laughing*) Yuh all sweet on one ernother, 'n Ah know it.

DELPHINE (*Seriously*):   Oh, Ah ain't saying Ah don't like him. But Joshuah can't see me, dear.

ELLEN: Aw, go on, Girl.

DELPHINE: All dem smiles yuh see, don't mean a thing.

ELLEN: Ah don't believe tha— How's he talk?

DELPHINE: He don't. He ain't never said nothin' t' me.

ELLEN (*Amazed*):   No?

DELPHINE: No.

ELLEN (*Puzzled*):   Maybe yuh ain't give him de right chance—?

[4] DELPHINE (*Tittering*):   Ah think he's skeered.

ELLEN: Skeered how?

DELPHINE: Cuz Ahm so young.

ELLEN: What?

DELPHINE: Ah think he think Ah ain't ole enuff.

ELLEN (*Thoughtfully*):   Tha could be—him being ouah leader 'n all that. Still, must be sompen wrong wid you. Maybe you too slow, girl?

DELPHINE: Ah can't put mahsef on him.

ELLEN: Shucks, Girl. Yuh green! Yuh get what yuh want, yuh better copy from Delialah.

DELPHINE: In de Bible—?

⁸ Ellen is a likable girl, warm-hearted, with affection for Delphine on their short acquaintance and, recently married herself, is all for romance. Delphine with more refinement and reticence than Ellen is initially shy and embarrassed, but is won to exchange of confidences with Ellen.

⁴ With her tittering "Ah think he's skeered" Delphine breaks down into the familiar amusement girls often manifest toward a man possibly in love. Delphine's diagnosis of Joshuah's holding back foreshadows what is actually revealed by Joshuah when he finally broaches the subject of marriage to her. Although Delphine strongly suspects Joshuah's interest in her, her uncertainty because he has said nothing is the basis for her responsiveness to Ollie when he appeals to her ambition to rise from the life she has known.

ELLEN: Sure. Yuh know how she got way wid Sampson.

DELPHINE (*Laughing*):   Lawdy! But yuh don't mean tha.

ELLEN: Ah don't—? Yuh know how long it took me t' git mah husband, Edgar?

DELPHINE: No—how long?

ELLEN (*Laughing*):   Ah met him like this evenin, 'n next mawnin Ah had him at de Altar!

DELPHINE: Oh, go long, Ellen!

ELLEN: Yuh don't bleve me, yuh axe Miss Patsy— (*Turning*) Ah got t' go— (*Laughing*) Ah don't b'lieve in walking when there's a rig for hire! Not this chile— (*Seeing* OLLIE *Off-Left*) Umph! Here's Ollie—.[5]

(*Exit—Up-Right.*)

[6] OLLIE (*Entering, he tosses gear on ground beside forge, and sees* DELPHINE):   Well, good morning, Beautiful!

DELPHINE: Hello, Ollie—How're yuh?

OLLIE: Surprised.

DELPHINE: Surprised bout what?

OLLIE (*Coming down*):   Finding you sitting out here all by your pretty self.

[7] DELPHINE (*Flattered*):   Oh, go on, Ollie.

OLLIE (*Joining her*):   Anyone would think you've something against me.

DELPHINE: What you mean—why?

OLLIE: You make it your business to evade me—you little heart-breaker.

DELPHINE (*Uneasily*):   Lawd, Ollie. What's got into yuh?

OLLIE (*Catching her*):   Come here to me, you little peach!

DELPHINE: Ollie, is yuh crazy?

OLLIE: The sweetest little peach in Georgia!

DELPHINE (*Evading his lips as he embraces her*):   Oh, Ollie! Ollie, stop! Don't yuh see de men in de field!

OLLIE: Kiss me!

DELPHINE: No!

OLLIE: Oh, you're going to be kissed!

[8] DELPHINE: No, Ollie! Don't—dooooon— (*He smothers the word with his lips. She struggles feebly, and succumbing, wilts in*

[5] Ellen doesn't think much of Ollie. Probably he has paid no attention to her, but essentially she is a simple and practical girl with no use for such airs as his.

[6] For the episode between Ollie and Delphine, Ollie is introduced in his best aspect. For all his fine clothes and airs he comes in carrying gear for the forge. It is possible to interpret his interest in the island settlers, prospective landowners and voters, as allied to his political ambitions, and the presence of Delphine may further motivate return visits, but he came before he knew of Delphine. There is actually nothing in the play to impugn the essential sincerity of his alliance with the freedmen. His approaches to Delphine at this time, first of flirtation, then of deliberate attempt to induce her to accept a position as his mistress, are in accord with his ideas of fashionable society. He would be proud of her as a beauty and would enjoy teaching her and molding her into a fine lady. It is when he takes advantage of Delphine on the night of the storm that he becomes thoroughly reprehensible, although his looseness of principle here is in marked contrast to the sober, substantial, and honorable character of his father.

[7] Delphine has been impressed by the glamour of Ollie and is flattered by compliment from him so long as it is just that and no more.

[8] Delphine succumbs momentarily in physical response to Ollie but she has character, the self-control to repel him and the self-respect to resent him.

sheer physical response. But in a moment, flushing with shame and anger, she breaks away and slaps him) Oh, yuh——!

OLLIE (*Rubbing his cheek*):   Now was that nice?

DELPHINE (*Glancing anxiously Off-Right*):   Yuh had no right t' put yore hands on me!

OLLIE (*Laughing*):   You little temptress—how could I help it?

DELPHINE (*Sharply*):   Yuh sposed t' be a gentleman, ain't yuh? Did Ah ever git out of mah place wid you? Did Ah ever give yuh de least cause to be so free wid me?

OLLIE: Oh, come now. It wasn't that bad. Why, I felt you let yourself go!

[8] DELPHINE (*Shocked*):   Oh, Ah hate you!

OLLIE: Well, I see I shall have to speak to Daddy Sykes.

DELPHINE: What yuh mean?

OLLIE: You understand very well what I mean.

[9] DELPHINE (*Worried*):   Tha ole man better not fool wid me!

OLLIE (*Amused*):   Oh, no? You make me desperate, and I'll have you *fixed*—I'll get some of Daddy Sykes love powder.

DELPHINE: Tha ole man can't do nothin t' nobody. Daddy Sykes is jes ignant. He full of talk. He jes try t' make folks think he know somepen bout *signs* 'n *Voodoo*.

OLLIE: You believe in him all right—though you needn't fear. I admit I'm crazy about you, and I've wanted to tell you so for some time. But what worries me, what I'm really concerned about, is your future.

DELPHINE: My future?

OLLIE: Yes. You haven't given it a thought, have you?

DELPHINE: Ah ain't had no cause t'—not lately.

OLLIE: No—why not?

DELPHINE: Oh, lots of reasons.

OLLIE: Like what? You're not going to tell me you're perfectly satisfied being lost over here on this God-forsaken island?

DELPHINE: No. But still, for one thing, the place ain't like it used to be. There's folks heah now, 'n we all gittin long so fine, someday Ah spose it's goin be real nice.

OLLIE: I thought you were smart. A beautiful girl like you—has it never occurred to you what you might make of yourself in Savannah—among the up-to-date—among people of class and distinction?

[9] Delphine is confused by the ignorance and superstition from which she has only half-emerged through the favored position she had held in the Burkhardt household. When after her seduction by Ollie in Act Two Delphine is inclined to think he had given her "love powder" she is sincere, although he more probably had not. Ollie's amused threat here, however, of resorting to some of Daddy Sykes's love powder could have contributed by psychological effect on Delphine to the seduction.

DELPHINE (*Laughing*):   Shucks! When Joshuah git through wid this island, Ah reckon yuh city ristocrats goin be wantin t' move ovah heah.

OLLIE: That's rich! Joshuah—Prospero disguised as a clod-hopper. He waves his magic wand, and, presto, he transforms the whole island! But, after all, you're not to be blamed. You've no way of knowing what life is like in Savannah—for people of my standing and culture—free men, who've never known what it is to call another "Master," who for generations have been educated abroad —in the best schools on the continent—as I was. Otherwise, you'd appreciate your chances and make an effort to get above this, this living like a common field-hand!

DELPHINE: Ollie, yuh know very well ain't nothing for a girl like me in Savannah.

OLLIE: You underestimate yourself. Why, with the proper clothes and my support—a beauty like you—why, you'd be the envy of Savannah society.

¹⁰ DELPHINE (*Laughing*):   Ollie, Ah do b'lieve yuh's tryin t' turn mah head.

OLLIE: You belong, Baby. You're not only good looking. You've a head on your shoulders. Why, you could even teach school.

DELPHINE: Now Ah know yuh tryin t' make a fool of me.

OLLIE: You think I'm joking? Why, after the war the Freed-men's Bureau is going to open schools all over the South. They're going to need teachers, thousands of them.

DELPHINE (*Impressed*):   But, Ollie, yuh know Ah can't even read 'n write.

OLLIE: That's no serious handicap. I could teach you as much in a month or two, and if you were willing to listen to me, in two years, I guarantee, you will have prepared yourself to take one of the schools.

DELPHINE: Oh, Ah'd give most anything if Ah thought Ah could rise that high!

OLLIE: You can, I tell you. If you're willing to study—

DELPHINE (*Enthralled*):   Oh, Ah'll study, Ollie. Ah'll study night 'n day—

[10] Delphine is sensible enough that Ollie does not succeed in the least in turning her head until he appeals to one of her deepest desires, to escape from ignorance. That the only idea of glamour with which he can reach her is that of learning to read and write and the hope of rising so high as to become a teacher is one of the substantial strokes in building Delphine's character. She is carried away by the prospect until as Ollie proceeds and she begins to suspect what his idea really is, she comes down to earth with solid sharp questions.

OLLIE: Good. I'll arrange a place for you and your sister to stay—

DELPHINE: You don't mean in Savannah?

OLLIE: Yes. Only it must be understood that this is a matter strictly between us—

DELPHINE: I don't git this.

OLLIE: If I'm to help you, there mustn't be any talk, neither here nor in town. I can't afford to have Papa get the wrong idea. I need his help too badly.

10 DELPHINE: Wrong idea about what? 'N why is somebody goin talk?

OLLIE: Oh, you should understand how people gossip. I've never mentioned this before. But you see—well, when we get the vote, I'm going to the legislature—that is, if Papa backs me. So I have to be careful. He's the big cheese in the State.

DELPHINE: Ah heard yore Papa run er barbershop.

11 OLLIE: He does. (*Hearing men approaching from field, he crosses up to look. Meanwhile—*) That's where he got his influence —(*Turning back, resolved to leave*) But come. Walk down to the landing with me.

DELPHINE: Ain't yuh goin wait 'n see Joshuah?

12 OLLIE (*Escorting her out. Down-Left*):   No. Tell him I left the gear on the anvil—

(*Exit together.*)

13 TAGGERT (*Entering and going to water barrel, but seeing children Off-Right as he crosses path between cotton house and forge*): Lawd, yonder go them chillun on de way t' de woods— (*Cupping his hands, he calls, as the other men file in wearily*) Beulah! Didn't Ah tell yuh not to go in dem woods! Come on back from thar!

SETLOW: Knowin tha boy of mine, t'woud'nt sprize me if he put em up t' it.

TAGGERT: Ahma have t' skin em yet. First thing Ah know one of em'll be pickin up er thorn er gittin snake-bit!

JOSHUAH: When Ah wuz dar aige de skin on de bottom of mah feet wuz thick'n er bullhide. (*He hands dipper of water to* TAGGERT, *who drinks before dropping to stretch out wearily*)

SETLOW (*Meanwhile*):   Us git this crop in thar'll be no more

[11] A nice touch of historical color, of the period when a barber-shop was the equivalent of a men's club.

[12] Interrupted in his campaign to win Delphine by the approach of the men from the field, Ollie hasn't given up. The episode introduces complication into the relation of Delphine and Joshuah, prepares for further complication, and ends suspended with question for the future.

[13] The entrance of the men from plowing has been prepared for by the opening view of them crossing the back of the stage; the audience knows what they have been going through and can appreciate their weariness. The immediate association with the children off-stage gives poignancy and meaning to their effort.

feet on de ground as far as mine's consarned. His barefoot days gone
foreber— (*Shaking his head wistfully*) But he'll never know.

JOSHUAH (*Joining them*):   No. None of this comin generation.
[14] But it won't be long now. With Gen'l Sherman chasin Johnson 'n
Bragg through Calina, 'n Grant hot behind Lee as er fiah in de
pineys, this war 'n all ouah troubles goin be over fore yuh know it—
(*Going to harness*) But what yuh all say, we git this section done
fore de sun gits too hot!

[15] LEM (*Hesitantly—as others bestir themselves*):   Mister Joshuah. . . .

JOSHUAH: What is it, Lem?

LEM: How bout gittin Daddy Sykes t' take mah place fer a day
or so?

PELTIER (*Laughing*):   It'll never happen! Daddy Sykes say he
wuked sixty years for nothin fore freedom, 'n now he bound to use
his wits!

ROSS (*Laughing*):   Tha ole rascal. Tha sounds jes like him.

LEM (*Bitterly*):   The ole man jes livin off us like er tick!

JOSHUAH (*Placatingly*):   Daddy Sykes ole 'n feeble, Lem. He
doin' bout much as anybody kin speck.

LEM: Not t' me he ain't. Ah's sick of it. Ah got t' have er rest.

ROSS: Shucks, Lem. Us jes on de varge of treein de coon!

JOSHUAH: Sure. Three more days 'n we'll be through plowin.
Then cept for de timber for de houses, we kin set back 'n take it
easy.

LEM: But Ah tell yuh, Mister Joshuah, Ah's come t' de end of
mah tether—Mah shoulder's killin me!

PELTIER: So's mine.

SETLOW: Yuh better say all de rest of us!

JOSHUA: Sure. Jes grit yore teeth, Lem, 'n come on.

LEM: But Ah been grittin mah teeth, Ah tell yuh!

JOSHUAH (*Soberly*):   So yuh jes goin walk off 'n leave us in de
lurch, hunh?

LEM (*Desperately*):   Ah can't hep it!

JOSHUAH (*Sharply*):   Any man say *can't* don't blong on this
ilun! But Ah been watchin yuh for de las week. 'N thar's one thing
clear: Yuh ain't got Ant Dosia's blood. Yuh's de youngest in de
gang. Yore muscles hard as er hickry jint. But from sun up t'

[14] The reference to the state of the war and its prospective early close prepares for the announcement at the end of the scene that the war is over.

[15] Every play that moves an audience has successive knots of emotion, points at which threads are suddenly pulled together into a moment that catches an audience unawares with a clutch at the throat, a tingle of the spine, a blurring of the eyes. Achieving the knot of emotion depends upon technique, construction, and a skilful playwright can produce such moments of emotional response as an end in themselves—that is sentimentality. When the knot of emotion is a moment of revelation into meaning in the play it is the playwright's most effective means of communication. The episode of Lem is skillfully built to such a revealing knot of emotion. The brief relaxation of the men from their plowing relaxes the audience. The problem of Lem is introduced almost casually, there is a diversion in the remarks about Daddy Sykes, and when Lem pursues his request for relief he is at first not taken seriously. Then when Lem is insistent comes Joshuah's outburst. For anything the audience knows, as for Joshuah and the other men, the denunciation is deserved, and the audience is carried with Joshuah's strong spirit. Then comes the sudden reversal. Lem has tried to make as little of his condition as possible, but stung by Joshuah's harsh words, and inarticulate, he exposes his shoulder to view. Ross's words, "Why de bon's bare!" jerks the threads of the situation into the knot of emotion, the abrupt realization to the audience of what Lem has uncomplainingly endured. The simple manliness of Joshuah's response is again charged with emotion for the audience, as is Lem's acceptance without grudge. At the same time that the individual character of Lem is revealed, the incident brings to a focus what all these men are enduring in varying degrees for their dream of a home. Because Lem is the youngest, a boy really, too young for the army, the audience is made to feel the strong foundation for the future, the coming generation.

sundown heah lately, all yuh been doin is stallin! (*Harshly*) What yuh miss is de bullwhip! Yuh's free 'n yuh got yore own patch o lan. But in yore heart yuh still ain't nothin but er triflin slave! Now if yuh want-er go, git!

LEM (*Hurt*):   Yuh kin hurt mah feelins, Mr. Joshuah. Thas all right. (*To others*) But Ah want yuh all t'—Ah want yuh all t' take er look at this. (*He exposes his fleshless collarbone*) Jes take er look!

ROSS (*Looking*):   Great Gawd A'mighty! . . . Why de bon's bare!

SETLOW (*Dumbfounded*):   It's er wonder yuh ain't cotched de lockjaw, Son.

JOSHUAH: Ah axe yore humble pardon, Lem. Ah didn't have de least idea.

SETLOW: Couldn't nobody know.

PELTIER (*To* LEM):   Yuh should-er spoke up fore now!

JOSHUAH (*To* LEM):   Yuh go on t' de Quarters. This ebenin we'll git yuh cross t' Savannah t' Cap'n Bryant. See if he can't git one of de Army doctors t' do somepen fer yuh. In de meantime, Ah hope yuh try t' fergit what Ah said.

¹⁵ LEM (*Going*):   Thas all right, Mr. Joshuah. Ah ain't paid yuh no mind.

(*Exit Right.*)

¹⁶ JAMES (*Dashing across Up-Right*):   Pappy, heah's Cap'n Bryant!

(LEM *re-enters.*)   (*Exit Left.*)

BEULAH (*Following him with other children, shouting gleefully*): Cap'n Bryant! Hi, Cap'n Bryant!

(*Exit Left.*)

LEM (*Looking off Left*):   He got a lady wid him!

PELTIER (*As he and others move up, obviously as excited and anxious to welcome the visiting* CAPTAIN *as the children*):   Er lady!

TAGGERT (*Calling Off-Right*):   Sarah! Hey, Sarah! Run heah, yuh all. Heah's Cap'n Bryant!

JOSHUAH: Ah wuz hopin we'd be done plowin fore this.

PELTIER: Why yuh say tha, Joshuah?

SETLOW: Still, we done beat de deadline.

JOSHUAH: Ah know. But we ought t' be ready t' plant.

[16] The incident of Lem with its emotion and function is complete and it is cleanly cut off with dramatic contrast when the children run in gleefully shouting their announcement of the arrival of Captain Bryant and a lady with him. Although no one knows yet that the lady is their teacher, the mood is right as introduction to that joyous occasion.

PELTIER: What yuh all make of de lady?

ROSS: Speck she bout one of de ristocrats.

[17] JOSHUAH (*Greeting newcomer*):   Well, well, Cap'n Bryant, if this ain't er Jack-in-de-box!

BRYANT (*Entering Up-Left with woman*):   In the Army, Joshuah, the first lesson you learn is: Take them by surprise!

JOSHUAH (*Laughing, as the young Union officer—who is perhaps 35—and his companion come down—*):   Well, Suh, yuh sure is got it down pat!

(DELPHINE *and several other of the older girls, together with the children, crowd in behind* LIBETH,[18] *who is a good-looking young white woman in her twenties and dressed in a plain dress of good material with bustle skirt.*)

JOSHUAH: But what's up—?

BRYANT (*Smiling*):   It's a big occasion.

JOSHUAH: Tha so. How come?

BRYANT (*Smiling*):   Whom do you suppose this lady is?

JOSHUAH: Now, Cap'n Bryant, don't tell me yuh done got married!

(*The* GIRLS *titter.*)

[19] BRYANT (*Embarrassed*):   This lady, Joshuah, is Miss Libeth Arbarbanel, of Hartford, Connecticut, the teacher you sent for.

[20] DELPHINE (*Exclaiming—she rushes to wipe bench with her apron*):   De teacher!

ROSS: Now Ah's seed er miracle!

LIBETH (*To* JOSHUAH, *extending her hand*):   How do you do, Mister Tain?

JOSHUAH (*Wiping his hand on his trousers*):   Lawd, Mam—this is too much for me!

BRYANT (*To* LIBETH):   I warned you, you'd create a sensation.

LIBETH: Captain, please!

DELPHINE: Won't yuh sit down, Mam.

LIBETH (*Taking seat on bench*):   Thank you, dear.

JOSHUAH (*As* WOMEN *enter*):   What yuh all reck'n, Folks. It's de teacher!

WOMEN (*Surprised*):   De teacher!

Lawdy!

Gawd bless her soul!

¹⁷ The likableness of Captain Bryant is immediately apparent, and the easy relation between him and Joshuah.

¹⁸ Libeth in a dress with long full skirts and bustle is picturesque and femininely appealing in the comparatively rough surroundings.

¹⁹ The fact that the lady is the teacher is held back and then, by Joshuah's incorrect surmise as to her identity and Captain Bryant's youthful embarrassment, is released with abrupt dramatic effect.

²⁰ The episode of the coming of the teacher contributes to the sense of progress and hope which is the function of Scene Three, it reveals what education means to the group, and it introduces white and colored people together in unison of spirit.

She done come sure nuff!

[21] SARAH (*Seeing the children swarming over* LIBETH): Beulah, what yuh chillun goin do? Git back 'n stop swarmin ovah de lady like hiving-bees.

PATSY (*Warmly*): Yuh can't blame de bees, Sarah, whar thar's honey! (*Laughter*)

JOSHUAH: Quiet, everybody! (*Turns to* BRYANT) Cap'n Bryant, will yuh—er—?

BRYANT: No, no, Joshuah. You're the officer of the day.

JOSHUAH (*Feeling inadequate*): Ah thot yuh might care t' say er word—t' sort of make us all acquainted—?

BRYANT: Later, perhaps.

JOSHUAH (*Embarrassed—to* LIBETH): Ah speck Ah ain't quite got yore name straight yit, Mam—

LIBETH (*Nervously*): It is awful. But it's Libeth Arbarbanel.

[22] JOSHUAH: Well, Miss Libeth . . . (*Carefully—feeling his way, but with gravity*) 'Low me, Mam, t' bid yuh welcome. Ah donno jes what Ah kin say, cept'n deep down in de hearts of ebery one of us, as Ah speck yuh kin see, there's er well of gladness 'n pride t' see yuh heah mongst us. Ah reck'n there ain't but one way to put it. Yuh's like father Abraham, de way we see yuh. He done broke ouah bonds 'n sot us free. 'N yuh's come t' hep us break de chains of ignance.

LIBETH (*Moved*): Mr. Tain, you make me feel very proud and very much ashamed. When I accepted your invitation, I did so thinking it was the only charitable thing a God-fearing woman could do. But you give me a new sense of my responsibility. Since listening to you, I know now, I should've gone down on my knees and offered thanks for the opportunity you were giving me. I say this in spite of any hardships which we may be called upon to undergo. All I ask is that you will trust me, and be diligent; for, for my part, I shall consider it my God-given privilege to do all in my power to help you, as you've so wisely said, break the chains of ignorance.

BRYANT: Hear! Hear!

JOSHUAH: Thank yuh, Mam. Yuh's er great woman, 'n Ah promise yuh, if we kin git haf de fairness yuh's showed in dem few words, we's gwine prove ouahsefs in de eyes of de world!

[23] BRYANT: I can bear witness to that. I've just returned from

21 The children's response to Miss Arbarbanel establishes her personality.

22 Joshuah and Libeth are confronted with a situation difficult to meet in words and manner. The effect of humility and dignity together expressed with simplicity and manifest sincerity achieved for each of them does much to create their characters.

23 The scene continues to build in the sense of progress and hope in Captain Bryant's congratulation on accomplishment and the gratification of Setlow's and Joshuah's responses. This brief sequence is cut off abruptly by the quick dramatic entrance of the Corporal and delivery of the telegram, then the poised moment of suspense, and then the climax in a soldier's terse but exultant announcement of victory for the Union. The freedmen are assured of the continuance of their freedom.

a trip of inspection. And General Sherman is going to be a proud soldier when he hears of it.

JOSHUAH (*Glancing around*):   Yuh all heah tha?

BRYANT: To put it bluntly, you're going to justify your emancipation in the eyes of all!

SETLOW: Glory to Gawd!

JOSHUAH: Cap'n, yuh make us feel mighty proud!

BRYANT: I intend that you should. You deserve to be congratulated. But while I'm about it, let me also give you a word of advice. In a few months you're going to have a crop—(*Seeing a* CORPORAL *enter to halt and salute smartly*) What is it, Corporal?

CORPORAL: Message for you, Sir. Major Cotton ordered it brought at once!

BRYANT (*Taking telegram*):   Thank you, Corporal. (*Opening it he reads, then exclaims*) Good Lord!

JOSHUAH (*Breathlessly*):   What is it, Cap'n?

BRYANT (*Moved*):   It's all over!

JOSHUAH: What, Cap'n? Not de war?

PELTIER (*Fearfully*):   We ain't loss?

BRYANT: Lost! (*Ecstatically*) We've won! Lee has surrendered his sword to General Grant. Victory has fallen to the Union—Long live the Union!

(*The* FREEDMEN *are stunned.*)

TAGGERT (*His voice low but ringing with profound fervor*): Surely, this is de hand of Gawd!

²⁴ DOSIA (*Dropping to her knees, in tears*):   We thank yuh, Jesus!

SARAH (*Clutching* BEULAH, *with tears of joy*):   Mah darling. There be no auction block fer yuh!

PATSY: No, Jesus! (*The memory of her own offspring like a vision before her mind's eye, she addresses them in apostrophe*) No more chains! No more scorn! Yuh free, Chillun—free t' walk de earth like every natural man!

SETLOW (*Like a clarion, caught in the grip of intense emotion*): Thus saith de Lawd God of Israel: Behold, I will open de way!

JOSHUAH (*Lifting the magnificent old spiritual, triumphantly*): "Go down, Moses,
Way down in Egyptland,

[24] The scene is charged with emotion, swelling up in the exclamatory phrases. Then the single voice of Joshuah leads out with "Go down, Moses." All are silent while his great voice carries through to "Let my people go." All the voices join in. Twenty-odd men, women, and children are standing freely in the clear central stage area, faces upturned in the sunlight of spring, their voices lifted in full release of their emotion in the spiritual, a magnificent scene ending.

Tell ole Pharoah
To let my people go."
> (*All the sufferings and pent-up joy surging up, after all the bitter generations of oppression, in one prolonged note of certitude, overflowing through the vehicle of the glorious song, their voices ring out and their tears flow unashamedly . . .*)

"When Israel was in Egyptland,
Let my people go.
Oppressed so hard they could not stand,
Let my people go.
Go down, Moses . . ."

[25](*Dimout.*)

ACT I
Scene IV

SCENE: The Same
TIME: April 14, 1865, or a week later
> [1](*At Curtain,* LIBETH *seen reading to children beneath tree*)

LIBETH (*Reading*):
"It was two by the village clock,
When he came to the bridge in Concord town.
He heard the bleating of the flock,
And the twitter of birds among the trees,
And felt the breath of the morning breeze
Blowing over the meadows brown.
And one was safe and asleep in his bed
Who at the bridge would be first to fall,
Who that day would be lying dead,
Pierced by a British musket-ball . . ." (*To children*)
That was Crispus Attucks. I want you to remember and be proud of the name, for he is one of our country's greatest heroes. The poet doesn't say any more about him. But there are other books that tell the whole story, and from them we know who he was and how he, a Negro citizen of Concord, was the first to shed his blood for *liberty and freedom for all* in our native land. (*Glancing at watch and rising*) But, we must get back to class—

RUTH: Oh, Miss Libeth, you didn't finish!

[25] Scene Three as previously pointed out, is essentially a scene of the group in a surge forward of progress and hope for the future. A foundation is laid in the opening view of the men at the plow, the determination and endurance with high spirits. With awareness of the men at their plowing off-stage as a background the scene pauses in the group movement for introduction of advance in the personal drama of Delphine and Joshuah. The following episode of Lem projects the determination and endurance into the future by its identification with youth. The introduction of the teacher lifts the scene into joyful happy spirit and with the promise of education for the children projects further into the future. In the jubilant climax of announcement of the end of war and victory for the Union the hope is given assurance.

Act I, Scene IV

[1] Scene Four is a personal interlude for Delphine and Joshua between two group scenes. The music of the full company singing at the close of the preceding scene should continue only part way through the blackout, ending softly, then a few seconds of silence and the light up on Libeth with the children. Opening the scene with Libeth and the children gives continuity from the preceding scene and her introduction as teacher, and effects a transition from the full stage to Delphine and Joshuah. The gentle relaxation and happiness of the opening of this scene is a realization of the confidence given to the hope of the settlers at the end of the preceding scene, also a release from tension.

LIBETH (*Going*):   We must keep to our schedule.

JAMES: But, Miss Libeth, that ain't fair!

LIBETH (*Turning*):   Ain't—?

JAMES: Isn't.

LIBETH: That's better. (*Going*) Since there are only two more stanzas, perhaps we may finish it inside—

BEULAH: Oh, Goody! Goody!

JAMES (*Going, and meeting leader*):   Hi, Mister Joshuah!

² JOSHUAH (*Entering Up-Right*):   How're you, Sonny— Good morning, Mam.

LIBETH: Good morning, Joshuah. What about my class?

JOSHUAH (*Laughing*):   Well, Mam. You know how tiz with ole folks. They still scratchin their heads. But don't worry. Ah speck everybody'll be there tonight.

LIBETH (*Going*):   Well, they'd better. I insist upon it. And you tell them I said so.

(*Exit.*)

JOSHUAH (*Smiling he goes Down-Left to retrieve wagon wheel beside porch of storehouse, and singing, rolls it up to forge*):
"Oh, some go t' church for t' sing 'n shout,
Way in de middle of de air . . .
Fore six month dey's all turned out,
Way in de middle of de air . . .
Oh, Zekiel saw de wheel . . ."

DELPHINE (*Emerging on porch of cotton house, and picking up refrain*):   "Yes, Lawd!"

JOSHUAH (*Hearing her, he drops wheel by forge and comes down, singing*):   "Zekiel saw de wheel . . ."

DELPHINE (*Singing above her smile*):   "Yes, Lawd!"

TOGETHER: "Zekiel saw de wheel
Way in de middle of de air!"

(*They conclude with a burst of warm-hearted laughter. He brings box Down-Center.*)²

³ DELPHINE (*Solicitously*):   Oh, yuh too warm—Look how yuh sweatin!

JOSHUAH (*Pleased*):   When Ah git t' wukin 'n singin I can't hep sweatin.

[2] The scene is light-hearted, Libeth and the children, Joshuah on his entrance, and the meeting between Joshuah and Delphine. Advance in familiarity and ease of relationship between Joshuah and Delphine is shown, which leads into Joshuah's for the first time undertaking to say something to Delphine of his thoughts and feeling about her.

[3] The preliminaries of courtship are homely and familiar.

DELPHINE (*Pressing him onto box*):   Here, sit down 'n lemme wipe yore forehead.

JOSHUAH (*Embarrassed*):   Yuh goin git yore hankcher dirty.

DELPHINE (*Laughing nervously*):   What if Ah do? Ah can always wash it, can't Ah?

JOSHUAH: Yuh know, yuh's a mighty fine gal t' be runnin round loose.

DELPHINE (*Slyly*):   Who'd want me?

JOSHUAH (*Laughing*):   Shucks, Ah bet yuh like de greasy pig. Yuh been t' a hund'd County Fairs, but ain't nobody cotched yuh yit!

DELPHINE: Now, Mister Joshuah, yuh know yuh spoofin!

JOSHUAH: Some might call it spoofin. But Ah call it good common sense—A gal like yuh get any man she want!

DELPHINE (*Probing*):   Any man maybe but de right one.

JOSHUAH (*Probing*):   Ah wonder if yuh'd know him, if he popped up now?

DELPHINE: A woman's heart don't fool her, Mister Joshuah. She take one glance at de *man for her,* and right away she say to hersef: "Thas him!"

4 JOSHUAH (*Soberly*):   Anybody can be carried away at first sight. But that don't mean they can't make a big mistake.

DELPHINE (*Laughing*):   Oh, thas jes a chance yuh have t' take.

JOSHUAH: Not if yuh use good common sense.

DELPHINE: What's a person's heart care bout common sense? If yuh love somebody yuh love em.

JOSHUAH (*Slowly*):   It looks tha way when yuh young. But when yuh git older 'n wiser, yore heart might sway yuh, but yuh listen t' yore head.

DELPHINE: Yuh think tha makes anybody any happier?

JOSHUAH: Ah wouldn't say that. But at least it keeps em from gittin hurt.

DELPHINE: But what makes yuh think they got t' get hurt?

JOSHUAH: How can they hep it, if they git somebody don't really love em?

DELPHINE: But you can't see inside of people! . . . All you can go by is de way yuh feel toward em—forget about your fears, 'n live in hope.

⁴ Delphine was right to Ellen in the preceding scene; Joshuah is afraid of the difference in their ages as an obstacle to love and marriage between them. His approach is tentative and indirect. Delphine does her best to bridge the gap, sincerely, earnestly, with no trace of coquetry, from the moment Joshuah settles to serious effort. There is innocence and dignity, poetry, and idealism towards love and marriage in this scene of courtship.

JOSHUAH: Yuh pretty deep, Delphine. Pretty deep. Yuh speak about hope but Ah wonder?

DELPHINE: Ah see yuh don't think Ah b'lieve what Ah say.

JOSHUAH: Tain't tha, Delphine. But les look at it like this. Take a man my aige, say. Spose he fell in love wid somebody no older'n you. Common sense'd tell yuh, wouldn't do him no good t' hope, now wouldn't it?

DELPHINE (*Laughing nervously*):   Thas accordin.

JOSHUAH (*Catching her as she goes behind him*):   Accordin t' what?

DELPHINE: Well, for instance—

JOSHUAH (*Hopefully*):   What—?

DELPHINE: Well, spose the somebody was really like yuh: Good-hearted 'n strong—er regular Moses t' his people? . . . Ah reckon most women'd be proud to have him. Ah reckon for most women it'd be like de story of de Mountain 'n de Sea.

JOSHUAH: Proud, eh?—Phumph!

DELPHINE: Why de grunt?

JOSHUAH: Marriage outer pride is like er body widout er soul. But love—that's er nother story.—But what's this bout de mountain 'n de sea?

DELPHINE (*Disappointed*):   It's jes er story.

JOSHUAH: Ah don't speck Ah ever heard that one.—How's it go?

DELPHINE: Oh, it don't matter.

JOSHUAH: But it do. Ah'd like very much t' hear it.—How's it go?

DELPHINE: Well—(*Her modesty driving her to cross behind him*) de Mountain was big 'n de Sea was free. But no matter how she'd pitch, every trial she make t' reach de Mountain ended right back in de ditch!

JOSHUAH (*Suddenly rising*):   Thas er *powerful story.*

DELPHINE: But—?

JOSHUAH (*Driving his fist into the palm of his hand*):   It just goes t' bear me out.

DELPHINE: Ah don't see how.

JOSHUAH (*Thoughtfully*):   This mountain of yores is sot in his ways. Nothin please him more'n stayin put—

DELPHINE: Ah see Ah picked de wrong story.

⁵ JOSHUAH: No. Hit's er timely parable. There's some like de mountain, 'n some like de sea, jes got t' go roving, jes bound t' be restless—specially when they young . . . Take yuh, if yuh got er good chance t' leave heah now, you'd be gone. But wid me—well, this Ilun 'n mah fawty. Well, they jes bout sum up mah heart's desire. Ah can't hardly wait t' git de gear fixed on the donkey yonder, cuz Ahm itchin t' git de mill started. Ah want t' build me er house, Delphine. Ah want t' build it (*Pointing Off-Right*) yonder, mongst dem oaks, facin de sea. Ah want t' build it low 'n ramblin, wid oak logs two feet thick 'n well seasoned, so it'll last. —Kin yuh understand that?

DELPHINE (*Impressed*):   Like de Rock of Ages, hunh?

JOSHUAH: Thas it. Like de Rock of Ages. Ah want t' build it wid er fireplace, where Ah kin sit through de long winter nights 'n watch de logs burnin, maybe catch de sound of de sighin winds.— Den, for summer, Ah want t' build me er porch, where Ah kin rair back, prop mah feet up, 'n look cross de water t' Savannah yonder, 'n watch de twinklin lights.

DELPHINE (*Thoughtfully*):   An thas all—?

JOSHUAH (*Lauding*):   Well, cose er man can't have much of er home widout er woman—Only—

DELPHINE: Ahm listenin—?

JOSHUAH (*Grimly*):   Only she got t' be de kind goin walk cross de doorsill 'n say wid me: "Heah, Lawd, at last is mah refuge!"

DELPHINE (*Shocked*):   Refuge! . . . Ah can't see her!—Ain't no woman want nothin like that!

JOSHUAH: No.—Why not?

DELPHINE (*Earnestly*):   Er woman want t' look forward t' havin er lil life!

JOSHUAH (*Upset*):   Now yuh show yore aige! Anybody git life got t' plant it.

DELPHINE: In er tomb—?

JOSHUAH (*Pained*):   Tomb—Phumph! But it's jes like Ah been sayin.

⁶ DELPHINE (*Defensively*):   But don't yuh see, Mr. Joshuah. Yore house is too gloomy. (*Earnestly*) Er house ought t' be like er wedding feast, bright 'n cheery; wid friends comin 'n goin. (*Carried*

⁵ Like the relaxation and the light-heartedness of the opening of the scene, that Joshuah broaches the topic of marriage to Delphine and dwells at this time on his dream of the home he would build on this island is a part of the function of the scene to express the spirit of confidence for the future engendered at the close of the preceding scene.

⁶ Delphine shows her possession of character. She is in love with Joshuah and wants to marry him, but when he draws his picture of marriage and it differs from hers she does not try to win him by acquiescence—get her man first, and let happen what may afterwords. She stands up to him in defense of her picture of marriage.

away by her deepest instinct and hopes) It ought t' have chillun, runnin everybody crazy, rompin 'n squealin from mornin till night! —Don't you gree wid me?

JOSHUAH (*Moved and smiling*):   Well, Ah admit hit's er mighty pretty picture—specially de part bout de chillun. (*Sobering*) But Ah still say, first we got t' git out de rain 'n try t' stay out. Once we git set, hit'll be time nuff t' set out de jug in friendship-whole-'n-hearty—!

SARAH (*Rushing in*):   Joshuah!

JOSHUAH (*Annoyed*):   Jes er minute, Sarah.

SARAH: But, Joshuah!

JOSHUAH: Never mind—lemme finish—

SARAH: Ah jes want t—

JOSHUAH (*To* DELPHINE, *as* SARAH *stands aside with a look of consternation*):   De pint Ah want yuh t' see: We got de lan 'n we kin build on it. But we got t' feel ouah way—like trying t' build er road through er vargin swamp. We got t' hack ouah way, 'n keep one eye on de sun—(*Turning*) Now what is it, Sarah? [7]

[8] SARAH: Ah come heah t' axe yuh ef yuh got er minute t' spare t' go yonder 'n see bout de pig done fell in de well!

JOSHUAH: Good Gawd! 'N yuh wait all this time t' tell me!

SARAH (*Accusingly*):   Yuh tole me t' shut up—Ah tried t' tell yuh!

JOSHUAH (*Running up to forge to pick up rope*):   Lawd, if yuh all ain't er pester t' mah soul! (*Running out*) Owen! Tom! Run heah! De pig's in de well!

SARAH (*To* DELPHINE):   All this time! Ah speck we goin have pork chops fer supper! (*They burst into laughter.*)

(*Blackout.*)

ACT I

Scene V

SCENE: The Same

TIME: That evening

[1] (*Prior to visibility it is clear that something in the nature of a catastrophe has struck the life of the* FREEDMEN.

PATSY *is heard leading them in the "Crucifixion," her rich contralto voice leadened with a note of profound sorrow.*

[7] The interruption from Sarah cuts off this conversation of importance to Delphine and Joshuah and leaves the question suspended with no assurance whatever for Delphine of the hoped-for outcome.

[8] Sarah and the pig in the well connects the scene with the group background again, and the homely humor at the end renews the note of light-heartedness by which the scene represents the settlers in their brief interval of fullest confidence before the reversal of the following scene.

Act I, Scene V

[1] The contrast of mood between the close of Scene Four and the opening of Scene Five is an especially strong dramatic effect. For the transition there should be a brief period of silence in the black-out, long enough for the mood of the end of the previous scene to subside, and the singing, then, should not fade in. From the first note, Patsy's voice should be heard clear and firm in the darkness, through the

[*Continued on page 341*]

Around her and dimly limned against the surrounding shadows, the FREEDMEN *are massed in clusters, their heads and bodies bent beneath the weight of the overwhelming disaster which characterized the shock of President Lincoln's assassination throughout the nation.*

The wealthy Negro freeman, OLIVER WEBSTER, SR., *is alone under the oak.*)

PATSY (*Singing*):   "They crucified mah Lawd, 'N he never said er mumblin word . . .

CHORUS: "Not er word,
Not er word . . .

PATSY: "They nailed him t' de tree
'N he never said er mumblin word . . .

CHORUS: "Not er word,
Not er word . . .

PATSY: "They pierced him in his side
'N he never said a mumblin word . . . etc."

JOSHUAH (*After a moment, entering with* LIBETH *and* EMANUEL):
What's this bout Father Abraham?

[2] CROWD (*Wailingly*):   He gone, Joshuah!
They done shot President Lincoln—
They done laid him low!
Ouah best friend gone, Joshuah. He gone! (*The* WOMEN *moan*)

[3] JOSHUAH (*Joining* WEBSTER):   Is this er fack, Mister Webster—?

WEBSTER: Yes, my friend. President Lincoln was shot down in cold blood last night.

JOSHUAH: Mah Gawd from Heabem—Ah can't b'lieve it!

LIBETH: How did it happen?

WEBSTER: He was shot in the back of the head, as he sat in his box at the theatre. This morning he died just before day.

LIBETH: How dreadful!

JOSHUAH: Who did it? Who could-er—?

WEBSTER: An actor by the name of Booth, according to the news. But I think he was hired for the job. I think the planters are in it up to their necks, and I fear we're in for bloody times!

DOSIA: Oh, Jesus, no!

[4] ROSS (*To* WEBSTER):   Yuh think dey after *us?*

first stanza with the choral response, and continuing without augmentation into the second stanza as the light comes up gradually on the scene. The visual effect reinforces the mood of the singing, the fading light and shadows of evening and the darker masses of the freedmen in groups, the outlines made heavy by the bent heads. Mr. Webster stands apart and alone, a solid figure of somber dignity, conservatively dressed in black with bared head. Question is created through the interval of singing; the audience does not know the cause of sorrow.

[2] With the mood prepared, announcement of the death of Lincoln comes with dramatic abruptness, immediately softened and at the same time made more penetrating by the unconscious poetry of folk expression of grief.

[3] Mr. Webster functions with Joshuah for establishment of the facts, Mr. Webster's terseness an effective contrast to the emotion in every speech from the freedmen.

[4] Ross's speech raises the question, turns the assassination from the shock of grief and an occasion for sympathetic emotion into a dramatic complication and potential reversal of the freedmen's fortunes.

TAGGERT: Who else, Man?

SARAH: Joshuah, what us goin do?

JOSHUAH: This is a hard 'n bitter blow. But les don't be skeered. Remember, we still got friends—folks like Gen'l Sherman 'n General Grant—folks like Miss Libeth heah.

[5] TAGGERT: Yeah. But what bout de lan?

PELTIER: De lan—?

LEM: Brer Tom, what yuh mean?

TAGGERT: What Ah want t' know—what we goin do bout it now dis happen?

JOSHUA: We goin er-head 'n raise er crop, thas what.

TAGGERT: Us never git this lan now!

JOSHUAH: Tom, what kind of talk is this?

TAGGERT: Ah ain't goin make no fool of mahsef!

LEM: Ah say de same. Ain't no use wukin for nothin!

TAGGERT: No!

LEM: What yuh say, Brer Ross?

ROSS: Ain't much sense tryin t' kill er bear less'n yuh big nuff t' skin him!

(*Silence.*)

JOSHUAH: Well, is yuh all through talkin like chillun?

PELTIER (*Quietly*):   Them skunks game nuff t' shoot de President, they must have sompen up thar sleeves!

TAGGERT: What yuh think, Mister Webster?

[6] WEBSTER: I can only repeat. It looks very bad!

TAGGERT (*Victoriously*):   Ah told yuh all so!

JOSHUAH: Tha can't be you talkin, Mister Webster.

WEBSTER (*Embarrassed*):   I'm only trying to be honest, Mister Tain.

JOSHUAH: What yuh think kin be gained by sech talk?

WEBSTER: The people have to know the truth!

JOSHUAH (*Sharply*):   Mr. Webster, we got this lan!

WEBSTER: Mr. Tain, I happen to be one of those who waited on General Sherman and induced him to settle you on the land. But I'd be less than a friend if I failed to admit it's a question as to how long you can expect to keep it!

JOSHUAH: Mister Webster, is yuh fergetting de Yanks?

[5] Taggert directs the question specifically to the land. Joshuah is confronted again by the problem of leadership of strengthening his followers.

[6] Mr. Webster's position introduces a fresh complication and a serious set-back to Joshuah's position. Mr. Webster is informed and logical, and a friend to the freedmen. He advises with earnestness as he honestly sees the situation. Joshuah has no desire for leadership for himself or as an end in itself. He has come naturally into leadership by force of will and a mind fixed upon a single concrete fact, the land, as objective for himself and others. When Webster, as an outside force, supports the fears of the freedmen Joshuah turns from the conflict of trying to put spirit into them, and without a word of support having come from one of them, unconsciously identifies them with himself, assumes speaking for them: "We got this lan' 'n anybody who speck t' be er leader roun heah got t' fight for ouah right t' hang on t' it."

WEBSTER (*Coldly*):   The Yanks have shaken hands with treason and said: "Let us forget!"

JOSHUAH (*Pained*):   Ah don't b'lieve it. It don't make sense!

WEBSTER: We're treading in deep waters, Sir. The assassination is proof of it!

TAGGERT: Cose!

JOSHUAH: This murder ain't nothin but er case of de pot of hate simmerin down t 'er mess of tryin t' git even.

WEBSTER: If only it were that simple.

JOSHUAH: Yuh got no grounds for saying it ain't.

WEBSTER: The facts speak for themselves. President Lincoln was the planters' friend.

JOSHUAH (*Shocked*):   What—?

WEBSTER (*Relentlessly*):   His policy toward them was always "forgive and forget!"

JOSHUAH (*Bitterly*):   Mister Webster, if Father Abraham's dead, he died cause of us!

DOSIA: Yes! Pity de po' sweet soul! (*She moans*)

PATSY: He desarved de full cup ob mercy. But dey's laid him low. Oh, weep for him! When us were lowly and bad oppressed, he stood up for us, and now he's gone to glory!

ROSS: He's gone—he's gone, and he won't be back no more . . . !

SARAH: Oh break de heart of me!

SETLOW (*Pointedly*):   You do well to moan, chillun . . . well may you shed de briney tears! De brigand done laid in wait for his life. But dem who call demsefs our friends look down on de byre wid scorn!

WEBSTER (*Getting the point*):   He stood against slavery and for that . . . Well, you've a right to revere him!

JOSHUAH: Den les do dat. He may be gone, but he done sot ouah feet on de highway to life 'n we goin tread hit wid courage.

WEBSTER: I agree with you in that, my friend. But I would remind you, courage without wisdom is useless.

JOSHUAH: We got to stick to our aims.

WEBSTER: Yes. But we must be flexible. We must go ahead. But with open eyes, and a readiness to anticipate our enemies and shift accordingly. If the planters are responsible, and I believe they

are, then there must be a plot, and in my opinion, they shot Mr.
Lincoln in spite of his friendliness because they want to frighten the
North into making an agreement.

JOSHUAH: Like what?

WEBSTER: Ask yourself. What do the planters want most?—
They want a full pardon for their rebellion and the restoration of
their lands.

PELTIER: It makes sense.

JOSHUAH: They can't get way wid it!

WEBSTER: That's not the point.

JOSHUAH: Meaning—?

WEBSTER: What over-all and long-range plan can we make to
defeat them? That is the big question before the race. Either we look
far ahead with wisdom, or the future of every Freedman in the South
is doomed!

(*Silence.*)

SETLOW: Is yuh got some idea for er plan?

WEBSTER: We must win the ballot.

JOSHUAH: De ballot—?

WEBSTER: Exactly. The whole country will support us.

JOSHUAH (*Darkly*):   So thas yore idea—

WEBSTER: It's not mine only. Just last week I met with several
of our leaders in Charleston, and they all felt it's the wisest course
we can take. The assassination of President Lincoln makes it only
clearer—only more mandatory.

JOSHUAH: 'N de meantime, yuh plan t' fergit bout de lan, is tha
it? Is tha what yuh call far-seein?

WEBSTER: We must work for political power. The question of
the land is too dangerous to handle right now.

JOSHUAH: 'N yet yuh call yoresef er educated man!

WEBSTER (*Annoyed*):   We cannot afford, Mr. Tain, to appear
before the whole country as being selfish.

[6] JOSHUAH (*Exploding*):   Selfish or no selfish. We got this lan'
'n anybody who speck t' be er leader round heah got t' fight for ouah
right t' hang on t' it!

LIBETH: But, Mister Tain. Perhaps he's right. You can't afford
to be partisan.

6 See note on page 343.

WEBSTER: It would be fatal. As it is, the planters are preparing to fight like cornered rats for the land.

JOSHUAH: Ah say, let em!

WEBSTER: But that will mean war all over again.

[7] JOSHUAH: Den let it be war den!

LIBETH: But are you sure that's what you want?

JOSHUAH: Ah'd sooner hab war den see mah people slip back in de mire.

WEBSTER: The trouble with you, Mister Tain, is you don't understand the importance of the ballot. All over the world it is prized as the people's most precious possession.

LIBETH: Indeed! That's very true.

[8] JOSHUAH (*Aroused to the depths*):   It's easy fer anybody t' prize somepen they ain't got. Ah remember tha bout Freedom. But votin—this much Ah know about tha. Votin ain't much. Ah's seed it all mah life, here in Gawgie 'n down in Lusana too. De man what holds de lan holds de office.—Look at de poor white folks. They vote. But what do they git out-er it? A gallon or two of corn likker come lection day, 'n atter tha, nothing but de same ole struggle 'n de same ole shack full of raw-bone babies.—Ah sayd it once 'n Ah say it ergain; let dem what have de ears t' hear, let em hear: We got this lan, 'n votin or no votin, we tend t' keep it!—We's lost Father Abraham. But we ain't going let tha discourage us. We goin moan his loss. But we goin do it in sorrow, 'n not in despair. Ah say tha cause despair 'n hope don't mix, 'n hope was de first big thing he give us. The planters might skeer some. But not us—not us, who's felt de lash, who know what tiz t' see er brother's brains dashed out, er father shot down in de middle of de field, 'n er mother hanged for liftin her hand gainst de Overseer. No! They don't skeer us, cuz we was brought up in de house of horror! [8] (*Suddenly pausing, he looks over the group and his eyes soften and a note of tenderness marks his tone*) Now t' git back t' Father Abraham.[9] He's lyin up yonder in Washington. Soon, they'll be puttin him in de cold, cold grave.

DOSIA (*Moaning*):   Lawd, Lawd!

PATSY: Wrap him in your arms, Sweet Jesus!

JOSHUAH (*Sadly*):   To some folks thas goin be de end of him. But not t' me 'n yuh—

⁷ We are accustomed to history of the Civil War and its aftermath from the point of view of the white people Northern and Southern, of a nation, and of government. Mr. Ward has written not a partisan play, but a play of dramatic unity, written within the frame of reference of the group of freedmen and the land. The audience is drawn into identification, experiences the episode and understands the characters from within that frame of reference. The Northern and the Southern white people have fought a war; there was something they were willing, with heroism, it is assumed, to fight for and die for. If the outcome of that war leaves untouched the deepest need of Joshuah and his people as he sees it, feels it, there is something for which he is ready to accept war, to fight for the possession of land or to die defending the right to it.

Joshuah is revealed in Scene Five in the essential character of the classical tragic protagonist, possessed by a single idea with an inner necessity which admits of no compromise, like Oedipus in his search for the criminal whose presence is responsible for the Theban plague, and Antigone and the necessity to her that the burial rites for her brother be performed. There is foreshadowing of doom in revelation of such character in Joshuah.

⁸ Although Joshuah is uneducated and history has been gradually supporting Mr. Webster, within the limits of his experience of direct observation Joshuah has a straight-thinking and clear-sighted mind. His argument from concrete fact on the ballot and land is strong. His speech rises to the height of dramatic power, however, when he draws up from the depths the source of his strength, the familiarity with suffering of those, with himself, for whom he speaks. At the climax of his speech—"No! They don't skeer us, cuz we was brought up in de house of horror!"—Joshuah is not arguing, he is no longer addressing Mr. Webster, he is looking within himself, his memory of the past. Mr. Webster will not be convinced, but he knows there is no more argument. When Joshuah comes to the sudden pause, the men and women about him are rapt, motionless and silent, some with eyes fixed on Joshuah, some staring straight ahead, some with bowed heads. Joshuah has reached into the depths of what they know, he has spoken for them. The preparation has been established for men to die with Joshuah at the end of the play.

DOSIA: No, Lawd!

JOSHUAH: For us, he's like er evergreen tree wid de roots planted deep in ouah hearts—

SETLOW: Amen!

JOSHUAH: So long as we live, he live; 'n Ah think thas goin be so for ouah chillun, 'n their chillun's chillun, on 'n on till de end of time.

(*The women sob.*)

SETLOW: Amen! Amen!

JOSHUAH: Thas all Ah know t' say, 'n Ah think thas all tha needs t' be sayd. But if any of yuh all want t' add er word, say it. Den, Ah think it would be mighty nice if us took de night off 'n sing some songs t' his memory.

DELPHINE (*After a moment broken only by the stifled sobbing, she lifts her voice in a note of ineffable sadness*):

"Steal away, steal away,
Steal away home t' Jesus.
Steal away, steal away,
Steal away home.
Ah ain't got long t' stay here."

(*Gradually the* ENTIRE GROUP *join in, and their voices ring tenderly over the island.*) [9]

"My Lawd calls me, He calls me by
The thunder,
He calls me by
The lightnin,
The trumpet sounds within-a mah soul.
Ah ain't got long t' stay here.

"Steal away, steal away,
Steal away home t' Jesus.
Steal away, steal away,
Steal away home. . . ."

[10] (*Slowly the Curtain is lowered.*)

[9] The sequence of tribute to Lincoln is the natural poetry of the Southern Negro folk sermon in which the responses of the congregation are a part of the rhythm and continuity of the expression of the emotion, and which characteristically leads into song.

The sobbing of the women is at once expression of the simple warmth and depth of their feeling for Lincoln whom they have never seen, and an outlet to stored-up old sorrow which Joshuah has touched. The final release to emotion comes in song, when first the single voice of Delphine is lifted in the soft piercing sweetness of the opening phrase of the spiritual, "Steal away, steal away." The light has faded almost to darkness as the other voices join in. Following upon a strong heightening of suspense as a carry-over of interest to the second act, the first act comes to rest for the interval.

[10] Scene Five is the end of an act, a true structural unit in the division of the play into two acts. The death of Lincoln is not the crisis of the plot-line of the play, which comes late, in Scene Three of Act Two, as is characteristic of plays as episodic in structure as *Our Lan'*. The scene of the death of Lincoln is a major turning point in the play, however, in the fortunes of the settlers and especially in mood. The first act is essentially a forward movement of high hope rising to higher confidence. The obstacles are internal and comparatively minor. The death of Lincoln is not immediate enough in effect to constitute the crisis of the play; the movement does not turn from this point and sweep onward to the catastrophe. In the second act progress continues, hopes rise, but every advance is met by a setback as forces from outside close in. The mood of the second act is that of intensifying conflict. The structure of ten episodes with considerable time intervals and the crisis four-fifths of the way through the play is greatly strengthened by the additional pattern of two balanced movements with a major turning point midway of the play.

ACT II
Scene I

SCENE: The same

TIME: A week later

[1] (*A storm is brewing. But now there is no wind, and only an overcast sky.*

From the distance comes the ring of the Freedmen's axes, felling timber for the houses they hope to build.

DADDY SYKES *is seated on porch of the cotton house, his feet on the top step, smoking his pipe.*

He appears oblivious of EDGAR, *who approaches, singing.*)

[2] EDGAR (*Singing Off-Right*): "Oh de blind man stood in de way 'n he cried:

Oh, Lawd, save me!" (*Entering, and wearing his Union Army uniform. He sees* SYKES) Seen mah wife?

SYKES: Ellen? She down t' de wharf.

EDGAR: Howcome yuh ain't in de woods wid de gang?

SYKES: What Ah need wid er house?

EDGAR: Ah never thot of tha. (*Hearing thunder*) Ah b'lieve it's goin storm sure nuff.

SYKES: Yuh see eny fightin?

EDGAR: Ah ain't seed nothin but er lot of boxes 'n crates!

SYKES: Made yuh wuk, hunh?

EDGAR (*Going*): Yeah. Ah never did git t' smell no powder.

SYKES: Speck yuh lucky. Dem Rebs is er tarble people.

EDGAR (*Turning*): Ah don't bar nothin on two feet mahsef, ole man. Cuz Ahm like de briar patch; step on me 'n Ahm bound t' snag yuh! (*Seeing others as he goes Up-Left*) Good evenin, Folks!

[3] OLLIE (*Entering with* DELPHINE): What does an ignorant field hand like Joshuah know about it? (*Joining* SYKES) Daddy Sykes, go tell Mr. Tain I said I must see him right away. Tell him it's about the sawmill.

SYKES (*Rising annoyed*): Mah mind tole me not t' set heah!

(*Exit Right.*)

OLLIE (*To* DELPHINE): My father says the whole scheme is doomed. These people will never get the land, now that Lincoln is dead. Didn't you hear him when he was over here last week?

Act II, Scene I

[1] The empty stage except for Daddy Sykes, after the ending of Act One, creates question, expectation; the sound of the axes reintroduces the note of hope. There is an atmosphere of tension from the brewing storm throughout the scene, however.

[2] Edgar's song opened the play, low and plaintive, and it opens Act Two, announcing Edgar's approach as he returns, the war over, to a wife and prospective home. This time the song, in spite of its theme, is vigorous and high-spirited in delivery.

[3] Ollie renews his attack on Delphine taking advantage of all the uncertainty for her future and that of her sister introduced by the assassination of Lincoln and the following turmoil. He delivers the final blow of discouragement that he has come to remove the lumber milling equipment loaned by his father. Delphine's feeling about Joshuah and her identification with the settlers comes out strongly, but she is shaken, although by no means won.

For the audience through the meeting between Ollie and Delphine there is the double interest of concern for Delphine, and the tension of knowing about the sawmill before the people of the island know about it, waiting for the entrance of Joshuah and the others and how they will meet the catastrophe.

DELPHINE (*Worried*):   Yeah. But—

OLLIE: Then you should see. The best Joshuah can hope for is a job on somebody's plantation. But perhaps you wouldn't mind spending your life with him in a filthy hut—with a dirt floor to walk on—where the only way you can prepare a meal is by stooping in front of a smoky fireplace?

DELPHINE: Ah didn't say Joshuah wanted to marry me.

OLLIE: Then you'll remain a housemaid.

DELPHINE: Ahm through being er housemaid.

OLLIE: You won't be able to avoid it. You've no education.

DELPHINE: Ahma git one. Ahma teach too—if it's de las thing Ah do on this earf! Miss Libeth already teachin me.

OLLIE: What're you going to do when your former master returns and breaks everything up?

DELPHINE: Marse Burkhardt might be dead, for all anybody know.

OLLIE: But can't you see? Even if he is, there's his family to take over. You've no chance, unless you listen to me. Say the word, and I'll be back for you tomorrow night, and take you and Roxanna both to Savannah with me.

DELPHINE: Sure, in the dark! Behime everybody's back!

OLLIE: You don't trust me. You think nothing of my friendship—

DELPHINE: Ah didn't say tha.

OLLIE: But you show it, when you refuse to listen. You'd rather think of these clodhoppers.

DELPHINE: Maybe Ah ain't ez proud as yuh, Ollie. Ah can't jes jump up 'n leave behind their back—sneak er-way in de dead of night like I got sompen t' hide.

OLLIE: There's no other way. But, of course, if you think nothing of your little sister's welfare—

DELPHINE: Why can't Ah jes tell Joshuah? You can trust him.

OLLIE: Not after today.

DELPHINE: Why not?

OLLIE (*Going up to look Off-Right*):   You'll see in a minute.

DELPHINE (*Watching him*):   What yuh fixin t' do?

OLLIE (*Turning back, and indicating donkey and bandsaw Off-Left*):   Take that donkey and bandsaw back.

DELPHINE (*Amazed, as he rejoins her*):   But, Ollie, howcome?

OLLIE: We have to get them out of Burkhardt's reach.

DELPHINE: But you know they all plannin on buildin homes!

OLLIE: We have to be practical. In times like these, you have to look out for yourself, or be dragged under. It's like I've been trying to get you to understand. For your own good, you'd better get wise, and make up your mind. I may not be free to come here anymore, after today.

DELPHINE: Yuh jes have t' give me more time!

OLLIE: But I tell you they may bar me away from the island.

DELPHINE: Ah know Joshuah. He wouldn't do nothin like tha. He's de biggest person yuh ever seed.

OLLIE: Look, Delphine. You're not concerned whether Joshuah or any of the others know about our plans. You're just afraid. You don't trust me. Yet you're scared to lose my friendship because you know I can do more for you in a minute than that big yokel can do for you in a year. Isn't that it, or the way it stands?

DELPHINE: Joshuah respect me—Ah say tha much for *him!*

OLLIE: You can't live on respect, my dear.

PATSY (*Shouting in distance*):   Hey, yuh mens! Whar yuh all runnin off t' in sech er hurry?

OLLIE: Damn it, they're coming—(*To* DELPHINE) I'm offering you everything, Honey—I'd ask you to be my wife, if I could. But I can help you. If only you'll let me, I'll give you an education and tomorrow when I'm independent we'll—

PATSY (*Shouting*):   Mister Ross! Don't yuh hear me? Whar yuh all goin?

(*Thunder.*)

JOSHUAH (*Entering with men*):   Hello, Ollie—(*He comes down, his hollow greeting as ominous as the approaching storm*) What's this bout de sawmill?

OLLIE (*Hesitantly*):   Well, it's probably going to prove a shock to you. But my father thinks the mill parts are no longer safe here. He's asked me to tell you he's sorry. But as long as the situation is so uncertain and as critical as it is, it's best that you return them.

CROWD (*Muttering*):   Thar now!

Well, well!

Phumph! Phumph! Phumph!

JOSHUAH: Yuh don't mean sompen else done come up?

OLLIE: He's only trying to protect himself. That donkey, you know, cost a fortune. We can't risk losing it or having it damaged. Mr. Venerable, his partner, and he have talked it over, and they figure it's the wisest course to take at the moment.

⁴ JOSHUAH (*Quietly*):   Ah kin see things might look dark, Ollie. But they can't be so bad anybody got t' be skeered.

OLLIE: You don't realize how things are going. You're isolated, cut off here on the island.

SARAH (*Leading women in*):   What's the matter?

TAGGERT: Ollie goin take de sawmill way.

ROSS: He jes goin throw us back.

SARAH: But, Ollie, howcome?

TAGGERT: Ah thot us wuz goin have all summer t' git lumber ready.

ROSS: Yeah. Now us gwine hab t' put up log cabins wid er axe.

OLLIE: You don't have to build now.

JOSHUAH: But tiz goin throw us back, Ollie. 'N less'n there's sompen yuh ain't tellin us, it's hard t' see how yuh all kin act like this.

OLLIE: You've no idea how high feeling is running on the mainland. Washington is a bedlam, and no one knows what the new President, Johnson, is going to do. He's a Southerner, you know— from Tennessee.

JOSHUAH (*Quietly*):   All threatenin storms don't break, Ollie.

OLLIE: Those who are sensible take cover, nevertheless, when they see clouds gathering. The planters are returning daily. Suppose this man Burkhardt comes back and finds the mill operating on his property?—Why he might take an axe or crowbar and smash that donkey to pieces!

JOSHUAH: Oh, no he won't. In de fust place, what's t' stop us from puttin er guard over it?

PELTIER: Yeah. We protect it, Ollie. We protect it wid blood!

OLLIE: You can't protect it from the law.

JOSHUAH: What law?

OLLIE: We've no legal right to set up a mill on another man's property. Burkhardt may go to Court and claim the mill and get it.

JOSHUAH: He never git way wid it. De Jedge Advocate wid us!

⁴ Joshuah meets the situation quietly, doing his job as leader, summoning every argument he can command. The line is drawn between courage and cautious self-interest in a crisis.

OLLIE: Yes. With *you*. You're Freedmen. It's the business of the Bureau to look out for *you*.

(*Lightning.*)

JOSHUAH: 'N dey'll look out for you all too. Cap'n Bryant stick up for anybody on ouah side.

OLLIE: That's a matter of conjecture, Mr. Tain.

JOSHUAH: Meanin—?

OLLIE: Simply, he may or he may not.

JOSHUAH: Well, look, Ollie. Spose Ah go back wid yuh 'n talk t' yore Pa?

OLLIE: It's impossible. He's out of town. He left yesterday for Charleston.

SETLOW: Well, what bout his partner?

OLLIE: You'd never get anywhere with him. He's dead set against it.

JOSHUAH: But Ah can try!

OLLIE: But I tell you it'd only be a waste of time. He was opposed from the start. Now he's blaming Papa and me for jeopardizing his whole future—It's no pleasure to me to come here and disappoint everyone. But I've no responsibility whatever in the matter.

[5] TAGGERT (*Sharply*):   Den if thas de case, yuh had no bizness bringin em heah!

OLLIE (*Stung*):   I was only trying to be of help to you, and you ought to be ashamed to make a remark like that.

PATSY (*Bitterly*):   Yuh de one ought t' be shame, Mister Ollie— gittin folks' heart set on sompen den go snatch it way.

(*The sky begins to darken.*)

OLLIE: Oh, be reasonable, Miss Patsy. You're not outdoors. You know you can get along in your huts for the time being.

SARAH (*Pained*):   Yuh kin say tha, Ollie. But yuh 'n yore Pappy 'n his partner, yuh all ain't never had t' spend de night in er leaky hut. Ain't none of yuh ever had t' go through sech misery as we did last winter. Yuh don't know what tiz t' see yore chillun suffer. Yuh ain't never had t' lay through de night listenin t' em whimper, wid de rain 'n snowy-wind sweepin in from every corner of de sea, 'n all yuh got t' keep em warm is er quilt of dry grass for kivver—

[5] The settlers, men and women, break into the emotional reactions of bitterness and recrimination, not entirely just but natural and understandable. Ollie is honestly hurt by the injustice and as sincerely concerned for the settlers as he is capable of being from his comfortable position, but nothing is changed as to the practical fact of removal of the sawmill.

If yuh had, Ollie, (*Bursting into tears*) yuh all'd have some pity. Yes, yuh would!

ROSS (*Bitterly*):   They thot us pay in er year or two. They think t' darsefs: dem Cuffees got lan. Pretty soon dey hab money. Now dey think us don't git lan, us ain't goin habe money. So dey pull dar freight!

PATSY: Thas de Gawd's trufe. Dey jes desertin us!

EDGAR: Yeah! 'N dey de ones wuz goin do so much t' hep us climb!

ROSS: Sure! So proud t' hep us. Whar all tha pride now, Ollie?

SETLOW: Ah came unto mine own 'n de received me not!

PELTIER (*Angrily*):   Us jes been fools. Us oughter knowed better'n t' speck anything from ristocrat mulattahs!

[6] OLLIE: Mr. Tain, why do you stand there and be silent?

(*There is a terrific flash of lightning, followed by thunder*)

JOSHUAH (*Glances at sky, then going*):   Come on some of yuh, gimmer er hand.

(*Exit Up-Right.*)

ROSS: But, Joshuah—de storm!

EDGAR: Looks more like er hurricane!

PELTIER: Damn if Ahm goin out dar.

(*The wind rises rapidly to fury.*)

[7] SETLOW (*Above wind to* OLLIE):   Yuh can't git cross tha water now! Yuh better figger on stayin de night!

(*The sudden deafening crash of lightning and thunder starts all stampeding.*)

PATSY (*Running out*):   Hab mercy, Lawd!

OLLIE (*Catching* DELPHINE):   Can you put me up for the night?

DELPHINE (*In wind*):   What yuh say?

OLLIE: Can you put me up in the Big House for the night?

[8] DELPHINE: Ah guess ah have t'.

(*Exit all.*)

[9] (*Blackout.*)

⁶ Joshuah realizes he has done all that he can do, the matter is settled and hopeless. He stands silent through all the attacks on Ollie and Ollie's defense controlling merely futile emotion of disappointment and anger. When Ollie appeals to Joshuah, with a mighty effort he restrains the outburst of anger that wells up within him, and without looking at Ollie or answering, he turns off in the direction of the sawmill with the curt command, "Come on some of yuh, gimmer er hand." He is oblivious to the breaking storm.

⁷ The humanity of Setlow appears: feeling as he does about Ollie at that moment, he remembers him as a fellow man who must be sheltered.

⁸ The scene ends in the blast of the storm and a whirl of excitement, in which Delphine acquiesces to putting Ollie up for the night in the Big House.

⁹ The end of Scene One is a sudden dramatic effect and the sound of the storm should rise after Delphine's last line to a moment of fury and be cut off abruptly by the blackout.

ACT II
  Scene II

[1] *The scene is the same and unchanged, except that growing cotton plants may be seen at the edge of the field by the forge. Nearby the women are singing. It is a bright sunny morning, six weeks later.*

WOMEN (*Singing Off-Right*):

"Oh, sometimes Ahm tosst'd 'n driven
Sometimes Ah don't know whar t' roam.
Ah's heard of a city called Heabem
Ahm tryin t' make it mah home . . . (*The women bearing hoes and with their skirts tucked around the waist, enter to cross and go off Up-Left—still singing*)
"True Believer, Ahm strivin t' make it mah home . . ." etc.

(JOSHUAH *emerges from the cotton house to come down and go up to forge to get his sledge hammer, as the singing dies down in the distance*)

ELLEN (*Entering and greeting him*):   Hello, Joshuah. Looks like we're in fer another hot one. (*She picks out a light-weight hoe*)

JOSHUAH: Ah reckon yuh can't git way from it this time of year —but if we kin jes scape er drought, everything goin be fine 'n dandy.

(Exit within.)

GEORGANA (*Entering Up-Left with* ROXANNA, *bearing a big basket between them*):   Good mawnin, Miss Ellen. How's yuh today?

ELLEN: Ahm jes fine. How de catch?

GEORGANA: We got one whopper. (*Displays fish*) Jes look at him.

[2] ELLEN: Lawd, he's big as er hoss. But, Roxanna, how's Delphine this mawnin?

ROXANNA: She ain't got no more fever, 'n she been settin up de last couple of days. But she still can't keep er thing on her stomach.

GEORGANA: Miz Patsy say, she think unbeknownst t' her, Delphine bout swallowed er fly!

ELLEN: Er upset stomach is er terrible thing. (*Going*) But if she settin up, it means she gettin better, 'n das de main thing!

(Exit.)

Act II, Scene II

[1] Scene Two opening on a bright summer morning with the cotton plants growing, the women singing as they go off with their hoes, and Georgana and Roxanna coming in with their fish, returns, for all the setbacks, to the progress and hope of an indomitable group of people. Joshuah is cheery and confident, prepared by proposal of marriage to Delphine for realization of his own highest personal hope of a wife whom he loves and a home. The entire opening of the scene prepares an ironic contrast for the reversal in Delphine's disclosure.

[2] Delphine's illness, probably from emotional disturbance, helps to keep sympathy for her and gives pathos to her position with Joshuah, as does her song.

Patsy's suspicion of the truth about Delphine gives the audience a foreshadowing ahead of Joshuah of the cause of Delphine's reaction to his proposal of marriage.

ROXANNA (*Getting basket*): Oh me! (*Seeing* LEM *Off-Right*)
Yonder go Lem. Looking like somebody in de hands of de slave
trader.

(*Exit together, Up-Right.*)

(*In a moment,* DELPHINE *enters, singing sadly, and her move-
movements show the results of her long illness.*)

² DELPHINE (*Singing as she drags herself down to sit beneath oak*):
"Sometimes Ah feel like er motherless chile
Oh sometimes Ah feel like er motherless chile
Sometimes Ah feel like er motherless chile
A long way from home! (JOSHUAH *emerges on porch to halt there
gazing upon her sympathetically, but she does not see him*)
"A long way from home!
A long way from home!" (*She flicks a tear from her eye*)

JOSHUAH (*Coming down, hesitantly*): Delphine. (*Startling her,
he joins her quickly*) Lawd, Delphine, forgive me for mah bad jedg-
ment—don't git up. Ah heard yuh singin 'n Ah was so glad t' know
yuh back on yore feet, Ah didn't stop to think—But lemme look at
yuh! (*Admiringly*) De same lil ole Delphine—cept for them tears
yuh ain't changed er lick! Lawd, how Ah do rejoice t' see yuh.
(*Going up to forge to get box*) But wait. (*Returning*) Here, put yore
feet on this box. Yuh oughter have er pillow. Reckon Ah could git
yuh one from de Big House?

DELPHINE: No, thank yuh, Joshuah. Ahm all right.

JOSHUAH: Den rair back cuz Ah got sompen t' tell yuh can't
wait.

DELPHINE (*Starting up*): No, please!

JOSHUAH: Oh, yes. Ah been holdin back too long already!

DELPHINE (*Rising and crossing Right*): No! No!

³ JOSHUAH (*Following her*): As Gawd is my jedge, Delphine,
Ah love yuh pass all understandin. 'N Ah want t' take yuh for mah
lovin wife!

DELPHINE (*Sinking on bench by porch, despairingly*): Oh,
Joshuah!

⁴ JOSHUAH: Ah know yuh think Ah don't trust yuh, Delphine.
But b'lieve me; if yuh seed me drawin back, it wuzn't for no lack
of faith in yuh as er woman. Ah wuz jes skeered t' try t' run gainst
nature. Ah figured yuh wuz titled t' a man yore own aige. But ever

³ Joshuah's words of proposal are formal and trite, quite out of character for his usual manner of speech, and absolutely natural.

⁴ Joshuah's whole speech of excusing himself for holding back, protesting his trust in Delphine, and offering what he feels in himself as justification for asking her to marry him becomes an irony in retrospect by the end of the scene.

since yuh been sick, there ain't been a night passed Ah ain't been
under yore window, hopin 'n prayin for yuh 'n looking de facks in
de face. There ain't many men livin got mah strength. They's few
'n far between got more *git up* erbout em. De ladder jes ain't been
built Ah can't climb. All Ah axe yuh is jes put yore trust in me 'n
say "Yes." Will yuh?

DELPHINE (*Regretfully*):   It's too late, Joshuah. De boat we
might-er caught done come 'n gone!

JOSHUAH (*Puzzled*):   Ah don't understand—? Yuh mean yuh
love somebody else?

DELPHINE (*Whispering*):   No, Joshuah.

JOSHUAH: Den what yuh talkin bout?

DELPHINE (*In tears*):   Don't ask me, Joshuah. Just forget everything. (*She sobs*)

JOSHUAH: Here, here—don't cry like tha. 'N don't try t' gimme
no answer now. Yuh been er very sick woman. (*Cheerfully*) In er
nother week or so yuh goin be yore oldsef ergain!

DELPHINE (*Firmly*):   Joshuah, soon's Ah git better Ahm goin
erway.

JOSHUAH (*Shocked*):   Lawd, Delphine! Now Ah know yuh
need t' git back in bed.

DELPHINE: Ah's got t' go, Joshuah.

JOSHUAH: But whar?—Oh, this don't make sense.—Whar yuh
go?

DELPHINE: "Whar" don't matter.

JOSHUAH (*Floundering*):   But, Delphine, is Ahm someway t'
blame?

DELPHINE: Yuh ain't got nothin t' do wid it, Joshuah.

JOSHUAH: Den tell me.

DELPHINE: Don't ask me, Joshuah. Just forget everything.

JOSHUAH: Ah got t' know!

DELPHINE: Yuh make it hard for me, Joshuah. Yuh force me.

JOSHUAH: But Ah's titled t' some idea!

DELPHINE: All right, Joshuah. Yuh want t' know. Well . . .
Ahma have er . . . baby.

JOSHUAH (*Stunned*):   Great Gawd, no!

DELPHINE: Ah knowed Ah wuz goin hurt yuh.

[5] JOSHUAH (*Sick*):   Phumph! Phumph! Phumph! (*Silence*) It can't be so. It can't be, Delphine!

DELPHINE: It's de truth, jes de same.

JOSHUAH (*After a moment*):   Yuh mind tellin me who de Daddy?

DELPHINE: No.

JOSHUAH: Den who?

DELPHINE: Ollie.

JOSHUAH (*Stabbed*):   Phumph! . . . But Ah might er knowed it . . . (*He shakes his head, sadly*) When this happen?

DELPHINE: De night of de storm.

JOSHUAH (*Raging inwardly*):   Ah oughter kill him. Ah oughter take him in these hands 'n crush every bone in his yaller body!

DELPHINE (*Quietly*):   Tha wouldn't set nothin t' rights.

JOSHUAH: Tell me. What he say bout it?

DELPHINE: He donno.

JOSHUAH (*Incredulously*):   Yuh ain't told him?

DELPHINE (*Coldly*):   Ah'd rather depart 'n go t' hell!

JOSHUAH: Den yuh don't want him—?

DELPHINE: Ah wouldn't have him now if Ah loved him!

JOSHUAH: Yuh don't have t' lie t' me, Delphine.

DELPHINE: Ah ain't.

JOSHUAH (*Cynically*):   Phey!

DELPHINE: It's de truth. He come in mah room—

JOSHUAH (*Sarcastically*):   'N cose he jes overpowered yuh!

DELPHINE (*Preoccupiedly*):   Ah made a fool of myself. He got me all mixed up. Strong ez Ah know mahsef, Ah think maybe somehow he bout gin me er dose of love powder.

JOSHUAH (*Snorting*):   Yuh must *think* Ahma fool!

DELPHINE (*Sincerely*):   Ahm jes tellin yuh like it happened.

JOSHUAH (*Sharply*):   Don't Ah know yuh could er screamed!

DELPHINE (*Pained*):   Oh, Joshuah, can't yuh understand. (*Her anguish rises to a wail*) Ah didn't know what t' do!

JOSHUAH (*Bitterly*):   Eh, hey! (*Silence*) But Ah never did have no chance wid yuh.

DELPHINE: Yuh hate me now, don't yuh? Yuh despise me!

JOSHUAH (*Preoccupiedly*):   Ah was right from de first. But Ah ain't de first ole man sot his heart on er young woman. Every

[5] Joshuah is an heroic figure and convincingly so because of his normal human failures, strong among which and completely natural and believable are his reactions of stunned sickness, rage against Ollie, and bitterness toward Delphine when the great moment of fulfillment of hope for which he has prepared himself is destroyed by her confession.

snaggled-toothed dog ever lived t' run cross er bone he couldn't chaw, come up ergainst de same thing!

DELPHINE: Ah's hurt yuh t' yore soul!

JOSHUAH (*Bitterly*):   How else yuh speck me t' be?—Ah thot yuh was sompen. But yuh had t' throw yoresef erway on er man who, Ah bet mah life, think he's too good for yuh t' even wash his drawers!—Yuh, who everybody been braggin on as er woman of cha-cter! Yuh who was so busy tryin t' raise yor sister up right! (*Sharply*) Er fine example yuh's turned out t' be—Yuh! Nothin but er wanton woman!

⁶ DELPHINE (*Angrily*):   Now jes er minute, Joshuah. Yuh may think yuh got cause t' be hurt. But that don't give yuh de right t' try t' spit in mah face. Maybe Ah am wanton-hearted, n' it twarn't no love powder—though Gawd knows sompen made me sick enough t' die! But yuh ain't neither kith nor kin t' me. Furthermore, yuh had yore chance, 'n yuh can't deny Ah had er right t' be skeered when nobody don't know what's goin happen today or tomorrow, n' me wid Roxanna t' depend on me.—Anyway, like it stand, whatever mistake Ah made is tween me 'n Gawd, 'n it's none of yore bizness!

JOSHUAH (*Crushed*):   Ah guess yuh right. Tain't none of mah business.

DELPHINE: Now Ahm goin back t' de house. But Ah jes want t' remind yuh. Ah told yuh Ah plan t' leave here, soon's Ahm strong enough. So yuh can set yore mind at rest fars de danger of mah settin er bad example is concerned. (*Softening*) On de other hand, Ah want yuh t' know Ah ain't got no hard feelins gainst yuh for what yuh said. Ah know how Ah'd feel . . . (*Her eyes brimming*) if things had been de other way round . . . (*Clutching his arm and leaning against his shoulder, as he stands like a rock braving the storm*) Ah want yuh t' know, too. Ah still think yuh's de finest man Ah's ever known!

(*Turning, she goes out Up-Right and he eases himself down to sit focused in pain and regret.*)

⁷ (*Blackout.*)

[6] This is Delphine's scene. She has been young and unformed, with a fine basis of character, but susceptible to uncertainties in her placement of values. She has her moment of human weakness, and nothing need be added to her own self-analysis and defense as she blazes out at Joshuah. At this moment her character crystallizes and she becomes the woman who will die with Joshuah at the end. There is self-respect in the spirit of her anger. Clarity of decision and self-determination follows, and then the fairness to Joshuah, her understanding, and her regret. Finally, the simple splendor of her farewell, "Ah still think yuh's de finest man Ah's ever known!" Delphine's judgment after the bitter things Joshuah has said to her leaves the audience in identification with his pain as the scene ends.

[7] Although Scene Two has no reversal in the fortunes of the group the reversal of hope in the personal story of Delphine and Joshuah gives it unity of mood with the course of the scenes of Act Two.

ACT II
  Scene III

¹ *The scene is the same, only now the soft tone of fall lends a warmth and rich sense of harvest. It is October and the Freedmen are ginning their cotton, baling it, and setting it outside for shipment to the mainland. Through earth and industry they have reaped a bountiful crop, and an unsuppressable joy bespeaks their realization that they have in their hands now, complete and undeniable, the economic means which can guarantee their new life.*

EDGAR (*With others at step of cotton house*):   Yuh all know what Ahm-a do soon's we sell de cotton?

EMANUEL: Ah bet Ah can guess!

EDGAR (*Enthusiastically*):   Ahm gwine t' Sawanny 'n buy Ellen er dress, 'n Ahm-a git me er new suit of clothes—For once in mah life Ahm-a see whut er new suit feels like.

LEM (*Excitedly*):   Ah jes want t' git t' Sawanny 'n see de sights!

ROSS: So some of dem tricksters kin git yore money, huh?

JOSHUAH (*Within cotton house*):   Hey, men. Here she comes!

ROSS (*As a bale of cotton plummets onto the porch, and the men jockey it off and into line with other bales*):   How many more, Joshuah?

JOSHUAH (*Emerging on porch, and wiping sweat from his brow*): Thas de las of em. How they look t' yuh all?

ROSS: Jes like pure white gold!

LEM (*Up-Center, as they set bale along side others there*):   Hey, everybody. Yonder Brer Setlow 'n Owens—'n dey got Ollie wid 'em!

EDGAR: Ollie—?

JOSHUAH: De stinkin rat.—It can't be.

LEM (*As* JOSHUAH *joins them*):   No? Look yonder.

PELTIER (*To* JOSHUAH):   Why yuh call him tha, Joshuah?

JOSHUAH (*Coming down*):   Oh, don't pay me no mind.

SETLOW (*Outside, approaching, triumphantly*):   "Lift up yore head, O ye Gates! Be ye lift up, ye everlastin doors, 'n de King of Glory shall come in!"

LEM (*Excitedly*):   They got good news!

SETLOW (*Entering with* OLLIE—*going on joyfully*):   "Oh bless ouah Gawd, ye people, 'n make de voice of His praise t' be heard!"

Act II, Scene III

[1] The opening of Scene Three in the warm autumn tones and sunlight, the bustle of handling the cotton bales, and the men working happily while they discuss in high spirits what they will do with the money from the cotton is the full picture of the promise held out before the sharp turn in the course of the scene in the direction of catastrophe.

LEM: What's de good news—'n whar de cotton agent?

SETLOW (*Ignoring him*):   "For Thou O Gawd has proved us: Thou has tried us as silver is tried—"

JOSHUAH (*Impatiently*):   Deed. But speak!

(OLLIE *looks on amused.*)

SETLOW (*Undauntedly*):   "Thou has caused men t' ride ovah ouah heads; we went through fiah 'n water, but Thou broughtest us into a wealthy place!"

EDGAR (*Boiling*):   Ollie, what is this?

² OLLIE: The land is yours.

ALL: No!

SETLOW: "Yes, de sparrow has found a house, 'n de swallow er nest for herself where she may lay her young!"

ROSS: Great Gawd from Whom all blessins flow! It can't be true!

OLLIE: But it is. Congress has passed the Civil Rights Bill with the Stevens' Amendment, which gives you the land!

³ EDGAR (*Waltzing with* LEM):   Shout hallelujah!

LEM (*Breaking away*):   Ahm gwine carry de news! (*Running off with a shout*) Hy, Delphine—Miz Sarah! We got de lan! We got de lan!

JOSHUAH (*Gazing across the field*):   Ouah lan! Gawd bless yuh, Thad Stevens!

TAGGERT: Joshuah, this calls for er celebration.

PELTIER: Yeah, Joshuah. How bout er barbecue wid music from town?

⁴ JOSHUAH: Ah reckon we'll have t' do sompen—(*Suddenly remembering*) By the way, Brer Setlow, what bout de Cotton Agent.

SETLOW: Us couldn't git none.

EDGAR: All de agents in Sawanny 'n yuh couldn't git *one*?

SETLOW: They say they ain't buyin less de Yanks say so.

ROSS (*Puzzled*):   Ollie, what yuh make of this?

OLLIE: The agents claim all Freedmen must have a permit to sell.

EDGAR: Well, Ah'll be damn!

JOSHUAH (*To* SETLOW, *avoiding* OLLIE *like the plague*):   Did you check wid Cap'n Bryant?

SETLOW (*Uneasily*):   Cap'n Bryant ain't here no more.

² Ollie does not know of the consequences of his wrong action toward Delphine, or that Joshuah knows, and continues in his sincere identification with the freedmen's welfare, now that there is no threat in it to his own interests. He is happy to be the bearer of good news.

³ The freedmen are all prepared in their high spirits over their crop for jubilation in response to the news of the passage of the bill granting them the land. This is the crowning moment of glory before the reversal.

⁴ An ominous note about the cotton agent in the midst of the rejoicing—prepares for the setback in the following scene.

JOSHUAH: No—?

SETLOW: Yes, Suh.

[5] OLLIE (*Volunteering*):   Captain Bryant has been removed.

ROSS: Ah don't like this.

JOSHUAH (*To* SETLOW):   But why?

SETLOW: Gawd knows—.

TAGGERT (*Angrily*):   Ah bet mah head gainst anybody's rope, this heah's some of dis President Johnson's doins!

EDGAR: Yeah! Tha Tennessee hillbilly settin in de saddle ridin high!

TAGGERT: Sure. Every time dey call er Reb's name, it's "Pardoned," sezee!

[6] EMANUEL (*Up-Center looking off*):   Joshuah, look yonder! . . . Soldiers!

JOSHUAH: Soldiers? (*They all plunge up to look*)

SETLOW: Dis don't make sense . . .

PELTIER (*Looking Off-Left*):   Joshuah, Ah don't like de looks of this.

JOSHUAH (*He gauges the situation outside for a moment, then in sudden decision, going*):   Come on. Git yore guns!

(*Swiftly they disappear. Shortly there's the sound and then the appearance of a group of white Union soldiers.*)

SERGEANT (*Commandingly, as they march in, bringing them to a halt near forge*):   Squads, halt! At ease. (*He salutes* CAPTAIN STEWART, *as the latter,* BURKHARDT *and* SAUNDERS *pass through the ranks*) Any further orders, Sir?

STEWART (*Coming down*):   Summon the Freedmen.

[7] BURKHARDT: Never mind, Captain. (*He goes to angle-iron*) This will bring them. (*He strikes iron, then turning indicates cotton*) Just look at that cotton! By rights every pound of it is mine!

STEWART (*Pointedly*):   There, Mr. Burkhardt, you put it in the nutshell!

BURKHARDT: I don't think I quite understand you, Captain Stewart.

STEWART: How do you planters expect me to co-operate with you, when you persist in such an attitude?

BURKHARDT (*Laughing, he turns to inspect his property*):   Oh,

[5] The removal of Captain Bryant is another ominous note, preparing for Captain Stewart.

[6] With the announcement of soldiers coming and Joshuah's order to get their guns the scene breaks sharply into dramatic action. The stage is empty briefly, the soldiers enter, and the colloquy between Captain Stewart and Mr. Burkhardt follows with the tension for the audience of expectation of the return of the freedmen with their guns.

[7] The return of Mr. Burkhardt and the question of what would happen then has been repeatedly foreshadowed through the play.

Mr. Burkhardt is introduced on the arrogance of forestalling Captain Stewart and summoning the freedmen in the old way of bringing in the field-hands. In all that follows he is immovably in the grip of his old ways of thinking. Captain Stewart seems to be representing the freedmen's interests against Burkhardt, in conflict with him, yet the entire course of the conversation is so at odds with the news Ollie has brought as to raise question and tension for the audience.

don't pay any attention to my remark, Captain. It's not easy to adjust overnight, you know.

STEWART: But you're not even trying to adjust. That's what's making my task so hard. The Freedmen sense it. That's why they're so intractable.

BURKHARDT: Oh, I wouldn't worry about the niggers. We know how to handle them.

STEWART (*Dryly*):   As slaves, perhaps.

BURKHARDT (*Kicking side of cotton house support*):   You don't change an ear of corn by removing the shucks.

STEWART: But you can change a man by removing his chains.

BURKHARDT (*Easily*):   That, Captain Stewart, is debatable.

STEWART: You may think so. But I think you're in for a big awakening.

BURKHARDT (*Hardening*):   Just how do you mean that?

STEWART (*Critically*):   Your entire policy is short-sighted. Take this cabal you've formed yourselves into, for example: This business of fixing the Freedmen's wages at five dollars per month. It's foolhardy to think you will be able to get them to work for it.

BURKHARDT: I see the niggers have been lying to you, Captain.

STEWART: The Bureau has sufficient proof. On the Mainland you're offering them six cents per day. That's peonage!

BURKHARDT (*Annoyed*):   I've no idea what you're talking about. But I'll say this. Knowing how lazy and shiftless the niggers are, he'll be a lucky planter who can break even at the rate.

STEWART: I can see that by that crop over there, which you were praising a moment ago.

BURKHARDT: That crop's an accident.

STEWART: Perhaps . . . However, it seems a good indication of the value of sound policy.

BURKHARDT (*Darkly*):   Such as confiscation—?

STEWART: I hold, Mr. Burkhardt, with your Alex Stephens: Your conduct toward the Freedmen should be kind, magnanimous, just! Then you may hope to organize them into a class of trustworthy laborers.

BURKHARDT: Alex's a dreamer.

STEWART: He recognizes the urgency of co-operating with the Bureau.

BURKHARDT (*Coolly*):   Your Freedmen's Bureau, Captain Stewart—if I may be permitted a moment of plain speaking—is nothing but a devilish device to control and humiliate us before our former slaves. It's frankly, an alien power!

[8] (JOSHUAH *and others enter—the men bearing arms.*)

STEWART (*Seeing them*):   Who's Joshuah?

JOSHUAH: Me, Suh.

STEWART: I'm Captain Stewart of the Bureau, and this is Mr. John Burkhardt, owner of the island. (*Attempting to flatter him*) He was just remarking how well you've done this year.

(*Rest of the women crowd in.*)

BURKHARDT (*Suavely*):   I don't see how you did it—and all by yourselves! But I can see we're going to get along—(*Drawing batch of papers from his breast pocket*) I've called you so you can sign these contracts—

JOSHUAH (*Hostilely*):   Contracts—for what?

BURKHARDT (*Easily*):   For you and your people to work the land.

JOSHUAH (*Glancing at his people*):   This heah's de first time Ah ever heard of folks needing er contract t' wuk thar own lan!

SAUNDERS (*Smugly*):   Ah tole yuh, Cuffee, this wasn't yore land.

JOSHUAH: Yuh hush, Man. We don't keer nothin bout what yuh tole nobody. This is ouah lan.

CROWD: Yeah. By Gawd! Yuh damn tootin!

JOSHUAH (*To* SAUNDERS, *indirectly*):   'N if yuh know what's good fur yuh, yuh better git on off this ilun 'n don't come back disturbin us in ouah homes no more.

SAUNDERS: By Gawd, Captain, are you goin stand thar 'n let this nigger insult me—a white man!

STEWART: I advised you, gentlemen, to let me handle things.

BURKHARDT: All right, Captain, You explain to them.

(OLLIE *enters.*)

PELTIER: We don't need no splainin!

EDGAR (*Ejaculating*):   They think we don't know de Gubment done passed de Stevens Bill—Heh!

SETLOW: Answer not a fool accordin to his folly.

[9] STEWART (*Sharply*):   Silence. And you, Elder, save your ser-

⁸ With the entrance of Joshuah and the freedmen armed there are two hostile forces on the stage. The soldiers are in ranks but at ease, the freedmen in an irregular group, the women in the background. Captain Stewart does not know that the news of the passage by Congress of the Stevens Bill has reached the island. References to Mr. Burkhardt as owner of the island and the producing of contracts to work the land are premonitory, but both the freedmen and the audience are in the dark.

⁹ The overwhelming reversal breaks, the President has vetoed the Bill, the land is ordered restored to the former owner. Captain Stewart proceeds to execute his function, hoping to carry out smoothly the limited arrangements for the welfare of the freedmen that have been placed in his hands. The freedmen with the cotton bales they have themselves produced behind them are now without need of exhortation from Joshuah, as fixed in their new ideas as Mr. Burkhardt in the old.

mon for Sunday. (*Shifting*) It's true there was such a Bill. But not any more. The President has vetoed it. He has thrown it out.

EDGAR (*Sarcastically*):   Heah yuh tell it; Gawd done put de fiah out in hell!

STEWART (*Glancing sharply at him, he turns to others*):   The President felt the Bill was a mistake. I'm not here to lie to you. General Howard sent me here to represent your interest. He is my superior, and the President told him to make arrangements to restore the land to its former owners . . . I know you expected the Government to give you the land. But that is not to be. It's not my duty to question why. All I can do is tell you, if you want to remain here, you must come to an agreement with Mr. Burkhardt, the rightful owner. Those contracts in his hand were drawn up by General Howard himself to safeguard your interest. You've already shown yourselves to be wise and industrious people. Under the terms of the contracts, if you remain the same, in three years you will be privileged to purchase your own forty acres if you so desire. Do you understand? Is it clear to all of you?

JOSHUAH: We already got this lan!

PELTIER: Yeah! (*Banging the butt of his gun down*) By Gawd!

PATSY: He ain't talkin t' me!

EDGAR: 'N nobody else. He got t' tell a taller tale den dat t' buck mah eyes!

[10] OLLIE (*Stepping forward*):   Just a moment, Folks. I think you're making a mistake—

JOSHUAH (*Ominously*):   Yuh keep out of this!

OLLIE: But if President Johnson has vetoed the Bill—

JOSHUAH (*Menacingly*):   Ah say mind yore own bizness!

OLLIE (*Ignoring him to appeal to others*):   It's your welfare, Folks—you can't just take the land—

JOSHUAH (*Grappling him from behind*):   Damn your stinkin soul!

OLLIE (*In pain*):   Look out! You're breaking my back!

SETLOW: Brer Joshuah! Brer Joshuah! You'll kill him!

OLLIE (*Desperately*):   Help!

ROSS: Joshuah! Turn him loose.

JOSHUAH (*Easing up*):   Ahma turn yuh loose. But if yuh ever

[10] In the midst of tension when Ollie innocently tries to intrude with what he sees as reasonable advice the restraint under which Joshuah has been holding himself in the presence of Ollie snaps and there is the sudden flare of violence.

put yore foot on this ilun ergin, Ahma mash yuh t' er yaller pulp!
(*Shoving him*) Now git—fore Ah change mah mind!

SETLOW (*As* OLLIE *reels off Up-Left*):   Yuh too hard on him,
Joshuah.

[11] JOSHUAH: Tha buzzard! He don't mean us no good. Take
mah word for it. (*Turning to* STEWART) Ez Ah wuz sayin t' yuh,
Suh. Gen'l Sherman give us his word: de Gubment wuz goin give
us er clear title t' this lan. We donno nothin bout yuh 'n this Gen'l
Howard bizness, 'n we ain't goin sign no contracts.

STEWART (*Coldly*):   You've just demonstrated what sort of man
you are. No one can reason with you. But I warn you, violence
won't get you anywhere in this case!

JOSHUAH: Ahm bankin on mah rights, 'n so's mah people!

STEWART (*Sharply*):   You're misleading your people! The Government is not going to give you the land. It is not going to do so
because the planters have lost so heavily in life and property during
the rebellion, while you have gained so much in your emancipation!

EDGAR: So us don't git nothin cept wuk?—Well, damn such
freedom ez dat!

JOSHUAH (*Angrily*):   We'll still be slaves till every man can
raise his own bale of cotton 'n say: "This is mine!"

ROSS (*As silence ensues*):   Ah thot all de Yanks wuz wid us.

PATSY (*Shrewdly*):   Tha ain't no Yank. Thas jes some Reb dey
done dressed up in Blue 'n brought here t' lie t' us!

STEWART (*Sharply*):   You know better!

JOSHUAH: Cap'n, yuh say yuh's er Yank. In yore heart who yuh
think is de real owners of this lan. Dem who been placed here by
de Gubment, or de planters who been fightin gainst de Gubment?

[12] STEWART (*Angrily*):   Bad soldiers must have misled you!

PATSY: Yuh better not let Gen'l Sherman heah yuh say tha.

STEWART (*Shouting*):   Enough! (*Catching himself*) Either sign
those contracts or get off the island!

JOSHUAH (*Ominously*):   'N spose we tell yuh, us ain't goin do
neither one?

STEWART: You'll sign all right. (*Warningly*) And if you commit any outrage, the Bureau will punish you with the utmost se-
verity!

[11] Joshuah turns from ejecting Ollie, in his physical strength unruffled by the effort, and calmly but firmly takes up the argument with Captain Stewart. His manifestation of violence, inexplicable, of course, on reasonable grounds to Captain Stewart, has damaged his position and Captain Stewart becomes more peremptory in consequence. Joshuah aroused to anger takes the stand which allows of no compromise: "We still be slaves till every man can raise his own bale of cotton 'n say: 'This is mine!' "

[12] Captain Stewart is young and caught in a situation too difficult for him. He loses control, becomes arbitrary, tries to carry the situation by assertion of authority, and finds himself against an immovable force.

JOSHUAH (*Quietly*):   Well, yuh might ez well git it straight. We ain't goin sign!

STEWART (*Feeling it a personal affront*):   You defy my authority?

JOSHUAH (*Quietly*):   We's free. Yuh got no 'thority over us.

STEWART (*After a moment*):   Have you finished?

JOSHUAH (*Quietly*):   Ez far ez *words* is consarned!

STEWART (*Ignoring challenge*):   Mr. Burkhardt. Use the lid on that barrel for them to sign. (*To others*) And you, Freedmen. Form a line up there. (*Seeing no man move*) I command you to line up there!

SETLOW (*Breaking ominous pause, repeating with quiet resolution*):   "Gawd is ouah refuge 'n strength, a very present hep in de time of trouble—"

STEWART (*Interposing, sharply*):   I command you to fall in line!

SETLOW: "Therefore will not we fear, though de earf be removed, though de mountains be carried into de midst of de sea!"

[13] STEWART (*Turning to Soldiers*):   Attention! (*The women break for cover, along with* BURKHARDT *and* SAUNDERS, *as the Soldiers obey*) Port Arms!

JOSHUAH (*Meanwhile*):   Fall in Guards!

(*In a flash the Freedmen square off for battle. Grimly the two groups stand at bay.* STEWART *seems to be searching for a sign of weakness.* JOSHUAH *is resolute and alert, with a sense of come what may.*)

STEWART (*In a quandary, but finally capitulating, commands his men*):   Fall back!

JOSHUAH (*As the Soldiers back Off-Left,* STEWART *covering their retreat, his back toward them protectingly*):   Steady, men. Hold yore fiah! (*His revolver in one hand and the other outstretched, he wards off the danger of an unwitting blast on their part.*)

[14] (*Exit Soldiers.*)

LEM (*In a moment*):   Dey runnin for de boat!

EDGAR: Joshuah, must we crack down?

JOSHUAH: No. Let em go.

SETLOW: Yeah. 'N let de will of Gawd prevail!

(*Blackout.*)

¹³ Captain Stewart has recourse to a show of force and is met in kind. The scene breaks into a drawn battle-line, the soldiers on one side, the armed freedmen drawn up opposite. This is the crisis of the play. It is a major turning point: the hopes and progress of the freedmen have reached their apex, from here the movement is one of accumulating forces against them. It is a point of choice, of redecision at a more serious and final level. The freedmen are confronted by war and, as Joshuah had foreshadowed, they choose war. What they are confronted with, and their choice, steps up the dramatic action to a higher pitch of rising tension from here to the end.

¹⁴ The soldiers retreat. There is for the moment relaxation of tension.

ACT II
Scene IV

[1] *A week ensues, during which the Freedmen, facing inactivity and their own sense of powerlessness to affect their bitter situation, have begun to exemplify a sense of high dudgeon. Although it is never quite successful in transcending their basic capacity for patience, it emerges, expressing itself in sharp, explosive outbursts and attempts to fix the blame for the adverse turn of affairs. Beyond this mood, the only noticeable change is the presence of a barricade, which they have erected by using the bales of cotton.*

EDGAR (*Armed as others around him, indignantly exploding*): All dis settin round like er yard full of chickens wid de pip: (*Barking*) Daddy Setlow, how long we got t' wait?

LEM: Thas what Ah wanter know!

SETLOW: Who can tell de ways of Gawd?—Be patient, Boy!

EDGAR: Damn patience. Damn hit t' hell 'n back!

PELTIER: Ah blame dis Peoria Bradley.

TAGGERT: Thas whar yuh wrong. Peoria Bradley's de only real man we got mongst de Colored in Sawanny.

EDGAR: He done had er whole week. 'N heah we is wid cotton nuff t' fill up anybody's warehouse!

LEM: Yeah. Look like he could-er done found *one* agent.

WEBSTER (*Outside, calling*):   Hello, in there.—How do you get in?

PELTIER (*At barricade*):   Come round de end thar.

LEM: Das Webster, ain't it?

TAGGERT: Yeah. He come see bout what Joshuah done t' Ollie.

EDGAR: If he know like Ah know, he better git on back cross tha water!

WEBSTER (*Entering*):   Where's Mister Tain?

PELTIER: Joshuah—? He be here in er minute.

WEBSTER: Perhaps one of you can inform me—Why is it, in spite of all I've done for you folks, you allowed my son to be assaulted?

EDGAR: He spoke up for de white folks, thas why.

Act II, Scene IV

[1] After the sharp rise into a boldly dramatic conflict at the end of the preceding scene, Scene Four is leaden-hearted. There is the tension of armed waiting throughout for what may happen, but nothing happens except the discouraging adverse turn on the attempt to sell the cotton. The work of the harvest is over. The clearing at the forge faces the boat landing, and the men are standing and sitting about within the barricade of cotton bales on guard. The women have gathered where their men are.

(JOSHUAH *enters Up-Right.*)

WEBSTER: Isn't it true Mister Tain was jealous over some girl here?

LEM (*Ejaculating*):   Jealous—thar now!

JOSHUAH (*Coming down*):   Ah'll answer tha mahsef, Suh.

WEBSTER: Well—?

²JOSHUAH (*Going*):   Come on wid me. Ah'll splain things.

WEBSTER (*Arresting him*):   Explain here. If my son is wrong, speak right out. I'm not interested in having anything hidden.

JOSHUAH (*Eyeing him*):   Yuh seem t' be sure of yoresef ez er Jersey bull.

WEBSTER (*Pointedly*):   Aren't you?

JOSHUAH (*Coolly*):   Ah's seed too many of em fall in de hands of de butcher!

WEBSTER: If you think you can bluff me, Mister Tain—

JOSHUAH (*Catching his arm*):   Awh, come on, Man—quit actin like er fool!

WEBSTER (*Resisting*):   Why can't you answer me here?

JOSHUAH (*Forcing him*):   Ah sed come on!

(WEBSTER, *sputtering some protest, is drawn off Up-Left.*)

EDGAR (*Laughing*):   Heh! Ah thot thar was goin be hell here t'reckly!

³ SARAH (*Sharply*):   Tha Ollie is er snake. 'N if Ah was Joshuah, Ah'd told his Pappy so right fore everybody. Ah'd er took him down er peg or two!

TAGGERT: How yuh know so much, old lady?

SARAH (*Indignant*):   Ollie ain't no earfly good. Ah know what Ahm talkin bout, ain't Ah, Ant Dosia?

DOSIA (*Sharply*):   Ah ain't in tha mess. So just leave me out.

SARAH: But yuh know Ah know what Ahm talkin bout.

ELLEN (*Sensing undercurrent*):   What is this, Miss Sarah?

PATSY: Dey got sompen up thar sleeve.

ELLEN: What is it, Miss Sarah. Come on 'n tell us?

SARAH (*Amused*):   Ask Ant Dosia.

DOSIA (*Sharply*):   Ah told yuh As wuzn't in this.

LEM (*Like the others, deeply intrigued*):   Oh, Mammy, go on 'n tell it!

SETLOW (*Warningly*):   If yuh all do know sompen, Ah'd advise yuh t' keep it t' yoresefs.

[2] Joshuah is created convincingly in *Our Lan'* as a leader and a man who rises into heroic stature because he is created first of all simply as a fine man with a fullness of revelation through small occasions as well as large. The episode with Mr. Webster is such an occasion. He is self-possessed, with complete freedom from pettiness. He retains respect and friendship for Mr. Webster, in spite of the matter of the sawmill, and he has confidence in him on the matter of Ollie if he knows the truth. He has to be a little peremptory with Mr. Webster's dignity out of his consideration for him, not to make public his son's conduct. Joshuah's character is built in such likable small touches as his friendly "Awh, come on, Man—quit actin like er fool!" as well as in the big things. Mr. Webster comes off well, too, in the outcome of the episode. In dignity and integrity, mutual respect and friendship with Joshuah, his conduct is all that it should be.

[3] The women's talk of Delphine and her situation in the manifestation of human foibles helps to keep the representation of indomitable heroism in the group of freedmen down to earth and tied to homely reality. The talk is a mixture of sympathy, spitefulness, excitement over drama, curiosity, and the relaxation of gossip. In the talk on a common subject a line of individualizing characterization runs through for each member of the group. It is the godly Setlow who rebukes the women—unheeded. It is the impulsive Sarah who is most spiteful, yet exclaims in contrition when Roxanna bursts into tears and runs out. The kindly Patsy is wide-eyed. Large comfortable Ant Dosia enjoys her importance as possessed of most information. The sequence serves to build out the process of waiting which is the basis of Scene Four, it covers the off-stage period for Joshuah and Mr. Webster, and in its simple, ordinary humanity it adds poignancy to the tragic fate which follows so soon.

SARAH (*Darkly*):   De truth goin out jes de same—Mother Nature goin see t' tha.

PATSY: Sarah, yuh can't mean what Ahm thinkin?

SARAH: Ah do if what Ant Dosia say is true.

DOSIA (*Exclaiming, though she too is secretly enjoying the drama*):   Yuh all hear this woman. Yuh witness!

SARAH: Yuh mean t' sit thar, Ant Dosia, 'n deny what yuh told me t' mah face?

DOSIA: Ah ain't denyin nothing!

SARAH: Yuh act like it.

DOSIA: All Ah know de gal told me somebody tricked her. 'N thas all Ah told yuh! But yuh had no bizness openin yore leaky mouf!

SARAH: Ah ain't hidin no skunk!

PATSY (*Dumbfounded, but piqued by the scandal*):   Jesus me! Yuh all can't mean what yuh sayin.

SARAH: If it's er lie, Ant Dosia told it.

DOSIA (*Coolly*):   De gal knittin feet for sox all right.

PATSY: Go long!

DOSIA (*Nodding*):   So hep me! . . . But who de cause, Ah donno no more'n yuh. It coulder been tha Ollie, but thas more'n Ah know.

LEM: Lawdy—tha nasty rascal!

(ROXANNA *bursts into tears and runs out, Up-Right*.)

SARAH (*Contritely*):   Lawd, us forgot all bout tha chile.

(*All are silent.*)

ELLEN: But yuh know. Ah thought she had her cap set on Joshuah.

SARAH: Tha Big House pizened hussy—Joshuah wasn't good nuff for her.

GEORGANA: Yuh all wrong. Pappy ain't wanted her. Pappy ain't care nuffin bout her.

LEM (*Ruefully*):   Ain't nobody had no chance wid tha high-yaller rascal!

ELLEN: This done took all de run out er me.

PATSY: Yuh said it, chile. Anybody had er told me Delphine would come up wid her *leg broke,* Ah wouldn't er b'lieved it!

DOSIA (*Sympathetically*):   De gal say whoever twuz must-er gin her er dose of love powder.

ELLEN: Love Powder!

PATSY: Den tha mean Daddy Sykes!

SYKES (*Indignantly*):   Ah been settin heah speckin sompen like dis. Ah knowed twan't be long fore yuh all dragged me in it.

SARAH: Awh go on, yuh ole spider-cookin hellion! Yuh mixed up in it all right.

⁴ JOSHUAH (*Re-entering with* WEBSTER, *the* COTTON AGENT, *and two ragged* CONFEDERATE SOLDIERS—*the latter barefooted*):   Heah's de Agent, Folks, what Peoria Bradley done sent us.

SETLOW (*Relieved*):   Thank God.

BROKER (*Examining cotton*):   You seem t' have a pretty good crop.

JOSHUAH (*Proudly*):   Us raised fifty-two bales—Fawty of em long staple. (*He follows the broker up beyond earshot, and they begin bargaining.*)

⁵ REB. I (*Indicating barricade*):   By Gawd, Ah see yuh all really mean t' shed white blood!

EDGAR (*As he and others tense*):   So what bout it?

REB. I: What yuh gittin riled erbout? We ain't got nothin ergin yuh Cuffees.

EDGAR (*Suspiciously*):   Yuh talk like yuh wid de planters—?

REB. I: Hell! For mah part yuh can kill all de planters in de Gawd damn South!

ROSS: We ain't atter killin nobody, Reb. We jes goin keep dis lan.

REB. I: 'N Ah don't blame yuh. De Yanks ain't got no right t' go kickin yuh off de place. They oughter be heppin yuh.

REB. II (*Agreeing bitterly*):   Sure Gawd oughter. Like Ah was tellin mah wife: "They should er took de lan 'n gin it t' yuh niggers 'n us." De damn planters got everything, 'n er poor son-of-a-bitch of a white man like me 'n yuh, Hill—why, hell, we can't even light in de swamp!

⁶ WEBSTER (*Conciliatorily, following* BROKER *down*):   I think Mr. Tain understands the difficulty of your position, Sir. But why not consider it from the long-range point of view.

BROKER: How's that?

⁴ The entrance of the cotton agent gives a brief lift to the scene, expressed in Joshuah's pride in the crop, but is almost immediately truncated to the generally low pitch of the entire scene.

⁵ The brief exchange with the two Confederate soldiers gives an economic and class instead of racial significance to the problem of the freedmen, and supports Joshuah's contention of the importance of the land.

⁶ The episode with the cotton agent reveals the obstacles before the freedmen even if they can hold the land. The agent is a helpless instrument of the adverse forces involved but receives something of the bitter disappointment that weighs Joshuah down.

WEBSTER: It can hardly be to your advantage to let them crush these people. The Freedmen are going to be the main source of your business tomorrow.

BROKER: If Ah didn't know that, Ah wouldn't be here, running the risk of becoming a marked man to the planters. But at the same time, Ah've got to recognize the fact, if Ahm caught with that cotton, they'll confiscate it.

JOSHUAH (*Sharply*): Tha crop's worth seven thousand 'n eight hund'd dollars!

BROKER: But Ah've no permit! What do you want me t' do— pay yuh market prices for cotton Ah have t' smuggle?

JOSHUAH: But, Suh. Yuh can pay more'n seventeen cents!—Cotton sellin for thirty!

BROKER (*Adamant*): It's your cotton . . . Ah'll give you seventeen for the lot.

JOSHUAH: We can't do it.

BROKER (*Going*): Then the deal's off— (*To* REBS) Come on, Boys.

TAGGERT (*To* JOSHUAH): What bout de chillun—?

JOSHUAH (*Arresting* BROKER): Wait, Mister . . . (*As the* BROKER *re-joins him*) How bout takin part of de crop—say, ten bales?

BROKER (*Thoughtfully*): It won't hardly pay. But, waal, just t' make a load, Ah'll give you fifteen for five.

JOSHUAH (*Pained*): Yuh jes said seventeen.

BROKER: For the lot.

SETLOW: Thas jes given it way!

TAGGERT: De chillun got t' eat!

JOSHUAH (*To* BROKER): Make it sixteen?

BROKER: Look, Ahm only tryin' t' do you a favor. Is it a deal or ain't it?

JOSHUAH (*Coldly*): It's a deal.

WEBSTER (*As* BROKER *counts out money*): I'm sorry, Mr. Tain —and I have to go now—But about that son of mine—well I hope you won't let the matter come between us, or fail to let me know if there's anything I can do in the future.

(*Exit.*)

ACT II

JOSHUAH (*Nods, as he counts money, and the* BROKER *and his men go up to begin taking cotton*):

[7] ROSS: Looks like everywhar we turn de white folks want t' give us de worst of it.

PATSY: Ah wouldn't feel too bad bout it. We ain't never had more'n jes bout nuff t' keep body 'n soul together. 'N when yuh come t' think bout it, we still got plenty cotton left.

PELTIER (*Bitterly*):   Ah'd jes ez soon see it all sot on fiah ez t' swallow this!

EDGAR: Neermind. De baddest dog meet his match some day!

JOSHUAH: Patsy's right. We got no cause t' give up heart. All we got t' do is hold on. (*Marshalling them out, he attempts to cheer them up by raising song*)

"Hold on!

Hold on! (*Gradually the* FREEDMEN *pick up song*)

Keep yore hand on de plow

Hold on!"

(*Dimout.*)

ACT II
Scene V

[1] *The Scene is unchanged. It is the following afternoon, and* SETLOW *is guarding a batch of supplies which he and others have apparently just brought from the mainland—a huge basket with smoked hams, etc., a barrel of flour, and large bags of beans, around which the women hover.*

SETLOW (*Sharply*):   Get back yuh all. Sarah, Ah mean it now! Get way 'n let de vittals be. Ah wouldn't fool wid nothin till Joshuah comes!

SARAH: Ah was jes lookin t' see if yuh all brung a lil sompen for de chillun. Dey bout t' run Miz Libeth crazy, shut up yonder in de Big House.

TAGGERT (*Guiltily*):   Here's a lil stick of mint Ah was goin give Alice.

SARAH (*Taking it*):   This'll never do. But, heah, Minnie. Take dis candy t' Miz Libeth.

GEORGANA: Lawd, peppermint! (*Drooling, as* MINNIE *takes candy*) Gimme jes er lick, Minnie.

⁷ Scene Four approaches conclusion in a deadening mood neither of hope nor defeat, the most difficult mood for renewal of energy. Even Joshuah cannot raise himself and his followers beyond dogged determination, on which level note the scene ends in the song, "Hold on!"

Act II, Scene V

¹ Scene Five of Act Two is one of the long scenes in the episodic structure of the play, actually slightly the longest. The length of continuous development is essential to build to the height of dramatic effect and emotion of the end of the play. The scene opens rightly on the homely reality and human frailty which gives poignancy to the heroic dignity to which these people rise. Also, the opening situation of supplies just brought from purchase on the mainland with the money from the cotton, the excitement, the thought of the children, gives concrete awareness of homes being built which prepares for the realization of tragedy in their destruction.

SARAH: No, Minnie! Go on t' de Big House.

(Exit MINNIE.*)*

[2] ELLEN *(Up-Right, sitting on bale, she sees* DELPHINE *in distance)*:   Heah come Miss Love Powder!

PATSY: Shame on yuh, Ellen. Shame!

ELLEN *(Saucily)*:   Oh, Miz Patsy, don't be fogey! *(Suddenly inspired by diabolical idea)* Ah jes thot of sompen—*(Springing down she comes forward)* Pappy!

SETLOW: What, daughter?

ELLEN: Ah betcha thar's one think yuh all forgot t' bring.

SETLOW: What?

ELLEN *(As* DELPHINE *enters—pointedly)*:   Betcha didn't git no diapers!

SETLOW: Diapers for what?

ELLEN *(Innocently)*:   Can yuh all beat this. Dey done gone all de way t' Savannah 'n ain't come back heah wid *diaper one!*

SARAH *(Catching her drift)*:   Lawdy! 'N rattle neither, Ah bet.

ELLEN: Too early for de rattle! But now diapers—*(Stabbingly)* 'n talcum. Who was it tellin me bout tha new brand of baby talcum— *(Innocently)* Wuz it yuh, Delphine?

DELPHINE *(In the dark)*:   Baby talcum—when?

ELLEN *(Casually)*:   Somebody wuz tellin me bout some new brand they say don't chafe. Oh, yeah, love powder. Thas what they call it.

SARAH *(Laughing)*:   Shucks, gal. Yuh want t' know de latest, yuh oughter see Daddy Sykes!

ELLEN: Daddy Sykes? *(Innocently)* Lawd, Daddy Sykes, whyn't yuh tell somebody yuh wuz in de love powder bizness?

(There is an outburst of laughter, and DELPHINE *tumbles. Her eyes swim, and for a moment she is transfixed with indecision.)*

[3] JOSHUAH *(Entering)*:   What's so funny?

(The laughter ceases suddenly.)

DELPHINE: Ah guess de joke's on me. *(She turns to go)*

JOSHUAH *(Arresting her, as he senses situation)*:   On yuh? *(To others)* What is this? *(Suddenly feigning laughter)* But Ah bet Ah know. Yuh done smoked us out, ain't yuh? Well, it's bout time. We been puttin it off till after de harvest. But's de truth; we's goin git married.

² In earthy folk people there is harshness as well as kindliness, both expressed with an outward freedom from restraint. It is the illusion of unglossed reality in the representation of the freed slaves throughout the play that gives conviction to their heroism. The harshest view the audience receives is in Ellen's and Sarah's jest upon Delphine. Ellen is young and not so much spiteful as thoughtless. Sarah of the mature women in the talk on Delphine in the preceding scene was the most impulsively spiteful and, consistently, she is the one among them who takes up Ellen's joke here. Once started Ellen and Sarah are both carried away with their own humor. It is also consistently the warm-hearted Patsy who protests, but the women as a group join in the laughter.

³ Joshuah does not impulsively, moved by Delphine's distress, on the spur of the moment pass over the disappointment and bitterness of Delphine's disclosure to him in the earlier scene. As the audience learns a little later, he had already thought it through and arrived at understanding of his own feeling and his decision. Nothing about Joshuah is ever superficial. What is revealed here is his sensitivity and quickness of wit for relieving Delphine of pain and resolving a difficult situation. Even Joshuah's authority of personality is not sufficient immediately to quell the turmoil of the women, and Lem and Edgar help to clear the stage for Joshuah and Delphine. The episode is a dramatically effective means of reintroducing the question of marriage between Joshuah and Delphine.

GEORGANA (*Shocked*):   Pappy, yuh don't mean it?

PATSY (*Impulsively embracing* DELPHINE):   Gawd bless yuh, Honey chile!

ROSS: Yuh all sure fooled everybody!

SETLOW (*Shaking hands with* JOSHUAH):   Deed yuh all did!

ELLEN: Oh, how kin you ever forgive me, Delphine—but Ah didn't know!

SARAH (*Joining them*):   Move, Ellen—Delphine, honey, yuh must forgive me—(*Whirling, to attack*) But, Ant Dosia, this is your fault!

DOSIA (*Angrily*):   Don't yuh tell tha lie!

JOSHUAH (*Interposing*):   Now hold on!

SARAH (*To* DOSIA):   Yuh told me, didn't yuh?

DOSIA (*Defensively*):   'N she tole me!

JOSHUAH (*Attempting to arrest the developing storm. Sharply*): What diffunce do it make who told who what! Now yuh know. (*His outburst brings a momentary silence*) Yuh all, take this stuff t' de Quarters 'n divide it tween yuh.

DOSIA (*Angrily*):   Ah jes want t' git it straight!

LEM (*Getting bag of beans*):   Oh, Mammy, come on 'n hush!

DOSIA: Don't yuh tell me t' hush!

LEM: Den come on!

DOSIA (*Going, belligerently*):   Ah don't bite mah tongue for no-body!

(*Exit.*)

EDGAR: Ellen, grab hold de other end of dis basket.

(*She complies, and they follow the others out, leaving* DELPHINE *and* JOSHUAH *alone.*)

⁴ JOSHUAH: Did yuh say sompen t' Ant Dosia?

DELPHINE: Yeah.

JOSHUAH: What yuh do tha for?

DELPHINE: Ah thot she might be able to help me—in mah con-dition.

JOSHUAH: You shouldn't er said nothin.

DELPHINE: Ah don't mind em knowin.—Though twas mighty fine of yuh t' try t' cover up for me.

JOSHUAH: Ah meant what Ah said.—If yuh can ever git over mah actin sech er fool last sommer.

⁴ The love-scene between Joshuah and Delphine is beautifully conceived and movingly written. Delphine says to Joshuah he is "jes erbout de biggest man Gawd ever made." His decision about their marriage is more than generosity of spirit. He realizes his own need of Delphine as well as hers for him and states both simply: "Ahm jes in love wid yuh," and "Yuh need me Delphine, 'n it'll be good for yuh." He has the largeness and clarity of mind to see their situation outside of all pettiness in full perspective of their own past and that of their parents and grandparents, to think of the coming child in terms of its need for a father, to see himself and Delphine not just as individuals but as part of a people who "always been up against it." Out of this perspective he has come to realize their need for each other as the surer and greater. All this has not been easy; Joshuah has been thinking, thinking for a considerable time, back into the areas of pain of his race. The racial identification which resolves the love story of Joshuah and Delphine integrates the personal plot-line in meaning with the tragic and heroic story of the group of freedmen and Joshuah's leadership.

DELPHINE: Joshuah, yuh jes erbout de biggest man Gawd ever made.

JOSHUAH: Ahm jes in love wid yuh, 'n soon's we git straight wid this Burkhardt—

DELPHINE (*Crossing*):   No, Joshuah. Yuh know tha can never be.

JOSHUAH (*Joining her*):   Yuh need me, Delphine, 'n it'll be good for yuh.

DELPHINE (*Sitting on bench*):   It won't work.

JOSHUAH: Yuh still thinkin bout de bitter words Ah said?

DELPHINE (*Thoughtfully*):   Ah jes know, for one thing, after this you'll never trust me.

JOSHUAH (*Quietly, gazing inwardly*):   Dey say er burnt chile dreads fiah. Thas true. (*Turning to her*) But if Ah bear de mark where Ah been singed, what must Ah think bout de scar on yuh?

DELPHINE: Ah's learned mah lesson, all right. But yuh forget there's one sharp stone goin always stick in your craw.

JOSHUAH (*After a moment*):   Yuh mean de chile? (*She nods*) Yuh wrong, Delphine. Ah admit Ah thot er lot bout it. But de chile goin need er father. 'N when er man means right by er woman, what's hers is his'n. Nothin else don't matter.

DELPHINE: Yuh's changed.

JOSHUAH: Ah jes been thinkin.

DELPHINE: 'N yuh'll go on thinkin.

JOSHUAH: No. This ain't nothin new. (*Quietly*) As er people we's always been up against it.

DELPHINE: Ah don't catch yuh.

JOSHUAH (*Explaining*):   De chile ain't mine. Thas so. But look back er ways, 'n what yuh see?

DELPHINE: Ah don't follow yuh.

JOSHUAH (*Gazing into the distant past*):   Take yore Mammy 'n mine—'n Ah reckon pretty near everybody else's Mammy—Ain't none of em ever had no *sayso* bout de father of thar chillun. (*Turning to her gently*) So whether it's er case of er high-yaller wid love powder, or ole Marster's whip, it's all de same in de end.[5] (*Her eyes swimming in response to his humanity, she creeps into his arms. For a moment they are silent, as he strokes her hair*) Yuh feel better? (*She nods*) Den Ahm glad. Mighty glad . . . Holdin yuh like

this's jes like de blossoms on er cheery tree. It's like Lusana mag-
nolias round sundown.

DELPHINE: Oh, Joshuah, yuh's like er warm wool blanket t'
mah soul!

JOSHUAH: Yuh's er comfort t' me too, Darling. Yuh's what mah
heart been wantin, 'n wid de hep of Gawd, yuh what Ahm goin keep
for de rest of mah life. Come what may.

DELPHINE: Yuh don't have t' tell me, Joshuah. Ah's knowed it
ever since de day yuh all come heah. But like de story Ah told yuh
bout de mountain 'n de sea, Ah couldn't b'lieve it'd happen t' me—
(*Profoundly moved, she smothers her face in his bosom*)

JOSHUAH: Mah darling. Mah lil Delphine!

DELPHINE (*Whispering*):   My Joshuah.[5]

(*Silence reigns between them. But in a moment a shot sounds.*)[6]

JOSHUAH (*Snapping erect, tense and listening, he is propelled to
his feet as two more shots follow in rapid succession—Yelling*):
Fall in Guards! (*Taking her and momentarily embracing her*) Run
hep Miz Libeth! Keep de chillun in de house—Better take em t' de
attic—Hurry now!

DELPHINE: Oh, Gawd.

JOSHUAH (*Sending her away*):   Hurry, hurry. Thar may be
shootin!

DELPHINE (*She clutches him to her then breaking away*):   Be
careful, won't yuh, Joshuah. (*Taking a long look at him, she turns
and runs off Up-Right*)

                                                            (*Exit.*)

EMANUEL (*Running in Up-Left*):   Dey comin, Mister Joshuah.

JOSHUAH: How many of em?

EMANUEL: Dey got five boat loads.

(*The other* FREEDMEN *pour in.*)

JOSHUAH: Everybody heah? Good.

EDGAR (*Up-Left at barricade*):   Ah see Burkhardt wid em.

[7] JOSHUAH: Phumph! Burkhardt, eh? Ah reckon they goin want
t' parley ergain. But lissen, men. Don't none of yuh all let tha fool
yuh. Thar must be thirty men out there. Yuh know what tha means.
Ah want yuh t' go t' yore posts, 'n jes remember: Ain't nobody ever
got nothin worthwile for nothin. Some of ouah leaders don't understand tha. They's turnin one Convention after ernother into de

⁵ Briefly the love of Joshuah and Delphine is fulfilled in spirit, expressed in the natural poetry of folk response to the beautiful and good things in their lives.

⁶ The sound of the shot cuts off sharply the love-scene with the beginning of the final movement in the story of the group. The climactic manifestation of Joshuah's character in the love-scene lifts him to a plane commensurate to the further climactic expression of his character in what follows, and the fulfillment of his love for Delphine gives him tragic poise. There is effective dramatic contrast from the moment of quiet which settles upon Joshuah and Delphine to the sudden breaking into activity with the freedmen rushing in.

⁷ Joshuah is not blindly obsessed in the desperate stand to which he leads the freedmen, but far-sightedly and sacrificially purposive, nor does he withhold from the men his own vision of the chances and meaning of what they are doing: " 'N it's hard t' stand yore ground when yuh know deep down in your heart de best yuh can do is serve as er lesson."

graveyard of all ouah hopes. Thar ain't er single one of em voted yet, cordin t' Mister Webster, t' give us de lan. It's got t' be up t' us. We ain't many. 'N it's hard t' stand yore ground when yuh know deep down in your heart de best yuh can do is serve as er lesson. Remember John Brown. Him 'n his lil handful stood up for ouah freedom 'n they sot de whole country on fiah! Git t' yore post now, 'n hold your fiah till yuh heah from me.

(OWENS, PELTIER, ROSS *and* EMANUEL *enter the Storehouse, Left, while* SETLOW *and others take position at the barricade.*)

LEM (*Panting, as he runs in*):   Ah thot they was gwine pick me off.

JOSHUAH: Yuh go wid dem in de storehouse.

(*Exit* LEM *Down-Left.*)

EDGAR (*At barricade*):   Heah dey come!

JOSHUAH (*Joins him to peep over barricade, then commands*): Halt! Whar yuh is, Yanks!

STEWART (*Outside shouting*):   I've something to say to you.

JOSHUAH: Well, git yore men back 'n den come on!

EDGAR (*In a moment*):   He bringin Burkhardt.

JOSHUAH (*Going down Right*):   Let em through.

LIBETH (*Entering, excitedly*):   Mr. Tain, what's going to happen?

JOSHUAH: Ah donno, Mam. But this ain't no place for yuh. Yuh got t' git back t' de Big House.

(STEWART *and* BURKHARDT *enter.*)

LIBETH: Perhaps I can help.

STEWART: Who're you, Madam—the teacher?

LIBETH: Yes, Sir.

STEWART (*Joining* JOSHUAH):   You don't think very much of her to expose her in this manner.

LIBETH: I came of my own accord, Captain.

STEWART: Well, please retire to a place of safety!

LIBETH (*Courageously*):   I'm sure there can be no necessity for that, Sir.

STEWART: It's my duty to warn you, Madam—(*Turning to* JOSHUAH) I see you've erected a barricade. What're you trying to do, bluff the Army? (JOSHUAH *is silent*) You do not reply!

JOSHUAH: Yuh go head, Cap'n. We listenin.

[8] STEWART: Well, be sure you get this straight. I've two platoons out there. But I've no desire to shed your blood. So what's the answer.

JOSHUAH: Yuh already know how we feel, Cap'n. (*Quietly*) This is ouah lan, 'n we tend t' stay heah like anybody else wid er just claim.

STEWART (*Snorting*):   Now it's a *just claim!* (*Glances at* BURKHARDT) I see I've encouraged you by remaining away all week. Well, contrary to what you may think, I delayed my return because I was determined to be fair to you. Last week after I left here, I wired Headquarters, explaining your case. In spite of my orders I did that. I even went so far as to wire General Howard himself. I've yet to receive a reply. But do you know what I *have* learned? General Howard himself has gone to Edisto Island, up the Coast, to do exactly what I'm supposed to do here. You can see for yourselves, if General Howard has gone to Edisto Island to see to it personally that the Freedmen there sign the agreements, you must do so also. You must either sign or vacate the island. It must be one way or the other. So make up your minds.

JOSHUAH: What yuh say bout Gen'l Howard 'n this Disto Ilun might be true. But dis ain't Disto Ilun. We done made up ouah minds bout dem contracts.

STEWART: You intend to defy the United States Government?

LIBETH: Mr. Tain. Think. What chance have you?

JOSHUAH: Miz Libeth, Ah told yuh t' git back in de house whar yuh b'long!

LIBETH: But, Mister Tain—

JOSHUAH (*Firmly*):   Yuh been too good t' us fer me t' hurt your feelins, Mam. Git back in de house 'n stay in er woman's place!

(*With a gesture of despair, she goes out Up-Right.*)

BURKHARDT (*To* JOSHUAH):   I wonder if you realize the leading niggers of the country are against this mad idea of confiscation?

JOSHUAH: This is Gawgie. We ain't had no Convention yit.

BURKHARDT: But you can see which way the wind is blowing. The most influential men of your race understand this question.

JOSHUAH: Dey's ignant.

BURKHARDT: Ignorant to you, and I suspect you can neither read nor write. (*Turning to others*) What about you, Boys? Are

[8] Captain Stewart is a humane man and experiences regret in the execution of the orders he has been given. Through most of the exchanges with Joshuah he addresses him with the respect of one soldier to another on opposite sides that so often characterized exchanges between gallant foes of the white North and South. Nevertheless, there is something of hastiness and impatience in his moving with drastic finality on the basis of report of General Howard's action to Edisto Island rather than waiting for direct communication once more with General Howard himself. There is convincing characterization of Captain Stewart as a young man who is irritated and thrown partly off his balance by the calm disregard of his authority.

you going to let this fellow lead you to your deaths? Have you thought about your families—your women and children? What's going to happen to them if you get yourselves killed off?

⁹ SETLOW: What Joshuah say goes for all of us—

STEWART (*Sharply*):   Speak for yourself! (*To others*) What've you men to say? (*As they are silent*) You leave me no alternative. (*To* JOSHUAH) We're going to retire.

¹⁰ JOSHUAH: Jes er minute, Cap'n. (*Under the weight of his responsibility*) Yuh say if we sign dem contracts, in three years we kin buy lan?

STEWART (*Eagerly*):   That's right.

JOSHUAH (*Turning*):   Den, Mr. Burkhardt. We got er lil money. Nuff t' pay yuh part down—

BURKHARDT (*Quickly*):   Hold on. I didn't say I wanted to sell.

EDGAR (*Ejaculating*):   Ah haaaaaaaaannnh!

BURKHARDT: If I sold, I'd have nowhere to go myself.

JOSHUAH (*Glancing at* STEWART):   Den, how bout part of de ilun?

BURKHARDT: I'm afraid I wouldn't be interested.

¹¹ JOSHUAH (*Swallowing*):   Jes er few acres—?

BURKHARDT (*Angry at being so exposed*):   But I'm not interested.

¹² JOSHUAH: Ah see yuh ain't mean t' be fair. (*Bitterly*) Yuh think yuh got de ups on us. But don't let tha fool yuh. 'N don't let what happen heah today fool yuh neither. (*Looking off, his eyes sharp with inner pain*) Cuz neither yuh nor all de rest of de planters put together goin ever kill de thing we's after. We know what's what. Yuh think if we ain't got no lan, we have t' wuk for yuh for nothin. But yuh never git way wid it. This is ouah lan. We done wukked 'n paid for it. Not only here, but all ovah this cruel South. De graves (*Pointing Off-Right*) ovah yonder is mah witness. De slaves sleepin in em declare Ahm right fore Gawd. It was us what first did de tillin t' make it give up de sweet sustenance of life, 'n yuh kin mark mah word: Though yuh won't even sell now, tha same sun yuh see yonder goin yit rise 'n find dem what does de tillin gatherin in de harvest—Yuh kin go, Cap'n. We'll hold ouah fiah till yuh git back t' yore men.

(BURKHARDT *goes out.*)

[9] The freedmen all stand with Joshuah, seeing clearly what their decision means. The heroic action belongs to the group. Joshuah as a leader represents them.

[10] The release of the final action is prepared, like a finger on the trigger, and stayed by one more hope introduced by Joshuah, again showing him as no obsessed man, but under pressure keeping his mind poised and clear-thinking for any possibly constructive development. Stewart sees where he is going and responds eagerly to the hope, not because it would mean successful execution of his authority, but because deep within himself he would give almost anything not to do what he has let himself become worked up to feeling he must do.

[11] Joshuah has no fanatic or egocentric pride. He humbles himself —and receives nothing. The last possible favorable complication is turned adversely.

[12] Again, as is characteristic at his times of greatest decision, Joshuah goes back beyond himself into the pain of the depths of his racial memory for his answer, and rises into magnificent unstrained poetry of speech. From the height of his vision he comes down quietly to the present and announces his decision: "Yuh kin go, Cap'n. We'll hold ouah fiah till yuh git back t' yore men."

STEWART: You're a bitter man, Tain. Think it over a little longer. I'll give you fifteen minutes if you wish.

[13] JOSHUAH (*Quietly*):   We's holdin ouah fiah, Cap'n, till yuh git back t' your men!

STEWART: So be it.

(*Exit.*)

JOSHUAH (*Covering his retreat*):   Hold it, men. Hold it!

[14] PATSY (*Entering, shattering the ominous silence*):   Gimme er gun, somebody!

JOSHUAH (*Sharply*):   Ah told yuh womens t' stay out de way!

PATSY: Gimmer er gun. Ahm in this fight.

(*A bugle blares.*)

JOSHUAH (*As shot sounds*):   Fiah, men! Fiah! Let em have it! (*His voice is drowned in the crack of rifle fire.*)

(*Blackout.*)

[15] (*The stage remains in darkness and there is no sound. But shortly as the lights come up we note that it is now late afternoon, and among the freedmen, PATSY is distinguished on an improvised stretcher, as she is borne off.*)

ROSS (*Emerging from storehouse*):   Joshuah!

JOSHUAH: What, Brer Ross?

SETLOW (*At barricade*):   Here come de boat back!

JOSHUAH: Did they get more men?

SETLOW: Ah don't see none.

JOSHUAH: Thas funny—(*Seeing PELTIER emerge from cotton house*) How yuh all faring?

[16] PELTIER (*Quietly*):   Yuh lookin at what's left.

JOSHUAH (*Stunned by realization of his losses*):   Lawd.

ROSS (*Hesitating*):   Ah hate t' say it, Joshuah. But there ain't no hope for us.

JOSHUAH: Yuh done lost Patsy—

ROSS: Tain't tha, Joshuah. But soon's dark fall, dey git us. Dey surround us.

SETLOW (*At barricade*):   Heah's Stewart ergin.

JOSHUAH (*Goes up*):   Come on in, Cap'n.

[17] STEWART (*Entering, he surveys scene*):   I've a cannon being put ashore! (*Pausing apparently to permit news to sink in*) I can blow you all to hell with one round. However . . . I've come to

[13] Joshuah's decision, Stewart's acceptance of it, and the beginning of rifle fire constitute the complication which precipitates the resolving action of the play. Battle to death is drawn.

[14] The unexpected entrance of Patsy and, rebuked, her "Gimme er gun. Ahm in this fight," draws a sudden knot of emotion, in part, because it is Patsy, the gentlest of the women.

[15] The final movement of the play from the Blackout to the end is on a plateau of dignity. The scene sustains physical action and violence, and heartbreaking events and emotions, without one touch that is melodramatic, sentimental, or strained. The action is not rushed, but moves forward in successive stages, with intervals of quiet, to inevitable conclusion.

[16] A knot of emotion—Peltier's quiet, "Yuh lookin at what's left."

[17] The introduction of the cannon determines immediacy to the end which, as Ross has already observed, has become inevitable. For Stewart it means no more certainty, but less loss of life for his men. His delivery of the ultimatum is impressive, concluding with the solemn traditional words of execution.

offer you your last chance. I want to appeal to you as one man to another. You've lost men and so have I. It's senseless bloodshed. I know how you feel. I know Mr. Burkhardt has refused to meet you halfway. But it's his land, and in the judgment of the Government, you must give over. (*Glances at sun*) I'm going to give you until sundown. That should be in about ten minutes. But take my solemn advice. The moment the sun disappears beneath the horizon, I shall order the gunners to touch off the cannon. And then, unless you shall have changed your minds, may God be with you and have mercy on your souls!

[18] JOSHUAH (*Quietly*):   Thank yuh, Suh, for your kindness. But fore yuh go, there's sompen Ah want axe yuh. Ah might have er couple of men who might want t' accept your offer. If they do, what yuh goin do t' em?

STEWART (*Quietly, after a moment*):   They will be free to leave the island.

JOSHUAH: Thank yuh ergin, Suh.

(*Exit* STEWART.)

[19] (*Turning to others*) Well, yuh all heard him, men. Tomorrow ouah folks goin be homeless ergin. They goin need yuh—?

SETLOW: Who can understand de ways of Gawd!

JOSHUAH: Meaning—?

SETLOW: Ah shall not be moved.

JOSHUAH: Peltier, yuh see mah pint, don't yuh?

PELTIER (*Bitterly*):   Ah come in this thing wid mah eyes wide open, Joshuah. Ah admit, Ah didn't think de Gubment would give us sech er raw deal, though Ah seed how dey treated eberbody in Missippi. But Ah guess Ah had de idea all de time, dey was gwine think twice bout forcin us. But I still think you're right, and if yuh can stay, Ah can too!

JOSHUAH: Well, yuh 'n Brer Setlow go hold de storehouse . . . Brer Ross, Ah won't axe yuh. (*Takes out roll of bills*) Here, take dis money. Do de best yuh kin by de womens 'n chillun. Yuh better try t' send Miz Libeth back home—(*Seeing* DELPHINE *run in*) [20] Go back, Delphine. (*She throws herself into his arms*) Here, Brer Ross. Take her long.

DELPHINE: They fixin t' blow yuh t' smithereens wid er cannon, Joshuah!

[18] There is high dignity in the quietness and courtesy of this last exchange between Joshuah and Stewart, in which the humanity of each is represented.

[19] Three men are left with Joshuah. Joshuah has made his position clear to Stewart, and for the last time Setlow and Peltier have the decision open before them, to die with Joshuah or yield. They choose death. Ross is not given opportunity for decision as he is reserved for the responsibility to the women and children.

[20] The entrance of Delphine introduces an unexpected complication and question of her going or staying, with the presence of time as the sun lowers. It is resolved by a profound and true, and deeply moving, perception in Joshuah of her right to stay. The personal story of Joshuah and Delphine as a focus of audience identification has been interwoven with the group scenes, has been drawn into integration with the group in meaning earlier in Scene Five, and now from this point to the end of the play the fate of the group and of Joshuah and Delphine are one in a single visual focus for the audience.

JOSHUAH: Ah know. Thas jes Yankee bluff. Yuh go hep wid de chillun.

DELPHINE: Ah ain't gwine widout yuh.

JOSHUAH: But yuh ain't in no condition t' be heah. Think of de chile!

DELPHINE: If yuh really thinkin bout de chile, then yuh come on wid me!

JOSHUAH: Yuh know Ah can't. (*Desperately*) Why don't yuh hep me by doing what Ah tell yuh?

DELPHINE: Ah want t' hep yuh, Joshuah. Ah do! Ah do!

JOSHUAH: Den go!

DELPHINE (*Breaking*):   Oh, Joshuah, yuh don't know mah heart. Don't try t' send me way. If yuh won't come wid me, lemme stay here. Don't try t' send me way. Lemme stay here whar Ah b'long, whether Ahm livin or dead!

JOSHUAH: Lawd, what Ahma do—? (*He tries to hand her to* ROSS, *but she eludes him and drops to the ground like a child reluctant to be moved*) Get up, Delphine!

ROSS: Pick her up, Joshuah. De sun almost down!

JOSHUAH: Get up, Delphine—Please!

DELPHINE: Ah rether be dead.

ROSS: Pick her up, Joshuah! (*Seeing him in helpless dismay*) De sun sinkin, fast, Joshuah. Dey fiah, dey kill her sure—do sompen!

JOSHUAH: Ah reckon ain't nothin Ah kin do. Yuh go on, Brer Ross.

ROSS: 'N leave her?

JOSHUAH: Yeah. She is mah woman. If she wanter stay heah, Ah ain't got no right t' drive her way.—Yuh git on.

ROSS (*Going in dismay*):   Gawd have mercy!

(*Exit.*)

JOSHUAH: Git up, Honey.

[21] DELPHINE (*Rising she dusts her skirt, then turns to him softly*): Yuh mad wid me?

JOSHUAH: No . . . Ahm proud of yuh! (*For a moment he holds her close to his bosom; then, leading her to seat beneath oak*) But yuh better sit.

DELPHINE: Ah want t' see what dey doin out there.

JOSHUAH: No. It's best not t' think bout em. Sit down 'n les talk.

[21] In love and facing death Delphine's childlikeness is infinitely touching, as is the conversation that follows, two lovers in the one short time they have together before death, and knowing it, engaging in the familiar universal desire of lovers to know all about each other before the time of their first meeting. This period is not a passive fatalistic waiting for death. There is literally nothing more Joshuah, or Setlow and Peltier inside the storehouse, can do until the cannon shot that is to come with the setting of the sun. Joshuah and Delphine are granted this much time; what they do with it is dramatic truth.

Surprisingly, from a technical point of view, here at the end of the play with dramatic effectiveness, the character of Joshuah is further rounded out with antecedent material.

DELPHINE (*Sitting*):   All right. Bout what?

JOSHUAH (*For a moment he stands watching outside, while she gazes upon ground at her feet, her arms wrapped about her knees*): Tell me bout de time when yuh wuz a lil girl heah on de ilun. (*Sits*)

DELPHINE: No. Yuh tell me how come yuh t' be sold down de river, like dey say.

JOSHUAH: Ah made some pike heads, 'n one of ole Marster's boys found em.

DELPHINE: What's er pike head?

JOSHUAH: It's er piece of sharp iron yuh fix t' er pole so yuh can stick de enemy.

DELPHINE: Oh. So yuh wuz plannin er risin gainst de Masters?

JOSHUAH: Yeah. We had de day all set. Us didn't need but er few more pike heads. But one day, Joel, de youngest of de boys found em where Ah had em planted in de well. They couldn't prove nothin zactly. But dey figgered couldn't nobody make dem pike heads but me, so dey sold me down t' Lusana.

DELPHINE (*She draws her shawl about her shoulders*):   But Georgana say your wife wuz killed.

JOSHUAH: She wuz. Poor Hannah—she throwed her life erway tryin t' save me. De High Sheriff come t' git me, 'n Ah broke 'n run. Hannah, she seed he was goin shoot, so she jumped in de way, 'n he killed her stone dead.

DELPHINE: She must er been er fine woman.

JOSHUAH (*Rising he peeps out*):   Yuh 'n her very much de same. (*Turning back to join her*) Yuh got de same sort of soft eyes 'n brown skin. Yuh got hips like her, 'n yuh carry yoresef like yuh mount t' sompen in de world!

DELPHINE (*After a moment*):   Ah reckon if things had er been diffunt, maybe me 'n yuh'd both been somebody, wouldn't us?

JOSHUAH (*Glancing at sun*):   Yeah. Ah speck so.

[22] DELPHINE (*Drawing her shawl about her*):   Ahm gittin er lil chilly.

JOSHUAH (*Putting his arms around her*):   Dis fall, yuh know. Winter jes er-round de corner.

[23] DELPHINE (*Wistfully*):   Yeah. Pretty soon de nights goin be frosty. Yuh git up in de mawnin 'n find de ground all covered wid white—(*Shivering*) Sing sompen, Joshuah.

JOSHUAH: Lawd, Honey, how can Ah sing?

[22] There is tension for the audience when Delphine remarks on getting chilly—a reminder that the sun is falling lower—and then pathos when she speaks of the future, the coming change of season, with death approaching close.

[23] The tenderness and delicacy of the interlude comes to a climax in the singing of "Deep River," the spiritual which so profoundly expresses all the pain and sorrow known in life by looking over the river of death to a promised land.

DELPHINE (*Swallowing*):   Yuh kin try—

JOSHUAH: It's funny—Ah can't seem t' think of nothin.

DELPHINE: Sing "Deep River."

JOSHUAH: All right—if de words can git through mah dry throat. (*He struggles for a moment, then lifts song*)
"Deep river, my home is over Jordan,
Deep river, Lawd; I want to cross over into campground.

"O Children, O, don't you want to go to that gospel feast,
That promised land, that land, where all is peace?"
    [24] (*A bugle sounds, and as it dies away there is the roar of the cannon. Simultaneously the wall of the forge is blown in, and shots ring out.*)

JOSHUAH (*Whirls to barricade, glances out, and turns to her*): Come on, git behind de tree—Dey chargin! (*He hustles her to tree Down-Left, then rushes back to retrieve his gun. Falling against the barricade, he fires one shot.*)

DELPHINE (*As a white* SOLDIER *appears on porch of cotton house and leaps to the ground—Screaming*):   Look out, Joshuah! (*Joshuah whirls. The* SOLDIER *lifts his rifle.* DELPHINE *dashes up, protectingly . . . But she is too late. The* SOLDIER *fires and* JOSHUAH *is hit. The latter tries to return fire. But his gun snaps. In a last sad gesture of futility, he hurls the empty weapon at the* SOLDIER *and falls.* DELPHINE *drops to his side to lift his head into her lap*) Oh, mah darling . . . Mah darling.

JOSHUAH: He got me, hunh? (*Dying*) Now . . . it's yore time . . . t' sing . . . Sing . . .

DELPHINE: Yes, Dear . . . (*Her heart bursting*) Ah sing.
(*As she swallows her pain and the first note flows from her lips,* SETLOW *is seen staggering off the porch to fall flat on his face and lie there.* STEWART *emerges behind him. He glances at the fallen freedman, then comes down.*)
    [25] STEWART (*To* DELPHINE):   Is he dead?
    [26] DELPHINE (*Ignoring him, her voice soars tenderly in requiem, as the Curtain Falls*):
"Deep river, my home is over Jordan,
Deep river, Lawd; I want to cross over into campground . . ."

                                                            (*Finis.*)

[24] Light has been fading through the period of Joshuah and Delphine together. The sound of the bugle announces that time has run out and prepares for the roar of the cannon—otherwise it would be too sudden a shock. There is the whirl of action in which Joshuah's first thought is protection for Delphine. Delphine in her turn, as the soldier aims his rifle at Joshuah, tries to save him with her own life, as Joshuah's first wife, Hannah, had done. There is not enough time for her intervention. Joshuah falls.

[25] Stewart's question to Delphine, "Is he dead?" is moved by more than the mutual respect of one soldier for another, by his recognition of the total quality of Joshuah as a man.

[26] With the death of Joshuah the play is resolved. Joshuah's singing "Deep River" for Delphine was deeply moving. The bravery, the control, of Delphine in her turn beginning to sing for Joshuah's passage over Jordan, her voice rising isolated in the quiet after the flare-up of big noise and action, then gradually soaring into release of emotion that carries her beyond awareness of the presence of Stewart or his question, comprise an effect that is heart-wrenching but filled with beauty, purity of emotion, and dignity. It has been built step by step with dramatic truth and naturalness to the characters and situation, and is proportionate to the subject and development of the play.

The visualizations and remarks on staging in the notes have no reference to either of the productions of *Our Lan'* and are personal to myself. Readers may prefer their own visualizations and ideas on staging, and they may go much further in detail than I have done. I have attempted only a suggestive degree of annotation toward realization of the play to the imagination through reading, and of analysis of structure toward meaning.

Our Lan' seems to me to be a tragic heroic drama rather than a tragedy. There is the quality of mind in Joshuah of singleness of purpose or idea and the sense of necessity upon him for his course of action by which he could have been treated as the protagonist of tragedy; but the sense of doom rises late in the play rather than constituting a unifying principle, awareness of social forces rather than of fate is strong throughout, the sense of the group is in strong balance to the focus on Joshuah, and the play does not have the tight swift structure that in general best serves the end of tragedy. Although adverse forces accelerate in the second act and doom seems to become increasingly inevitable, the play is characterized by alternation of hope and reversal, even to a small hope faintly and briefly held on the verge of the final movement of resolution, when Joshuah proposes purchase of land to Mr. Burkhardt. The emotional effect at the end is not the catharsis of tragedy, the purification of pity and fear through universalization of suffering as common to man together with his power to transcend fate in integrity of will. The integrity of will is there but the suffering is particular. The climactic emotional effect at the end of *Our Lan'* is that of overwhelming sadness made bearable by beauty in the purity of emotion in Delphine's singing and by admiration and awe before the heroism not only of Joshuah but of the men and a woman who have died with him.

Our Lan' has another purpose to serve than that of tragedy, and its structure and temper are right to its own end. *Our Lan'* is the story of the heroism of a group of people the foundation of whose heroism is the indomitable capacity to endure, to work, and to sustain determination and optimism in the face of obstacles and setbacks. The object is to draw the audience into a sense of full acquaintance, of living with this group of people, for which a considerable number of scenes are needed. For realization of the nature of their heroism, both number of scenes and passage of time are needed. The somewhat leisurely episodic structure accomplishes these ends. It has been noted in the preceding analysis how the episodic structure, with its inherent weakness of a late crisis, has been skilfully strengthened by the division into two movements with a major turning point and climax both in plot-line and mood midway in the play.

The group are ordinary people, not a selected company, and need leadership, not a leader who determines their direction, but who sustains them in the direction of their own capacities. Joshuah is a man in whom the best capacities of his people are fulfilled in highest degree. He truly represents them as well as leads them. The play is the story at once of the heroism of a group and of an extraordinary heroic man. For full realization to the audience of Joshuah the personal story with Delphine, interwoven through and integrated with the group, is needed, and the final focus when they have become most representative on Joshuah and Delphine as isolated figures on the stage.

The people of the play are a folk group, that is, uneducated and unsophisticated, living in direct contact with the earth as their source of sustenance, close to the fundamental relationships, experiences, and emotions of life. To express them the play has in its temper the qualities of simplicity, directness, and naturalness, an illusion of artlessness. For its purpose the play is entirely in the convention of realism. The control of the function of singing in the play is especially significant. Song was integral to the lives of the people of the play and its use in the play does much to create them. Music is actually used artfully throughout the play as dramatic expression and intensification; it binds scenes together structurally, giving closer unity to the episodic movement, and it unifies the play in mood. But every song in the play the people in real life might readily have sung in such a situation and at such a moment as that in the play.

As natural to the lives of folk people as song is the poetry of speech, in rhythm, in melody, and in imagery. The play is unified by beauty of speech in its continuous flow, and as the greater occasions of dramatic expression arise, on the folk foundation and in unity with it, the language rises to moving heights of power or opens up depths of emotion and insight. Finally, there is a quality in the temper of the play for expression of its people which one feels strongly as no illusion of art, but a unified sincerity.

The play is not without flaws. They are occasional in speech, a touch of stiffness or a trite sentence or phrase for one of the non-folk characters. Miss Libeth Arbarbanel after her introduction and her scene with the children loses life; her further characterization is in too few lines and those inadequate in quality.

Except for Miss Libeth the characterization even of briefly seen persons is highly successful. Captain Bryant, Captain Stewart, Mr. Burkhardt, his overseer Saunders, the two rebel soldiers, all are given representative character and individual life with precision. Each of the group of settlers on the island, men and women, has a clear line of character running through and can be easily visualized, as though the playwright knew them personally. Delphine is created with naturalness in her unsophisticated simplicity, with delicacy for her weakness and problems, and with sure touch for her maturing and growth into a great woman.

Joshuah is a character of dramatic stature. With his simplicity and common humanity there is something of classical antiquity in him. Joshuah is most fully expressed in the quality and the word from Aristotle's *Ethics*—magnanimity, greatness of soul with freedom from pettiness. Joshuah as an individual is created in profound identification with his race. At every crisis of decision he finds the way to go from deep wells of memory farther back than personal memory. At the same time he transcends his race, is a universal man. Similarly, the play *Our Lan'* is a play justly of racial pride which becomes also a play for pride in humanity.

A Note on the Technique of Reading a Play

A play should be read the first time in a manner and under circumstances to approximate as closely as possible experience in the theater. The techniques of a play, as compared to a novel, are determined by the expectation that it will be experienced through a theatrical production. The novel is to be read in isolation and at leisure. Its length is such that ordinarily it is read in parts over a considerable period of time. The skilful novelist adjusts his work to interrupted experience by chapters, and builds the whole upon effects which can survive on the continuity of memory rather than depending on a close sequence of emotion. The novelist can utilize tempos and involvements which require a slow and studied reading, or even turning back pages and rereading.

The playwright, on the other hand, has written for his basic effect to be gained in the brief uninterrupted experience, except for planned intermissions, of the two-hour performance in the theater under the stimulus of group response. He has built carefully constructed climaxes which mount from one emotional pitch to another and would be destroyed by interruption. He has pulled threads of situation and speech sequence together into a knot of emotion; if a thread is cut, the knot will fall loose. He has developed effects by the juxtaposition of scenes. He has utilized such visual projections as the shock of an unexpected entrance upon the stage, the abrupt cutting off of a scene

429

by a blackout, the gradual withdrawal by a slow curtain, and he has written speeches which capitalize upon those physical materials of his craft.

The successful reading of a play depends upon imagination in terms of the theater. A play, then, should be read through the first time without pause beyond such act intermissions as production would allow, maintaining approximately theater pace, and in a situation favorable to concentration with freedom from interruption. If a play is jointly experienced by someone reading it aloud, the one who reads has the responsibility of uninterrupted theater pace.

The theater provides powerful aids to focus of attention. The reader of a play is on his own. The play is an economical literary form; if well written, every word counts, in the stage directions as well as the dialogue. The playwright has expended hundreds of hours over months, even years, determining those words, choosing, rejecting, rewriting, pounding the script down to the final form which will have for the audience the effect of a spontaneous flow of dialogue, but in which every word has been closely considered for its function to the meaning of the play. It is necessary in reading that every word register on the mind clearly and sharply. To get exactly what the play says while maintaining an approximation of theater pace without pause or rereading there is just one answer—energetic concentration.

A play with value beyond the pleasant passing of two hours contains more than is to be gained from a single theater experience, but it has been written to communicate the basic intention, effect, and meaning through such an experience. It is hard to get away from first impressions, and the first reading of a play should be performed in a manner to establish a right direction. After that, if the play has the worth and interest to the reader, comes the analysis, rereading, and development of interpretation and imaginative projection in one's mind which can lead to a fuller experience in a subsequent reading, just as the experience of a great play grows in successive theatrical productions.

A Note on Reading Manuscript Plays

In the theater of the Dionysian festivals of ancient Athens the archon, the chief state official, read the scripts and selected those to be produced in the annual competitions which gave us the plays of Aeschylus, Sophocles, Euripedes, and Aristophanes. Shakespeare and Molière, as managerial shareholders of their respective companies as well as their principal playwrights, were also playreaders. Shakespeare must have had a part in the reading of scripts by which plays of Ben Jonson and of Beaumont and Fletcher were produced by his company, and it was the discernment of Molière that first opened the theater to plays by Racine. In Molière's century in France the patronage of a cultivated aristocracy which provided a good deal of the support for theatrical production was based on discriminating reading. Molière and the Prince de Conti, a patron of Molière's company for a time, read and discussed plays together, and Louis XIV gave his favor to *Les Précieuses Ridicules* from reading the play in manuscript. In the eighteenth and nineteenth centuries the actor-managers characteristically chose the plays for production.

Today in this country in the commercial theater the producers determine the plays for production, receiving scripts for their own reading through various channels of recommendation, from play agents, from the authors, from a staff playreader or play department, or by farming out scripts to semiprofessional playreaders. Scripts are recommended by actors who see a part in the script, by family and friends, and as a popular joke with some truth in it, by secretaries and office boys. Anyone in New York with a point of contact is liable to take a hand in recommending scripts, but it is the producer who makes the choice. In off-Broadway and art theaters sometimes a single person as manager or director selects the plays, more often a board; in community and university theaters, usually a board or committee.

For theater and drama to exist three things are necessary: plays must be written, there must be a situation for production, and plays must be read and selected for production. These three functions are interdependent and inseparable; that of playreading is equally determinative with the others of the quality of theater and the future of drama, and at the present time has received least recognition as an area for training and specialized capacity.

Nine years ago I introduced reading of manuscript plays into my Modern Drama course at the University of Michigan. The course had been conducted to the end not only of acquiring a knowledge of the history and plays of modern drama, but through the approach of experiencing, understanding, and evaluating each play by a disciplined procedure, development of the capacity for independent critical interpretation and estimation. Clearly the final test is on a manuscript play. I have selected each year two scripts from the advanced playwriting at the university, at least one of which is ordinarily a play to be produced on the year's program, and have placed them in the hands of the students near the end of the course by duplicated copies. American drama cannot achieve its potential scope and variety if limited for survival to selection for New York City production, and community and university theaters fall short of their appropriate function and full vitality if they depend for contemporary plays solely on try-out in New York. The students' reports on the manuscript plays are made as though each student were a member of a playreading board or committee for a non-commercial theater recommending for or against production of the new play.

I suggest to the students that estimating a manuscript play is exactly the same as estimating an established play except that it is entirely between the reader and the play. It should be read without prepossession as to the experience of the playwright, his knowledge of theater, or how high in excellence the play may be. Great plays were first plays in manuscript, and some of them were selected for production without previous reputation of the author. There is always the excitement of discovery. For recommendation, however, neither a great nor a perfect play should be demanded. Few of the established plays produced are both great and perfect, and many are neither, yet properly have their place in the theater. On the other hand, a manuscript play to be recommended should worthily fill a place on the program for the audience of the theater organization, if the audience is paid the respect of assuming for them some spirit of adventure. Finally, the play should be considered as written, read for what it is, with restraint on any possible impulses toward vicarious playwriting.

From 1950 to the present year each manuscript play copy has carried an introductory address to the students as follows:

To the Students of English 135:

This is a manuscript play. It is one of a set of copies that have been made for the use of English 135 to make available to each student the experience of critical reading of a manuscript play.

The future of American drama will be determined by the general public, by the educated and theater-interested people who constitute the governing boards and playreading committees of community theaters. As the vitality of dramatic writing in this country in number and varied character of plays of value has become increasingly disproportionate to the scope of production offered by the commercial theater in New York, community and university theaters are turning increasingly to the production of new plays. What this trend may do for the interest and character of noncommercial theater programs and the significant development of American drama depends upon an adequate number of people who can read a manuscript play with sound judgment and confidence for selection for production. Among several objectives, one of the functions of a course in Modern Drama can be training in the ability to read a play, the culmination of which is the reading of manuscript plays.

Every established play was once a play in manuscript. The greater number of the dramatists whose works are studied in the

Modern Drama course gained initial recognition through other than commercial theater production. In critically appreciative reading of plays the height of pleasure is in the fresh approach to a play which no one has ever seen produced, for which there is no background of established reputation or critical review; and in the theater there is no experience comparable to that of seeing a play which has been previously read in manuscript.

This manuscript play which has been selected for your reading is such as might be recommended to your consideration as a member of a noncommercial theater board. With each script is provided a report form of a type commonly used both in professional playreading offices in New York and by noncommercial theater playreading committees.

The report form is a standard 8½ x 11-inch sheet of paper. On the front side one fourth of the page is given to the factual data anyone considering a play for production wants to know for practical considerations of finance, staging, casting, and program, as follows:

PLAY REPORT by _____ Course: Date:

Author: Title:

Type of play:

Number of characters: —— men, —— women, —— m. principles, —— w. principals, —— children, —— animals.

Number of acts and scenes:

Number and type of sets:

The remaining three-fourths of the front side of the sheet is under the heading *Synopsis*. Three-fourths of the reverse side is under the heading, *Analysis;* for the remaining fourth the heading, *Recommendation*.

Through the years I have been pleased to receive letters from former students of their functioning in a variety of situations in bringing new scripts to production. If this book should contribute to such functioning for any reader, I will feel especially rewarded for the time and effort of its writing.

Index